KOREA

KOREA

The East
Asian Pivot

JONATHAN D. POLLACK, *Editor*

NAVAL WAR COLLEGE PRESS
Newport, Rhode Island

The contents of this volume represent the views of the authors. Their opinions are not necessarily endorsed by the Naval War College or by any other agency, organization, or command of the U.S. government.

Printed in the United States of America

Policy Studies Series

NAVAL WAR COLLEGE PRESS
Code 32
Naval War College
686 Cushing Road
Newport, R.I. 02841-1207

Library of Congress Cataloging-in-Publication Data

Naval War College (U.S.). Asia-Pacific Studies Group. Asia-Pacific Forum (2004 : Newport, R.I.)
 Korea : the East Asian pivot / Jonathan D. Pollack, Editor.
  p. cm. — (Policy studies series)
 Papers presented at the Naval War College's Asia-Pacific Forum, the annual conference of the college's Asia-Pacific Studies Group, held in Newport, R.I., on 26–27 August 2004.
 ISBN 10: 1-884733-36-0
 ISBN 13: 978-1-884733-36-9
 1. Korea (South)—Politics and government—1988—Congresses. 2. Korea (South)—Economic conditions—1960—Congresses. 3. Korea (North)—Politics and government—Congresses. 4. Korea (North)—Economic conditions—Congresses. 5. East Asia—Foreign relations—Congresses. 6. World politics—21st century—Congresses. 7. Strategic planning—Congresses. I. Pollack, Jonathan D. II. Title. III. Policy studies series (Naval War College (U.S.))
 JQ1725.N38 2004
 951.904'3—dc22
                                        2005034471

Cover and typographical design by
Chapman and Partners of Warren, Rhode Island.
Map image by Cristina A. Hartley, Naval War College
Visual Communications Division.

Contents

Acknowledgments

The Asia-Pacific Studies Group wishes to express its deep appreciation to the Naval War College Foundation, through the generosity of the Raytheon Company, for its financial support in sponsoring the conference and in publishing this volume. This is the second conference symposium published with support from the Foundation and from Raytheon; a third volume in this series, based on a conference planned for the spring of 2006, is anticipated. The Korea conference benefited significantly from the timely and highly efficient support of Captain J. R. Mathis, USN; Mitchell Ewing; Major Steve Park, USA (then a student at the Naval War College); and Andrew Erickson—support for which I am most grateful. Thanks are also owing to Pelham Boyer and others on the staff and supporting organizations of the Naval War College Press for their prompt and meticulous labors on the manuscript and for seeing it through to production. It should go without saying that all views expressed in this volume represent the personal views of the authors and should not be attributed in any way to the Naval War College, the Department of the Navy, or the U.S. government as a whole.

JONATHAN D. POLLACK
Chairman, Asia-Pacific Studies Group
Naval War College

ASIA-PACIFIC

FORUM

KOREA
The East Asian Pivot

Foreword

Korea: The East Asian Pivot is the second in the Policy Studies Series of the Naval War College Press and extends the focus on East Asia evident in the first volume of this series, *Strategic Surprise? U.S.-China Relations in the Early Twenty-first Century* (2003), also edited by Jonathan D. Pollack. The appearance of these books underscores the commitment of the Naval War College to strengthening the regional studies component of its educational and research mission and, more generally, to supporting ongoing changes in Navy education designed to improve the regional, cultural, and linguistic expertise of the sea services in the contemporary security environment. It is to be hoped that these volumes will contribute to the professional development of officers of all the services, as well as to the wider debate on fundamental issues of national strategy and policy.

The papers in this volume were first presented at the Naval War College's Asia-Pacific Forum on 26–27 August 2004. The forum is the flagship conference of the College's Asia-Pacific Studies Group, convened periodically to focus on a major issue in Asia-Pacific strategy, with particular attention to future policy implications. The conference drew upon many leading specialists on Korean affairs and on regional politics and security, drawn from institutes and universities across the United States and from countries of the Asia-Pacific region, including the Republic of Korea, Japan, China, Australia, and Canada. In addition to faculty and students from the War College, participants at this event also included Senator Jack Reed (D-R.I.); and representatives from the office of the Chief of Naval Operations, U.S. Forces Korea, U.S. Pacific Command, the National Intelligence Council, the Department of State, and the corporate sector.

This conference concentrated on the potential for major change on the Korean Peninsula: in the politics and economics of the two Koreas; in the respective defense strategies and military capabilities of North and South; and in the strategies and policies of

China, Japan, Russia, and the United States toward the peninsula. Despite the intense focus in recent years on the North Korean nuclear weapons issue, this was not a primary focus of the conference deliberations. By placing peninsular and regional dynamics in their larger context, and by examining how various policy considerations and actions are shaping the peninsula's future, the participants shed light on Korea both in the near term and in the longer term. Deeming Korea "the East Asian pivot" is not hyperbole—few issues have greater inherent potential to shape politics, economics, and security within the region in coming years than the evolution of both Korean states, their relationship with one another and with the major powers, and the corresponding strategies of the major powers toward the peninsula. The findings should therefore be of direct relevance to policy planners, political-military analysts, and scholars on both sides of the Pacific.

CARNES LORD
Director, Naval War College Press

PART ONE

The Setting of Korean Politics

1

Korea's Looming Transformation

Jonathan D. Pollack

Nearly sixty years after the establishment of rival states on opposite sides of the 38th Parallel and fifteen years after the end of the Cold War, the ground is shifting in Korea. For a half-century, the two Koreas (aided for much of this time by their respective great-power benefactors) inhabited separate worlds, characterized by a heavily armed coexistence. The resumption of major military conflict, sustained internal upheaval, abrupt unification, and nuclear weapons development were all deterred or averted, enabling both regimes to pursue extraordinarily divergent strategic paths. North and South, as well as the major powers, thus maintained nominal stability on the peninsula, though in light of Korean history and geography it was an unnatural stability.

To numerous observers, two principal factors (one highly worrisome, the other decidedly more optimistic) have an inherent potential to redefine the long-prevailing status quo. The negative factor is North Korea's renewed nuclear weapons development. Given the implications of nuclear weapons proliferation for regional security and for the future of the nonproliferation regime, concern about this ominous prospect is wholly understandable. Since the collapse of the Agreed Framework in the fall of 2002 and North Korea's withdrawal from the Nuclear Nonproliferation Treaty (NPT) in early 2003, policy attention has focused on the nuclear weapons impasse and whether a negotiated outcome is achievable. In September 2005, after two years of fitful, intermittent discussions in Beijing, diplomats from six states signed a statement of principles on a potential denuclearization accord. As the subsequent round of talks in November 2005 highlighted, negotiations over a true accord (as distinct from a composite statement of expectations) will be protracted, contentious, and quite possibly nondefinitive.

This volume does not devote sustained attention to the nuclear weapons issue, although it is discussed in some of the chapters. Rather, the nuclear issue is symptomatic of a larger transformation under way on the peninsula, and in the relationship of both Koreas to the outside world. To some analysts, this transformation concerns the second and decidedly more optimistic possibility: the expectation of major change that will unambiguously tie the North to the outside world. However, this volume does not posit a certain or inevitable outcome to this process. It instead delves into the complex dynamics in the national strategies and power trajectories of North and South, and the parallel shifts in the strategies and policies of the United States, China, Japan, and Russia, the four major powers with enduring national interests on the Korean Peninsula.

The far-reaching power realignment between North and South furnishes the primary context for this study. By every measure other than aggregate military capabilities, the power of the South (historically the far less developed half of the peninsula) has pervasively outstripped that of the North. For all intents and purposes, the decades-long competition between the two Koreas has ended, though the stark division of the peninsula remains intact. Both states still claim legitimacy and authenticity, but the meaning and significance of these claims have changed profoundly. South Korea, though prone to periodic internal upheaval over the decades, has emerged as an increasingly consequential industrial and diplomatic power, moving well beyond decades of highly authoritarian, military-dominated politics. By contrast, North Korea (though compelled by circumstances to adapt at least marginally to the outside world) remains mired in the regime's systemic pathology, unable to break definitively with its past while fiercely defending its sovereign prerogatives.

But what do the South's successes and the North's failures portend? How might the South exploit its increased advantage, and how does the North escape from the liabilities of its past while trying to ensure the survival of its polity? What do these cumulative changes and future possibilities imply for American policy? The North's acute economic crisis and increasing marginalization, the South's profound generational and leadership shifts, and major alterations in great-power policies toward both Koreas (including major changes in U.S. defense strategy and force deployments) all attest to the peninsula's altered political, economic, and strategic realities. Korea may indeed represent the last lingering frontier of the Cold War, but this legacy is rapidly dwindling. The reality of major change—for both Koreas, for the region, and for U.S. strategic interests—is inescapable, even if such change has yet to materialize fully, and even if the full possibilities remain uncertain.

This volume is a collaborative effort, drawing upon leading political, economic, and military analysts from the United States and the Asia-Pacific region. It explores the long-term transitions under way in both Koreas, the factors that are shaping this change, and the potential implications for the future political and strategic geography of Northeast Asia. The analytic approaches and policy perspectives of various authors differ significantly, and I have made no effort to force a consensus among them. All, however, recognize the major departures from long-extant realities that are placing ever-increasing pressure on the political strategies and security arrangements that have dominated the peninsula since the end of the Korean War.

Weighing the implications of peninsular change must begin with the anomalous circumstances of the past century. Notwithstanding the ebb and flow of various dynasties and repeated pressures from or outright domination by external powers, Korea has retained cultural, linguistic, and societal coherence throughout most of its history. Its subjugation by Japan in the first half of the 20th century and the peninsula's subsequent division into Soviet and American occupation zones were sharp departures from this historical pattern. The creation of rival systems in North and South reinforced this deviation, placing the two systems on starkly different paths in ideology, diplomacy, and economic development. It is difficult to imagine more divergent approaches to political, economic, and social organization than those pursued by the two Koreas over the past half-century. As Robert Scalapino notes in his introductory essay, these separate political strategies reflected the disparate responses of early-20th-century Korean political activists to the peninsula's weakness, division, and vulnerability to external penetration. The North and South remain the legatees of this tumultuous history. Starkly different concepts of Korean nationalism hover over the contentious events of the past one hundred years and will continue to shape Korea's future.

THE POLITICS OF NORTH AND SOUTH: A TALE OF TWO SYSTEMS

At present, the Republic of Korea (ROK) and the Democratic People's Republic of Korea (DPRK) continue to inhabit separate worlds. But can these distinct identities persist, and what might supplant them? These themes are explored in the chapters by Andrei Lankov, Narushige Michishita, and Byung-Kook Kim. Lankov and Kim examine the political dynamics of North and South, respectively, and each concludes that the prevailing systemic identities either have already changed beyond recognition or will ultimately unravel. Michishita concentrates on the North's approaches to deterrence, risk-taking, and diplomacy and is more tentative in his judgments. But he also recognizes that North Korea's future prospects are intimately tied to the outcome of the nuclear negotiations.

Lankov focuses on developments within North Korea. He explores the enduring pathology of the North Korean system, highlighting how its self-isolation and internal control have enabled leaders at the top to sustain their hold on absolute power, thereby defying widespread expectations in the early 1990s that the collapse of North Korea was only a question of time and circumstance. He concludes that the engagement strategies of Kim Dae Jung and Roh Moo Hyun, the ROK's two most recent presidents, will contribute more to the erosion of central control in the North than a policy designed to stigmatize and isolate the DPRK. His expectations of major change therefore derive from a "bottom up" rather than a "top down" view of politics. Beneath the veneer of absolute control in Pyongyang, Lankov sees powerful social forces that are deeply estranged from the regime—forces that will become even more alienated as information about the outside world (and especially about the ROK) further disseminates within the North, and as South Korea's economic weight and influence in the North increases.

In a longer-term sense, Lankov concludes that it will be impossible to prevent the spread of "subversive information" in the North. In addition, as those producing for the domestic market increase their economic autonomy from the state, ideological loyalty to the regime will become increasingly suspect. He asserts that "sub-elite intellectuals," the closest approximation to an educated, urban middle class in the DPRK, will be the pivotal trigger to large-scale change and the ultimate demise of the North Korean system. In Lankov's view, the hopes in South Korea for "a peaceful, gradual, and relatively inexpensive evolution for the North Korean regime are likely to be undermined by a force [the Southerners] do not really take seriously: the North Korean population itself." He believes that the citizens of the North (in a manner comparable to events in Germany a decade and a half ago) will ultimately seek "unification with the fabulously rich southern half of the peninsula." Lankov concludes that the ROK must begin to plan in earnest for the outcome that the South's leadership seeks to avoid.

Michishita focuses on the North's approaches to military policy and negotiations with the outside world, not on the long-term viability of the DPRK. Unlike Lankov, he offers a more leadership-centered view. He highlights the characteristic patterns in North Korean actions, which he deems far more comprehensible and logical than is widely assumed. He argues that the risks and rewards for the DPRK are far larger in the renewed nuclear crisis than they were during the events of 1993–94, with "bigger carrots . . . put on the table together with bigger sticks." The situation has injected ever-more-pronounced tensions within North Korean decision making, as the DPRK leadership wrestles with the potential implications of a negotiated outcome. Michishita concludes that "the path to a larger breakthrough remains very uncertain. Kim Jong Il might again prove himself to be a man of tactical flexibility and strategic ineptitude." Thus, his assessment remains contingent on a pivotal but still very obscure factor: the underlying strategic calculations of senior leaders in Pyongyang.

Kim's chapter chronicles the extraordinary odyssey in South Korea's internal politics, focusing on the incumbent president, Roh Moo Hyun, and the political forces allied with him. He concentrates on the convulsive year of 2004, when Roh and his political adversaries were locked in an intense confrontation over the country's future as well as its history. Since Roh Moo Hyun's election in late 2002, internal politics have experienced repeated upheaval, as Roh has sought to harness disparate societal elements to achieve a lasting transformation of South Korea's political norms and institutions. There has been a profound internal political realignment, manifested primarily by the growing power of younger Koreans (known as the "386 generation") who have no memory of or identification with the military-dominated politics of the past, with the Korean War, or with the era of economic backwardness in the ROK. Despite their youth and political inexperience, those in their 20s and 30s are highly organized and seem determined to reshape the country's politics. The effects of this age cohort and its political clout have been felt very quickly: Uri, the President's political party, did not even exist at the time of Roh's election, but it was able to assume majority control of the National Assembly in the spring of 2004.

However, President Roh's erratic actions and discordant political style have contributed directly to the stunning erosion in his political support since 2004, making him a lame duck well before the end of his term. Though Roh has recovered from previous political setbacks, the South Korean public has wearied of his confrontations with political adversaries, leaving the country divided and dispirited. Paradoxically, the previously dominant political forces in the ROK (known as the "5060 generation") have not yet been able to translate Roh's political liabilities into a sustained political recovery. Though the 5060 forces retain ample influence in certain areas (notably, control of several of the country's most prominent newspapers), they often seem marginalized and rudderless.

South Korea's long-term political future, therefore, seems increasingly up for grabs. But this political upheaval has had pronounced and potentially lasting effects. Massive shifts in leadership attitudes and in public opinion have taken place over the past half-decade, with national security strategy moving away from the close interdependence forged between the ROK and the United States during the Cold War. Kim's detailed assessment of public attitudes since Roh's election underscores this conclusion. There are very pronounced generational cleavages over various political identity issues, including policies toward North Korea, ROK defense policy, attitudes toward the United

States and China, and repeal or modification of the South's long-standing national security laws. Public opinion exhibits extraordinary volatility and variation, preventing political leaders from achieving meaningful consensus on national-level policy. Beyond doubt, South Korea's democratization since the late 1980s has been an extraordinary accomplishment. But Kim argues that modernization and democratization have combined to render South Korea's *guksi*, or national essence, largely irrelevant, without a new concept to supplant it. This has contributed to a crisis in national identity. Roh Moo Hyun has succeeded in burying the old order, but at ample cost. As Kim observes, Roh "has turned South Korea's political identity on its head. . . . [O]nce anticommunism was judged unfit, and illegitimate for an economically prosperous, militarily secure and democratically vibrant South Korea, many . . . Cold War beliefs no longer looked obvious."

Moreover, the search for new directions has triggered an internal blood-letting, leaving the country's political elites deeply divided. As Kim concludes, "by negatively rather than positively redefining South Korea's self as an opposite of its past, Roh ironically brought back to life its Cold War culture of hatred and distrust. . . . South Koreans fight over what they hate, not what they stand for." Kim has painted a disquieting picture of a political system "trapped in a crisis without an exit." These domestic divisions have also made it impossible for the South to develop a coherent long-term strategy toward the North, simultaneously leaving alliance relations with the United States vulnerable to manipulation by domestic forces.

Roh's actions are rooted primarily in his determination to disentangle South Korean politics from its Cold War past, rather than a considered assessment of strategy toward the North. This has provided Pyongyang with added breathing room as it seeks to ensure its long-term survival without being obligated to sustained reciprocity or transparency in its dealings with the South. Despite the DPRK's resumption of its nuclear weapons program and the enhancement of its ballistic missile capabilities, substantial segments of South Korean public opinion no longer connect these developments to ROK security. Moreover, through his advocacy of a "policy of peace and prosperity" since early 2003, Roh Moo Hyun has not let the protracted nuclear weapons impasse impede the opening of political or economic doors to the North. In few areas is the divergence between U.S. and South Korean views more pronounced.

Many in South Korea assert that the North has no practicable alternative to threat reduction and economic engagement with the ROK, which they expect to lead inexorably to reconciliation between the two Koreas. Growing numbers of South Koreans no longer conceive of North-South relations in adversarial terms. The immediate consequence of this shift in attitude is the ROK's increased commitment to regime sustainment in the

North, and it also helps explain the South's parallel gravitation toward China. The South has pursued its initiatives toward Pyongyang without appreciable attention to the North's political and military actions. Thus, the DPRK has achieved an ample political breakthrough with Seoul, since the North can anticipate open-ended support from the South. But might the South's role in the North ultimately trigger unforeseen consequences in the DPRK, as Lankov believes? Or will leaders in Pyongyang, despite the acute needs and extraordinary vulnerabilities of the DPRK, be able to confine the ROK's role to tourism, special industrial zones, and infrastructural projects, thereby limiting the South's reach into North Korean society? Alternatively, might a hybrid political identity evolve that neither Korea has yet to define? Has the North offered assurances and concessions to the South that Seoul has not revealed to the United States? What reciprocity (if any) is the South seeking from the North? There are no clear answers to these questions. Two conclusions, however, seem incontestable: the destinies of the two Koreas are increasingly intertwined; and the United States has only a limited understanding of the possibilities and consequences of the ROK's growing engagement with the DPRK.

NORTH KOREA'S ECONOMIC PROSPECTS

North Korea's longer-term economic prospects are pivotal in any assessment of the peninsula's future. The economic system remains in serious crisis, though this has yet to trigger a political meltdown. Though there has been a modest economic recovery since the late 1990s, this has not been the precursor to a larger economic transformation. The DPRK has persisted with grim resilience ever since the collapse of the Soviet Union and in the face of sharply diminished support from Russia and China, weathering a decade of acute economic contraction and societal privation. The DPRK leadership calculates that limited marketization, ample international assistance, and the continued allocation of major economic and industrial resources to the military sector (in relative terms, larger than that of any other country in the world) will enable the regime to maintain its hold on power.

Can North Korea indefinitely sustain such an approach without plunging into deeper economic crisis? Marcus Noland, Nicholas Eberstadt, and Phillip Wonhyuk Lim offer contrasting perspectives on these questions. Noland chronicles the DPRK's economic decline, Pyongyang's efforts to rejuvenate the national economy, and its pursuit of external support to help sustain the regime. He notes "the rupture of the traditional social compact," which has exacerbated various social inequalities in the North and, potentially, placed political stability at risk. These departures from *juche* (self-reliance) and the heightened emphasis on a "military first" campaign have "overturn[ed] the traditional paths to power and status: captains and entrepreneurs have now replaced party cadres and bureaucrats as preferred sons-in-law." As Noland concludes, "North Korea appears to be evolving toward some kind of unique post-communist totalitarian state . . . a strange revival of dynastic feudalism in the form of a nonsocialist patrimonial state." He does not offer detailed predictions, noting that there is no certain relationship between economic decline and political challenges to the regime. As he further observes, the system's prospects are also contingent on the strategies of external actors toward the North. Unlike Lankov, he deems political instability much more likely if international pressure on the North increases, and far less likely under conditions of sustained engagement with the outside world.

Eberstadt addresses a comparable set of questions, but from a different vantage point. He acknowledges that he has long predicted the collapse of the North Korean state, without this singular event coming to pass. He argues that the phenomenon of state collapse is highly contingent, noting that such an outcome (as in other historical cases) may have been "imminent but averted." Like Noland, he dates the North's economic decline from the 1980s, concluding that by the mid-1990s the DPRK was on a trajectory of economic collapse, defined as "the breakdown of the division of labor in the national economy." But he concludes that the major surge in external financial assistance to the DPRK in the mid- to late 1990s (primarily from the ROK and the United States) enabled the North to stave off this threat, thereby improving the possibility of longer-term survival. Eberstadt argues that profits from weapons sales, illicit economic transactions, and the prospect of renewed compensation for deferring further nuclear weapons development may enable the DPRK to persist as a state. But he remains profoundly skeptical that the September 2002 economic reforms (which included efforts to remonetize the North Korean economy) constitute meaningful change. While acknowledging that his predictions about the end of the system have not been validated, he concludes that "the specter of an economic collapse is a ghost that haunts the DPRK to this very day," which can only be remedied by more fundamental internal changes than he believes the regime is prepared to undertake.

Lim offers a much more positive assessment of the North's economic prospects. He believes that the policy changes of recent years reflect a fundamental shift in economic direction, though he also argues that the success of the new strategy will depend in substantial measure on resolution of the nuclear crisis and the resultant ability to attract significant amounts of foreign capital. He reviews various economic reforms related to price reform, increased autonomy for plant managers, and accommodation to market forces, suggesting that announced policy changes largely ratified developments that had already taken place. But he acknowledges very large uncertainties in any longer-term forecast. He hypothesizes four prototypical scenarios based on the degree of leadership commitment to major reform, and the attitudes and policies of external powers, especially the United States, toward assistance to the North. Satisfactory resolution of the nuclear crisis is therefore central to Lim's estimates of the longer term, even as he remains cautious about the prospects for a successful outcome. But none of his hypothetical outcomes posit the end of the North Korean system. Even in the most pessimistic of scenarios (characterized as the "arduous march"), the North grimly persists, even as it would remain largely isolated from the outside world and unprepared to yield its nuclear weapons capabilities. As he argues, it is not North Korea that has collapsed, but the models that have long anticipated the inevitability of state collapse.

The positing of alternative scenarios is an admittedly imperfect substitute for systematic observation and measurement. But heightened economic aid and humanitarian assistance, small-scale marketization, and a partial breakout from international isolation have clearly contributed to state survival. South Korea and China both calculate that external aid (especially in the energy and food sectors) can stave off a renewed humanitarian crisis, an assumption also shared by nongovernmental organizations. Neither Seoul nor Beijing is prepared to significantly constrict the flow of economic resources into the North, and Chinese entrepreneurs in particular have near-term opportunities to penetrate the North Korean domestic market.

The shift in the Six-Party Talks toward a more incentive-based approach (reflected in the September 2005 denuclearization declaration) appears to improve North Korea's prospects for survival. Despite the unease over continued nuclear weapons development in the North expressed by all five states negotiating with the DPRK, these issues have been largely trumped by more local concerns, a conclusion not lost on the North's representatives at the nuclear talks. Pyongyang's pursuit of a nuclear weapons capability, though intrinsically worrisome, reflects the acute vulnerabilities of an embattled regime, whose power and influence are increasingly circumscribed. But for how long and to what end can contradictory policy goals be sustained? Will North Korea prove capable of indefinitely garnering external assistance without having to forgo its nuclear weapons potential? For Pyongyang, economics and security are closely linked, but this relationship also depends on the calculations and actions of the South and the major powers. An open-ended, aid-based strategy does not necessarily posit a certain outcome, but it does render abrupt change far less likely. The policies of external powers therefore define the parameters of the North's interactions with the outside world. But the potential effects remain contingent on the DPRK's own actions, and on whether external aid will ultimately induce unanticipated internal change, irrespective of Pyongyang's preferences.

THE MILITARY RIVALRY

The North-South military confrontation (one that has also centrally involved U.S. forces) is among the enduring legacies of Korea's division. The armed face-off has been integral to the way both Koreas have defined and defended their respective identities and claims to legitimacy. Conventional deterrence, though at exceedingly high force levels, has been maintained by both sides for more than five decades. This has encompassed massive North Korean forward deployments in locations proximate to potential invasion corridors; significant American forces arrayed on the opposite side of the 38th Parallel; and large-scale ROK military forces subordinated to U.S.-designed and led command arrangements. All three factors are now undergoing significant change, but without a clear security end point. These issues are explored in the chapters by Seung Joo Baek and Yong Sup Han.

Baek traces the evolution of North Korean strategy and military capabilities since the early 1960s, when the DPRK launched its "four-point military guidelines." Notwithstanding its then-extant alliances with Moscow and Beijing, the North undertook an extraordinary commitment to military self-reliance, including in defense industrial production. Baek describes the realization of the DPRK's military strategy in subsequent decades, especially during the 1960s and 1970s, when the DPRK enjoyed high rates of economic growth. He also highlights the North's commitment to building a nuclear weapons infrastructure and to ballistic missile development in subsequent decades. Though he asserts that North Korea has not wavered from its declared commitment to military superiority over the South, he concedes that the DPRK's stunning industrial and economic contraction during the 1990s has redefined Pyongyang's military options.

Baek also notes the continued debates among ROK analysts on the security implications of the North's economic decline. It seems ever more problematic for the DPRK to sustain massive military forces (in relative terms, larger than any other state in the world), let alone undertake meaningful modernization of its increasingly suspect conventional capabilities. Baek sees North Korea increasingly wedded to an asymmetric military strategy that can compensate for its growing conventional vulnerabilities, thereby preserving its military options *in extremis*, but presumably geared more toward deterrence and defense than to an offensive strategy against the South. But he also highlights the persistence of an array of highly coercive options in North Korean military strategy, posing the issue of whether these are legacies of a bygone era reiterated largely for purposes of domestic legitimacy, or ones that remain integral to the North's plans in the event of renewed conflict, no matter what its source. Either conclusion underscores the persistence of latent instability on the peninsula, which Pyongyang continues to exploit for political-military advantage.

Han traces the growing changes in ROK defense policy and plans, including major up-heaval in the U.S.-ROK alliance. Despite the South's extraordinary economic growth and the emergence of more robust ROK military capabilities, he paints a somewhat dispiriting picture. He describes a persistent military threat posed by the North against the South, growing strains in the U.S.-ROK alliance, and the prospect of an opera-tional North Korean nuclear capability that would inhibit American military reinforce-ments in a future crisis. Han sees the ROK military leadership whipsawed between the mounting expectations of U.S. defense planners (who want South Korean forces to ful-fill defense responsibilities long assumed by the United States) and the need to adhere to the civilian leadership's increasingly relaxed assessment of the DPRK military threat. He notes that Seoul has long aspired to a more autonomous national defense concept and capability, but he voices skepticism about the realism of such a goal. He also con-cludes that the ROK military leadership never anticipated that the United States would move as vigorously as it has to reduce its forces deployed on the peninsula, or that U.S. officials would formulate a defense concept that explicitly moves beyond peninsular roles and missions. These changes convey the policy tensions that increasingly underlie ROK-U.S. defense planning.

Han highlights the incongruity between the continued risks of large-scale armed con-flict on the peninsula while the South's leadership seems intent on a defense strategy that is devoid (at least for presentational purposes) of a defining threat. He acknowl-edges that "the U.S. influence on South Korea's defense planning, force structure, crisis management, and doctrine has been dominant for so long that many observers cannot imagine South Korea's defense without the alliance." He expresses a fervent hope that both countries can achieve a shared vision of a future alliance but concedes that the outlines of such a vision are only dimly discernible. With U.S. and ROK threat percep-tions at cross-purposes, Han's forecast for the alliance and the future role of the ROK military seems uncertain and potentially disquieting. A far less politically potent mili-tary leadership in the South adds to an increasingly unsettled security forecast, with no obvious consensus on the road ahead.

KOREA AND THE REGIONAL POWERS

At different historical junctures, China, Japan, and Russia have all assumed major po-litical, military, and diplomatic roles in Korea, especially in periods when the peninsula has been prone to external penetration or outright domination. Contemporary politi-cal and strategic calculations are premised on different assumptions, particularly with the ROK pursuing a far more independent political identity. For example, Moscow and Beijing were instrumental to the late Cold War and early post–Cold War diplomatic realignments on the peninsula, enabling the ROK to achieve pivotal breakthroughs with both of its former adversaries. At present, Japanese diplomacy (in which Prime Minister Koizumi has been directly involved during visits to Pyongyang in 2002 and 2004) seeks an equivalent breakthrough with the North, suggesting that the DPRK also hopes to exploit possible inroads with neighboring states.

The major regional powers are therefore weighing their respective interests and comparative advantage under far more dynamic political and strategic circumstances. To varying degrees, each power recognizes the need to revisit its strategies toward Korea, deriving from concerns about peninsular stability, future power alignments on the peninsula, and longer-term trends in U.S. regional strategy. The calculations of each major regional power (and the corresponding responses of North and South) underscore that the peninsula remains an arena for major power collaboration and competition. But primary initiative has passed to China and, to a lesser extent, to Japan, with Russia increasingly relegated to a subordinate position. These issues are explored in ample detail in the chapters by Phillip Saunders, Jae Ho Chung, Victor Cha, Gilbert Rozman, and Alexandre Mansourov.

Among the regional powers, China has assumed an especially prominent role. Saunders traces the evolution of Chinese policy toward the peninsula, deeming it a microcosm of the changes in Beijing's domestic and foreign policies of the past two decades, as well as a means to solidify China's position and presumed leverage with both Koreas. The stakes for Beijing in Korea have increased immeasurably, simultaneously providing China with increased latitude in dealings with both North and South and underscoring the potential risks to Chinese interests if its principal policy assumptions are not validated. Saunders sees China motivated both by near-term concerns and by the opportunity to shape the peninsula in the longer run. He analyzes the contradictory impulses underlying Beijing's increased cultivation of the North, notwithstanding China's predominant focus on expanded political and economic ties to the ROK. As he observes, "North Korea is now viewed [by China] as a problem to be managed rather than as an ally or strategic asset." He notes the expectations of some Chinese policy analysts of an internal economic transition in the DPRK akin to that experienced in China, though most observers remain guarded about these possibilities, at least in the near term. In particular, he emphasizes Beijing's efforts to forestall various worst-case outcomes, encompassing regime collapse, a "nuclear domino effect" that might attend a failure to inhibit nuclear weapons development in the North, or a decision by Washington to initiate the use of force to eliminate Pyongyang's weapons program. These concerns underlie China's ever-more-prominent involvement as mediator and facilitator of the Six-Party Talks.

Even as Beijing seeks to elicit U.S. cooperation in the diplomatic process, the latent possibilities of a heightened Sino-American rivalry also shape Chinese policy calculations. Saunders notes the ample debate among Chinese policy analysts about the factors determining Beijing's longer-term options on the peninsula, especially should unification ultimately materialize. Notwithstanding China's growing awareness of its longer-term advantage on the peninsula, Saunders concludes that Chinese analysts still conceptualize Korea more as an arena for great-power competition, with particular attention to the potential for a coordinated U.S.-Japanese strategy to inhibit the extension of Chinese regional influence. This begs the issue of whether China is fully weighing Korea's longer-term power potential, as distinct from the immediate opportunity to attenuate the alliance bonds between Washington and Seoul and to deny Japan a larger peninsular role.

Chung focuses on the major changes in South Korean perceptions of China evident over the past decade. Despite the presumed commonality of interest between the ROK and Japan as American allies and fellow democracies, public opinion in South Korea exhibits far less negative remembrance of China's Korea intervention and of the China-DPRK alliance, compared to the intense hostility still directed against Japanese colonial rule. In Chung's view, the ROK's initial reassessment of China was triggered largely by economic calculations, but these have long since been abetted by heightened awareness of China's reemergence as a major power and the opportunities this presented Seoul to diversify its policy options. Beijing's unmistakable cultivation of Seoul has been highly validating to South Korea and helps explain the minimal attention among ROK analysts to the security implications of the rise of China, despite the substantial enhancement of Chinese military capabilities. (The appreciable expansion of China-ROK military-to-military relations is a primary manifestation of this phenomenon.) Some in the ROK also believe that China can play a significant role in restraining North Korea, thereby helping justify the South's increasingly benign view of peninsular security.

However, Chung notes that some leaders in Seoul continue to exhibit caution toward China's rise. For example, widespread Korean enthusiasm about trade and investment opportunities with Beijing might diminish somewhat if China's rapid growth begins to impinge on the ROK's presumed economic advantage. But Chung concludes that the ROK views the renewed links with its major-power neighbor as a means to limit Korea's "psychological dependence" on the United States. The rapprochement with China thus reflects a deeper reassessment of ROK foreign policy goals that (barring major shifts in Chinese policy) seems likely to be sustained, especially in light of the United States' deeming Japan its East Asian security partner of choice. Under such circumstances,

Chung concludes, the increasing congruence of ROK and Chinese policy interests will persist, without Seoul having to choose between its relations with Beijing and Washington. Policy makers in Seoul clearly believe that more diversified political-security ties, with South Korea positioned between the United States and China, will enhance the ROK's leverage with both states. This is not a risk-free strategy for South Korea, but it increasingly resonates within Seoul policy circles, as well as reflecting public sentiment.

Cha explores a similar range of issues, with particular attention to ROK judgments about Japan and their resultant effects on Seoul's strategic choices. In his view, recent U.S. force restructuring decisions on the peninsula and American moves toward an increasingly interdependent security relationship with Tokyo have triggered renewed fears of abandonment in Seoul, compelling the ROK to reassess its security alternatives. China's "inexorable gravitational pull" (especially in the economic realm) creates the prospect of a heightened South Korean identity with continental Asia (i.e., China) and a distancing from the ROK's previous affiliation with maritime Asia (i.e., the U.S.-Japan alliance).

However, Cha does not believe that an unequivocal "Korean shift" is inevitable. He evaluates Seoul's security deliberations in relation to offensive versus defensive realism, arguing that the ROK is more likely to pursue the latter course. He concludes that power-balancing goals will dominate ROK security calculations, leading Seoul to retain its primary security affiliation with Washington and Tokyo. He also argues that commonality with Tokyo as a fellow industrial democracy and the longer-term concern about Chinese economic domination of Northeast Asia will diminish Korea's willingness to subordinate its interests to Beijing's preferences. In the event of peninsular unification, Cha asserts that Seoul's reasons for limiting its dependence on China will be even more compelling. As he observes, "realists . . . appreciate future uncertainty and know that North Korea will not be around forever. In a unification scenario . . . a united Korea faces the prospect of an 800-mile contiguous border with a militarily and economically burgeoning China whose intentions are not transparent." He concludes that such a possibility will diminish sentiment for an unequivocal ROK tilt toward Beijing.

Cha also devotes attention to Japan's relations with North Korea. He does not see Tokyo possessing leverage with Pyongyang comparable to that of Washington or Seoul. But he concludes that Japanese financial support could prove pivotal for longer-term multilateral aid packages to the North, thereby giving Pyongyang ample incentive to address Japanese policy concerns. These encompass the threats to Japanese security posed by the DPRK's ballistic missiles, but also the fate of Japanese citizens abducted by the

North in earlier decades, which remains a matter of intense domestic concern within Japan. Cha notes the widespread criticism that Prime Minister Koizumi's visits to the DPRK triggered within Japan, but he believes these criticisms are largely unwarranted. He concludes that a coordinated U.S.-Japanese policy toward the DPRK has led to uncharacteristic flexibility on the part of Pyongyang, with North Korea unable to separate Tokyo from Washington. On this basis, Cha believes that Japan and the United States have developed a viable long-term strategy toward the North that makes forward movement contingent on the DPRK's addressing the concerns of both countries.

Rozman explores Chinese and Japanese strategies in ample detail. He contends that analysts in both systems have not fully revealed the deeper calculations underlying these political and strategic assessments. In his view, both states are locked in a highly competitive dynamic that now shapes their respective approaches to the two Koreas. As he observes, "China and Japan have resumed their regional competition . . . [while] the United States and Russia, which had carved Korea in two, also remain intent on playing a role in shaping its destiny. The region is returning to triangularity at its core. . . . China and Japan must deal with a defiant North Korea, shape relations with an emboldened South Korea, and draw on the distant but overwhelming power of the United States, as well as a Russia insistent on a continued role." Rozman contends that East Asia's two predominant powers interpret Korean realities in light of how each perceives the potential role of the other. To China, a divided peninsula or one subject to Japanese control dictates direct Chinese involvement, so as to reduce Tokyo's opportunities to consolidate its advantage on the Asian mainland. To Japan, a Korea under predominant Chinese influence heightens Tokyo's marginalization on the Asian continent, compelling Japan to somehow ensure a major political and economic presence on the peninsula.

Rozman argues that China steadily gained the advantage on the peninsula over the course of the 1990s, requiring Tokyo to seek inroads to counteract the consolidation of Chinese influence. But Japan was inhibited by the dominant U.S. position in Korea and the starkly adversarial environment on the peninsula that persisted even after the end of the Cold War. Rozman interprets Prime Minister Koizumi's September 2002 trip to Pyongyang as a bold effort to inject Japan into peninsular politics, an initiative that the Prime Minister has endeavored to sustain throughout the prolonged nuclear impasse. He contends that China and Japan approach the crisis with very different objectives in mind: "China sought to transform the regional security order, reducing U.S. hegemony and, to the extent possible, undercutting America's bilateral alliances." By contrast, he sees Japan compelled to operate in the shadow of American power, with Tokyo conceding China's lead role in the multilateral process now taking shape. As Rozman concludes, "China occupies the pivot and has no intention of relinquishing it." He contends that Beijing feels that its larger regional strategy is well served by a "united, proud, and strong-willed [DPRK that] demands equality in foreign relations as well as respect. This suggests that China has no way to persuade the North to abandon its nuclear program without a deal that is in its national interests." Beijing therefore favors a deliberate, longer-term approach to addressing the nuclear issue, whereas Washington and presumably Tokyo fear that anything short of an unequivocal resolution of the crisis will enable North Korea to again evade its obligations while garnering ample political and economic compensation along the way.

However, Rozman contends that Tokyo is also seeking to ensure its strategic equities on the peninsula and that this has entailed continued internal debate over the wisdom of tethering Japan to U.S. policy goals. This in particular pertains to the possibility of a future Sino-Japanese rivalry in Northeast Asia. He sees Japan as far warier about the prospect of unification than is China: "[M]any in Japan expect a unifying Korea to become more nationalistic against their country and to favor ties with China. They had taken South Korea for granted as a state limited by the threat from the North and unable to leave the U.S. embrace, but now they are scrambling to find a way to retain influence [in South Korea] and to develop a direct connection to North Korea." This provides the relevant background for Koizumi's efforts to cultivate relations with Pyongyang and to rebuild ties with Seoul, which have been badly frayed by the Prime Minister's repeated visits to the Yasukuni Shrine, renewed controversies over Japanese history textbooks, and heightened tensions over competing territorial claims in the waters between Japan and Korea. The outlook for Japan's relations with both Koreas remains problematic, but leaders in Tokyo have few alternatives if they are to develop the means to influence peninsular developments in the longer term. Tokyo is uneasily straddling alternative approaches to regional security, still unable to articulate a longer-term Japanese strategy toward the peninsula. As Rozman concludes: "The critical questions are not who wants a nuclear North or who wants unification soon, but who is interested in using an active North Korea to shape the region. China is, the U.S. is not, and Japan may be, depending on its North Korean and South Korean ties."

Mansourov explores Russia's diminished position and involvement on the peninsula following the Cold War, and Moscow's disinclination to engage in renewed rivalry over Korea. He describes Russia as "a strategic player with limited economic stakes in Korea," unwilling to undertake high-risk infrastructural or industrial investments in the North and equally unlikely to be more than a second-order trading and investment partner of the South. He highlights how leaders in Moscow have put forward "a well-calibrated two-Korea policy." Mansourov characterizes Russian policy toward the North as "passive, reactive, and cautious," with major policy initiatives occurring only through periodic senior leadership interventions. In the early stages of the renewed nuclear crisis, Moscow failed in its efforts to assume a mediating role. In a word, Russia lacks the requisite resources and opportunities to assume a genuine leadership role, tacitly conceding this position to China. Moscow does seem committed to meaningful threat reduction and nonproliferation on the peninsula, which presupposes attentiveness to Pyongyang's security requirements. But Russian policy is equally unprepared to condone, let alone support, coercive moves or threats from any party, including the DPRK.

Russia nevertheless seeks to protect its fundamental security interests on the peninsula, which will remain subordinate to its larger stakes in bilateral relations with China, the United States, and Japan. As Mansourov concludes: "Both the maintenance of the existing status quo and unification are acceptable policy alternatives to Moscow, as long as Russian influence is preserved in Pyongyang and Seoul, and no other great power (either China or the United States) is able to establish its dominance over the entire peninsula." Under conditions of unification, it might be possible to envision a somewhat heightened Russian role, especially in view of Moscow's direct experience with the dissolution of the Soviet system. But large-scale political change will be determined largely by forces beyond Moscow's control.

However, the present environment is hardly static. Stability may be a notional shared interest of all parties in Korea, but it is an imprecise and ultimately unsatisfactory label. Change (if not outright turbulence) is afoot at virtually all levels, and no state with enduring interests on the peninsula can deem itself a bystander. Developments on the peninsula will have larger reverberations across Northeast Asia as a whole; Korea is where various forces and interests converge as well as compete.

THE UNITED STATES AND SOUTH KOREA:
ALLIANCE REDEFINED OR ALLIANCE IMPERILED?

The U.S.-ROK alliance does not stand apart from these ongoing changes. However, the modalities and mechanisms of the alliance have often lagged well behind major shifts in great-power relations and internal developments within South Korea. William Pendley traces the stresses encountered by the United States and the ROK as both nations have sought to adapt to the post–Cold War world and to the South's democratic transition. He notes the alliance's singular success in deterring armed conflict for a full half-century and in facilitating the ROK's extraordinary economic and political transition. Though these purposes remain integral to the alliance, he foresees major challenges that put the sense of shared purpose at increased risk. Pendley chronicles the evolution of the North Korean nuclear issue over the past decade or more, including the increased divergence in U.S. and ROK approaches to the dispute and repeated efforts by Pyongyang to weaken the alliance. Though he does not argue that the military relationship can carry the alliance on its own, he believes that explicit, mutually agreed understandings are an absolute prerequisite. He does not envision these understandings as a one-way street. In Pendley's view, "increased coordination and consultation" must be more than a slogan; it needs to be the hallmark of a "modernized alliance."

Pendley places particular emphasis on three areas: (1) threat perception; (2) internal change within South Korea; and (3) the implications of U.S. global strategy for military planning on the peninsula. Each highlights the challenges to ensuring the alliance's viability and relevance. He argues that "the Korea-U.S. alliance is strongest when faced with a common threat that is acknowledged by both Seoul and Washington," yet this shared perception seems increasingly absent. He faults the United States for being slow to adjust to Korean nationalism and democratization, including to ROK expectations of the U.S. transition from a leading to a supporting role in command arrangements and in the alliance division of labor. He challenges both leaderships to reinforce deterrence on the peninsula. Though he does not express abject pessimism about the future, he concludes that a credible alliance could well be at risk unless the two countries work vigorously to renew and refurbish these ties.

Pendley does not believe that both countries and both militaries are simply "going through the motions," but he does recognize that inertia cannot be a substitute for strategy. Beneath the veneer of shared alliance goals, however, the evidence of divergence continues to accumulate. For many years, the ROK leadership was almost preternaturally disposed to accommodate U.S. expectations, but this era has passed. The test for the longer term is whether either or both leaderships are able to reconcile or bridge their differences. Failing that, both countries will have to adjust to a different reality and a different future that neither desires.

Any assessment of the alliance's future must begin by recognizing the fundamental asymmetries of interest and power between the United States and South Korea. First, the United States is a superpower, whereas the ROK is a local or regional power. To South Korea, the United States has always loomed very large in its thinking and planning; to the United States, South Korea is important, but it is one commitment among many. Second, the United States was the dominant force in designing the alliance and determining its overall purposes and directions, with the ROK in a subordinate position. The ROK found this more acceptable when it was weak, vulnerable, and nondemocratic, but it is progressively less satisfied by an unequal relationship. Third, the United States defines its security requirements in global terms, whereas Korea's strategic horizons remain far more circumscribed. This third asymmetry is also reflected in competing American and Korean visions of future East Asian security.

To some observers, many of these underlying tensions and differences will only be clarified by peninsular unification. Korea at present remains an incomplete or unfinished state. At a conceptual level, both Washington and Seoul have long made reference to the shared goal of a unified, democratic Korea, and unification may ultimately transpire. There would be undoubted clarity in a one-state solution, though this still begs the issue of how such an outcome would transpire and what the dominant strategic orientation of a unified Korea might be. At the same time, though unification can be imagined, it is not yet at hand. The Six-Party Talks attest to the reality of the DPRK, and the notional contours of a multilateral agreement obligate all signatories to peaceful coexistence and recognition of one another's legitimacy. However, some of the most contentious issues between Washington and Seoul concern their respective strategies toward the North. For example, the United States asserts that, as a condition for achieving normal relations with Washington, North Korea must make a "strategic decision" to definitively yield its nuclear weapons potential. But few anticipate such an unequivocal action on the part of the DPRK. It is particularly doubtful that leaders in Seoul will insist upon it as the entry fee that Pyongyang must pay for enhanced relations, including the provision of ample economic assistance. The preferred ROK approach is anathema to the United States, underscoring the growing divergence in national strategies.

Major differences are also reflected in the changes in U.S. defense strategy on the peninsula. The Bush administration is in the midst of a significant realignment in its global military deployments, with U.S. forces in the ROK near the forefront of these deliberations and decisions. By the end of 2008, a third of the U.S. forces that were stationed in Korea at the outset of the administration will have been withdrawn from the peninsula; additional American units will have been redeployed well to the south of their long-standing locations in the ROK. U.S. officials argue that the capability to surge forces over long distance and the ability to exploit new defense technologies to defeat a renewed attack by the North enable the United States to reduce the size and mix of forces deployed in Korea without diminishing deterrence or weakening the U.S. capacity to reinforce in a crisis. The United States no longer accepts the logic of open-ended deployment of U.S. forces at fixed locations in service of a military strategy that it believes has long outlived its utility. American officials also argue, not without reason, that South Korea is wealthy and powerful enough to shoulder increased defense burdens.

The reduction in U.S. force levels on the peninsula is further symptomatic of larger shifts in U.S. regional strategic priorities. The Department of Defense has conveyed to South Korean defense officials its desire to build air and sea hubs on the peninsula that would be designed to facilitate military operations in unspecified "regional contingencies."

This has left South Korean planners triply uneasy: first, because U.S. forces would be increasingly focused on nonpeninsular missions; second, because many in South Korea believe that the United States seeks to envelop Seoul in contingency planning directed against China; and third, because Seoul is increasingly uneasy about the prospect of more coercive strategies to eliminate North Korea's nuclear weapons potential. In all the above areas, South Korean officials perceive an increasing divergence in U.S. and ROK goals, thereby eroding the strategic underpinnings of the alliance. President Roh Moo Hyun's advocacy of a "balancer" concept captures the essence of the South's policy dilemmas. In this concept, the ROK is the country "in between," in both a physical and strategic sense, intent on developing an alternative to threat-driven defense planning. Taken to its logical conclusion, a balancer strategy challenges the fundamental underpinnings of the alliance.

Thus, the sustainability of the U.S.-ROK alliance in its extant form is far from assured. The security relationship increasingly lacks a strategic concept and rationale that is fully accepted by both leaderships. South Korea envisions a strategy that combines continued security ties with the United States and nonadversarial ties with all its neighbors, including North Korea. The United States sees the necessity of a strategy that encompasses collaboration with the ROK, but not to the exclusion of U.S. security requirements that involve the peninsula and go beyond it. Despite extensive bilateral negotiations between both countries in recent years, a deeper strategic conversation has yet to transpire. Without a frank discussion of the strategies, interests, and goals of both countries that might define the alliance in the 21st century, U.S.-ROK relations could be increasingly adrift, leading both into uncharted waters that neither would welcome. Indeed, neither country is addressing how such tensions and controversies are evaluated and exploited by Pyongyang and Beijing.

Beyond dispute, the Korean Peninsula is at the center of changes that are reshaping regional geopolitics. The transformation of the peninsula is not a question of if, but of when and how. Many of these prospective changes remain poorly understood in the United States, and American decision makers have often been slow to respond to the evidence of ferment and realignment. Though the United States retains a major stake in Korea's future, the American role (especially the military role) is likely to be exercised increasingly from a distance. Moreover, compared with the past, the United States will be far less able to determine the pace and directions of change. The future will entail a Korean peninsula that is ever more "Koreanized." This volume endeavors to elucidate these possibilities and their consequences, not to divine solutions for regional security. But a very different Korea looms, portending major change across the region and in American strategy in Northeast Asia.

2

Korean Nationalism
Its History and Future

Robert A. Scalapino

The Korean peninsula occupies a unique geopolitical position. Few, if any, societies—ancient or modern—have been surrounded by three larger, more powerful nations. Historically, China served as suzerain for Korea, with countless generations of Korean monarchs and *yangban* (nobility) paying homage to the great empire on their northern border. China did not occupy Korea, nor did it impose its government on the Koreans. For these reasons, it had deeper influence both culturally and politically. Confucianism became the dominant philosophic creed throughout Korea, and monarchical supremacy the key to political unity.

With the decline of China's power and prestige at the end of the 19th century, Korea was subjected to the increasing influence of Russia and Japan. The era of Russian primacy was brief, commencing with the defeat of China in the Sino-Japanese War of 1894–95 and ending with the Russian defeat at the hands of Japan a decade later. Even prior to that event, Japanese influence was rising, reflecting the growing military and economic power of the Meiji government. Here was a nation that, after abandoning isolation, sought to learn from the more advanced nations of the West while retaining key Japanese characteristics. In progressive stages, Japan took power in the Korean peninsula, culminating in full-fledged annexation in 1910. A separate and independent Korea no longer existed.

From its first manifestations, modern Korean nationalism was shaped by this history of subjugation. At an early point, Korean national consciousness formed around the principle of "repel the barbarians." Even more than China, imperial Korea sought to exclude outsiders. China's failure to constrain the barbarians was a prominent factor in its declining influence in Korea. In modern times, animosity was directed primarily against Asian "foreigners"—especially the Japanese, since it was they who posed the greatest threat—but a broader xenophobia remained implanted in the society.

Unlike the situation in Japan, the Korean monarchy lacked full-fledged support in the early modern period, and while such events as the assassination of Queen Min by the Japanese in 1895 evoked strong protests, internal opposition to the Korean government was recurrent, as the Tonghak rebellion of that same period made clear. As the thrust of Japan became more threatening, King Kojong sent a letter in October 1905 to President Theodore Roosevelt seeking American assistance against the Japanese. However, the United States, now deeply committed in the Philippines, did not wish to become involved with Japan over Korea.

Fundamentally, Korea had three broad options in seeking to defend its territorial and cultural integrity. One possibility was maximum isolation, and that option had been pursued throughout the centuries, causing Korea to acquire the label "Hermit Kingdom." It was attempted in some degree by North Korea until the recent past. In the age of globalization, however, it has become increasingly unrealistic. A second possibility was to seek positive and relatively balanced relations with the three neighboring powers. The problem with this policy was that it rarely succeeded, as events during and after the late 19th century illustrated. One power became dominant and came to wield primary influence. Japan provided the final evidence. The third option was to seek the support of a distant, nonthreatening power to balance contending neighboring forces. King Kojong's effort in this regard was replicated by post-1945 Korean leaders, including Kim Dae Jung and Roh Moo Hyun.

Meanwhile, Korean nationalism also had to overcome daunting domestic obstacles. First, the monarchy did not receive universal support; hence, the type of personal symbol so vital to Japanese nationalism was not fully available. More important, the intertwined forces of factionalism and regionalism interfered with the achievement of national consciousness. Personalism dominated politics as well as other relationships, and loyalty to one leader was coupled with antagonism toward others. Moreover, provincial identifications dominated national ones, with the commitments to localism powerful up to the present. Thus, a candidate might receive 90 percent of the votes in his district and 5 percent in that of his opponent.

Notwithstanding these handicaps, nationalism gradually emerged, with its exponents initially coming largely from the *yangban,* scholar, and student classes. Nationalist impulses among the lower classes existed but often took relatively primitive form, such as in the Tonghak Rebellion of 1894–95, when a mystical religious cult emerged as a political force promoting antiforeign activities. As nationalism assumed a broader, more cohesive dimension, however, certain external influences often served as stimulants, among them Christianity and Western-style democracy. The first mainstream nationalist movement within Korea was the March First Movement. Massive demonstrations began on 1 March 1919 and lasted for approximately one year, with calls for independence and relief from alien oppression. Many of the leaders, coming from student and religious groups, had been influenced by Woodrow Wilson's Fourteen Points, which included a call for self-determination.

The March First Movement had repercussions among the overseas Koreans, who were widely dispersed at that point. In addition to those in the United States and Japan, a sizable number were in northern China, Manchuria, and Siberia. Some activists, such as Rhee Syngman, had long been active in the United States, promoting Korean independence among fellow countrymen. When a Korean provisional government was set up in Shanghai on 10 April 1920, Rhee was designated premier. A provisional legislative assembly, composed of representatives of the eight Korean provinces, Siberia, China, and the United States, was also created. However, the Shanghai Provisional Government was riven by factional quarrels and growing ideological divisions. At an early point after the Bolshevik revolution, Koreans in Manchuria and Siberia made contact with the Russian Communists, receiving economic and military assistance. In June 1918, Yi Tong Hwi, later to be premier of the Provisional Government, organized a Korean People's Socialist Party in Khabarovsk. The following year, the group changed the party name to the Korean Communist Party.

As the years passed, the rift between the Koreans affiliated with the Communist movement and those committed to liberal democracy or more conservative causes deepened. With the Manchurian Incident of 1931 and the Japanese occupation of Manchukuo, Korean nationalists found a potential ally in China. The Chinese government began to provide Korean nationalists with financial and political support. On 10 November 1932, factional differences were temporarily set aside and the Korean Anti-Japanese Front Unification League was created, with the Korean National Revolutionary Party established shortly thereafter. However, the ideological divisions could not be contained, and two large blocs emerged, the majority being in the leftist camp.

These developments had limited impact on the Koreans on the peninsula. As the Pacific War approached, large numbers of Koreans were recruited into the Japanese armed forces or sent to Japan as laborers. Nationalist activities were almost wholly conducted abroad, not in Korea. In April 1941, at a conference held in Hawaii, support was pledged to the provisional government now operating in Chungking, and Rhee

Syngman was designated diplomatic agent to that body. The Koreans associated with the Communists, mostly operating in Manchuria in the form of small guerrilla groups, remained quite separate from the others.

The stage was thus set for the events that followed the Japanese defeat in 1945. The division of occupied Korea was a product of the wartime alliance involving the Soviet Union, the United States, and other parties. Russia had agreed to enter the war and, in return, play a role in post-war Asia-Pacific affairs. Its entry, only six days prior to the war's end, resulted in a rapid march into Manchuria, toward the Korean border. Russia could easily have occupied the entire Korean peninsula, presiding over a unified Korea of a decidedly new type. U.S. troops were no nearer than Okinawa, and the United States had no detailed plans for implanting forces in Korea. However, because Russia wanted American support and cooperation in the post-war era, an agreement was hastily reached to have a joint occupation, with the 38th Parallel the dividing line. At the outset, it was assumed that the occupation would be temporary, ending when an independent, unified Korean government could be established.

In late December 1945, an agreement was reached at the Three Ministers' Conference in Moscow to establish a trusteeship for Korea for up to five years, under a "provisional democratic government" created with the assistance of a Joint Commission consisting of U.S. and USSR representatives. At this point, Korean nationalism demonstrated its new vitality. Throughout the country, South and North, strong protests were voiced. It was alleged that trusteeship made Korea a vassal of other nations. A typical comment was issued in the newspaper *Haebang Ilbo*, asserting that the United States had promised independence to the Philippines immediately, a nation "several thousand years behind Korea in terms of history or civilization."

Even the Korean Communists initially opposed the trusteeship plan. However, at the beginning of January 1946, the party was brought into line by Russian pressure, despite continuing internal opposition. In contrast, the United States failed completely to get the non-Communist groups in the South to support the plan. While the trusteeship plan severely damaged the Korean Communists in terms of public opinion, the non-Communists of the South remained divided. Rhee Syngman had emerged as the leader of moderate and conservative groups by early 1946, but efforts to form a strong coalition between liberal conservatives and the left continued to falter.

The course of nationalism developed in distinctive ways, first in North Korea, then in the South after 1945. Kim Il Sung and his small band of comrades came into North Korea some weeks after the Japanese surrender, entering with another contingent of Russian troops. Kim, however, was different from the Soviet Koreans who came in sizable numbers in the opening months of the Occupation. He and his band had been in a training camp near Khabarovsk for nearly five years, but Kim's youth had been spent in North China and Manchuria. At this point thirty years of age, young Kim had accepted Russian guidance and, with it, Marxism-Leninism. However, his group, known as the Kapsan Faction, maintained a largely separate identity from those who were more thoroughly Russianized Koreans.

Initially, leadership in the North was in the hands of Cho Man Sik, an ardent non-Communist nationalist of moderate persuasion and very popular with his supporters. At an early point, however, Soviet support went strongly to Kim, perhaps because he was perceived as malleable—young and without a firm domestic base. Thus, when Cho was ousted in early 1946 because of his opposition to trusteeship, Kim Il Sung was supported by the Russian authorities in taking power. The Kim Il Sung era had begun.

When Russian troops departed in 1948, Kim had established himself as the key leader, but he faced competition from the separate South Korean, Yenan, and Soviet-Russian factions. The Korean War represented for Kim a short-term defeat but, in certain respects, a long-term victory. Seeing the disunity of Republic of Korea (ROK) political forces and taking full account of the withdrawal of American troops from the South and, more important, the assertion of Secretary of State Dean Acheson that South Korea was not within the U.S. defense perimeter, Kim decided to unify Korea by force. He managed to gain the approval of a somewhat dubious Stalin by insisting that even if the Americans sought to intervene, they would arrive too late; victory would already have been achieved. Mao and his Chinese colleagues were also informed of Kim's intentions and accepted them, although they did not expect to become involved.

As conflict erupted, Kim Il Sung issued strong nationalist appeals, calling upon the Korean people to unite under a socialist banner and create a strong nation independent of all external pressures. North Korean practices, however, were far from unifying, with those who had opposed Communism eliminated in a variety of ways. Meanwhile, victory turned quickly into disaster for North Korea in the aftermath of General MacArthur's Inchon landing. The Northern forces were forced into a precipitous retreat, and when the United States decided to cross the 38th Parallel, American forces quickly pushed the defeated Democratic People's Republic of Korea (DPRK) troops back to the Yalu, on the China border. At this point, China entered the war, unwilling to see a unified Korea under non-Communist (and American) control, and the war ended with the reestablishment of two Koreas.

While the war proved enormously costly to Kim and his forces, in terms of both lives and physical destruction, it enabled him to begin the process of eliminating his Communist rivals. The first to feel Kim's wrath was the South Korean faction, headed by Pak Hon Yong, a veteran revolutionary with an extensive following. Pak had come to the North and initially assumed an important role. In September 1952, however, he and his key supporters were charged with conspiring to overthrow the Kim leadership, and several were immediately executed. Pak himself was not tried and executed until December 1955. One powerful faction outside the Kim Il Sung circle had been eliminated. In 1956–58, key members of the Yenan and Soviet factions were eliminated, either through imprisonment or through a return to their home bases. By 1958, Kim Il Sung had no major opposition. His Korean Workers Party was in total control. Kim now proceeded to establish a regime of his own choosing, nominally a part of the international socialist movement but in reality a system resting upon xenophobic nationalism, more traditional than modern.

Until the Korean War, the DPRK was highly dependent upon the Soviet Union, both for security and for economic assistance. During and after that war, however, reliance shifted extensively to China. Thus, as the Sino-Soviet rift widened in the late 1950s, the DPRK tilted to the Chinese side. Yet even with respect to China, Kim took care to maintain a certain separateness. An important part of DPRK nationalism was the effort, reminiscent of the Hermit Kingdom, to keep outsiders from entering the country too extensively. The dominant slogan became *juche,* or self-reliance. In addition, the DPRK assumed all of the attributes of an absolute monarchy. In contrast to earlier times, the new monarch sought—and for the most part obtained—the total loyalty of his followers. He was defined by the media and in all official statements as omniscient, all-caring, and capable of leading his people to new glory. Both Kim Il Sung and his son, Kim Jong Il, have sought to cement their power by tying the military closely to them, making it the principal element in the upper political hierarchy and awarding it special economic privileges. This is officially labeled the *songun* ("military first") policy.

The economic policies followed by the North until recently helped to underwrite xenophobic nationalism. By keeping market forces minimal and precluding extensive foreign trade and investment through a host of restrictions, economic intercourse with outsiders, even with the South Koreans, was extremely limited. In recent years, however, Kim Jong Il has been forced to recognize that the old economic order is no longer feasible. The DPRK has been a failing society economically, with severely threatening social repercussions. Consequently, both internal changes and efforts to open the doors to foreign traders and investors have commenced.

It remains to be seen how successful these efforts will be. Moreover, the most extensive efforts have been with respect to North-South relations. Following the opening of

South Korean tourism to Mt. Kumgang, plans have been laid for a special economic zone headquartered at Kaesong, immediately across from the Demilitarized Zone (DMZ), with South Korean businesses encouraged to undertake investments, taking advantage of cheap North Korean labor. Rail and road lines across the DMZ are also being reopened. In addition, high-level North-South military talks have been held, with agreement on steps to prevent accidental conflicts at sea and on the suspension of propaganda broadcasts along the border. These activities, both economic and in the security realm, have been hailed in the North under the banner of "Reconciliation and Future Reunification." Similarly, agreements on marching together at the opening of the Olympics and holding joint student meetings symbolize the current mood. Unquestionably, the "Sunshine Policy" of ROK President Kim Dae Jung and the "Peace and Prosperity Policy" advocated by his successor, Roh Moo Hyun, have greatly facilitated the North's new approach.

There remains, however, an enormous gap—political as well as economic—between the two Koreas. Thus, reunification at best will be a lengthy process, barring the collapse of the North or armed conflict, neither of which seems likely. The progress in North-South relations may well continue, but there are many hurdles to be crossed, and the appeal to nationalism and to the unity of the Korean people, will not alone suffice. For the near future, nationalism in the DPRK will continue to focus on loyalty to leadership, past and present, and the need to maintain total unity to combat the threat of the United States. Japan is also portrayed as having not unequivocally renounced its past evils and, hence, to be carefully watched. Suspicions regarding Japan constitute one of the few sentiments shared, in considerable measure, by North and South, despite growing economic interaction and the efforts of President Kim Dae Jung and Japanese Prime Minister Koizumi to improve bilateral relations.

Meanwhile, if economic intercourse with the external world goes forward, the repercussions in the DPRK are likely to be similar to those taking place in China and Vietnam. New ideas and approaches will gradually be introduced from the outside, and with economic growth, pluralism will develop within the society. Greater attention will have to be paid to public concerns. In the case of the DPRK, given the economic conditions (per capita GDP in 2003 was estimated to be only 1/13 that of the ROK, or slightly over $800 per annum) and the deep traditionalism embedded in the political system, there are many political hazards in pursuing a course of opening up. In all probability, this is the key reason why Kim Jong Il and his associates have been so hesitant and have searched so extensively to develop a possible model that will prove effective. It is also probable that opening in its diverse forms has evoked differences of opinion in the top echelons of the DPRK elite, although these have been carefully concealed.

Another problem largely unique to the DPRK is the future of dynastic succession. Will one of Kim Jong Il's sons replace him, and will he be as widely accepted? Traditionalism in this as in other respects is not likely to withstand the process of modernization forever. At a minimum, the extreme personalization of politics must be modified to enable a greater institutional role. In the DPRK, nationalism has long been the pillar upon which power has rested, with ideology twisted to fit nationalist requirements. No doubt this will continue, yet if the emphasis is to be increasingly on the goal of reunification and the unity of the whole Korean people and nation, there will be a serious problem in meshing certain past DPRK nationalist themes, such as the omnipotence of the leader, with the democratic system of the ROK.

Nationalism in the South proceeded along a decidedly different path. The foremost champion of Korean nationalism in the ROK initially was Rhee Syngman, who had spent more than four decades leading the movement for Korean independence and democracy. Yet Rhee, like many charismatic figures, represented a paradox. While wedded ideologically to democracy and freedom, he was personally autocratic and fiercely independent, rarely willing to accept the advice of others unless it coincided with his views. Hence, he soon came into conflict both with American Occupation authorities and with Washington. Alternatives, however, proved impossible to establish.

Rhee's nationalism rested on the thesis that the Korean people had the right to govern themselves, free from all outside interference, including that of the United States. Unfortunately, he was not able to put together a lasting and effective coalition that could advance and carry out effective policies. The Korean War provided an interlude, admittedly disastrous for the people, and Rhee returned to authority angered by an armistice that he felt denied the South Koreans a deserved victory. As the 1950s drew to a close, economic conditions in the ROK worsened, and political unrest increased. Student riots took place, with casualties and growing hatred. Finally, Rhee was persuaded to resign, leaving Korea for Hawaii.

The ensuing brief era of Chang Myon was marked by the failure of a democratically inclined leader. Chang could not find a path between the left and the conservatives and therefore lost the support of both. A military coup took place in May 1961, and for the next eighteen years, the head of the ROK was a military man, Park Chung Hee. Park was a simple man and far from democratic in his instincts, but he launched the ROK on its remarkable path of economic development. His prime ambition was to raise the ROK's economic status, both to benefit the Korean people and to raise South Korea's position in the Asia-Pacific region. In this he succeeded, and this is the principal reason that, in a poll conducted a few years ago, the Korean people chose Park as their favorite leader in the post-1945 era.

Park was also strongly supportive of the U.S.-ROK security alliance and cooperated with the American military in a variety of ways. Like most other Korean leaders, however, he pursued his own domestic policies, largely ignoring American complaints about human rights violations. A crisis did emerge when ROK intelligence agents abducted Kim Dae Jung, then in exile, from his Tokyo hotel room in 1973 and put him on a ship with the intention of ending his life. U.S. authorities, alerted to the event, shadowed the ship and made it clear to the Park government that Kim Dae Jung's death would have serious consequences. He was spared, although given a lengthy prison sentence after reaching Seoul.

In this period, nationalism in the ROK was directed mainly at building up leadership, stimulating pride in economic accomplishments, and condemning the North. Gradually, however, the ROK evolved toward a more pluralistic society, a product in considerable degree of the nation's economic advances and the emergence of a large, educated middle class. Journalists, academics, and university students began to protest certain political restrictions. At the time of Park's assassination in late October 1979, martial law had been declared in the southern region due to a series of public demonstrations over the ouster of Kim Young Sam, the key opposition leader, from the National Assembly, as well as other issues. When General Chun Doo Hwan took power in 1980, political instability was rife. After some initial liberal moves, Chun cracked down on protesters, closing universities and outlawing most political activities. The Kwangju uprising followed, with many hundreds killed.

During this stormy period, Chun received the support of the American government, both passive (nonintervention) and active (receiving Chun at the White House in February 1981). Thus, many activists became bitter at the United States, with students in particular blaming the United States for such events as the Kwangju killings. By the late 1980s, the United States, aware of the risks, was warning the Chun government that it could not meet broad middle class protests with military force. Thus, when Roh Tae Woo became president in 1988, he pledged the creation of a democratic government. It was under his successor, Kim Young Sam, elected in 1992, however, that the political tide shifted appreciably, paving the way for Kim Dae Jung and Roh Moo Hyun.

During this period, nationalism in South Korea was taking on new dimensions. Coupled with the call for more political rights was a rising demand for greater international recognition. Inevitably, the issues of American power and policy emerged, especially among the younger generations. This new emphasis first came to the fore in the early period of the Kim Dae Jung administration. Kim had made as one of his goals the inauguration of a new policy toward North Korea, labeled the Sunshine Policy. This policy was based on three principles: no tolerance of any armed provocation by the North; no support for unification by absorption; and the promotion of reconciliation and cooperation with the North. Kim's summit meeting with Kim Jong Il in June 2000 symbolized a new era in inter-Korean relations. Developments such as South Korean tourism to Mt. Kumgang and meetings between divided families received increased emphasis.

In contrast, political trends in the United States moved in an opposite direction with the election of George W. Bush in November 2000. In its final months, the Clinton administration had sought to negotiate with Pyongyang and even undertook a high-level meeting in the DPRK capital between Secretary of State Madeleine Albright and Kim Jong Il. The effort fell short of success, with the issues of the North's abandoning its ballistic missile program incomplete, and verification and recompense for abandoning the nuclear program unresolved. However, it was presumed that if Vice President Gore had been elected, these efforts would have continued.

The Bush administration sent very different signals. Kim Dae Jung's trip to Washington to meet with Bush in March 2001 was poorly timed, since the new administration had no policy toward the North in place at that point. While promising to undertake a thorough review, Bush clearly viewed the Sunshine Policy as deeply flawed. Moreover, his subsequent designation of North Korea as a part of the "axis of evil" and his negative personal remarks about Kim Jong Il created a widening fissure in official U.S.-ROK relations on how to handle North Korea; they also stimulated anti-Americanism in the ROK. At this point, many South Koreans, especially among the younger generations, were inclined to downplay the threat of the North and speak longingly of the need to bring all Koreans together. Nationalism in the ROK was taking a new tone in certain circles, especially among youth and the left.

As time passed, the Bush administration sought to mollify allies and others by indicating that it was prepared for negotiations with the DPRK to address the festering nuclear weapons issue, and that it had no intention of using force against North Korea. Step by step, some progress was achieved in meetings convened in Beijing: the three-party talks, the six-party talks (including the placing of U.S. and DPRK proposals on the table, which may provide a basis for compromise), and the signing of a denuclearization agreement by all six parties in September 2005. But major issues of verification, timing, and the order of actions and responses of the two parties remain extremely difficult to resolve.

In this context, the North Korea issue remains one factor in the continuing, if somewhat diminished, wave of anti-Americanism in the ROK. Many harboring negative feelings toward the United States blame Washington for placing obstacles in the way of North-South rapprochement. The argument is that if the United States would show greater flexibility and cease appearing as a threat to the North, progress could be made on both security and economic matters, and the path toward Korean reunification could be opened more fully. Many who hold this view are motivated by romantic or ideological considerations, prepared to regard Northerners as brothers and willing to overlook or minimize the colossal political and economic differences in the two societies. Nationalism in its current form, however, clearly underwrites these views in certain circles. The idea of one Korean people and nation, with enhanced prestige and power both regionally and globally, is naturally appealing.

The most outspoken proponents of North-South reconciliation and opponents to U.S. "dominance" are to be found in the younger generations. Those under 30 years of age in the ROK at present constitute over 45 percent of the population. For them, the Korean War is long-forgotten history but the American military presence is a contemporary fact. The percentage of those having negative feelings toward the United States and Americans in this group has risen substantially in the recent past. Recent polls indicate that while the U.S.-ROK security alliance retains the support of nearly two-thirds of the Korean people, there is a strong feeling that the United States is too dominant and uses Korea for its own interests. Moreover, when asked in the fall of 2003 which leader, Kim Jong Il or George W. Bush, was more threatening to peace in Korea, the results were 42.1 percent Kim and 38.0 percent Bush.

Policies toward North Korea are not the only matter stirring nationalist responses. Incidents involving the U.S. military in the ROK, such as the deaths of two South Korean girls hit by a U.S. military vehicle (with the driver exonerated from guilt by a U.S. court), evoked strong protests. The presence of more than 7,000 troops and their families at the Yongsan base in the heart of Seoul has naturally heightened the sense of the American presence and has increased resentment. Thus, the recent decision to relocate American forces in the ROK, removing them from the DMZ region to the south and closing the Yongsan base, along with some reduction in overall forces, while a part of a shifting U.S. global strategy, is a wise move politically. To be sure, some South Koreans now voice concern about the reliability of the U.S. security commitment and the costs involved in a heightened ROK security responsibility, but a reduction in American visibility is a step in the right direction in terms of South Korean sentiments, assuming that its timing is appropriately considered and actions are taken after full consultation with the ROK government.

In broad terms, both the ROK leadership and a sizable portion of the population want the U.S-ROK relationship to be one of partnership rather than of patron-client, with the ROK government fully independent and free to set its own policies. Here again, prevailing nationalist currents are very strong. At the same time, as noted earlier, all leaders, including both Kim Dae Jung and Roh Moo Hyun, have insisted that a U.S.-ROK security alliance remain vital to Korean interests, and in this, they have the support of a majority of the South Korean people. Moreover, to demonstrate loyalty to the alliance, President Roh, with the support of his Uri party, sent a contingent of ROK military units to Iraq for noncombat duties, despite opposition to that war by a majority of the electorate.

Looking ahead, Korean nationalism is likely to continue to flourish, but its precise course will depend on future political developments. The policies and public diplomacy of the American government will be highly important. A willingness to consult in depth on all moves affecting South Korea and to listen to ROK proposals would be enormously helpful. Further, to move in the direction now being signaled with respect to North Korea—namely, a willingness to negotiate and show some flexibility while still maintaining a firm stance on such issues as verification—can be most important to the American image in South Korea and elsewhere.

The actions of the DPRK will also be critically important in influencing the patterns of ROK nationalism. Will the process of opening to the outside economically be accompanied by other evidence of flexibility? Will the image of an enemy and a threat be replaced in growing degree by the image of cooperation and reconciliation? Here, nationalism has a powerful resonance, namely, the concept of one people, long separated because of both external and domestic circumstances, desiring a return to unity. But how can the huge differences be bridged? Certainly not in short order, unless it be through collapse or conflict, neither of which is desired. Only a lengthy evolutionary process seems possible, and in this, realism must prevail over romanticism. This will be a continuing challenge for the ardent nationalists of South Korea.

Meanwhile, an increasing number of South Koreans regard China as the most important external force influencing Korea, even more important than the United States. The reasons are multiple. China's economic relations with the ROK in terms of trade and investment now predominate over all others. Furthermore, China's growing military power together with its huge population ensures that it will play a major role in Northeast Asia, including the Korean peninsula. Today, China is the chief patron of the

DPRK in economic terms, and, hence, a state with significant influence when it chooses to exert itself. Thus, in both North and South Korea, a historic issue presents itself: can China be a friendly, supportive partner, or will it be a recurrent threat? As noted earlier, this issue has run through Korean history, and there is little chance that it will disappear, although China has worked vigorously in recent times to present an image of a benign power dedicated to the five principles of peaceful coexistence.

Korean leaders in the South have recently opted for a combined strategy of soliciting good relations with China while maintaining a strategic alliance with a distant power, the United States. In contrast, the North has no true allies at present. It is well known in Pyongyang and elsewhere that while China is a major source of aid, privately Chinese leaders have many criticisms of the DPRK, in terms of its economic policies, its political structure, and its nuclear weapons program. North Korea may therefore seek to move toward balanced relations with all major states, including the United States and Japan, in the near future.

Korean nationalism remains strong in both North and South, but it varies in its emphasis between traditionalist sentiments and a greater willingness to adjust to the modern world. Within the nationalist tides there still runs an antiforeign current, but the broader demand for equality and independence is in accord with the positions of nationalists elsewhere. In all settings, moreover, there are conflicting forces. Among young South Koreans, for example, some of those exhibiting the strongest anti-American sentiments are at the same time deeply influenced by contemporary American culture. Despite recurrent political turmoil, the ROK is likely to continue as a democracy, and with economic growth also progressing. It is in North Korea that the most extensive changes are likely, whether in a few years or a few decades. Thus, the great challenge for Korean nationalism will be how to adjust to these facts.

PART TWO

The Political Strategies
of the Two Koreas

3

Can North Korea Be Reformed?

Andrei Lankov

The past decade has witnessed a dramatic shift in perceptions of North Korea and its future prospects. In the early 1990s, collapse of the regime was widely anticipated, but it is now generally assumed that such a collapse is unlikely and indeed undesirable. A policy of engagement and unilateral concessions is seen as the only realistic way to deal with North Korea. Many experts and policy makers assume that the leadership in Pyongyang will be able to introduce economic reforms and maintain control for the foreseeable future. This is seen as the preferred scenario, since the gradual evolution of North Korea would presumably make eventual unification less costly and would also help to reduce security risks in Northeast Asia.

However, such expectations are based on assumptions about North Korean society that are seriously flawed. The major fallacy is the expectation that the North Korean population will remain docile throughout a protracted process of gradual reform. To explain the reasons why these assumptions are dubious, this chapter will explore the economic, societal, and political forces that North Korea must inevitably confront, though we do not know when or how these considerations will unfold. But it is also necessary to consider the prevailing logic of expert opinion about North Korea, principally as assessed from "the outside."

ROK VIEWS

In the early 1990s, euphoria ran high in Seoul about the likelihood of large-scale political change in the North. It was widely expected that the collapse of North Korea, the world's principal surviving Stalinist regime, was imminent. Geopolitical dreamers in

Seoul speculated about a unified Korea that would quickly surpass Japan in both economic and military power and would soon occupy its rightful place as the "hub of East Asia." Leading specialists both in Korea and abroad animatedly discussed the form and consequences of the inevitable North Korean collapse.[1] However, these expectations proved mistaken, even though they seemed entirely reasonable at the time. Indeed, North Korea was politically the most repressive and economically the most inefficient of all Communist societies. Despite its loud rhetoric of "self-reliance," it was completely dependent on Soviet aid. Thus, it appeared destined for a speedy demise in the new post–Cold War environment.

Contrary to expectations, the North Korean regime demonstrated a surprising resilience, albeit at a cost of many hundreds of thousands of lives. While economically more efficient Communist regimes have been wiped out, the North Korean leadership has managed to withstand internal and external pressures, and even secured the first Communist Party dynastic succession amidst famine and economic collapse. Secondly, the experience of German unification soon demonstrated that any absorption of the North would be painful and very costly, even though all estimates of the costs of unification were largely guesswork. Nevertheless, few would now disagree with what Seung-Ho Joo wrote in 1998: "Korean unification after the German model will be a heavy blow to the Korean economy. . . . The Korean people cannot afford to lose their hard-earned economic prosperity in the interest of immediate national unification."[2]

A major policy switch therefore occurred in Seoul in the mid-1990s. The new strategy toward the North was based on the assumption that a North Korean collapse would be prohibitively dangerous and costly and therefore should be prevented or (if possible) deferred. This was the major rationale behind the "Sunshine Policy" of President Kim Dae Jung, culminating in the Pyongyang summit of 2000. When Roh Moo Hyun was elected Kim's successor in December 2002, he very early declared his intention to continue the engagement policy, which he asserted "had no alternative."[3] Kim Dae Jung's policy has been continued, even if its official name has been changed to the "Policy of Peace and Prosperity."

The Sunshine Policy, the practical realization of the pro-engagement approach toward the North, is usually associated with the nationalist left, which has been dominant in South Korean politics since 1997. However, the conservative opposition, despite its occasional broadsides against the "appeasement of the Pyongyang dictatorship," is no more willing to deal with the consequences of a North Korean collapse. Indeed, the policy of unilateral concessions began under the administration of President Kim Yong Sam (1992–97), who was by no means a leftist.

The change in official strategy was accompanied by a similar shift in the academic community's perceptions of North Korea. By the mid-1990s, North Korean specialists began to suspect that the collapse of the Pyongyang government was not imminent. In 1997, Marcus Noland expressed what an increasing number of experts felt by that time: in spite of all the seemingly insurmountable problems, North Korea would somehow "muddle through."[4] From the mid-1990s, the "soft landing" was increasingly perceived as a desirable and feasible outcome, and this new mood encouraged both Seoul and Washington to move from containment to engagement.[5] By the late 1990s, the pendulum of expert opinion had reached an opposite extreme: a majority now assumed that the North Korean regime could survive for a long time, perhaps for decades.

THE PREMISES OF ENGAGEMENT

The promoters of engagement hope that the North, if treated with the right proportion of pressure and incentive, will undertake reform more or less along the lines of China or Vietnam.[6] According to this model, the introduction of a market economy, combined with the intake of foreign investment, will eventually raise North Korean living standards. Under this scenario, the yawning economic gap between the two Koreas will gradually diminish, making an eventual unification less costly. Tae-Hwan Kwak and Seung-Ho Joo expressed this logic when they wrote in 2002, "North Korea's soft landing, or gradual adoption of a market economy and liberal democracy, is desirable and feasible. . . . Economic reforms and an open-door policy, no matter how limited they may be, will set in motion the transformation of the Stalinist regime. As its economic structure begins to change under the impact of market-oriented economic policies and increased contacts with the outside world, its political and social structure is bound to change."[7] Such a policy was expected to cushion the economic impact of a German-style "unification through absorption." It was also seen as politically safe, since it reduced the risks of a military confrontation. (There were, and are, widespread fears that if cornered the Pyongyang leadership would initiate some military provocation or even launch a full-scale war against the South.) Thus, the mild approach is seen as a way to dissolve a potentially explosive situation.

The engagement-policy advocates were and remain quite imprecise on the timing of this transition process. It is assumed that within the framework of the Sunshine Policy, the affluent and democratic South will coexist with the poor and authoritarian but self-reforming North for a "long time," probably for decades. A clear majority of South Koreans now believe that "there is no need to hurry with unification"—an opinion expressed by 69.8 percent of the participants in a 2001 poll.[8] The same opinion is quite persistent: a large poll conducted among the undergraduates of the South Korean universities in November 2004 indicated that merely 6.6 percent believed that unification should be achieved "as soon as possible," while 53.4 percent favored "gradual unification" and 36.4 percent said that they would prefer "peaceful coexistence" of the two Korean states (in other words, no unification at all).[9]

However, these hopes are based on an implicit, seldom-enunciated assumption that the current North Korean regime will be able to retain control and stay in power during the reform process. Some changes in the political and social structures of the North are expected and are seen as beneficial, similar to the changes that have taken place in China since Mao's death. But it is still believed that Kim Jong Il or his successors will be able to avoid any serious breakdown of the political system, and that the reform process will be gradual, orderly, and essentially controlled by the Pyongyang government. The scenario thus assumes that the contemporary process of reform in the North will be comparable to that under way in China and Vietnam. In most studies of the unification issue, Pyongyang's ability to control the situation is not even questioned.[10] However, the assumption that the North Korean regime will be able to remain a coherent political entity while imposing the above-mentioned reforms is not well grounded.

There is a major difference between China and Vietnam and North Korea. The difference is the existence of a prosperous and democratic "other Korea" just across the border, with an obvious ability to exercise a powerful demonstration effect on the impoverished North. Neither Vietnam nor China was exposed to a demonstration of such economic prosperity and political freedom a few hundred miles away. South Vietnam ceased to exist in 1975. When Deng Xiaoping began his reforms in China, Taiwan was still an authoritarian state without the private wealth it enjoys today, and it was too small to be seen as relevant. The Chinese and Vietnamese both knew of the prosperity of the capitalist West, but these were "other" countries, with different cultures, histories, and heritages, and hence their success was not seen as directly relevant to the problems of China or Vietnam.

The Effects of Information Control

From the very inception of the North Korean state, stories of the alleged sufferings of the impoverished and exploited Southerners have played a major role in Pyongyang's propaganda. The South was depicted as a land of terror and poverty, where penniless students sold their blood to pay for their textbooks, and sadistic Yankees drove their tanks over Korean girls just for pleasure. The Year One textbook used in elementary education by the regime presents North Korea's children with an enlightening picture:

"A school principal in South Korea beats and drives from school a child who cannot pay his monthly fee on time."[11] In high school, students learn that "nowadays, South Korea is swamped with seven million unemployed. Countless people stand in queues in front of employment centers, but not even a small number of jobs are forthcoming. The factories are closing one after another, and in such a situation even people who have work do not know when they will be ousted from their position."[12] These stories are inventions, pure and simple: primary education in South Korea is free, and even in the worst moments of its economic history the number of unemployed people in the South did not even remotely approach seven million. These are examples taken at random, yet for decades the North Koreans have been bombarded with similar stories about South Korea's destitution.

This propaganda was largely believed until the early 1990s, even when some doubts had begun to emerge. For example, many people noticed that the rioting South Korean students, sometimes shown on North Korean television, were extremely well dressed by prevailing North Korean standards.[13] However, such propaganda could efficiently function only in an ideologically sterile environment, one in which the North Korean populace was completely deprived of any information that could undermine the official picture. The North Korean leaders never underestimated the importance of strict information control or, rather, a self-imposed information blockade. Historically, all Communist countries have tried to cut their populaces off from unauthorized sources of information, but few went to the extremes of North Korea. In this regard, it even surpassed Stalin's Russia.

The contribution of foreign broadcasts to the demise of the Soviet Union and other Communist systems has been very significant, but the North Korean authorities have always been extremely cautious in dealing with foreign media. In 1985, an official in Pyongyang reacted to my disclosing to him that in the Soviet Union citizens could buy a shortwave radio set and tune into any station. (Jamming was not mentioned in the conversation, but in practice, Soviet jamming was only a nuisance, not an insurmountable problem.) Slightly bewildered by such an incomprehensible display of flexibility on the part of Soviet officials, he declared: "And what if the content of the broadcast is bad or unclean?" The North Korean authorities had been taking good care of the spiritual hygiene of their populace from the early 1960s. Radio sets sold in North Korean shops have no free tuning and can be used only for receiving the official Pyongyang channels. To the best of my knowledge, this system is unique to North Korea, since even under Stalin shortwave sets were readily available to the public. Only in the military might some North Koreans have access to normal radios, and some of these undoubtedly use this access to listen to South Korean and other foreign broadcasts. But when caught they are punished severely. As late as 1995, the North Korean movie writer Chŏng Sŏng San was sentenced to twelve years' imprisonment when he was caught listening to a South Korean broadcast while doing his military training. (Chŏng was lucky: he managed to escape and eventually defected to the South.)[14] In less relaxed times the punishment could be worse: in 1988 a soldier received a twenty-year sentence for listening to a broadcast from Seoul and sharing the news with local farmers.[15] Radio sets with free tuning could always be purchased in the hard currency shops, but these sets had to be submitted to police stations, where the sets' tuning mechanism was disabled. After being subjected to such obligatory surgery, a Japanese- or Chinese-made radio set can also only receive two or three official Pyongyang channels. Though this procedure is still followed, the policy is no longer relevant, since far too many small radios are now smuggled into the North.

Other potential sources of unauthorized information are also blocked with unusual thoroughness. Foreign media, including the periodicals of supposedly "fraternal" countries, have not been publicly available in North Korea since the early 1960s. All foreign publications, with the exception of purely technical materials, are kept in special departments within libraries, available only to those trusted individuals who have the requisite security clearance from the police. This system generally follows the old Soviet pattern, but in the USSR only publications on politically sensitive issues were deemed dangerous enough to be kept in special departments. Even the channel controls of television sets sold in border areas are sealed, to make sure that they cannot be used to watch Chinese programming in Korean. (Because of technical differences, South Korean television programs cannot be viewed on North Korean sets.) No private access to the Internet is available even to the most privileged North Koreans, despite some development of local computer networks in the past few years.

This efficient system of information management is remarkably different from the situation in a divided Germany, where the East Germans could easily access information from the West. As Dominik Geppert has written: "Western radio, and especially TV, was even more important for the mass of the population. Whereas state power managed to some extent to prevent Western printed material from entering the country, the people of the GDR were able to tap into the electronic media without major restrictions. The East German historian Stefan Wolle has recently pointed out that West German radio and television maintained the cultural unity of the German nation throughout forty-five years of division."[16] East Germany endured this situation for so long because the economic gap between the two parts of the country was much narrower and because everybody expected the Soviets to intervene in the event of a spontaneous pro-unification movement in East Germany.

The self-isolation policy of the North is based on the assumption that the outside world is hostile toward the Pyongyang regime and is ready to hasten its demise by waging a propaganda war and fostering dissent. At one time, this assumption was generally correct. However, over the last decade the situation has changed remarkably. Nowadays, the predicament of the North Korean rulers is ameliorated by the fact that their major adversary, South Korea, no longer actively seeks to promote dissent within the North, with the full understanding that a democratic revolution in the North is not deemed in the interests of Seoul. It is clear that the supporters of the Sunshine Policy do not want to rock the boat and are ready to turn a blind eye to human rights abuses in the DPRK. It is well known that the right-wing "conservative" press is much more willing to report human rights abuses in the North, while the leftists usually prefer to remain silent on this issue or even occasionally dismiss such accusations as "fabrications" or "exaggerations." There is little doubt that South Korean leaders, especially those from the left-leaning "progressive" camp, are now willing to tacitly accept whatever measures may be necessary to silence internal opposition in the North, as long as such suppression is done quietly and without attracting much attention from the outside world. South Koreans who visit the North as tourists or as members of technical assistance teams are instructed to be careful and, essentially, abide by the wishes of the North Koreans, avoiding any controversial situation.

Seoul is also increasingly reluctant to admit refugees from the North, who were once welcomed with generous subsidies and loud fanfares. In August 2004, Rhee Bong Jo, the ROK Vice Minister of Unification, stated, "it is against government policy towards North Korea for nongovernmental organizations (NGOs) to prompt or prod North Korean defectors to flee to South Korea." He echoed the remarks of his boss, Unification Minister Chung Dong Young, who had made similar comments just a few days earlier. This was not an exclusive initiative of the officials in the Unification Ministry. Around the same time, Foreign Minister Ban Ki Moon also blamed the NGOs for their defector-related activity.[17]

It would be a mistake to believe that such an approach is typical only of the current government and its leftist supporters, many of whom had been Pyongyang sympathizers in the 1980s. Similar views are expressed frequently across the political spectrum, often on the assumption that defectors would become a serious burden on the underdeveloped South Korean welfare system and a source of manifold social problems.[18] There is a bitter irony in the fact that the major supporters of such a cynical, if nonetheless pragmatic, approach to the North Korean human rights situation are the same political forces that inside South Korea loudly advertise themselves as staunch protectors of human rights against infringements by dictators.

However, the spread of information about the outside world is dangerous in itself to the North Korean leadership, and this spread will naturally follow increased contacts with the outside world. It does not really matter whether the traditional adversaries of Pyongyang intend to nurture dissent in the North or, alternatively, whether they prefer the status quo to continue indefinitely and thus are ready to scale down their propaganda acidity. The spread of information occurs anyway, even if there is no government-sponsored propaganda campaigns specifically directed against the North. This information from abroad undermines the government's legitimacy, and even the most carefully regulated contacts with the outside world nourish grave doubts about the supposed superiority of North Korea's social and political system.

The Liabilities of North Korean Political Mythology

Thus, there is good reason to be skeptical of Pyongyang's ability to control its citizens should the populace become better informed about the outside world and, above all, about South Korea. Even some elements of Pyongyang's own propaganda unwittingly undermine its ability to strictly regulate the flow of information. First, North Korea cannot fully utilize nationalism as a major source of the regime's legitimacy, since the Pyongyang propagandists have spent their reservoir of ink insisting that the South and North belong to the same nation. To be sure, the Southern leaders are generally portrayed as "traitors" who sold out their noble Korean identity to the wicked Yankees, and South Korean life is described as "corrupt" and devoid of national purity. However, such statements will not be particularly persuasive against the background of Seoul's prosperity and freedom. In China and Vietnam, the affluence of the capitalist West is well known but is not generally seen by the populace as relevant to the problems of their own countries. Western prosperity can always be explained away in Marxist-cum-nationalist terms as a product of the sinister imperialist and neocolonialist policies and as a result of the brutal exploitation of the non-Western world and its resources. Because of the existence of South Korea, however, the situation in the North is different.

Second, the North Korean ideology of *juche* is not a religion in a strict sense, comparable to fundamentalist Islam. It does not imply retribution and rewards in the afterlife, and its claims to superiority are based not on some godly approval, but on its supposed ability to provide a better material life for the people. In 1962, Kim Il Sung reportedly promised to deliver "a house with a tiled roof, soup with meat and silken clothes" for every North Korean. This emphasis on material and economic success is what has made the myth of North Korean prosperity and South Korean poverty so indispensable to the regime's survival. It is not by accident that the North Korean banknotes bear the inscription, "We do not envy anybody in the world!"

Third, the unification propaganda could backfire. If the unification of Korea is the supreme goal of the entire nation, is it really important under whose tutelage it is achieved? If the South and the North are two parts of the same country, why is the North so poor and the South so rich, and why should Northerners endure hardships and deprivation while their Southern brethren enjoy such prosperity? The customary references to imperialism and neocolonialism are unlikely to be effective in this context, and the combination of a growing awareness of the Southern prosperity and the traditional pro-unification rhetoric might make people see South-driven unification as an acceptable and desirable option: it will be unification, after all, not a foreign occupation.

The Effects of Economic Change

The gap between the two Koreas and the corresponding difference in living standards is huge, far exceeding the difference that once existed between East and West Germany and led to the ignominious collapse of the former. The per capita gross domestic product (GDP) of the South is approximately US$10,000, while in the North it is estimated to be between US$500 and US$1,000.[19] Obesity is a serious health problem in the South, while in the North the ability to eat rice every day is a sign of unusual affluence. South Korea, the world's fifth-largest automobile manufacturer, has one car for every two adults, while in the North a private car is less accessible to the average citizen than a private jet would be to the average American. South Korea is the world's leader in broadband Internet access, while in the North only major cities have automatic telephone exchanges and private residential phones are still a privilege reserved solely for cadres. This South Korean reality represents a remarkable difference from the North Korean propagandists' picture of long queues of exhausted people standing in front of employment offices in the vain hope of landing a job, or of innocent schoolchildren severely beaten because of their parents' inability to pay their tuition fees.

The market reforms and foreign investment encouraged by the "Sunshiners" are almost certain to be economically beneficial, but an unavoidable side effect will be a further deterioration of the carefully constructed system of information control and, hence, the death of the official *juche* myth. As observed by Samuel Kim, reform would require North Korea "to change its national identity until it becomes just like South Korea's."[20] Would the North Korean population, especially its better-educated sector, agree to live indefinitely in a less affluent and more restrictive version of South Korea when a German-style unification appeared to present them with a much easier path to instant success and prosperity?

Increased foreign investment will unavoidably give rise to a large number of foreigners coming into contact with North Koreans. From Pyongyang's point of view, the situation is made worse by the fact that most investment is likely to come from the South, which is also the major source of politically subversive information. (Few other countries express any interest in investing in North Korea.) The market-style reforms will also lead to a decrease in effective police control over the populace, thus further destabilizing the regime. If Pyongyang is going to follow the "friendly advice" of the Sunshiners, it will be only a question of time before its people learn the truth about the real situation in the supposedly impoverished and exploited South.

There have been some recent signs that the self-imposed information blockade is beginning to erode, largely because its maintenance is very expensive and the North Korean government is running short of money. For example, it appears that authorities have abandoned attempts to check all privately owned radio sets on a regular basis. For decades, such random home checks were undertaken to ensure that officially purchased radios had not been modified so that they could receive foreign broadcasts. These checks used to be conducted once or twice a year, but now these costly exercises do not make much sense: small transistor radios are smuggled in from China in large quantities, and they are very easily concealed.[21]

An even more important phenomenon is the speedy spread of South Korean video-tapes, which now constitute the major part of the video consumption in North Korea. Over the last few years, a large number of used VCRs (often, but not always, brought from China) have become available in the internal North Korean market, with some observers estimating that in Pyongyang one out of 10 to 15 households now has a VCR.[22] South Korean soap operas or an occasional U.S. movie with (South) Korean subtitles forms the backbone of the video consumption in North Korea. The South Korean actors and actresses are well known and much admired, and their hairstyles and fashions are eagerly imitated by the Pyongyang youth. There have been reports that the Pyongyang youngsters even compete among themselves as to who is best able to reproduce the fashions and manners of the recent South Korean shows.[23]

The large-scale illegal migration across the Chinese border has also greatly contributed to the gradual spread of more reliable information about the outside world. The number of North Korean refugees in China at its peak likely reached 150,000–200,000, and a large part of these people were regularly involved in the transborder movement, traveling to China and back, often smuggling goods and currency.[24] This means that a half million or more North Koreans have visited China over the past decade. These refugees have seen the results of market reforms in China and are painfully aware of North Korea's backwardness and poverty. Returned refugees also have some inkling of South

Korea's prosperity. Some of them have had contact with South Korean missionaries, diplomats, tourists, and businessmen who now flood the provinces of northeast China. Some of the younger refugees have even surfed South Korean Internet sites. They are less likely to believe the official propaganda, and they are too numerous to be silenced or isolated.[25]

Even some South Korean consumer products are making their way into North Korea. The North Korean authorities long prevented South Korean merchandise from getting into the country, since its quality is itself a testament to the absurdity of the officially approved worldview. However, northeast China is now flooded with South Korean consumer products, and many of these are eventually smuggled into the North. The North Korean reaction to the goods is often that of surprise ("Better than Chinese!" or "Not much different from Japanese!") and is often mixed with national pride.[26] There is even a new trend of cheating buyers by presenting Chinese items as goods produced in South Korea.[27]

Not surprisingly, it is the North Korean elite who lead the changes. As noted previously, North Korean students are beginning to style their hair according to the current South Korean fashion, and Northerners with VCRs prefer to watch South Korean love stories rather than the locally produced epics about the heroic exploits of the Kim dynasty. South Korean songs, often thinly disguised as "Yŏnbyŏn norae" ("songs of the ethnic Koreans from China"), are well known in the North.[28] In April 2002, the Pyongyang authorities issued a formal list of South Korean songs that could be sung in the North. This is remarkable, since as late as 1995 a North Korean citizen could be sent to a labor camp for the crime of singing a South Korean song (and in a bizarre and truly Stalinist twist, one such song was included in the officially approved 2002 list).[29] By and large, North Korea still remains information-poor, but the walls are crumbling as never before.

REFORM AND IDEOLOGICAL CHANGE

Is it possible to check the spread of subversive information while still promoting economic reforms? It seems unlikely. The development of minor private and semiprivate businesses and the decollectivization of agriculture are likely to have positive effects without provoking undue political concerns in the immediate future, and such reforms are now taking place in North Korea, albeit on a limited scale. According to a recent report by the World Food Program: "Each cooperative farm household is entitled to a private garden of 30 *pyong*: this equates to about 100 square meters or 0.01 hectares. There are approximately 1.67 million such households in the country. In addition, a significant proportion of urban dwellers also have access to garden plots, albeit usually smaller than those cultivated by farm households."[30] There have been some recent (and unconfirmed) reports that the scale of these private plots has been increased to 400 *pyong* (some 1,400 square meters), and that in some cases the authorities experiment with the individual responsibility system in the agricultural cooperatives.[31] However, in the long run these small-scale reforms will constitute a danger, since they diminish the government's ability to control the daily life of the population.

Even limited reforms bring a relaxation of ideological pressures. Political indoctrination sessions once occupied two or three hours every day, but it is now becoming increasingly difficult to ensure that people attend these tedious and time-consuming activities. The same is true in regard to many other public rituals that used to define the daily life of North Koreans, including tributes to the portraits and statues of the Great Leader and mass rallies. The more privileged must still attend these functions, since they have something to lose, but the North Koreans at the bottom of the official hierarchy do not care much any more. Indeed, a worker from a long-defunct plant is aware that the state bureaucracy has the means neither to reward his "politically correct behavior" nor to punish his refusal to participate in a state ritual. If such an individual survives economically, it is largely through the pursuit of small-scale business activities or handicrafts. He or she is essentially independent of the old state-run economy and hence is immune to subtle threats and incentives of promotion or demotion, and the increases or decreases in rations that ensured daily compliance for decades. This also means that citizens are much less subject to the standard indoctrination procedures. In this new situation minor transgressions are increasingly likely to go unpunished, or even unnoticed, by the authorities. The growth of markets and other forms of unofficial economic activity further increases the number of people who are able to avoid the control of the once-omnipresent ideological and civil bureaucracy and at the same time strengthen their independence.

Even such a seemingly apolitical measure as the de facto abolition of the travel permit system in the countryside might have political implications. Until recently, no North Korean was allowed to leave his county of residence without such a permit, to be obtained from his local government unit. These travel permits, generally known as *t'onghaengjung*, had to be produced when train or intercity bus tickets were purchased. However, from the mid-1990s the requirements were greatly relaxed, partly due to rampant corruption but also because of some changes in policy.[32] Without such a relaxation no private trade (and subsequently the survival of the population) would be possible. This newly acquired ability to travel has also brought opportunities for exchanging information with people from other parts of the country.

However, it is still unlikely that minor reforms alone are sufficient to bring about any serious transformation of the North Korean economy. In the longer run, large-scale foreign investment will be necessary to sustain growth, and when that has occurred, contacts between North Koreans and outsiders (overwhelmingly South Koreans) will become unavoidable. There is no doubt that the North Korean authorities will strive to restrict these contacts, and it is also likely that South Korean authorities will be cooperative in this regard. However, in spite of all efforts, such interaction with prosperous outsiders will be inevitable. Many observers assume that a reformed North Korean regime will still be able to suppress open dissent of the politically active minority, while the majority of the population is kept docile by increased living standards, augmented by a slow yet steady improvement in their political rights. This situation would largely parallel that which existed in China and Vietnam in the 1980s and 1990s. However, the very existence of the South makes such a scenario quite implausible. The undeniable fact of a prosperous South could trigger within the North Korean public a belief that their grave problems could be solved rapidly and easily through unification and the wholesale adoption of the South Korean social, economic, and cultural system. The South is not a threat because of some particular policy pursued by the government in Seoul; it constitutes a mortal threat simply because it exists.

HOW CHANGE MIGHT BEGIN

It is easy to imagine how discontent about the North Korean system, as well as information about the almost inconceivable South Korean prosperity, will begin to spread within the North. It would originate with the relatively well-heeled groups who are allowed to interact with South Koreans and foreigners, and would then filter down to the wider social strata. Once people come to the conclusion that they have no reason to be afraid of the usual crackdown, followed by the slaughter of real or alleged rebels and their entire families, they are likely to react more in the East German style than the supporters of the Sunshine Policy are willing to consider. The North Korean leaders are thus very realistic in their evaluation of the situation. At first glance, their zero-tolerance policy toward dissent appears to be continuing. Indeed, the fear of retaliation is one of the two major factors that keep the system intact. But there are reasons to suspect that the zeal of supervisors is declining as well. For example, illegal border crossings, once a capital crime, are now viewed increasingly as a minor transgression. Although occasional reports of executions of apprehended defectors do surface, these appear to be the exception and usually involve those who are accused of espionage or subversive activities (like those people whose execution in March 2005 was secretly filmed).[33] The majority of the defectors who are apprehended by border guards or are extradited from China are detained for only a short term—normally, a week or two. If they are not found guilty of any serious offense, they are sent for "labor reeducation," a period of forced labor lasting only a few months. According to a recent study that summarizes the available data about the treatment of deportees, an astonishing 40 percent of them return to China after their release from detention.[34]

However, it is the North Korean sub-elite intellectuals, the approximate analogue of the educated urban middle class, who probably constitute the main danger to the regime. It is often believed that the North Korean ruling class is essentially monolithic, and its political unity has been one of the major factors explaining the regime's resilience. Such unity is explained by the fact that an unusually large part of the top officialdom consists of people who are related to Kim Il Sung's family, or to families of his former guerrillas. They are on the top only because of their personal connections, and they stand little chance of surviving the regime's collapse. But the situation at the lower levels is different. Middle- and low-level cadres, factory managers, teachers, engineers, and intellectuals have much less reason to adhere to the existing system, and they have ample reason to be discontent.

Until the 1990s, the North Korean educated urbanites were relatively affluent, since the right to live in a major city, and in Pyongyang in particular, was a major privilege. They had, by North Korean standards, a reasonable supply of food and daily necessities. They were often extolled in the propaganda of the regime, which appears to have been more appreciative of (but not more permissive toward) the intellectuals than most other Stalinist governments. But this is no longer the case. During the 1990s economic crisis, the urban population was hit hard, since it depended heavily on the public distribution system, which almost ceased to function during this period. After the "economic reforms" of 2002 (which is perhaps a misnomer for this set of ad hoc measures and concessions to changing realities), the position of urban wage earners deteriorated even further, since wages could not keep up with the growing consumer prices.[35] The opportunities for urban dwellers to secure additional income through trade are slim, due in part to their own cultural biases, but also because the educated urbanites usually lack the initial capital and have no skills that would be marketable in North Korean society.

At the same time, these people are more educated, and are thus better able to assess the situation critically than members of other social groups. In the former USSR, as well as in other former socialist countries, the reform movements were initiated or enthusiastically supported by the same strata of urban college graduates who from very early days had felt a great disappointment in the Communist system. Their expectations were often naive and their hopes exaggerated, but this was irrelevant when these discontented factory managers, college professors, engineers, and clerks formed huge rallies demanding democracy and a market economy. There is no reason to believe that their Korean counterparts will not react in a similar way once the pressure of terror is relieved.

AN EAST GERMAN PRECEDENT?

Some observers of North Korea argue that public outbursts or protests are unlikely, since the North has no organized opposition of any kind—apart, perhaps, from some clandestine Christian groups, scattered and not particularly interested in militant political activism. However, this difference may not matter a great deal. The peaceful East German revolution of 1989 was not organized by any powerful network of dissenters, but it was a result of a general outburst of dissatisfaction about a government that was seen as increasingly inefficient, illegitimate, and unable to rely any longer on the threat of foreign intervention to suppress dissent. Although the East Germans enjoyed arguably the highest standard of living in the Communist bloc, it counted for nothing once its people learned that living standards in West Germany were vastly higher. Also, in the new political situation in which they found themselves, they were not afraid of a Soviet-led military crackdown. Moreover, the East German revolution was not preceded by any significant outbreaks of public discontent. As late as 1989, the East German regime received the normal 99 percent approving vote in the uncontested elections. Unlike the permanently restive Poles, until late 1989 the vast majority of East Germans outwardly appeared docile and content with the regime. But this docility later proved to be a political illusion. Once the first open disturbances began, politicization of the hitherto passive populace occurred very fast. A historian of the East German collapse has remarked on this sudden and seemingly unexpected nature of events: "For decades there had been virtually no challenge to Communism in the GDR, and then, in the space of a few months, the regime seemed to implode. The 'silent majority' of East Germans, believed to be socially atomized and politically complacent, had taken to the streets and toppled Honecker and his hard-line faction."[36] The East German experience reminds us that mass political mobilization can be achieved in a very short time and among a seemingly apolitical and disorganized population.

Many Sunshiners come from the Korean left, which for the last two decades has been worshipping the "masses," or "minjung," as the major driving force of history. Nonetheless, these same people have fallen into the trap of equating the "North" with the current Pyongyang government (essentially, a small hereditary oligarchy) while dismissing the sub-elite and general populace as politically insignificant and incapable of any action. However, their plans of a peaceful, gradual, and relatively inexpensive evolution for the North Korean regime are likely to be undermined by a force they do not really take seriously: the North Korean populace itself. There is a latent desire to be rid of a repressive and economically inefficient system and solve the grave problems through unification with the fabulously rich southern half of the peninsula. Even the South Korean unwillingness to accept the Northerners will hardly influence this general situation. What will Seoul do if faced with a large-scale pro-unification movement in the North? There is hardly any alternative to the acceptance of such a movement and its demands, even if the South Korean policy makers see such aspirations (perhaps correctly) as based on illusions, false hopes, and inflated expectations.

If North Korea moves toward an internal collapse followed by German-style unification, what are the likely political implications? The policy of engagement still remains the best available option, since any outside pressure on North Korea is likely to lead to Pyongyang's attempts to reestablish greater control over its society. It is also possible that the North Korean leaders would risk a military confrontation if they felt themselves under pressure. Last but not least, engagement and encouragement of foreign (overwhelmingly South Korean) investment in the North will somehow cushion the trauma of unification. In short, the calculations of the Sunshine Policy advocates are probably correct, but their long-term goal—that of a gradual, prolonged, and managed unification process—seems unfeasible. Thus, it will be important to prepare for any contingencies that might suddenly develop and leave precious little time to react.

These contingency preparations could include a number of measures. For example, the refugees seeking to enter the South, now seen largely as an economic liability, might become a pool of useful cadres for the postunification process. Currently, not much training is offered to these individuals, and they usually cannot succeed in the highly competitive environment of the South Korean school system. But they are best positioned to act as intermediaries between the North Korean populace and the future administration of a united Korea. Some policies required in the event of North Korea's implosion should be undertaken, as well. This should include a guarantee of complete immunity from prosecution for all former senior officials of the Pyongyang regime. Perhaps the property rights of the Kim family should also be protected by law so as to render them and their supporters less willing to fight to the last man, even if maintaining such laws becomes a growing challenge as more information on the North Korean regime and its crimes surface after unification. But not much can be done at this stage. The only thing we can be sure about is that North Korea's future will be full of unexpected turns. It will scarcely be the slow and orderly transition most North Korea experts anticipate and would clearly prefer.

NOTES

1. See, for example, Byung-joon Ahn, "The Man Who Would Be Kim," *Foreign Affairs* 73, no. 6 (November/December 1994), pp. 94–108.

2. Seung-Ho Joo, "Korean Foreign Relations Toward the Twenty-First Century: Reunification and Beyond," *American Asian Review* 16, no. 3 (Fall 1998), p. 106.

3. In an interview with *Le Monde* immediately following his election as ROK president, Roh stated: "There is no alternative to the Sunshine Policy and the initiative has not failed." Cited in "No Alternative to Sunshine Policy: Roh," *Korea Times*, 24 December 2002.

4. Marcus Noland, "Why North Korea Will Muddle Through," *Foreign Affairs* 76, no. 4 (July/August 1997), pp. 105–118.

5. See Kenneth Quinones, "North Korea: From Containment to Engagement," in *North Korea after Kim Il Sung*, ed. Dae-Sook Suh and Chae-Jin Lee (Boulder, Colo.: Lynne Rienner Publishers, 1998). This volume included articles by prominent North Korea specialists in the United States and, despite minor disagreements among the contributors, most decisively favored the engagement policy. The volume arose from workshops held in 1995 and 1996, indicating that the change of mood in the academic community began quite early.

6. Among the publications supporting this thesis, see in particular Kim Ick Soo, "Pukhan-ŭi Chungguk-ŭi model toip: kanŭngsŏng, hangye mich' namhan-ŭi yŏkhal" [The Introduction of the Chinese Model to North Korea: Probability, Limitations, and the Role of South Korea], *Tongbuka kyŏngje yongu*, no. 2 (2001), pp. 325–73.

7. Tae-Hwan Kwak and Seung-Ho Joo, "The Korean Peace Process: Problems and Prospects After the Summit," *World Affairs* 165, no. 2 (2002), p. 80.

8. Hong Yŏng-rim, "6.15 1 chunyŏn yŏron chosa" [Public Opinion Poll to Mark the First Anniversary of the 15 July Summit], *Chosun Ilbo*, 11 June 2001, p. 3.

9. "Kukmin t'ongil yŏron chosa pogosŏ" [Report About a Nation-Wide Poll on the Unification Issue], *T'ongil Hanguk*, no. 2 (254) (2005), p. 89.

10. In the above-mentioned article about the desirability of Chinese-style reform in North Korea, Kim Ick Soo does not even mention popular discontent as a factor that might influence the decision-making process in Pyongyang.

11. Kang Ch'ŏl-hwan, "Pukhan Kyogwasŏ sok-ŭi Namhan [South Korea in North Korean Textbooks]," *Chosun Ilbo*, 7 December 2001, p. 54.

12. Yi Hyo-bŏm and Ch'oe Hyŏn-ho, "Pukhan kyokwasŏ-rŭl t'onghan ch'ŏngsonyŏn kach'igwan yŏngu: Kodŭng chunghakkyo kongsanjujŭi todok 3,4 haknyŏn chungsim-ŭro. Pukhan yŏngu hakhoebo" [A Study of the Youth Value System through North Korean Textbooks: Centered Around the Textbooks for the 'Communist Moral' for the Year 3 and 4 of the High School], *Pukhan yongu hakhoebo*, no. 2 (2000), p. 250.

13. I heard such remarks from North Korean students in the mid-1980s.

14. Cho Ho-yŏn, "T'albukcha sahoe chŏgŭng yŏsŏs kogae nŏmŏya" [Five Rites of Passage in the Social Adaptation of the Defectors from the North], *Kyonghyang sinmun*, 17 March 1999.

15. *Ichhyojin irum* [Forgotten Names] (Seoul: Sidae chŏngsin, 2004), pp. 138–39.

16. Dominik Geppert, "Opposition and Resistance in the GDR," *Historian*, no. 73 (2002), p. 28.

17. Yoon Won-sup, "NGOs Warned Not to Encourage NK Defections," *Korea Times*, 19 August 2004.

18. When in October 2004 an unusually large number of North Koreans defected to the South, an editorial in *Korea Herald* expressed the prevailing sentiments: "It looks like the problem of defectors is entering a truly difficult stage, where humanitarian considerations should be adjusted along with a more realistic attitude toward seeking a long-term solution." *Korea Herald*, 27 October 2004. The editorial implies that South Korea should do something to reduce its attractiveness for the refugees.

19. There are varying estimates of the North Korean GDP. In 2000 the figure was estimated at $757 per capita, compared to South Korea's $9,770 per capita. Sang T. Choe, Sukhi Kim, and Hyun Jeong Cho, "Analysis of North Korea's Foreign Trade: 1970–2001," *Multinational Business Review*, no. 1 (2003), p. 105.

20. Samuel S. Kim, "The Future of the Post-Kim Il Sung System in North Korea," in *The Two Koreas and the United States*, ed. Dong,

Wonmo (Armonk, N.Y.: M. E. Sharpe, 2000), pp. 46–47.

21. On the spread of small radios and interest in South Korean broadcast, see: "T'albukja 67% Puk-e issŏssŭl ttae Namhan Radio Ch'ŏngch'wi" [67 Percent of All Defectors Listened to the South Korean Broadcast while in the North], *Tonga Ilbo,* 28 February 2003, p. 49. Unless specified otherwise, all Korean periodicals were accessed via the KINDS database (www.kinds.or.kr).

22. An interview with Han Yŏng-jin (defected from the North in 2002), 20 August 2005, Seoul.

23. About such imitations, see Cho Won-ik, "Nam taejung munhwa yŏlp'ung" [Great Popularity of South Korean Mass Culture], *Segye Ilbo,* 8 December 2003, p. 6; Hong In-p'yo, "Nam Chosŏn sangp'um chohayo," "Pukhan-e punŭn 'Namp'ung'" ["South Korean Goods Are Great": The Craze about Things South Korean in North Korea], *Kyonghyang sinmun,* 17 March 2004, p. 3; "Puk kowich'ŭng sinsedae 'nam p'aesyŏn chohsŭpnoeda" [Among the Young North Korean Elite, "South Korean Fashion Is Cool"], *Segye Ilbo* 16, 16 September 2003, p. 8. During 2002–2005, such reports have become increasingly common.

24. The most serious attempt to count the refugee population was undertaken by South Korean sociologists in China between November 1998 and April 1999, when the famine was in its height. According to this study, between 143,000 and 195,000 refugees were then taking shelter in Northeast China. *Tumangang-Ul Konnoon Saramdul* [People Who Have Crossed the Tumen River] (Seoul: Chŏngdo ch'ulp'an, 1999), p. 27. A collection of interviews with defectors conducted in Northeast China in 2003 includes a number of interviews with people who cross the border regularly. "Puk-chung kukkyŏng choyŏk-ŭl kada" [Traveling in the Areas Near Sino-Korean Border], *Keys,* no. 1 (2004).

25. For information on the use of the Internet facilities by North Koreans in China, see Han Chang-hŭi, "Puk silsang alliryŏ . . . T'albukja homp'i kaesŏl" [To Tell About the Real Situation in the North . . . A Defector Establishes a Home Page], *Kukmin Ilbo,* 6 July 2004, p. 8; and Yi Mi-suk, "Kasŭmi Ullin T'albukja e-meil" [An Emotional E-mail from a Defector], *Munhwa Ilbo,* 28 May 2002, p. 2.

26. Kang Ch'ŏl-hwan, a South Korean journalist of North Korean origin, conducted a series of interviews with defectors, asking them when and how they came in contact with South Korean products for the first time. See Kang Ch'ŏl-hwan, "Namhan sangp'um ch'ŏs kyŏnghŏm. Turyŏpjiman puttŭs" [The First Experience of South Korean Merchandise: Fear and Envy], *Chosun Ilbo,* 24 April 2002, p. 59.

27. About this trend, see Kang Ch'ŏl-hwan, "Pukhan chang madang-sŏ Namhan sangp'um 'pult'i' nanda" [A Shine of South Korean Goods in North Korean Markets], *Chosun Ilbo,* 17 April 2002, p. 53; Hong In-p'yo, "Nam Chosŏn sangp'um chohayo": "Pukhan-e punŭn 'Namp'ung'" ["South Korean Goods Are Great": The Craze About Things South Korean in the North], p. 3.

28. On the spread of South Korean pop music in the North in the late 1990s, see Kang Ch'ŏl-hwan, "Yong-ŭi nunmul, T'aejo Wang Kŏn pidio ingi" [The Tears of Dragon, the Great Popularity of a Video about T'aejo Wang Kŏn], *Chosun ilbo,* 17 June 2002, p. 59.

29. Concerning approval of the list, see Kim Yŏng-sŏk, "Kim Jong Il Namhan kayo 20 kok haegŭm" [Kim Jong Il Lifted the Ban on 20 South Korean Songs], *Kukmin Ilbo,* 14 June 2002, p. 2. Chi Nam-hae was arrested and sent to prison camp for three years for singing a South Korean song in 1995. See *Ichhyojin irŭn* [Forgotten Names], p. 24.

30. Food and Agricultural Organization (FAO/WFP), "Crop and Food Supply Assessment Mission to the Democratic People's Republic of Korea," Special Report, 22 November 2004 (Rome: World Food Program, 2004), p. 8.

31. Yu Hŭi-yŏn, "Puk, 2002 nyŏn ihu nongŏp kaehyŏk pakch'a" [North Korea: After 2002 the Agricultural Reform Speeds Up], *Munhwa Ilbo,* 4 April 2005, p. 8.

32. Kim Mi-yŏng, "Kukkyŏng tosi 'Pyŏngyang an purŏpta" [Border Cities 'Do Not Envy Pyongyang'], *Chosun Ilbo,* 7 September 2001, p. 53. The numerous stories of the defectors also do not leave much doubt that North Koreans can secure a travel permit with relative ease or bribe police posts to let travelers pass without asking questions about travel permits.

33. The footage attracted much attention in the South, especially after it was acquired by the popular online daily "Daily NK." See "Syegye ch'oech'o Pukhan konggae ch'ongsal hyŏnjang konggae" [For First Time in the World, a Public Execution in North Korea Is Shown], *Daily NK,* 18 March 2005.

34. "T'albujadŭl-ŭi T'alch'ul Kwajŏng-gwa Songhwan Hu-ŭi Unmyŏng" [The Escape of the Refugees from the North and Their Fate after Extradition], *Keys,* no. 6 (2002), www.nknet.org/kr/keys/lastkeys/2002/25/03.php.

35. On the position of wage earners in North Korea after reforms, see Chŏng Chae-kwon, "Pukhan sahoe pyŏnhwa / "ilhanmank'ŭm punbae" pinbuch'a hwakdae" [Changes in North Korean Society / The Gap between Rich and Poor Is Increasing under the "Distribution According to Labor"], *Hangyorye sinmun,* 1 July 2003, p. 6; Kim Pŏm-su, "2003 chigŭm P'yŏngyang: chung" [Pyongyang Now, in 2003: Part 2], *Hanguk Ilbo,* 5 March 2003, p. 15.

36. Steven Pfaff, "Collective Identity and Informal Groups in Revolutionary Mobilization: East Germany in 1989," *Social Forces,* no. 1 (September 1996), p. 92.

4

North Korea's Military-Diplomatic Campaign Strategies
Continuity versus Change

Narushige Michishita

On 10 January 2003, the Democratic People's Republic of Korea (DPRK), or North Korea, announced its withdrawal from the Treaty on the Non-Proliferation of Nuclear Weapons (NPT), returning to a situation comparable to that of 1993, when it had first declared its intention to withdraw from the NPT. On 10 February 2005, the DPRK for the first time claimed unequivocally to possess nuclear weapons, which it deemed necessary for national security. On 19 September 2005, the DPRK agreed at the Six-Party Talks in Beijing to a joint declaration obligating the North to denuclear-ization and to rejoining the NPT. Within hours of this announcement, however, North Korea insisted that it would not forgo its nuclear weapons capabilities without the United States providing the North with one or more light-water reactors for power generation. All these actions and statements reflect North Korea's employment of a highly developed, if frequently idiosyncratic, military-diplomatic strategy by which the DPRK seeks to shape relations with the United States, the Republic of Korea (ROK), and Japan. Can we identify an underlying logic or strategy to these actions, or does North Korean behavior derive primarily from immediate political-military require-ments that change as its circumstances and security calculations change?

To address these questions, this chapter will shed light on patterns and characteristics of North Korea's military-diplomatic campaigns, discuss their implications for the on-going nuclear crisis, and explore whether and how they are likely to undergo signifi-cant change in future years. We argue that North Korea's political objectives have not changed in recent years; hence the pattern of its military and diplomatic actions will not fundamentally change. We will also contend that North Korean leaders are good tacticians but poor strategists. Their crisis behavior and their inability to make bold decisions in response to offers of multilateral engagement will largely determine the outcome of the second nuclear confrontation under way since 2002.

CHANGING CHARACTERISTICS OF NORTH KOREA'S MILITARY-DIPLOMATIC CAMPAIGN STRATEGIES

Political Objectives

North Korea's political objectives in employing force have changed significantly over time.[1] While North Korea's political objectives were predominantly hostile in the 1960s, cooperative elements began to appear in the 1970s, particularly in relations with the United States, which became more fully apparent in the 1990s. The first important turning point came in 1974, when North Korea initially proposed the conclusion of a peace agreement with the United States. Although the North Koreans probably did not expect substantial improvement in their relationship with Washington at that time, they certainly thought it possible to remove or reduce the U.S. military presence in South Korea by cutting a deal with the United States like North Vietnam did by signing the Paris Peace Accords in 1973. North Korea's ultimate goal was to maintain the current regime by improving its relations with the United States.

This direction became much clearer in the 1990s when North Korea's political objectives included "complete normalization of diplomatic relations between the DPRK and the United States," and the "U.S. promise to take balanced policies toward North and South Korea."[2] However, the important difference between the 1970s and the 1990s was that while the North Koreans tried to change the status quo on the Korean Peninsula by improving its relations with the United States in the former instance, they tried to maintain the status quo by doing the same in the latter. While the North Koreans seriously tried to unify the peninsula, including by force, in the 1970s, they tried to avoid South Korean–led unification by absorption in the 1990s.

Second, purely military objectives have diminished in importance over time for Pyongyang, while diplomatic objectives now loom larger in North Korea's military actions. The primary objectives involved in the seizure of the U.S. intelligence-gathering vessel *Pueblo*[3] and the shooting down of the U.S. Navy EC-121 reconnaissance aircraft[4] in the 1960s were military: to stop or hamper U.S. intelligence operations. The 1970s were a transitional period. North Korea's political objectives in the "West Sea incident" in 1973–76[5] were basically diplomatic and potentially economic. North Korea's objective in the Axe Murder incident[6] was definitely more diplomatic than military. In the 1990s, diplomatic objectives came to the fore more clearly. North Korea's military-diplomatic campaigns in the 1990s focused more on trading military capabilities for diplomatic gains. In addition, obtaining economic benefits became one of the major objectives in the latter decade. While the North Koreans did not demand monetary compensation in exchange for the return of the *Pueblo*'s crew, in nuclear and missile diplomacy they demanded light-water reactors, heavy fuel oil, and other assistance to support their economy.

Patterns of Military Actions

North Korea's military actions have been consistent with its political objectives, particularly in terms of their intensity and targeting. The intensity of the military actions and the number of casualties have diminished over time. North Korean actions in the late 1960s caused a large number of deaths on both the U.S. and South Korean sides. However, the number of casualties resulting from North Korean military actions in the 1970s was much smaller than that in the 1960s. In the 1990s, there were only a few casualties on the U.S.-ROK side caused by North Korean military actions, despite the long and high-profile military-diplomatic campaigns conducted in the decade. The number of deaths totaled 507 in the 1960s, 94 in the 1970s, 17 in the 1980s (excepting the deaths suffered in terrorist attacks), and zero in the 1990s.[7]

There were two major reasons for this trend. One was that the need to actually resort to brute force to achieve diplomatic objectives diminished once North Korea acquired military capabilities of significant strategic importance, such as nuclear weapons and longer-range missile forces, whose potential use had sufficient compellent effects. The other is that the emergence of more cooperative political objectives made it diplomatically unwise for the North Koreans to inflict significant human and/or physical damage on U.S. forces in particular, and on South Korea to a lesser extent. Killing Americans would have been clearly detrimental to the normalization of U.S.-DPRK relations.

Another indication that the North Koreans tailored their military actions to their political objectives is seen in the shifts in targeting patterns. In the 1960s, there was no target discrimination. Both Americans and South Koreans were the targets of North Korean military actions. However, the North Koreans started to distinguish between the U.S. and South Korean targets in the 1970s, and the discrimination became clearer in the 1980s. After 1981 the North Koreans stopped attacking Americans, and the focus was put on the South Koreans alone. This North Korean tendency not to target Americans continued in the 1990s. While the North Koreans continued to physically attack the South Koreans, they did not attack Americans. As a consequence, the gap between the military target and the diplomatic target has widened. While the importance of the United States as a diplomatic target has grown, its importance as a military target has diminished.

Military Capabilities

North Korea's propensity to use or threaten force has nevertheless remained high, particularly when opportunities were created by acquisition of new military capabilities. Examples abound. North Korea's assaults along the Demilitarized Zone, the *Pueblo* incident, and the shooting down of the EC-121 in the late 1960s were preceded by a major military buildup based on the Party military lines adopted in 1962.[8] In the early 1970s, the naval actions around the Northwest Islands (five offshore islands under the United Nations Command that are situated much closer to the North Korean coast than to the South Korean coast) were made possible by the procurement of high-speed guided-missile boats. The nuclear and missile diplomacy in the 1990s was enabled by the development of nuclear and missile capabilities that had accelerated in the 1980s.

In this context, it is noteworthy that North Korea was relatively inactive in using its conventional military forces in the 1980s. The changing military balance on the Korean Peninsula explains the inaction or relative calm in that decade. By 1986, South Korea had finished its second midterm Force Improvement Program, and the United States and South Korea had incorporated more offensive elements into the U.S.-ROK military strategy.[9] South Korea had been outspending North Korea on national defense since 1976, and the overall military balance was shifting in favor of the U.S.-ROK side. Moreover, North Korea was beginning to put a larger share of resources into ballistic missile development and weapons of mass destruction, including nuclear and chemical weapons, with diminished emphasis on conventional forces.

Deterrence as a Central Component

Despite North Korea's focus on the offensive aspect of military strategy, the development of an effective deterrent has been a critical enabling factor in Pyongyang's military actions. In exercising military force, North Korea had to minimize the risks of the U.S.-ROK side's undertaking strong retaliatory actions. For example, the United States and South Korea seriously considered military actions in response to the North Korean raid on the Blue House, the seizure of the *Pueblo*, the shooting down of the EC-121, the Axe Murder incident, and the North's nuclear development program. However, in all cases, Washington and Seoul eventually dropped the military option.

One of the sources of North Korea's deterrent capabilities was the Party military lines. Kim Il Sung explained the "military lines," the "arming of the entire population," and the "fortification of the entire country" as "the most powerful defense system from the military strategic point of view, a system which is capable of thwarting any enemy attack."[10] Until the 1990s, one of the most important reasons why the United States and South Korea did not take punitive military actions had been the realization that the costs and risks of renewed war with North Korea were considered prohibitive. However, the sources of North Korea's deterrence capabilities have changed over time. By 1994, North Korea had lost its ability to defend against a U.S.-ROK counteroffensive. In June 1994, Gen. Gary Luck, Commander in Chief of the U.S.-ROK Combined Forces Command, assessed that North Korea could be defeated even if it used the one or two nuclear weapons it might have possessed.[11] In other words, North Korea had lost its denial capabilities by then, with deterrence by denial replaced by deterrence by punishment. North Korea's deterrence capability now came from its ability to punish Seoul and inflict enormous casualties on U.S.-ROK forces, although it did not have a chance to win a major military conflict. In the 1990s, North Korea deployed a large number of long-range artillery and multiple rocket launchers along the Demilitarized Zone, taking Seoul hostage. Despite the confidence that the U.S.-ROK side had in prevailing in war, North Korea successfully deterred surgical and coercive actions with its ability to "punish."[12]

Extensive Exploitation of Legal Factors

Legal factors mattered significantly in North Korea's military actions. This may seem contradictory to many observers of North Korean behavior, but the DPRK judges such considerations a significant factor in its larger strategy. North Korean officials have proven extremely knowledgeable about legal issues and well versed in exploiting them to their advantage. Quite frequently, North Korea's military-diplomatic campaigns involved legal issues in important ways. In the West Sea incident of the 1970s, the failure of the Armistice Agreement to define maritime boundaries was exploited and the validity of the Northern Limit Line was challenged. Behind the scenes was the emergence of the twelve-nautical-mile territorial sea boundary as a new international norm in the early 1970s, and the North sought to exploit the opportunity. The North Koreans also took advantage of provisions in the NPT in putting time pressure on American negotiators. The sustained actions in the Joint Security Area and around the Northwest Islands in the 1990s were designed to undermine the Armistice by highlighting its defects. In particular, the naval operations in the Northwest Islands areas in June 1999 aimed to exploit the weakness of the Northern Limit Line in a much more sophisticated manner than in the 1970s.[13]

North Korea's ability to make use of legal factors derives partly from the nature of its decision-making system, in which a small number of specialists tends to stay in the same position for a long time, resulting in a deep understanding of technical issues and the retention of organizational memory.[14] A former North Korean diplomat who defected to the South revealed that there were many older officials in the MFA, and that almost 90 percent of the officials in the ministry stayed in the same bureau throughout his or her life. Such a personnel management system certainly creates rigidity. However, it also helps guarantee consistency, continuity, and a significant level of professionalism.[15]

The Element of Surprise

The element of surprise has almost always been an important ingredient in North Korea's military actions. The seizure of the *Pueblo*, the shooting down of the EC-121, the Axe Murder incident, the announcement to withdraw from the NPT, and the launch of the Taepo Dong missile all to varying degrees entailed surprise for those monitoring North Korean behavior. In recent years, the North Koreans have taken into account political developments both in the United States and in South Korea in deciding when to initiate an action. The nuclear diplomacy and missile diplomacy commenced shortly after new administrations came into office in the United States and South Korea. In this way the North Koreans seem to have caught U.S. and South Korean policy-makers off balance. Surprise was used effectively, and it worked well in advancing the DPRK's political goals. Behind North Korea's effective use of surprise are the nature of its decision-making system, its military capabilities, and the tactical skill of its officials.

Domestic Politics

Domestic political considerations have been of secondary importance in North Korean military actions. In 1993, Kim Jong Il was elected Chairman of the National Defense Commission only a month after North Korea announced its withdrawal from the NPT.[16] In 1998, Kim Jong Il was reelected to the same position just after the Taepo Dong missile was launched, and the launch was extensively used for domestic propaganda and agitation purposes.[17] However, it is not true that the North Korean leaders resorted to force when they had domestic political problems. North Korea's use of force increased when Kim Il Sung's leadership position had been consolidated in the 1960s, while there was not much use of force in the 1950s after the Korean War, when a serious domestic power struggle was taking place in North Korea.[18] Also, when Kim Jong Il formalized his position in the Korean Workers' Party in the early 1980s, North Korea continued to undertake provocative actions.[19]

Moreover, North Korea's military actions could have worked against domestic political objectives because some of the actions failed. The Axe Murder incident was a major failure. The North Korean navy was defeated in the 1999 battle in the Yellow Sea. Unconventional actions such as the Rangoon bombing in 1983 and the bombing of the Korean airliner in 1987 also failed disastrously. These cases would have given ammunition to Kim Jong Il's domestic rivals if such rivals had actually existed.

Some observers argue that the North Korean leadership has used military actions to tighten internal order. However, this argument is also flawed. For one, the North Korean leadership exercises stringent control over the media. Since information and media content are tightly controlled, the North Korean authorities can simply make up "foreign military aggression," or other comparable allegations, to tighten domestic control. For another, if the information is not controlled perfectly and an actual military confrontation is needed to tighten the internal order, then the military failures will also be known to the public, discrediting political authority.

The International Environment

The contention that the North Koreans take military actions when they face negative international developments does not often hold true. Pyongyang has initiated military actions when the international environment was favorable to its interests as well as when it was not. For example, the Axe Murder incident took place in an environment most favorable to North Korea. The nuclear diplomacy began when the international situation was extremely negative. The Taepo Dong launch occurred when the international environment was quite favorable because of the adoption of the engagement/Sunshine Policy on the part of the United States and South Korea. When the missile was launched, high-level U.S.-DPRK talks were taking place in New York. The June 1999 naval provocations took place shortly after former U.S. Secretary of Defense William Perry visited Pyongyang. In addition, the international environment does not necessarily determine the outcome. The Axe Murder failed disastrously despite the favorable international environment, while the nuclear diplomacy turned out to be a success under the most unfavorable international circumstances.

Caveat: Even Rational Actors Can Miscalculate

More often than not North Korea's crisis behavior is rational. However, the leadership does make serious mistakes. One typical example is the Axe Murder incident. At the time of the incident, the international environment was quite favorable to North Korea, and it attempted to exploit a military opportunity in the Joint Security Area to its diplomatic advantage. However, the tactical mistake of killing American servicemen in an extremely brutal manner turned the entire venture into a disastrous failure. The naval clash in June 1999 was another case in which the North Koreans made a major error. Although it is difficult to know North Korea's internal assessment, circumstantial evidence suggests that the DPRK mistakenly assumed that the South Korean side would not have as strong a military reaction as it actually did. The result was disastrous: the North Koreans lost lives, naval vessels, and their reputation for military prowess. Moreover, other unconventional actions have also failed. Assassination attempts on South

Korean presidents have never succeeded; neither have guerrilla infiltrations done so in any meaningful way; and the bombing of a South Korean airliner in 1987 decisively shifted the attitude of the international community against North Korea.

In this sense, the claim that the North Koreans have always been highly effective in using force and Kim Il Sung and Kim Jong Il are "military geniuses" is simply not credible. The North Korean leaders have been voracious users of force at various times, but this does not mean that they have been any better at using it than others.

THE MID- TO LONG-TERM EFFICACY OF NORTH KOREA'S MILITARY-DIPLOMATIC CAMPAIGNS

North Korea's military-diplomatic campaigns have in some cases produced negative mid- to long-term consequences by provoking reactions from other concerned countries. In the 1960s, sustained assaults along the Demilitarized Zone caused the U.S.-ROK side to fortify the DMZ. In the 1970s, North Korean naval and air activities provoked South Korea's effort to fortify the Northwest Islands and modernize its naval forces deployed in the area. The local military balance in the area therefore became far more favorable to the South Korean side by the time naval vessels of North and South Korea engaged in battle in June 1999. The launch of the Taepo Dong missile in 1998 encouraged the United States and Japan to boost their research and development efforts on ballistic missile defense.

These cases have demonstrated the importance of paying attention to mid- to long-term negative consequences in assessing the effectiveness of North Korea's military-diplomatic campaigns. Short-term success could turn into mid- to long-term failure. In this sense, the existence of military or other potential countermeasures can make an important difference in determining the longer-term effectiveness of any military-diplomatic campaign.

Implications for the Continuing Nuclear Crisis

The single most important determinant of success in North Korea's military-diplomatic campaigns has been military advantage. Where the North Koreans possessed military advantage, chances were high that their military actions would succeed. In other words, the military balance, instead of negotiating skills, played a decisive role in determining the outcome of North Korea's military-diplomatic campaigns.

The nuclear and missile diplomacy are relevant cases in point. The nuclear diplomacy of 1993–94 resulted in the Agreed Framework. The missile diplomacy of the late 1990s almost produced significantly improved relations between the United States and North Korea. However, North Korea failed to obtain any meaningful diplomatic or economic benefit from its military actions in the Joint Security Area, the Demilitarized Zone, and the Northwest Islands areas in the 1990s. Pyongyang devoted just as much diplomatic effort and negotiating skills in its campaigns in these areas as in the nuclear and missile diplomacy, but without comparable success. The level of sophistication and complexity involved in the former was by no means lower than that involved in the latter.[20]

What distinguished these cases was the existence of the nuclear and missile capabilities in the former that exerted tremendous compellent effects on the concerned countries. The armed demonstrations in the Joint Security Area, the skirmishes in the Demilitarized Zone, and the naval clash in the Northwest Islands areas were not at all trivial. However, in terms of strategic significance and compellent value, these military actions were no match for the significance of the nuclear and missile capabilities. This does not mean that tactical factors were irrelevant. Sophisticated diplomacy and effective use of surprise were indispensable in successfully translating the nuclear and missile capabilities into substantial diplomatic and economic gains. However, tactical factors such as negotiating skills were at best secondary determinants of the effectiveness of North Korea's military-diplomatic campaigns.

Relating Military Actions to Political Objectives

Currently, North Korea is repeating its nuclear diplomacy of 1993–94. So far, there is no indication that North Korea's political objectives have changed significantly since 1994. Regime survival, normalization of relations with the United States and Japan, and acquisition of economic assistance from abroad still remain its primary goals.

In October 1993, North Korea informally unveiled its demands relating to the nuclear issue with the United States. At that time, it proposed (1) the conclusion of a peace agreement or a treaty that includes legally binding assurances on the nonuse of, and nonthreat of, force against the DPRK; (2) the provision of light-water reactors to the DPRK to finalize the resolution of the nuclear issue; (3) a full normalization of diplomatic relations between the DPRK and the United States; and (4) a U.S. pledge of an equidistant policy toward North and South Korea.

At the Six-Party Talks held in August 2003, North Korea presented a proposal for a "package solution" to the nuclear issue. According to the proposal, the United States was to (1) conclude a nonaggression treaty with North Korea; (2) establish diplomatic relations with it; (3) guarantee economic cooperation between the DPRK and Japan, and between the two Koreas; and (4) compensate for the loss of electricity caused by the delayed provision of light-water reactors and complete their construction. In return, North Korea would (1) allow nuclear inspections and not make nuclear weapons;

(2) fully dismantle its nuclear facilities; and (3) freeze the test-firing of missiles and stop their export.[21]

In short, the core elements of North Korea's policy objectives—nonuse of force against it, the supply of energy, and the normalization of diplomatic relations with the United States—have not changed from those it had pursued ten years ago. Moreover, almost all of these goals were noted in the joint statement of September 2005 agreed by North Korea and the other five participants at the Six-Party Talks in Beijing.

The Pattern of North Korea's Military Actions

If the DPRK's political objectives remain largely unchanged, patterns in North Korean military actions will also likely remain more or less the same. North Korea's targeting pattern remains constant. In June 2002, a North Korean patrol boat attacked a South Korean naval vessel in the Yellow Sea, killing six men on board.[22] In March 2003, four North Korean fighters suddenly engaged a U.S. RC-135S reconnaissance aircraft in the Sea of Japan and attempted to force the aircraft to land in North Korea.[23] (It involved elements of the 1968 *Pueblo* incident and the 1969 EC-121 incident put together.) The North Koreans killed South Koreans, but they did not physically attack Americans. Also, based on past negotiating history, it is no surprise that the second round of nuclear diplomacy has already proven more protracted than the first. It took nineteen months of the "first" nuclear diplomacy between the time of North Korea's announced decision to withdraw from the NPT to the conclusion of the Agreed Framework. This round of diplomacy has already exceeded two years, with no end in sight.

Compared to the first nuclear crisis, North Korea's bargaining position is stronger in some aspects but weaker in others. On the one hand, weaponization of nuclear materials seems to have advanced; reprocessing of spent reactor fuel into plutonium has advanced significantly; uranium enrichment has been added to the North's nuclear options; No Dong missiles have been deployed in large numbers; and the Taepo Dong missile has been flight-tested. On the other hand, North Korea's conventional military forces have weakened, and the overall military balance has shifted in favor of the U.S.-ROK side.[24] Moreover, the size of the North Korean economy has shrunk appreciably, and the country has become dependent on economic and humanitarian aid from abroad. North Korea seems to have become more susceptible to sanctions.

The single most important determinant of success in North Korea's military-diplomatic campaigns has been military advantage. Given its enhanced nuclear and missile capabilities, it is possible that North Korea believes it will get a better deal than the Agreed Framework in the ongoing process. However, such an outcome will come true only if North Korea decides to give up much more of its military capabilities than it did ten years ago. Such a possibility also assumes that the United States will be prepared to go farther to achieve denuclearization in the second crisis than in the first, but this remains to be seen.

Redefining Deterrence

In April 2003, the DPRK Ministry of Foreign Affairs argued that a "physical deterrent force" was needed to protect the security of North Korea.[25] It was a significant departure from the past, since North Korea had always used the word "deterrent" with a negative connotation.[26] North Korea seems to have used the word to both justify its possession of nuclear weapons and enhance the credibility of its deterrent capabilities. This conclusion was further substantiated by North Korea's February 2005 claim to possess finished nuclear weapons, although the DPRK did not undertake a weapons test to demonstrate definitively that it possessed such capabilities.

Since 1994, North Korea's deterrent capability has been undermined in some aspects but strengthened in others. On the one hand, active adoption of the Revolution in Military Affairs (RMA) has provided U.S. armed forces with far more effective offensive and defensive capabilities. Improvements in counterbattery forces deployed south of the Demilitarized Zone have undercut North Korea's ability to "punish" the South. Adoption of the "preemption" doctrine in the U.S. National Security Strategy of 2002 has increased the possibility of the United States taking military actions against North Korea and, therefore, has made it riskier for North Korea to operate on the brink.[27]

On the other hand, North Korea might have taken Tokyo hostage, in addition to Seoul, with a large number of No Dong missiles already fielded in North Korea. Also, given the recent developments in South Korea—the rise of anti-American sentiment and the election of Roh Moo Hyun, who has been more assertive toward the United States than previous South Korean presidents—any attack on Seoul in reaction to coercive actions taken by the United States against North Korea would be "intolerable" to the South Koreans. Taken as a whole, North Korea's deterrent capability based on its ability to punish still seems credible.

The Role of Legal Factors

North Korea will likely continue to use legal issues to its advantage. First, North Korea declared its withdrawal from the NPT on 10 January 2003. However, it is not clear whether the withdrawal actually took effect on 10 April. The Bush administration did not take a position on whether North Korea's withdrawal notification met the requirements of Article X of the NPT, and the United States has not tried to reach agreement on North Korea's legal status under the NPT after 10 April.[28] Room was left to be exploited. Indeed, even though North Korea susbsequently claimed to possess nuclear weapons, it later declared that it would be prepared to agree to denuclearization under certain specific conditions, deeming the elimination of nuclear weapons part of the final legacy of Kim Il Sung.

North Korea has tried to undermine the armistice by exploiting the Northern Limit Line issue and will likely continue to do so. In February 2003, North Korean fighter aircraft crossed the Northern Limit Line two days after the Korean People's Army (KPA) Panmunjom Mission suggested that the North Korean side would abandon its commitment to the Armistice Agreement if sanctions were imposed by the United States. The KPA claimed that imposition of sanctions would amount to a "blockade," which is banned by the Armistice Agreement.[29] These actions had much in common with the West Sea incident in the 1970s and the 1990s.

Continued Reliance on Surprise

As in 1993, North Korea started the second nuclear diplomacy with the element of surprise. In October 2002, in talks with Assistant Secretary of State James Kelly, North Korean officials unexpectedly acknowledged that they had a program to enrich uranium. After three months, North Korea declared its withdrawal from the NPT. Its later claim to possess nuclear weapons (although hinted in prior statements) also surprised many observers. North Korea views its capacity for surprise as a means to keep other concerned countries off balance. We should therefore expect future instances of such a tactic. Thus, the use of surprise is nothing new, and it will continue to play a role. However, the North Koreans use both positive and negative surprise. They tend to use tough and soft tactics alternately: first, they use negative surprise to raise the stakes, and then they use positive surprise to cash in on tension or crisis. Policymakers must be prepared both for positive and negative surprises.

The Domestic Political Context

On 3 June 2003, a decision was announced to hold the election for the Eleventh Supreme People's Assembly (North Korea's parliament) on 3 August.[30] This seems to be another instance of North Korea attempting to make domestic use of international tension. North Korea had held the election for the Tenth Supreme People's Assembly one month prior to the Taepo Dong launch in 1998. The first session of the newly elected Assembly was convened five days after the launch. North Korea might use tension resulting from the nuclear issue to bolster internal solidarity yet again; the repeated calls endorsing the "military first" policy reflect this tendency.

The International Environment

North Korea embarked on an exploratory uranium enrichment program during the Clinton–Kim Dae Jung era.[31] Therefore, the claim that North Korea was reacting to a negative international environment did not hold true on this occasion. When North Korea sought to import centrifuges, it saw an opportunity to prepare yet another tool to be used for both military and diplomatic purposes.

The Future Role of Military-Diplomatic Campaigns

Despite its clear concern about the spread of nuclear weapons capabilities to the DPRK, the United States does not seem ready to apply "preemption" and regime change to North Korea. The increased efforts to reach agreements at the Six-Party Talks, including U.S. declarations of "no hostile intent" toward the North and even a declaration that the United States would explore normalization in the event of successful denuclearization, highlight the shift in U.S. strategy in 2005. If the talks do not yield a major breakthrough and North Korea proceeds with further nuclear weapons development and challenges U.S. interests in other areas, the "preemption" strategy might gain increased support. But the use of flight-testing missiles as a bargaining tool seems to have diminished since 1998. Another missile launch would prompt heightened development of missile defense systems on the part of the United States and Japan, which China would definitely view in negative terms. Using missile launches as part of the North's military-diplomatic campaigns would not work as well as it did in 1998.

PROSPECTS AND IMPLICATIONS

The second nuclear crisis has presented the nations of Northeast Asia with a "high-risk, high-return" situation, where bigger carrots are put on the table together with bigger sticks. Despite periodic signs of mounting tension, a peaceful solution to the nuclear issue is possible. Moreover, there is a potential for more substantial agreements among the concerned countries in a "more-for-more" arrangement. North Korea has more to offer now than ten years ago, while its neighbors have already offered more than ten years ago. On paper, all affected countries are at least prepared to consider the possibilities of a much larger breakthrough than was achieved in 1994.

However, the current situation involves higher risks. If the North Koreans are to raise the price of their bargaining chips by scaring the international community, which has seen a North Korean nuclear game once already, they might have to bring the situation much closer to the brink than before. If the international community is to prevent North Korea from cheating again, it might have to get tougher than before. The United

States is playing a lead role in the international effort to resolve the nuclear issue, but it now relies far more fully on China to advance this process. Structural analysis strongly suggests that a negotiated settlement is possible and potentially more beneficial to all parties than the previous one. However, if all involved countries fail to make good use of diplomatic opportunities, Northeast Asia might end up far worse off than ten years ago.

In this context, it is important to ask two questions: whether Kim Jong Il is a rational leader in a crisis situation, and how much risk the North Korean leaders are willing to take in seeking to reach agreement with neighboring states.

Kim Jong Il's Crisis Behavior

North Korea's leaders, including Kim Jong Il, are much more capable of rational calculation and action than is often claimed. In recent years, Kim has met all the top leaders of major countries deeply involved in the Korean peninsula except the United States. Kim's frequent international exposure has demonstrated that however idiosyncratic his aims might be, he is a calculating and rational actor. One remaining concern is the fact that Kim Jong Il has no experience of making a decision to back off in a major international crisis.

In two previous major crises on the Korean Peninsula, Kim Il Sung made the decision to back off. In August 1976, two U.S. Army officers were killed in the Joint Security Area in Panmunjom by North Korean guards wielding axes. In one account of the Axe Murder incident, when Kim Jong Il received a report that the U.S. military police and South Korean workers had started to cut off the branches of a poplar tree in the Joint Security Area, he ordered, "Show them the Korean way. Don't care about the South Korean workers and give the Yankees a lesson. And don't use guns."[32] After some wrangling, the clash started. The North Korean guards grabbed the axes that the South Korean workers were carrying and brutally killed the U.S. officers.

In reaction, the United States mobilized its armed forces and concentrated them in and around the Korean Peninsula in a major show of force. Then the U.S. forces in Korea, together with South Korean special forces, undertook an operation to cut down the poplar tree. An extremely tense situation was created during the operation, which could have escalated into a free-for-all exchange of fire had there been one accidental shot in the area. On 21 August, Kim Il Sung, in the name of the Supreme Commander of the Korean People's Army, sent a message to the United Nations Command side, saying that it was "regretful" that the incident occurred in his attempt to end the crisis.

In May 1994, North Korea began removing the spent fuel rods from the 5-megawatt nuclear reactor. In June, it announced its withdrawal from the International Atomic Energy Agency (IAEA), taking the situation to the edge. In response, the United States reinforced U.S. Forces Korea and came up with a plan to impose sanctions on North Korea. Then in July, Kim Il Sung invited former U.S. President Jimmy Carter to defuse the tension and succeeded in paving the way for the Agreed Framework. It is widely believed that Kim Jong Il had directed the nuclear escalation until his father met with former President Carter. In both crises, it was Kim Il Sung who made the decision to back off.

Although we have yet to see if his son has the same capacity, Kim Jong Il has experienced several mini-crises that he has managed well. The first post–Kim Il Sung crisis was the September 1996 submarine incident. A North Korean *Sang-o*-class special-purpose midget submarine ran aground off the east coast of South Korea while approaching the coast to recover infiltrators. South Korean President Kim Young Sam mobilized approximately 60,000 South Korean troops. In the end, twenty-four infiltrators were killed and one was captured. On 29 December, the North Korean Ministry of Foreign Affairs issued a statement expressing "deep regret" and pledging efforts to prevent the recurrence of similar incidents.

In June 1999, a naval battle took place between the North and the South in the Yellow Sea, resulting in a large number of casualties on the North Korean side. Despite the casualties, the North Korean side did not show too many signs of confusion and even tried to exploit the incident for diplomatic purposes. In June 2002, a North Korean patrol boat attacked a South Korean naval vessel in the Yellow Sea, killing six men on board.[33] The head of the North Korean delegation to the inter-Korean ministerial talks sent a message to the South Korean side, saying, "Feeling regretful for the unforeseen armed clash that occurred in the West Sea recently, we are of the view that both sides should make joint efforts to prevent the recurrence of similar incidents in future."[34] The North Koreans did not show any intention of escalating the situation. Rather, they somewhat casually expressed regret to the South Korean side; the weight of the remarks was much lighter than those expressed by Kim Il Sung in 1976 or the North Korean Ministry of Foreign Affairs in 1996.

Given these episodes, we can conclude that Kim Jong Il has acted rationally in recent mini-crises. However, in these cases North Korea confronted with South Korea instead of the United States. In the case of the 1996 submarine incident, the United States even mediated between the two Koreas. In this sense, Kim Jong Il has yet to prove himself to be a rational actor in a big crisis with the United States.

How Far Can North Korea Go?

If North Korea continues to do what it has done in the past decade, the question is, how far can it go this time, and toward what ends. North Korea has failed to make use of some golden opportunities in the past. The North Korean leaders have remained tentative and inconsistent in pursuit of their ultimate goal: normalizing relations with the United States and acquiring a large amount of economic assistance from the outside world.

For example, the Agreed Framework provided that the United States and the DPRK would "move toward full normalization of political and economic relations." The two countries agreed to reduce barriers to trade and investment, open a liaison office in each other's capitals, and upgrade bilateral relations to the ambassadorial level. In fact, the United States eased some economic sanctions against North Korea, but these measures did little for the North Korean economy. The United States and North Korea had completed most of the technical arrangements needed to open liaison offices in each other's capitals by April 1995; however, North Korea was reluctant to actually implement the agreements.

In addition, as Wendy R. Sherman later argued, a substantial agreement between the United States and North Korea was "within reach" in late 2000.[35] In 1998, North Korea embarked on a diplomatic offensive vis-à-vis the United States. The Taepo Dong 1 launch activated comprehensive U.S.-DPRK talks on bilateral relations. The preparations for the Taepo Dong 2 launch accelerated the U.S.-DPRK talks, culminating in the September 1999 simultaneous announcements by the United States to partially lift economic sanctions and by North Korea to freeze missile flight-testing. The North Korean effort to improve its relations with the United States was helped by South Korea's Sunshine Policy and the Perry process. As a result, the United States and North Korea issued a joint communiqué in October 2000 in which the two countries decided to "take steps to fundamentally improve their bilateral relations."[36] Further details of the possible breakthrough were discussed during Secretary of State Albright's visit to Pyongyang and in the sixth round of the U.S.-DPRK missile talks. From North Korea's perspective, these were enormous achievements, given the status of the U.S.-DPRK relations just several years earlier. However, the two sides failed to reach an agreement in the end, and U.S.-DPRK relations did not experience a major breakthrough.

North Korea's tentativeness and possible indecision do not stop with its policy toward the United States. When North Korea attempted economic reform in the 1980s and in the 1990s, it did so, at best, half-heartedly. So, the question is: how far can North Korea go this time? Have the North Korean leaders somehow left behind their wary approach of the past and become bold enough to seize the opportunity created by the second nuclear crisis, which holds out the prospect of far more substantial security and assistance from the other five participants in the negotiating process?

North Korea's initiation in July 2002 of measures to improve its economic management methods offers some possible clues. The significance of these reform measures lies in the fact that they are implemented nationwide and are not limited to exclusive economic zones, as in previous reform efforts. These measures will potentially have a much larger effect within North Korean society and might trigger significant, possibly adverse, political consequences. The country's top priority is to sustain the regime of Kim Jong Il. However, progress in economic reforms could undermine the regime's control over society, while those displaced on account of the economic reforms may challenge the rule of the Kim Jong Il regime. In this sense, North Korean policymakers have decided to take risks.

Moreover, North Korea's neighbors have agreed on an engagement policy toward the DPRK. South Korea, China, and Russia are the staunchest supporters of engagement. The United States and Japan also voice support for the policy, though with important reservations. South Korea initiated its version of an engagement policy toward the North in 1988, which grew into the Sunshine Policy under the Kim Dae Jung administration and the Policy of Peace and Prosperity under the Roh Moo Hyun administration. By visiting Pyongyang in September 2002, Japanese Prime Minister Junichiro Koizumi made it clear that the Japanese government was committed to the engagement policy. He offered normalization of bilateral relations and provision of economic assistance if North Korea fully addressed the nuclear issue as well as issues of immediate concern to Japan. Given North Korea's accelerated pursuit of economic reform, sizable economic assistance from Japan would presumably be very attractive to the North. In May 2004, Koizumi visited Pyongyang again, revealing his position that normalization could come into reality at any time during his term in office. So far, the United States has maintained the toughest stance vis-à-vis North Korea. However, it has also pronounced its willingness to move toward normal relations with the North, including a package of economic and energy assistance in addition to security assurances.

Yet North Korea's responses thus far remain mixed. It spent ample time in the first two years of renewed nuclear crisis harshly attacking U.S. policy, and failed to respond conclusively to overtures by its neighbors, instead preferring to steadily advance its nuclear weapons goals. The renewal of the Six-Party Talks in the summer of 2005, culminating in the denuclearization declaration of September, suggests a possible turn toward a negotiated agreement. But the path to a larger breakthrough remains very uncertain. Kim Jong Il might again prove himself to be a man of tactical flexibility and strategic ineptitude. Delaying tactics might work to give the North Koreans marginal benefits, but they will not produce a strategically significant outcome.

If North Korea chooses to resolve the current nuclear situation by peaceful means, it will have chosen to take the engagement option and obtain the significant economic assistance. However, even in this positive scenario, North Korea's leaders might still prove half-hearted reformers by spending the economic assistance in maintaining the status quo rather than rehabilitating its economy and society. If they are left to their own devices, this is the most likely outcome. But will the North continue to keep the outside world at arm's length or even farther? Do the risks of engagement mean that the DPRK will still seek to stand apart from the larger international community, content to play yet again for tactical advantage in its continued strategy for national survival? These are the questions that remain to be answered.

NOTES

The views expressed in this paper are exclusively those of the author.

1. For the history and analysis of North Korea's military-diplomatic campaigns, see Narushige Michishita, "Calculated Adventurism: North Korea's Military-Diplomatic Campaigns, 1966–2000," Ph.D. dissertation submitted to the Paul H. Nitze School of Advanced International Studies, Johns Hopkins University, May 2003.

2. C. Kenneth Quinones, *Kitachousen: Bei-Kokumushou Tantoukan-no Koushou Hiroku* (North Korea's Nuclear Threat "Off the Record" Memories) (Tokyo: Chuuoukouronsha, 2000), p. 259.

3. On 23 January 1968, only two days after North Korean armed agents mounted an assault on the South Korean presidential residence, North Korean naval vessels captured the U.S. Navy intelligence-gathering ship *Pueblo* and its crew in the Sea of Japan. To get the crew and the ship back, the United States agreed to hold direct talks with the DPRK in Panmunjom. The crew, but not the ship, returned to the United States in December 1968 after the conclusion of the talks, which lasted eleven months. The *Pueblo* incident was a total victory for North Korea. By capturing the ship, North Korea succeeded in

hampering U.S. intelligence activities, diverting U.S.-ROK attention away from Vietnam and straining U.S.-ROK relations.

4. On 15 April 1969, air-to-air missiles fired by two North Korean MiG-21 fighters shot down the U.S. Navy EC-121 reconnaissance aircraft in the Sea of Japan. All the crew members aboard were killed. Although U.S. leaders gave thoughts to military options, they were rejected in the end.

5. In October 1973, North Korea initiated long and systematic military-diplomatic campaigns in the areas surrounding five offshore islands in the Yellow Sea. These so-called Northwest Islands—Baengnyeongdo, Daecheongdo, Socheongdo, Yeonpyeongdo, and Udo—are located much closer to the North Korean west coast than to the South Korean west coast but remain under the military control of the Commander in Chief, United Nations Command (CINCUNC) according to the Armistice Agreement signed in July 1953.

6. In August 1976, in what was called the Axe Murder incident, two U.S. Army officers were killed in the Joint Security Area (JSA) in Panmunjom by North Korean guards wielding axes. North Korea tried to use the incident to reinforce its diplomatic offensive by claiming that the United States was preparing for war and that the U.S. presence in South Korea was a root cause of the confrontation

on the Korean Peninsula. However, the brutal killing of the U.S. servicemen backfired on North Korea. The reaction of the international community to the North Korean action was extremely negative. North Korea's diplomatic offensive against the U.S. military presence in South Korea lost its momentum thereafter.

7. Lee Mun Hang, *JSA-Panmunjeom, 1953–1994* (Seoul: Sohwa, 2001), p. 373 (for the 1953–1992 period); and data obtained from the ROK Ministry of National Defense, dated 29 August 2002 (for the 1993–2000 period).

8. *Rodong Sinmun*, 16 December 1962, p. 1. According to Kim Il Sung, the military lines ordered "to train the People's Army into a cadre army, to modernize armaments, fortify military positions, arm the entire people, and to garrison the whole country. " Kim Il Sung, "Let Us Strengthen the Revolutionary Forces in Every Way so as to Achieve the Cause of Reunification of the Country," concluding speech delivered at the Eighth Plenary Meeting of the Fourth Central Committee of the Workers' Party of Korea, 27 February 1964, in *Kim Il Sung Works*, vol. 18 (Pyongyang: Foreign Languages Publishing House, 1984), pp. 222–23.

9. Gugbang Gunsa Yeonguso (National Defense Military History Research Institute), *Geongun 50-nyeonsa* (Fifty-Year History since the Foundation of the Armed Forces) (Seoul: Gugbang Gunsa Yeonguso, 1998), pp. 354–65; Chung Min Lee, *The Emerging Strategic Balance in Northeast Asia: Implications for Korea's Defense Strategy and Planning for the 1990s* (Seoul: Research Center for Peace and Unification of Korea, 1989), pp. 195, 198; and Peter Hayes, *Pacific Powderkeg: American Nuclear Dilemmas in Korea* (Lexington: Lexington Books, 1991), pp. 91, 93.

10. Kim Il Sung, "The Present Situation and the Tasks of Our Party," Report to the Conference of the Workers' Party of Korea, 5 October 1966, in *Kim Il Sung Works*, vol. 20 (Pyongyang: Foreign Languages Publishing House, 1984), p. 361.

11. Ashton B. Carter and William J. Perry, *Preventive Defense: A New Security Strategy for America* (Washington, D.C.: Brookings Institution Press, 1999), p. 130.

12. Ibid., pp. 128–29.

13. For example, see Proceedings of the Eighth General Officers Talks, 2 July 1999, provided by the UNCMAC.

14. Bong-Geun Jun, former Blue House staff, interview by author, Seoul, ROK, 16 May 2002.

15. A defected former North Korean diplomat, interview by author, Seoul, ROK, 15 May 2002.

16. *Pyongyang Times*, 10 April 1993, p. 2.

17. "Successful Launch of First Satellite in DPRK," *KCNA*, 4 September 1998; and "Kim Jong Il's Election as NDC Chairman Proposed," *KCNA*, 5 September 1998.

18. Dae-Sook Suh, *Kim Il Sung: The North Korean Leader* (New York: Columbia University Press, 1988), pp. 137–57, 212–37.

19. In the Sixth Party Congress in 1980, Kim Jong Il was elected to the Presidium of the Political Bureau, to the Political Bureau, as secretary in the Secretariat, and to the Central Military Commission.

20. For the sophisticated nature of North Korea's military-diplomatic campaigns, see Proceedings of the Sixth through Eleventh General Officers Talks, 15, 22 June 1999; 2, 21 July 1999; 17 August 1999; 1 September 1999; and UNC, "Report of the Activities of the United Nations Command for 1999," these materials provided by the UNCMAC; "Special Communiqué of KPA General Staff," *KCNA*, 2 September 1999; and "KPA Navy Command's Important Communiqué," *KCNA*, 23 March 2000.

21. "Keynote Speeches Made at Six-way Talks," *KCNA*, 29 August 2003.

22. ROK Ministry of National Defense, "The Naval Clash on the Yellow Sea on 29 June 2002 between South and North Korea: The Situation and ROK's Position," 1 July 2002. One of them died a while later in hospital.

23. Eric Schmitt, "North Korean Fliers Said to Have Sought Hostages," *New York Times,* 8 March 2003, p. A1.

24. In February 2000, the director of the Defense Intelligence Agency testified, "North Korea's capability to successfully conduct complex, multi-echelon, large-scale operations to reunify the Korean peninsula declined in the 1990s." Vice Admiral Thomas R. Wilson, Director, Defense Intelligence Agency, "Military Threats and Security: Challenges Through 2015," Statement for the Record, Senate Select Committee on Intelligence, 2 February 2000.

25. "Statement of FM [Foreign Ministry] Spokesman Blasts UNSC's Discussion of Korean Nuclear Issue," *KCNA*, 6 April 2003.

26. For example, the KCNA reported, "The U.S. claim that its forces in South Korea are a 'war deterrent force' is nothing but sophism intended to justify its military presence in South Korea and its moves to ignite another Korean war." "Removal of Danger of War from Korean Peninsula Called For," *KCNA*, 20 January 2002.

27. White House, *The National Security Strategy of the United States of America* (Washington, D.C., 2002).

28. Department of State Daily Press Briefing, Richard Boucher, Spokesman, Washington, D.C., 9 April 2003.

29. "Spokesman for Panmunjom Mission of KPA Issues Statement," *KCNA*, 18 February 2003.

30. "Election of Deputies to 11th Supreme People's Assembly of DPRK to be Held," *KCNA*, 4 June 2003.

31. "Interview on ABC's This Week with George Stephanopoulos," Secretary Colin L. Powell, Department of State, Washington, D.C., 29 December 2002.

32. Jung Chang-Hyun, *Gyeot-eseo Bon Gim Jeong Il* (Kim Jong Il Seen from the Side), rev. and enl. ed. (Seoul: Gimyeongsa, 2000), pp. 201–202.

33. ROK Ministry of National Defense, "The Naval Clash on the Yellow Sea on 29 June 2002 between South and North Korea: The Situation and ROK's Position," 1 July 2002.

34. "Working Contact for Ministerial Talks Proposed to South Side," *KCNA*, 25 July 2002.

35. Michael R. Gordon, "How Politics Sank Accord on Missiles with North Korea," *New York Times*, 6 March 2001, pp. A1 and A8.

36. "U.S.-DPRK Joint Communiqué," Washington, D.C., 12 October 2000.

5

The Politics of National Identity
The Rebirth of Ideology and Drifting Foreign Policy in South Korea

Byung-Kook Kim

The summer of 2004 was extremely hot and humid in South Korea. The "*sinjuryu*," or New Mainstream, of South Korea's volatile political society, described by its foes as the "Talibans" and even "Jusapa,"[1] frontally challenged the country's remaining Cold War ideological taboos. The Presidential Truth Commission recognized Song Yun Kyu, a former leftist guerrilla, and two North Korean spies tortured to death in prison in 1974, as heroes in the struggle for democracy. In the commission's view, the acts of resistance by Song and the North Korean agents exposed South Korea's violation of its constitutional provisions on freedom of thought and conscience.[2] The leading conservative newspapers were in an uproar, conceding that the deaths were unjust acts of state violence, but heatedly denying the democratic intentions of those exonerated by the Truth Commission. The uproar soon turned to cynicism when it was disclosed that the commission had employed progressive dissidents, once charged with "espionage" and "liaison" with radical subversive organizations during the 1980s, as its investigators.[3] To the dismay of the conservative papers, President Roh Moo Hyun warmly greeted the completion of the Truth Commission's two-year investigation. As Roh observed, "The media reported I will negatively judge your work. . . . I have no such intentions. Whether it occurred as part of a struggle for democratization or not, any past violations of human rights by an illegal exercise of public power need to be thoroughly investigated."[4] Many observers interpreted his words as a pledge to expand the Truth Commission's mission beyond the investigation of human rights abuses under Park Chung Hee,[5] delving instead into South Korea's darkest days of national division and civil war between 1945 and 1953.

THE WAR OVER NATIONAL IDENTITY

Barely two weeks later, another front opened in the ideological struggle. The ruling Uri Party, with 151 National Assembly Members, joined forces with the newly established Democratic Labor Party to endorse a "Truth Law on Collaborators and Traitors during Japanese Colonial Rule-by-Force."[6] By exposing various acts of betrayal committed by the collaborators before 1945, its advocates argued, South Korea would at last free itself from not only its shameful past but also its "perverse" present. In this revisionist view, Rhee Syngman's forging of an alliance with former soldiers, bureaucrats, and business leaders of colonial Korea enabled many of Imperial Japan's collaborators to become part of South Korea's "vested interests";[7] this, they contended, prevented the emergence of a genuinely democratic state.

The truth finding allegedly required an investigation of more than 100,000 people.[8] The draft bill enraged Park Geun Hae, the Hannara Party leader and daughter of Park Chung Hee, a first lieutenant in Imperial Japan's Manchurian army before liberation. Two of South Korea's three leading newspapers, *Chosun Ilbo* and *Donga Ilbo*, also fought back vigorously, condemning the Uri Party for making an "infantile" moral judgment without taking historical context into consideration. But the revisionist campaign gained greater force as Roh Moo Hyun's allies, protégés, sympathizers, and labor union followers, who controlled South Korea's two largest television networks, launched their own media war against *Chosun Ilbo* and *Donga Ilbo*.

In the same month, Koguryo, a dynasty that ruled over Manchuria and part of Korea between 37 BC and AD 668, became a political issue between South Korea and China and within South Korea. China's Ministry of Foreign Affairs triggered an outburst of public anger and resentment when it deleted Koguryo from its website on Korean history, in tandem with an academic and media campaign to redefine it as a "local government" of imperial China.[9] The anger soon turned away from China and toward Roh Moo Hyun and his Uri Party. In response to Chinese moves, the Uri leaders behaved very circumspectly, maintaining their "composure," "responding toward China in a learned way," and "always bearing in mind China's status as South Korea's main trade partner."[10] Many Uri legislators had been much harsher on America. The "386" Uri leaders[11] had opposed South Korea's dispatch of troops to Iraq because it "helped George W. Bush's reelection." On 21 July the U.S. House of Representatives unanimously passed a North Korean Human Rights Act, which various Uri legislators immediately condemned as an unjust "interference in North Korea's domestic affairs." Some legislators briefly considered submitting a bill to urge the U.S. Senate not to vote on the North Korea Human Rights Act.[12] The conservative camp cynically recalled the Uri Party's caucus of April 2004, where 63 percent of its newly elected National Assembly Members identified China and only 26 percent America as South Korea's most important partner.[13] The month of July simply reconfirmed the belief of South Korean conservatives that the Uri Party was an anti-American leftist party infatuated with China.

Park Geun Hae summed up Roh Moo Hyun's mix of action and inaction on these issues as "sabotaging South Korea's national identity," warning of a "total war" if South Korea continued drifting in a "strange way."[14] Was Roh undertaking a genuine act of redefining national identity? Why had his ruling coalition's rewriting of South Korea's modern history become such a hotly contested issue? What were the longer-term implications for South Korea's foreign policy and its place in East Asia's rapidly changing power configuration? Had South Korea become a willing part of what one scholar called a "Pax Sinica"?[15] This chapter will explore these issues. The first section provides an overall map of South Korea's national identity that formed in South Korea's tragic years of Japanese colonialism (1910–45), U.S. military occupation (1945–48), and civil war (1950–53), and identifies the generic weaknesses of that identity. The next section highlights how this identity broke down under the powerful force of "generational change," encompassing South Korea's increasing economic affluence, democratization, North Korea's setbacks after the Cold War, and the war on terrorism. We then offer a top-down perspective, analyzing Roh Moo Hyun's historical rectification campaign as a strategy to rescue his failing presidency and to pursue a fundamental ideological realignment in favor of the Uri Party.

CONSERVATIVES WITHOUT CONSERVATISM

South Koreans are what Anthony D. Smith once called an "ethnie," a people with a historically inherited homeland living with a common set of myths, customs, and language, as well as a shared collective memory of history.[16] South Koreans looked at themselves as a *kyorae* or *dongpo*,[17] Tangun's sons and daughters with a proud memory of once ruling over what is today China's northeast region.[18] The clear ethnic identity, however, did not guarantee an easy transition to modernity. On the contrary, South Koreans struggled very hard to make a modern nation out of their ethnie, which required the transformation of their ethnie into a body of equal citizens.[19] Their republic was formally inaugurated in 1948 as a liberal democracy and a market economy, but the choice of state ideology and identity was primarily forced by events, rather than embraced and endorsed by its people. For South Koreans with an agonizing memory of Japanese colonial exploitation, there was no tradition worth being revived and rebuilt. Confucian beliefs were judged a cause of the Chosun dynasty's disgrace by obstructing the advance of *silhak* ("practical science") and by breeding factional political strife. There was thus no other future for which they could strive in 1948.

As a divided nation confronting a Stalinist rival to its north, South Korea had to choose liberal democracy and a market economy as its raison d'être, to legitimate in its own eyes the separation from North Korea. Moreover, as a child of the Cold War, South Korea's baptism into American liberalism offered the surest means to secure a loyal patron abroad.[20] The choice of liberal democracy and market economy constituted a strategy for national survival.

This proved a momentous decision. Unlike Taiwan's Kuomintang regime, which possessed its own locally generated modern political ideology, *San Min Chu I* (Three People's Principles), South Korea was totally dependent on American liberalism to justify breaking apart its primordial identity to construct a new republic in the southern half of the Korean peninsula. This ideological dependence on America translated into a revolution in its educational system immediately after 1948. Entire curricula were redesigned with the goal of acculturating South Koreans to liberal values and norms, thus sowing the seeds of a very contentious civil society. As new ideas galvanized individuals and empowered society, South Korea's ruling elite found its crisis of legitimacy worsen continuously, because it could not or would not deliver what it pledged constitutionally. Rhee Syngman turned authoritarian in 1952, and Park Chung Hee in 1972. Similarly, reformist rhetoric did not allow Chun Doo Hwan to shed his tyrannical image. The birth of a contentious civil society thus occurred in tandem with a crisis of regime legitimacy.[21]

Despite these internal conflicts, South Korea escaped the disease of perpetual regime turnovers. Rhee Syngman ruled for twelve years, Park Chung Hee for eighteen years, and Chun Doo Hwan for eight years. The presence of a "hard state" with an extraordinary capacity for repression aided their longevity, but repression alone could not explain their long tenure. Anticommunism was the political glue that enabled South Korea's political elite to weather its repeated crises and even prosper. Born out of a bloody civil war, the culture of distrust and hatred against communism gave a reason for South Korea's separation from its northern brethren. The North was an "axis of evil," frontally denying the *ilryun* ("human ethics") through its war-making on fellow Koreans. After experiencing horrific violence and destruction during three years of civil war, South Korea acquired McCarthyism of its own and became entrapped in a culture of hatred against all forms of socialism.[22] The Korean War was a rare moment in history when a fundamental transformation of a nation's ideological terrain occurred and became "frozen" in culture and institutions, as characterized by Seymour Martin Lipset and Stein Rokkan.[23] The armistice was signed in 1953, but South Koreans continuously relived their civil war as if it had never ended, transforming this experience into political myths, symbols, and rituals. As Park Chung Hee's military junta declared in its first public manifesto, anticommunism was defined as South Korea's *guksi* ("national essence") as long as North Korea possessed an upper hand in military rivalry.

The military threat from the North justified the compromise of South Korea's other liberal ideological tenets. Although Rhee Syngman possessed an impeccable record of resistance against Japanese colonial rule and maintained a hard line toward Japan after 1945, he made peace with former imperial soldiers, bureaucrats, and businesspeople accused of collaboration with Japan, lest he lose his mini–cold war with Kim Il Sung. The unholy alliance offered an additional advantage of consolidating his domestic power base. Fearing a purge much like one in North Korea, former colonial elites gave Rhee Syngman their unswerving loyalty and weeded out his foes from South Korea's inner circle of power, including Kim Ku of the Shanghai Provisional Government.[24] Expediency dominated the staffing of the state, making Rhee's rhetoric of anti-colonialism hollow, if not hypocritical, and disadvantaging South Korea in the struggle to acquire nationalist legitimacy. This pretense of anticolonialism ended when Park Chung Hee, seizing power through a military coup d'état, normalized relations with Japan in 1965, in pursuit of trade, investment, and colonial reparation funds even at the risk of massive protests.[25]

The ideal of liberal democracy thus became a victim of anticommunism. The authoritarian rulers of South Korea justified restrictions on basic rights as a prerequisite of national security and harshly repressed its dissidents, student leaders, and progressive political activists. Each left a deep scar on South Korean politics. After Cho Bong Am garnered 22.5 percent of the votes in a two-way presidential race in 1956 under a then-radical platform of peaceful unification, Rhee Syngman's court ordered his execution on charges of being a North Korean spy.[26] Park Chung Hee also orchestrated highly calculated moments of rightist rage and fear. In an effort to cripple the defiant intelligentsia, the Korea Central Intelligence Agency abducted dissidents from abroad under charge of "sympathizing with North Korea" in 1967, and rounded up more than a thousand students for "organizing underground cells in a conspiracy for a people's revolution" in 1974. Like Cho Bong Am under Rhee Syngman, Park Chung Hee's archrival Kim Dae Jung was imprisoned and later placed under house arrest for holding a "leftist" idea of unifying the two Koreas under a framework of "federation." Repression became institutionalized with the launching of Park Chung Hee's Yushin regime in 1973; in its seven years of existence, a total of 1,173 activists were imprisoned. For 203 jailed for violating South Korea's draconian National Security Law,[27] suffering became particularly intolerable, because their crime became their family's disgrace as they were "guilty by complicity" (*yeonjwajeo*), justifying tight surveillance by security forces.

The ruling elite of South Korea, with its self-image as a conservative force, thus suffered from a profoundly contradictory ideological platform. Confronting North Korea's Stalinist regime, it saw itself as a conservative in the Cold War ideological spectrum, but the ideology it claimed as its own was anything but conservative. In a postcolonial agrarian society abruptly cut off from Japan's imperial division of labor and suddenly pushed onto a world of sovereign nations without any prior experience of political freedom, neither liberal democracy nor market capitalism constituted a tradition worthy of conservation. The two were a future to work for rather than a past inherited, but South Korea's political elites took these fundamentally progressive ideas as their project of modernization. In so doing, they inadvertently legitimized the moralistic critique of their political rivals and intellectual foes of both liberal and radical orientation. Except for very brief moments of popular uprising and regime collapse in 1960, 1961, 1979, and 1980, this seemingly untenable political situation of justifying the illiberal reality in terms of liberal beliefs continued for four decades, before a decisive democratic breakthrough occurred in 1987. The elites maintained hegemony because they delivered protection from a much greater evil, North Korea's Stalinist regime. For most South Koreans, their rulers' violations of human rights were minor when compared with the bloody occupation by North Korea's People's Army in 1950. In the case of Park Chung Hee, modernization offered an additional rationale for enduring authoritarian rule.

THE CRISIS OF SUCCESS

The crisis in South Korea's national identity came not with failure, but with success. In less than four decades, South Korea was transformed from a client state living off U.S. aid into an OECD member with a dynamic, advanced industrial base. Politically, too, South Korea stunned even its own people by bringing down Cold War taboos one after another to strengthen basic rights after the democratic breakthrough of June 1987. Likewise, South Korea began to equip its armed forces with America's high-tech weapons and advanced managerial know-how and skill. Correspondingly, South Korea saw its international status rise continuously, recognized by Moscow in 1990 and by Beijing in 1992, while being applauded as an economic model for Third-World countries by international organizations. With North Korea breaking down from within, after the sudden cutoff of Soviet military and economic aid, South Korea thought it had triumphed in its mini–cold war. By 2001, even the Ministry of Unification publicly questioned whether there was any military *jujok* ("primary enemy").[28]

That taste of success, however, became a catalyst for political discord rather than harmony, because it destroyed South Korea's national consensus of anticommunism. Anticommunism was judged an ideology either unfit or illegitimate for an economically prosperous, militarily secure, and democratically vibrant South Korea. No longer fearing the North, many looked beyond anticommunism for a new raison d'être. The questioning of anticommunism ignited an ideological chain reaction, making many question the presence of U.S. military troops, the legal restriction on basic rights, and the conservative interpretation of South Korea's historical past.

These ideological changes surfaced in South Korea as a generation gap, given the nation's highly compressed economic, political, and military transformation. The country was "four families living under one roof" when the presidential election of 2002 made Roh Moo Hyun a political Cinderella. The primary line of conflict was between its younger "386" and older "5060" generations.[29] These two age cohorts were different breeds. The 50-to-60 age cohort, born before 1953 and entering university before 1972, lived through the darkest days of Japanese colonialism, U.S. military occupation, and civil war. The democracy they experienced in their formative college years was also Chang Myon's inept Second Republic (1960–61), which proved incapable of pulling society out of the paralyzed economy, with a per capita GNP of $83 before it was overthrown by a military coup d'état.[30] The subsequent era of *buguk gangbyong* ("prosperous nation, strong military") under Park Chung Hee's authoritarian rule inculcated the 5060 generation with a conservative ethos of order, security, and growth. Moreover, the formative years of the 5060s coincided with periodic wavering in America's security commitments, which only strengthened their conservatism.

The United States excluded South Korea from its "Acheson Line" of defense in 1950, thus contributing directly to Kim Il Sung's invasion in June. In 1971, the United States unilaterally pulled out the 7th Army Division under President Nixon's "Guam Doctrine," provoking a war scare, and justifying (however briefly) Park Chung Hee's launching of a Yushin regime in 1972 for total national mobilization. President Carter shocked even the U.S. Congress and military establishment when he announced a complete withdrawal of U.S. ground forces in 1977. Mindful of this historical record, many of the 5060 generation subsequently interpreted DoD's East Asia Security Initiative (EASI) of 1990[31] and the Global Posture Review (GPR) of 2003 as extensions of this long history of weakening U.S. security commitments.[32] Neither policy reformulation spoke of a complete withdrawal of U.S. troops from South Korea. In the case of the GPR, the central concept was to strengthen America's military alliance with South Korea by equipping much-reduced U.S. forces with new, advanced weapons. The 5060 generation, however, interpreted both policy changes through ideas formed during and even before Park Chung Hee's authoritarian rule, and imagined each to be a precursor of America's abandonment of South Korea. This profound sense of security vulnerability, in turn, kept alive their ethos of order, security, and development.

The 386 generation had vastly different formative years. Entering college between 1982 and 1991, when South Korea's per capita GNP grew from $1,847 to $7,183, much of this age cohort never experienced absolute poverty. They also lived under a failing or failed political regime, but their failed regime was Chun Doo Hwan's brutal Fifth Republic, established through a bloody massacre of Kwangju protestors in 1980, not a democratically elected regime.[33] The Fifth Republic was deemed politically incompetent and breakable, ironically denying its own legitimacy through the pledge of "liberalization" that it found necessary to fend off the challenge of democratic forces. Moreover, coming of political age during Ronald Reagan's presidency, most 386ers never feared America's military abandonment of South Korea. Unprecedented affluence and military security prevailed, liberating this age cohort from their parent generation's obsession with order, security, and development. What made them especially rebellious was their distinctive understanding of the U.S. political role in South Korea. Acculturated into Latin America's dependency theory and liberation theology and later into North Korea's *juche* ideology of national independence, and then spreading throughout college campuses under the shock of the Kwangju tragedy, many 386 student activists looked on America as an accomplice in Chun Doo Hwan's despotic rule. Chun Doo Hwan's transfer of a South Korean army division, nominally under U.S. command, into Kwangju in May 1980 without prior American approval hardly ameliorated their perception of American intentions. After all, they argued, Reagan chose Chun as his first head-of-state visitor in 1981, thus revealing his active support for Chun's authoritarian rule.

This revisionist reinterpretation of the U.S. role initially began as a debate among progressive academics and intellectuals, but quickly spread among 386 university students to become a generic characteristic of their generation. Ironically, the source of their radicalization was Chun Doo Hwan's Fifth Republic. To fight against Chun's repressive security forces, 386 dissidents continuously escalated their ideological protests, initially toying with dependency theory and liberation theology, then embracing Marxist ideas and Leninist organization, and later landing in North Korea's home-grown *juche* ideology of a Nietzsche-like superego. Searching for an ideology that frontally negated the Fifth Republic, they eventually split into two groups. The "NL" line called for national liberation modeled after North Korea, whereas its rival "PD" line strove for a *minjung* (people's) democracy.[34] These two forces went beyond the delegitimation of the ruling political elite into the negation of not only the negatively defined national identity of anticommunism, but also the positively defined national self-image of lib-eral democracy, market capitalism, and alliance with America.

Most of this generation soon gave up the NL and PD lines when Eastern Europe's Communist regimes collapsed from within and North Korea decayed under a systemic crisis after 1991. However, their spirit of resistance and their contempt of South Korea's identity survived, influencing their interpretations of what a vote for Roh Moo Hyun in the presidential election of 2002 meant, whether America's war against Saddam Hussein's Iraq and its subsequent request for a dispatch of South Korean military troops in 2003 and 2004 were just, and how to interpret Roh's historical rectification campaign of 2004.

Table 1 illustrates South Korea's generational divide. The share of people identifying with "progressivism" reached 29.3 percent for the 386 generation in 2002, whereas only 14.2 percent of the 5060 power bloc adopted this identity. The 386 generation was a strong advocate of basic rights, with 53 percent demanding the repeal or substantial amendment of South Korea's National Security Act and 43.9 percent recognizing workers' right to strike even in the state-managed public sector. The 386ers were fervent "postmodernist" believers in gender equality, with a mere 5.5 percent defending South Korea's family laws, which acknowledged only males as heads of household. The 5060 generation constituted the polar opposite across all three rights issues. The advocates of repeal or a substantial amendment of the National Security Act reached only 26.4 percent, whereas strikes by public-sector workers secured support of only 19.7 percent. The older cohort predictably defended South Korea's conservative household registration system five times more frequently than the 386 age cohort. The size of the generational gap was equally large in foreign policy areas, with 5060 people calling for an immediate end to all aid to North Korea twice as frequently as 386 members. Strong supporters of South Korea's alliance with America numbered 76.3 and 42.3 percent in the two age groups, respectively. The only issue area in which the generational gap narrowed considerably was social welfare, understandable given South Korea's communitarian Confucian cultural heritage. Here a national consensus existed, with public opinion tipped markedly leftward.

More troublesome for South Korea's domestic politics and relationship with its American ally, the 386 and 5060 cohorts each controlled powerful organizational resources and commanded compelling ideological images. Having dominated politics as supporters or foes of South Korea's "three Kims," who retired from public life only in 2002 after thirty years of regionalist rivalry, the 5060 generation controlled top layers of South Korea's *juryu* (mainstream) institutions, including political parties, business corporations, state ministries, and newspapers. The 5060 cohort proudly took credit

Table I   **Generational Gap between South Korea's 386 and 5060 Age Cohorts, 2002–2003**

	Immediately End All Aid to North Korea		Maintain or Strengthen Alliance with America		Increase Social Welfare Budget		Amend or Repeal the National Security Act		Public Sector Workers Right to Strike	
	May '02	May '03	May '02	May '03	May '02	May '03	May '02	May '03	May '02	May '03
386	11.1	17.4	42.3	63.5	76.7	61.1	53.0	59.4	43.9	37.6
5060	23.7	31.7	76.3	91.0	60.0	45.6	26.4	30.5	19.7	20.1
All	15.0	22.2	56.4	76.3	70.2	56.8	41.8	45.5	34.2	28.8

	Maintain the Household Registration System[a]		Oppose Generation Change in Leadership		Identify Oneself as a Progressive[b]		Frequent E-mail & Internet Opinion Site Users[c]		Watch TV News & Read Newspapers Daily	
	May '02	May '03	May '02	May '03	May '02	May '03	May '02	May '03	May '02	May '03
386	5.5	7.7	11.1	16.3	29.3	30.8	39.1	39.5	68.8	60.8
5060	27.8	39.9	27.8	43.2	14.2	15.5	9.5	5.8	66.1	68.7
All	14.9	20.5	18.4	25.8	24.9	24.4	34.4	32.2	64.3	60.9

Source: National surveys conducted by the East Asia Institute in collaboration with *Hankuk Ilbo* on 27–28 May 2002, and 2003.

a. The Household Registration System, originally introduced in Korea's colonial period, legally organizes the household around its male head. such, it is criticized as a fundamental obstacle in bringing gender equality and protecting the rights of single mothers and divorcees.

b. The survey asked the respondent to identify her ideological preference on the 0–10 scale, with "Very Progressive" rated as zero, the "Centris five, and "Very Conservative" as ten. The respondent was given the choice of choosing any number between zero and ten.

c. The "frequent" users are those who said they used e-mail and Internet opinion pages "every day" or "almost every day" in the survey.

for South Korea's quadruple successes of economic growth, military security, political democratization, and diplomatic breakthroughs. The 386 cohort, by contrast, made up strategic mid-layers of its *juryu* institutions, and also led nongovernmental organizations (NGOs) that exploded from 3,800 to 6,159 between 1996 and 1999. Shaken up by a spread of centrist ideas after Kim Young Sam reinstituted civilian rule in 1993, many 386 dissidents sought new life in NGOs.[35] Moreover, this age cohort acquired its own medium of expression and propaganda when Kim Young Sam pursued a forceful broadband Internet policy and built a cutting-edge IT infrastructure. With nearly all of South Korea's approximately 1,200 townships linked into one integrated network by 2002, and with Internet users exploding from 13,801 in 1998 to over ten million by 2002,[36] many 386 NGO leaders had their voices heard without conservative newspapers "distorting" with editorials and columns. The stage was set for a generational war.

ELECTORAL SUCCESS AND THE CRISIS IN GOVERNANCE

The polarization of public opinion set only the overall context of political conflict in South Korea, not its detailed content. The generation gap could have remained latent, had Roh Moo Hyun and his 386 aides not purposely magnified, inflamed, and organized it.

Roh was as much a creator as a product of ideological polarization. When Kwangju threw its support to him in the New Millennium Democratic Party (NMDP) presidential primaries in March 2002, allegedly under the direction of Kim Dae Jung's "invisible hand,"[37] Roh Moo Hyun was instantly transformed from a political outcast into a Cinderella. The image of a Kyongsang native backed by Cholla residents galvanized the young voters, who were by then thoroughly alienated from ideologically shallow regionalist elections and the morally illegitimate money politics of the established political leaders. Moreover, once his bid for power became credible, Roh Moo Hyun purposely made his complex personality a political issue. He was a genius in populist mobilization, winning two new supporters every time he made one enemy, and constantly making and remaking the list of enemies as his political fortunes went up and down throughout the presidential election campaigns. When Rhee In Jae, of the mainstream faction, revealed the wartime leftist criminal record of Roh Moo Hyun's father-in-law in a nationally televised NMDP primary debate to win back his front-runner position, Roh Moo Hyun retorted: "I married my wife knowing her father's past. She is a happy mother of our children. Should I abandon her? Am I qualified for presidential roles if I abandon such a woman and not qualified if I love her?"[38] That effectively ended what little was left of Rhee In Jae's credibility and instantly made Roh Moo Hyun a challenger of repressive Cold War taboos. Similarly, when anti-American protestors demanded the trial of two American GIs for "negligent homicide" in running over two schoolgirls with an armored vehicle, Roh Moo Hyun expressed his discomfort with the conservative newspapers' coverage of anti-Americanism with a powerful rhetorical question: "Why so much fuss about anti-Americanism?"[39]

Roh Moo Hyun was also a risk taker, "betting everything he had whenever challenged or given an opportunity," to quote his lecture before Yonsei University students.[40] The press called him a master of the "All In" strategy, and he lived up to his rhetoric. When prosecutors charged Roh Moo Hyun's aides for illegally raising political funds during the presidential campaign, he proposed holding a plebiscite for a vote of confidence.[41] Coming after an uninterrupted fall in his public support ratings, which were as low as 16.5 percent in October 2003,[42] the vote of confidence would have been political suicide under normal circumstances. However, with public prosecutors chasing after the Hannara Party's illegal campaign funds, estimated as over fifty billion won (ten times more than the charge brought against his aides), Roh Moo Hyun's gesture to hold a vote of confidence made Hannara look unrepentant. The opposition was portraying its 2002 presidential candidate, Lee Hoi Chang, as a victim of political repression. To ethically compromise the Hannara Party even more, Roh Moo Hyun pledged to resign if his illegal funds surpassed one tenth of his opponents'.[43]

The president obviously had no intention of holding a plebiscite or resigning from his post. The Constitutional Court predictably found his proposed vote of confidence unconstitutional in November 2003.[44] There was also no surprise in prosecutorial politics. Roh Moo Hyun's aides were charged in May 2004 with illegally raising 4.6 billion won from *chaebol* contributions, which was less than one tenth of Lee Hoi Chang's illegal fund-raising.[45] Roh Moo Hyun had thus transformed his personal calamity into an opportunity by dragging his foe into a "who-is-dirtier" debate. The game paid off handsomely. The investigation resulted in a trial of twenty-three National Assembly Members, making Roh Moo Hyun look cleaner.

The mix of populism and risk-taking served Roh Moo Hyun well, especially during election campaigns. Whenever he was challenged on South Korea's Cold War ideological taboos, he responded with rhetoric that was colorful yet ambiguous, strong yet elusive, polarizing yet shallow. He lashed out against Rhee In Jae as a ghost haunting South Korea with its repressive Cold War past, but he did not offer his views of Kim Jong Il's Stalinist regime. He scorned as rightist paranoia any charges of anti-Americanism directed against progressive NGOs, but he also kept his distance from them lest he too looked like an anti-American radical. He was a master of ideological ambiguity, clothing a progressive platform in conservative discourse and vice versa. He saw his call for a revision of South Korea's Status of Forces Agreement (SOFA)[46] as perfectly in line with the alliance system, because "demanding a revision by definition assumes continuous American military presence."[47] There would be no SOFA to revise if there were no U.S. military troops stationed on South Korean soil. When a group of NGOs sought Roh's support for a nationwide signature drive urging America's recognition of South Korea's primary jurisdiction over criminal cases involving GIs, Roh Moo Hyun refused, because it was "inappropriate for a presidential candidate to behave like a NGO activist, however strongly he sympathized with their cause."[48] By contrast, Lee Hoi Chang, who had accused Roh of anti-American agitation, publicly urged Hannara loyalists to join in the signature drive.[49]

The ideological ambiguity of Roh Moo Hyun's presidential campaign explains his political coalition's extreme level of heterogeneity. Figure 1 contrasts Roh Moo Hyun's supporters with Lee Hoi Chang's as of June 2003, when a majority of people still gave him a positive approval rating as president. The horizontal axis maps out attitudes on the National Teachers Union (NTU), with the right end showing a negative opinion and the left end a positive view. The vertical axis gives attitudes on the U.S. military presence, another area where public opinion polarized in South Korea. Quadrant 2 houses South Korea's "traditional conservatives" with a mix of pro-American security views and antilabor ideas (35.9 percent). Quadrant 3 resembles the "orthodox progressive" (21.6 percent), combining a desire for greater autonomy in national security policy with a strong support for labor movements. With South Korea's political democratization, economic prosperity, and military security, a large portion of South Koreans moved away from the Cold War line of cleavage between Quadrant 2 and 3. For the quarter of South Koreans identifying with Quadrant 1, defending the U.S. military presence was entirely compatible with a show of support for labor unions—including South Korea's radical teachers, known for anti-American tendencies. The NTU's call for *chamgyoyuk* ("true education") apparently won support even among many who harbored conservative security ideas. The social conservatives in Quadrant 4 (18.5 percent), advocating an immediate or incremental American military withdrawal while opposing labor activism, constituted another "unorthodox" force defying the easy Cold War categorization of conservatives and progressives. The ideological ambiguity of Roh Moo Hyun played very well with such an evenly divided society during elections. He drew support more or less evenly across all four of the quadrants in Figure 1. By contrast, Lee Hoi Chang, who exhibited a decidedly conservative image in spite of his late efforts to make a U-turn on his relations with NGOs in 2002, drew 49.7 percent of his supporters from Quadrant 2. That cost Lee Hoi Chang the presidential election.

Figure 1   **Heterogeneity of Political Support for Roh Moo Hyun and Lee Hoi Chang, June 2003**

		National Teachers Union	
		Favor Strongly or Favor on Balance	Oppose Strongly or Oppose on Balance
U.S. Forces in Korea	Should stay or should remain for a considerable period	Quadrant 1 Roh Supporters 26.9% Lee Supporters 21.0% All 24.0%	Quadrant 2 Roh Supporters 29.9% Lee Supporters 49.7% All 35.9%
	Should immediately or incrementally withdraw in stages	Quadrant 3 Roh Supporters 23.0% Lee Supporters 13.8% All 21.6%	Quadrant 4 Roh Supporters 20.3% Lee Supporters 15.5% All 18.5%

Source: A public survey with a random sample of 1,005 conducted by the East Asia Institute in collaboration with *Joongang Ilbo* in June 2003.

Roh Moo Hyun's strength in building a majority coalition of heterogeneous forces during elections became a source of weakness once he won the election and tackled the task of governance in a divided society. As a candidate, he made Lee Hoi Chang look like a stuffy, distant, and dull conservative entrapped in Cold War prejudices. Once he was in power, however, the strategy of ambiguity no longer worked, because he was the president who had to make difficult choices on contentious national issues. In this postelection game of trade-offs, his initial choice of governance strategy looked like that of triggering a leftward realignment in South Korean politics. President-elect Roh Moo Hyun launched his transition team with progressive professors and researchers from South Korea's hitherto politically marginalized provincial universities and state think tanks. The choice of Lee Jong Seok, Seo Dong Man, and Seo Ju Seok as members of moderate Yun Young Kwan's Subcommittee on Foreign Affairs and Trade assured the continuity of Kim Dae Jung's Sunshine Policy, but with a newly added nationalist, if not anti-American, ideological bent. The Subcommittee on Macroeconomic Policy had Lee Jeong Wu, an ardent advocate of distributive justice, as its coordinator. Likewise, industrial policy fell under the control of Kim Dae Hwan, a progressive labor expert with a long record of advocating a comprehensive reform of *chaebol* conglomerates, including their opaque governance structures marred with cross shareholding, insider trading, and cross loan guarantees.[50] Moreover, with Roh Moo Hyun's blessing, Lee Kwang Je prepared for a takeover of South Korea's presidential secretariat with his 386ers.[51]

Roh Moo Hyun sounded brave in his nationally televised "Talk with People" in early 2003, promising a sweeping change in South Korea's SOFA, the wartime operational command structure, and even the Mutual Security Treaty with the United States.[52] Hoping for a breakthrough in economic policy, Kim Dae Hwan called for a progressive dismantlement of the institutional mechanisms through which *chaebol* conglomerates controlled affiliate companies.[53] Following his presidential election pledge of serving as a "neutral mediator" between Washington and Pyongyang on nuclear issues, Roh Moo Hyun openly criticized President Bush's hawkish views on North Korea and volunteered South Korea's "lead role" in peacefully resolving the nuclear issue.[54]

The left turn, however, lasted only very briefly. The first backlash came from abroad only weeks before the inauguration, with U.S. Defense Secretary Rumsfeld's call to move American ground troops southward, away from North Korea's forward-deployed artillery, as part of an effort to build an "equal partnership" with the South Korean ally. Roh Moo Hyun disparaged South Korea's alliance system as unequal, and Rumsfeld was determined to make it more equal, but in an unanticipated direction. The redeployment was a step toward more equal burden-sharing in the eyes of U.S. policymakers, because America's ground forces as deployed were vulnerable to a North Korean blitzkrieg.[55] A month later, a DoD delegation shocked South Korea by proposing to complete an agreement on troop redeployment by September.[56]

The Rumsfeld shock came as North Korea was busily engaged in another round of nuclear blackmail. With IAEA inspectors expelled from North Korea, Pyongyang had a free hand in playing its game of brinkmanship in January and February, withdrawing from the NPT, transferring 8,000 spent fuel rods into a reprocessing facility, and even reactivating its hitherto mothballed 5-megawatt reactor.[57] The U.S. proposal for troop redeployments in the middle of a nuclear crisis was immediately interpreted as a precipitous decline of American trust in South Korea, triggering mounting concern among foreign investors over military deterrence. For every notch that international credit agencies downgraded confidence in the South Korean economy, South Korea was estimated to shoulder an additional half-billion dollars in interest payments.[58] To make foreign investors even more jittery, in the same month of February, SK Group's top executives were charged with account fraud and insider trading, mocking South Korea's claims of success in upgrading prudential regulations and spreading rumors of an impending prosecutorial crackdown on other *chaebols*.[59] Nearly three million people also confronted overdue credit cards, excessive mortgage indebtedness, and related financial liabilities.[60] These adverse trends, coupled with the signs of a drift in the U.S.–South Korea alliance, triggered a nosedive in the stock index.[61]

Upon being sworn into power on 25 February 2003, Roh Moo Hyun swiftly altered course. In response to President Bush's formal request for war support, he moved to dispatch army engineers and medics to Iraq despite strong NGO opposition.[62] Roh Moo Hyun also called for postponing all talks on U.S. troop redeployments until North Korea gave up on its nuclear program. To his conservative foes' surprise, on 19 April he seemed to accept even America's longstanding call for transforming South Korea's armed forces into a regional balancer in Northeast Asia, ready to back up American military power in other political trouble spots.[63] The conservative predecessors had avoided, if not opposed, this step, lest China see South Korea as following America's lead to contain China.

In tandem with the Pentagon's pursuit of transformation, Roh Moo Hyun pledged to make the South Korean armed forces into a high-tech war machine, armed with modern information technology, thus preparing for eventual U.S. troop relocation and downsizing in the Korean peninsula. He looked as if he accepted Rumsfeld's new global military strategy, seeking only to slow down its implementation until after North Korea gave up its nuclear weapons program. He also put off the negotiation on SOFA until after peaceful resolution of the North Korean nuclear crisis.[64]

When attacked for ideological contradictions, Roh called himself a "pro-American independent"[65] who accepted South Korea's primary responsibility of deterring North Korea, as well as its backing of American regional military endeavors in distant areas. Well before his May 2003 summit with President Bush, Roh Moo Hyun realized he could not keep up his ideological ambiguity without provoking a security-economic crisis. To meet the challenging tasks of governance, he needed a friendly United States. The U-turn on foreign policy inevitably threatened his coalition by driving away many of his progressive supporters.

In May 2003, Roh Moo Hyun also became hopelessly trapped in labor politics. Even more than in foreign policy, he zigzagged, enraging both progressives and conservatives. Emulating his maneuverings over alliance policy, Roh began with a progressive platform of "correcting South Korea's imbalance of social power." The transition team agreed, recommending state prosecutors refrain from holding labor leaders in custody when investigating illegal but nonviolent labor strikes and disputes.[66] Once in power, however, he was burdened with the presidential responsibilities of economic recovery, and those responsibilities conflicted with his electoral promises. To allay investor fears, he pledged a "resolute response" when a militant Solidarity of Freighters closed down southern ports, only to accept its entire list of demands three days later.[67] The state zigzagged even more when the NTU opposed bringing all schools and students into a single nationally administered digitized information system on the grounds of protecting basic rights and privacy. The Minister of Education initially ruled out any reversal of the policy and then accepted the National Human Rights Commission's call for a comprehensive reappraisal, only to backtrack again to reconfirm the original plan for an administrative overhaul of South Korea's educational system.[68]

The zigzags of May triggered organized labor to launch protests to end Roh Moo Hyun's political wavering and force him to side unambiguously with labor interests. The railroad workers' union was on strike even after Roh Moo Hyun abandoned his program of privatizing South Korea's badly managed railroad system. This time, Roh Moo Hyun lashed back with a crackdown. Enraged, the Korean Confederation of Trade Unions (KCTU) got taxi drivers, textile unions, and metal workers to take turns in a "relay of strikes."[69] Health and medical workers, subway unions, and freighters followed days later with strikes as well.[70] On 21 August, Hyundai accepted union demands to cut workdays to five days per week, increase wages, and seek prior union agreement on the transfer of production facilities to overseas locations. Workers at Kia and Daewoo followed suit in subsequent weeks.[71]

Under attack on all fronts, Roh Moo Hyun despaired: "Everyone is interested only in flexing one's muscle. The state cannot but become paralyzed and sabotaged. I worry I cannot adequately perform my presidential role."[72] The internal cohesion of Roh Moo Hyun's coalition was threatened by actions he deemed necessary in an era of globalization. In May, the president promised to revise the laws to bring labor market flexibility.[73]

A month later, feeling "betrayed" by labor unions, who he thought were trying to "break and teach [him] a lesson,"[74] Roh Moo Hyun attacked South Korea's labor movement as having lost its sense of "moral integrity and responsibility"[75] and refused to protect "any labor movements led by a leadership interested only in furthering its interest."[76] He talked bravely of "taking away labor privileges" and "meeting investor needs";[77] but in Shinhan Holding Company's takeover of illiquid Choheung Bank, Minister of Finance Kim Jin Pyo "persuaded" Shinhan to guarantee the Choheung employees not only job security and wage hikes, but also a share of executive and managerial posts in the newly merged financial institution. Despite Roh Moo Hyun's warnings against labor militancy, the precedent of a labor union "dictating" key terms of mergers and acquisitions was set, prompting other similarly distressed workers to contest corporate restructuring and downsizing.

Paradoxically, Roh Moo Hyun the risk taker and the transformer needed political stability if he was to prevent his heterogeneous electoral base from breaking apart from within. He thought he could satisfy both progressives and conservatives with his colorful but ambiguous rhetoric; but that rhetoric got him in trouble as both progressives and conservatives claimed a role in his electoral victory and demanded payment for their support, in the form of specific policy initiatives, after the inauguration. To a certain extent, his heterogeneous supporters set off a conflict to force Roh Moo Hyun to unambiguously side with their platform. The United States was a master of brinkmanship, too, imposing its preferences on alliance structure, troop composition, and SOFA issues with a "take-it-or-leave-it" attitude. In this game of brinkmanship, it was far more effective than any of Roh Moo Hyun's domestic constituencies because of its indispensable role in South Korea's military security and economic prosperity. The president accommodated Rumsfeld's demands, but with a plea for a slowing of the pace of change. To save face, Roh claimed that he accepted Rumsfeld's program for his vision of an "independent" South Korea. The adjustment of alliance structure and troop composition, pursued in tandem with America's military transformation, he argued, opened a way to a more equal alliance, because it presumed South Korea would be taking over much of the American role of deterrence.

By contrast, conflicts with labor unions only sharpened. Roh declared that various militant unions were illegitimate and "no longer a true labor movement." The KCTU ridiculed the president as an "amateur shaman butchering workers" with "contradictory words and actions."[78] In a rare moment of labor unity, the conservative Korean Federation of Trade Unions (KFTU) agreed, accusing Roh Moo Hyun of "only creating discord by destroying all rules and norms."[79] The dilemma of governance had thus turned into a crisis of governance in a mere six months of his presidency. By the summer of 2003, Roh's approval ratings plummeted to 41.9 percent,[80] 50.1 percentage points below his February ratings.[81]

MOBILIZATION

As Roh Moo Hyun prepared for his second year in power, he already looked like a lame duck. In Figure 2, the dotted line traces the trajectory of public presidential performance ratings, measured by a randomly selected national sample,[82] and the solid line that of presumably more informed expert appraisals of presidential performance in six issue areas.[83] The average ratings were very grim, ranging between 25 and 40 (respectively, "bad on balance" and "mediocre") on the scale of 0–100, at both public and expert levels in all six issue areas.[84] When respondents were asked to identify Roh Moo Hyun's best performance area among the six issue areas, 53 percent of the general public sample and 55 percent of Roh Moo Hyun's government advisors replied "none." When asked to identify his worst performance area, the general public selected politics and administration, finance and fiscal policy, and labor and welfare by a ratio of 40 : 12 : 9. The government advisor group, by contrast, selected politics and administration, trade and corporate policy, and foreign affairs and security by a ratio of 27 : 19 : 18.

Figure 2   **Presidential Approval Ratings: General Public and Experts**

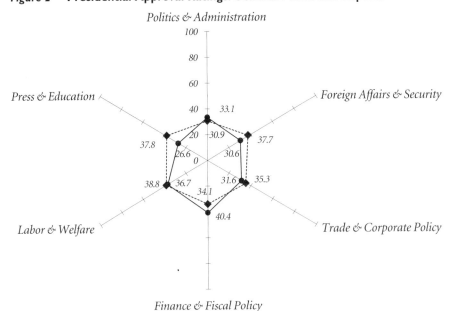

Roh Moo Hyun was rescued, however briefly, by his foes' lack of prudence, imagination, and perseverance and by his ability to exploit those weaknesses through risk-taking bordering on recklessness. The catalyst for a swift change of public mood was the collapse of the New Millennium Democratic Party (NMDP), from which Roh Moo Hyun's followers split in the middle of prosecutorial investigation of the NMDP's illegal political fund-raising in November 2003.[85] Cholla region voters deserted the NMDP en masse as the Uri Party seemed their region's only hope of sharing power after Kim Dae Jung retired from politics. With a general election only five months away, Roh Moo Hyun had young Uri legislators link his native South Kyongsang Province with Cholla supporters under the slogan of *dongjin* ("Marching Eastward").[86] Having once led an austere life as democratic activists and dissidents, many Uri leaders commanded a sense of moral superiority over the NMDP by being free from irregular fund-raising and ethically compromised regionalist activities. Having mastered politics through the art of *undong* ("movements"), they excelled in stirring up mass support through playing on symbols, rituals, and images. To transform South Korean electoral politics into a two-party race between Hannara and Uri, Roh Moo Hyun chose Jeong Dong Young of North Cholla Province as his party's chairman while placing Governor Kim Hyuk Kyu of South Kyongsang Province as top of the Uri party list for the general election of April 15, 2004.[87] Roh Moo Hyun drummed up both candidates as presidential aspirants in order to lure Cholla from the NMDP and South Kyongsang voters from Hannara.

The NMDP saw its future threatened. As late as December 2003, public opinion polls reported a three-way deadlock, with the electorate split into Hannara, NMDP, and Uri supporters by a ratio of 19.8 : 14.4 : 15.7. This balance of power broke down after Jeong Dong Young and Kim Hyuk Kyu received a seal of approval from Roh Moo Hyun as the Uri Party's next-generation leaders. A mass exodus of support drove the shift of power from NMDP toward Uri. Whereas Hannara's level of support fluctuated between 15.5 and 19.6 percent throughout January and February, the NMDP saw its level of support shrink to 9.3 percent and remain there for the next three months. The NMDP's loss was entirely taken up by the Uri Party, whose support base jumped to 25.8 percent by 14 January.[88] This shift of loyalty, moreover, occurred while Roh Moo Hyun's public approval ratio remained at 31.6 percent.[89] With Kim Hyuk Kyu and Jeong Dong Young newly recruited as its twin next-generation leaders, the Uri Party succeeded in projecting itself as a young reformist political force. To reverse its fate, the NMDP introduced a motion of impeachment against Roh Moo Hyun for breaking South Korea's legal regulations on presidential neutrality in elections, and for condoning his close political aides' irregular activities in political fund-raising. The public reacted in a complex way, disapproving Roh's performance by a ratio of 57 : 25 and demanding his apology by 61 : 30, but also opposing the NMDP's motion of impeachment by 54 : 28 and expecting the National Assembly's rejection of the motion by 50 : 24.[90] Most legislators thought impeachment was unlikely until Roh Moo Hyun insulted Hannara and the NMDP with a defiant press conference on 11 March. He refused to apologize because "[he] did not know what [he] did wrong." To avoid a popular backlash, Roh Moo Hyun promised to respect South Korea's general election of 15 April as its people's verdict and consider all courses of action, including resignation, after the election.[91] The enraged opposition passed the NMDP's motion of impeachment on 12 March, which made Roh look a victim rather than a villain in the eyes of the electorate.

Public sentiments altered dramatically overnight. With the Uri Party condemning the impeachment as a "legislative coup d'état" led by South Korea's vested interests, the NMDP saw its already-meager base of electoral support contract further. The Cholla region, in particular, lost all hope for the NMDP's electoral comeback and bet its future on the Uri Party. With no hope of reconstructing Kim Dae Jung's ruling coalition, centered on Cholla voters, the NMDP chose a second-best option of entering the Uri Party as a minority shareholder. By contrast, Hannara (identified as a party of Kyongsang voters since its establishment in January 1991) commanded a minimum base of popular support required for survival. However, this regionalist party identity also placed a tight upper ceiling on how much public support it could garner in elections. In fact, with NGOs judging the Hannara Party's support for the motion of impeachment to be hypocrisy—questioning its foe's legitimacy when it was responsible for an even greater evil of money politics—Hannara struggled to hold onto its regional base, let alone reach beyond Kyongsang voters. Whereas the NMDP saw its level of support drastically decline three times (see Figure 3)—September 2003 (NMDP antimainstream faction's party split), January 2004 (Jeong Dong Young and Kim Hyuk Kyu's rise within Uri), and March 2004 (motion of impeachment)—Hannara's level of support hit bottom in February (18.9 percent) and March (19.9 percent) 2004. Even then, it did not fall much below 20 percent, because Kyongsang voters stood by it.

The National Assembly elections of 15 April 2004 turned South Korean party politics upside down. Uri took away most of the NMDP's Cholla region voters while defeating Hannara in the competition to get nonregionalist voters through building its party image as a clean underdog fighting an uphill battle against South Korea's corrupt establishment. Uri tripled its seats, from 47 to 152, whereas the NMDP's strength declined from 62 to 9 seats. The Uri Party succeeded in taking over the Chungcheong Provinces from the United Liberal Democrats (ULD) with its pledge to relocate the capital city to within the provinces' borders. The general election reduced ULD seats from 10 to 4.

Figure 3   Presidential Approval Ratios and Public Support for Political Parties

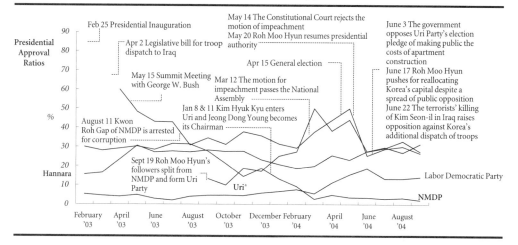

Source: The presidential approval ratios and political party support levels of February and March 2003 are from *Donga Ilbo*. Those of May 2003–September 2004 are from the Korea Society Opinion Institute. The data for April 2003 are not available. *Donga Ilbo* held surveys on 22 February and 28 March 2003. The Korea Society Opinion Institute's data are of 30 May, 20 June, 21 July, 20 August, 22 September, 6 October, 17 November, and 1 December in 2003 and 16 January, 13 February, 24 March, 12 April, 25 May, 29 June, 27 July, 17 August, and 21 September in 2004.

a. The survey of February and March 2003 asked respondents to evaluate presidential performance on a four-point scale: very positive, more or less positive, more or less negative, and very negative. The approval ratios are calculated by adding up those who gave a very positive or a more or less positive evaluation. The other surveys asked respondents to choose between a positive or a negative appraisal. The approval ratios are simply the sum of those who appraised positively. The Korea Society Opinion Institute did not include the question on presidential performance on its survey of 12 April 2004, because Roh Moo Hyun's presidential authority was suspended after the passage of NMDP and Hannara's motion of impeachment.

b. The Uri Party was formally established on 11 November 2004. However, since the split of NMDP on September 19 until 11 November 2004, the Korea Society Open Institute included its direct predecessor, an informal legislative group led by Jeong Dong Young and Kim Keun Tae, in the survey list of political parties.

Among the three regionalist parties, Hannara alone survived, with a total of 121 seats, but that represented a decrease of 24 seats.

The newly introduced "one-man-two-vote" system, whereby a voter cast one vote for a district candidate and another for a political party, enabled one-third of the electorate to split-vote to balance regionalist calculations with their nonregionalist hopes. The primary beneficiary of this new procedure was the Democratic Labor Party (DLP), a leftist party with public support of 2.1–5.9 percent in 2003 public polls. Hitherto excluded from all power and responsibility, the DLP was without any record of policy blunders or moral misconduct. This image became the source of its power. Alienated voters chose it as a vote of protest. The DLP elected eight National Assembly Members through its party list, while only two district candidates survived. Those who sided with Uri, Hannara, NMDP, or ULD in district elections accounted for 78.3 percent of its party list votes.[92]

The National Assembly election of 15 April 2004 opened a new "progressive" era in South Korea's political history. ULD, the embodiment of Cold War conservatives, failed to even elect its president, Kim Jong Pil. With labor activists and NGO leaders in the DLP's party leadership, the democratic socialists established a legislative foothold.[93] Roh Moo Hyun also succeeded in electing twenty or more of his close confidantes. To appease South Korea's angry public, even Hannara had purged many of its old guard, nominating a sizable group of young "reformers," thus making a shift of power greater in both scope and depth. The number of new faces in South Korea's 299-member National Assembly reached 187 (62.5 percent), an increase of 13.5 percentage points since the general election of April 2000. Moreover, fifty-three legislators were once "Talibans" and "Jusapas," with records of violating laws on political assembly and national security in the struggle for democratization. Kim Jong Pil (ULD) retired from public life, while Kim Dae Jung (NMDP) reconfirmed his intention to stay out of or above politics as an ex-president. The third of South Korea's "three Kims," former President Kim Young Sam (Hannara), continued speaking out against Roh Moo Hyun, but nobody had listened to him since the Asian financial crisis of 1997, which made him a symbol of incompetence. The era of the three Kims was over.

What kind of a power shift had occurred in the legislative elections? Figures 4 and 5 sum up surveys of National Assembly members conducted by Sim Jeyeon and others in collaboration with *Joongang Ilbo* and published in February 2002 and August 2004.[94] The researchers modeled their findings on Kenneth Janda's work, asking for respondent views on ten or more contested policy issues[95] and then calculating the average of all responses to construct an ideological index.[96] They also conducted public telephone surveys with a similar questionnaire in both years.[97] The results show continuity as well as change. South Korean party politics had moderately polarized already in 2002 as a result of Kim Dae Jung's recruitment of "new blood" in his 2000 general election campaign. Between January 2002 and August 2004, the average Hannara National Assembly member moved to the right by 0.1, and the average NMDP legislator to the left by 0.2, respectively ending with an ideological index of 5.4 and 3.5.[98] In spite of this increase of "average" ideological distance, there existed a sizable common ground for compromise and accommodation, because 160 (73.1 percent) of the 219 legislators surveyed in January 2002 were centrist, moderately conservative, or moderately progressive. The same three clusters declined, but still remained a solid majority (60.8 percent), among the 209 Uri and Hannara respondents in Sim Jiyeon's survey of August 2004. Moreover, Uri barely commanded a majority of 152 legislators. A defection of a few of its moderates, estimated as 44.4 percent of its National Assembly members in Figure 5, could veto any contested bills even if Uri forged a center-left coalition with the DLP. Thus, Uri's success in 2004 did not signal a momentous transformation of South Korean party politics. Rather, it showed widespread public indignation over money politics.

The contour of public sentiments, as traced in Figure 6, demonstrates even more clearly that South Korean party politics dramatically realigned in 2004 without a corresponding ideological change in society. The "average" voter moved leftward by 0.1 to 4.6, with the single largest group of voters located in the range of 3.6–4.5 rather than 4.6–5.5, as they did in 2002. The voters' distribution curve flattened, but even then, those with centrist, moderately conservative, or moderately progressive views numbered 69.6 percent in August 2004, a decline of 9.6 percentage points since 2002. Whereas South Korea's National Assembly continued to show a moderate level of ideological polarization, the general public exhibited a slightly left-leaning consensus. Thus, South Korea's electoral shock of 2004 was driven more by voters' indignation over the motion of impeachment than any fundamental ideological transformation. The motion of impeachment initiated by mortally crippled NMDP, ULD, and Hannara buried all issues, and voters of all ideological leanings rallied around Roh Moo Hyun out of outrage on 15 April. For many, Roh Moo Hyun was a lesser evil; he apologized for illegal fundraising and even pledged, however rhetorically, a vote of confidence.

Figure 4   **Ideological Terrain, February 2002**

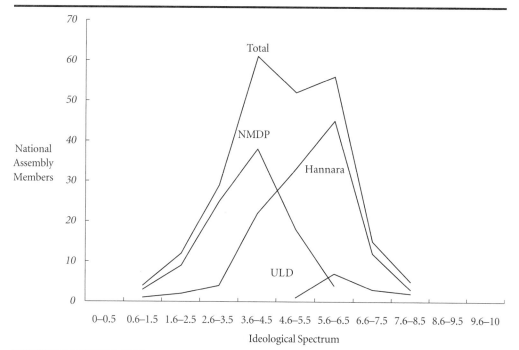

Figure 5   **Ideological Terrain, August 2004**

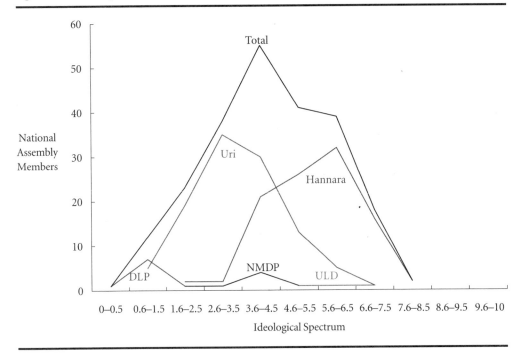

Ideological Spectrum

Hannara and the NMDP exacted revenge with a motion of impeachment for investigating their deals with *chaebol* conglomerates.

The general election became a watershed in South Korean politics only because Uri won a majority when Roh Moo Hyun was in control of South Korea's imperial presidency. According to Sim Jeyeon's ideological survey published in February 2002, Roh Moo Hyun was a radical with an ideological index of 1.5, isolated very far from his NMDP legislators (see Figure 5), and also from South Korea's voters (see Figure 6).[99] This ideological distance, however, did not prevent Roh from imposing uniform guidelines on Uri's ideologically heterogeneous National Assembly members. Roh could make or break anyone's public career with his control over a wide range of instruments of power, including the Prosecutor's Office, the National Tax Agency, and the National Intelligence Service (NIS), even when the public ratings of his performance remained dismal. The state prosecutors were indicting National Assembly members en masse for illegal fund-raising, as well as for violations of South Korea's newly revised election laws.[100] The NIS put the legislative branch in a permanent state of siege, dramatically expanding its wiretapping activities.[101] The press was also targeted for wiretapping if the NIS thought "national security" required it. With his

Figure 6   **Public Attitudes, 2002 and 2004**

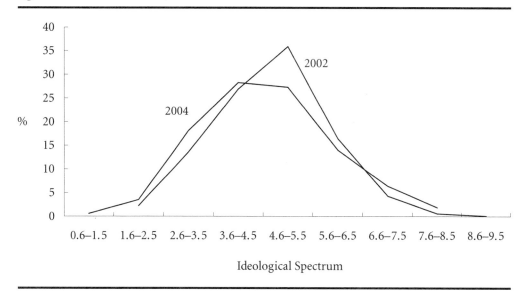

control over such bureaucratic powers, Roh Moo Hyun was able to align his potentially unruly Uri Party behind his risky "all-in" strategy of political change.[102]

Upon resuming his presidential powers in May after the rejection of impeachment by the Constitutional Court, Roh Moo Hyun called for reconciliation. The peace did not last long. Hannara's Park Geun Hae built up her popularity, whereas Roh Moo Hyun lost ground with a series of policy blunders. The opposition movement against the relocation of the capital mounted as conservative NGOs, newspapers, and the Hannara Party saw the issue as an opportunity to break the progressive forces' historical control over Seoul.[103] More critically, an Iraqi terrorist group released a gruesome videotape of its execution of Kim Seon-il, a Christian missionary employed by a South Korean company supplying goods to U.S. troops in Iraq, even as the Ministry of Foreign Affairs and Trade gave a rosy report on negotiations with his kidnappers. Accusations of incompetence or even cover-up were particularly damaging because they corresponded with general public sentiment and with Hannara's long-established line of criticism (see Table 2 and Figure 2). Roh Moo Hyun's approval ratings nosedived from 50.1 percent to 25.4 percent by 29 June.

To recover his popular support, Roh Moo Hyun entered another stage of calculated risk-taking. Having zigzagged, if not U-turned, in foreign policy and labor politics in 2003, with dire consequences for his electoral coalition's internal unity, Roh Moo Hyun chose a course of policy inaction or conflict avoidance in those two issue-areas as his best option. When that was not made possible by the United States or labor

Table 2 **Government Advisers' Evaluation of Roh Moo Hyun's Performance as of February 2004, by Individual Party Issues**

Politics & Public Administration		Foreign Affairs & Security		Economy	
Building a Cooperative Relationship with the National Assembly	-32	Making South Korea Northeast Asia's Regional Center	-19	Provision of Unemployment Relief	-38
Instituting an Effective Governance System	-24	Appointment of Key Policymaking Personnel	-15	Inducing Macroeconomic Recovery	-35
Overcoming Regionalist Politics & Elections	-9	Troop Reallocation & Reduction of U.S. Forces in Korea	-5	Aiding Individuals with Bad Credit after a Burst of Household Credit Market	-32
Expanding Public Participation in Politics	9	Normalization of Relations with North Korea	1	Real Estate Market Stabilization	-4
Ensuring Political Neutrality of "Power Agencies"[a]	11	Six-Party Talks in Beijing to Stop North Korea's Nuclear Development	7	Reallocation of South Korea's Capital to Chungcheong Province	-2
				Tax Reform	1

Society		Education		Press	
Achieving Economic Security for the Workers	-26	Reducing the Private Sector's Share of Educational Expenses	27	Roh Moo Hyun's Legal Suit against the Press	-23
Managing Industrial Conflicts between the Workers & Management	-25	Strengthening Public Schools & Education	-21	Ensuring Political Independence of Public TVs & Radios	-18
Provision of Economic Relief for the Poor	-24	Reforming the College Entrance System	-18	Restricting the Media's Informal Contacts with Civil Servants	-13
Elimination or Reforming the Household Registration System	6	Strengthening Provincial Universities & Colleges	-6	Use of the Internet to Inform the Public of Government Policy	2
Encouraging Female Participation in Society	10	Looking after the Socially Alienated Classes	-6	Introducing News Briefing at the Presidential Secretariat & Ministries	3
Promoting Local Decentralization for the Provinces	11	Promotion of Special Education for the Gifted	3		

Source: An expert survey conducted by the East Asia Institute on 26 January–9 February 2004, through both Internet and telephone in collaboration with *Joongang Ilbo.* The survey targeted 1,178 professors, researchers, corporate executives, and NGO leaders who worked as advisers for 22 state ministries. 253 experts, or 21.4 percent of the total responded.

Note: See Endnote 87 for the calculation of the expert groups' "simple average evaluation" of Roh Moo Hyun's performance on each of the individual issues.

a. The "Power Agencies" include South Korea's Public Prosecutor's Office, National Intelligence Service, National Tax Service, military counterintelligence agencies, and police, among others, which served as repressive agencies of political surveillance during authoritarian rule and even after democratization in 1988.

unions, he held onto his rhetorically colorful but substantively shallow and even contradictory policy of "independence within a robust U.S.–South Korea alliance." The fear of driving an unbridgeable wedge between pro-labor and antilabor groups within his coalition made him alternate between hawk and dove positions on industrial conflicts. Confronted with no easy choice, Roh Moo Hyun zeroed in on the campaign of "historical rectification" to find a new line of cleavage that could provide a stable support base for his ruling coalition. As part of this effort, the Truth Commission gave revisionist verdicts on the leftist victims of white terror during the Cold War. Uri Chairman Sin Gi Nam followed with a proposal to repeal the National Security Act. The party worked with the DLP to jointly propose the "Truth Law on Collaborators and

Traitors during Japanese Colonial Rule-by-Force." The radical wing of Uri even condemned the U.S. House of Representatives North Korean Human Rights Act as interference in North Korea's domestic affairs.[104] The voice of caution was intermittently heard from Uri Party members until Roh Moo Hyun unambiguously came out in support of the radical wing. Park Geun Hae responded with her own threat of a "total war" if Roh "continuously sabotaged South Korea's national identity."[105]

For Roh Moo Hyun, the campaign of historical rectification constituted an instrument to transform Uri's 2004 electoral victory into permanent hegemony. Unlike foreign and labor policy, where a stark political choice risked an implosion of his ruling coalition, historical rectification looked like a low-risk strategy involving few foes and many friends. Only "collaborators," "traitors," and their descendants had a direct stake in how South Korean history was rewritten. Moreover, political conflict over history issues did not directly damage national security or economic competitiveness, because unlike the issues of *chaebol* reform, labor market flexibility, and the U.S. troop presence, the targets for ideological defamation were already dead or very old, without a veto power on economic growth and national security. To preempt any negative effects, Roh declared that he would not raise history issues with Japanese Prime Minister Koizumi.[106] The benefits of a successful rewriting of history, by contrast, were huge. The campaign of historical rectification could arrest, if not reverse, Park Geun Hae's rising popularity by condemning her father as a traitor. The two leading conservative newspapers could lose moral credibility too, if their founders were damned as collaborators. Even before the Truth Commission was established, the new Uri chairman Lee Bu-young had already deemed Park Chung Hee a "man of betrayal and disguise . . . who served as an elite Japanese first lieutenant, only to transform himself into a freedom fighter of Kim Ku's Independence Army with Japan's defeat in war, then to lead a communist cell within South Korea's military until he was arrested by Kim Chang-yong's Counter Intelligence Corps, whereupon he betrayed his comrades to save his life."[107] To make the Hannara Party extremely edgy and even fearful, Uri's bill for the Truth Commission authorized Roh Moo Hyun to name all nine commissioners with majority consent of the National Assembly.[108]

The July offensive produced mixed results. Some of Roh Moo Hyun's earlier supporters returned to the fold,[109] raising his approval ratings by 4.8 percentage points to 30.2 percent in August, thus confirming the existence of a strong minority group of ideologically committed revisionists. The upward trend, however, quickly reversed under partisan conflicts, economic uncertainty, and terrorist threats. Moreover, the Uri Party's level of public support began moving in tandem with Roh's approval ratings for the first time since its establishment in November 2003. In other words, Uri lost its separate identity once it became a majority party and its radical wing lined up behind Roh Moo Hyun's July offensive (see Figure 3). The campaign succeeded in reunifying his core supporters but failed to expand the basis of support, partly because it was based on a wrong estimate of public priorities. To be sure, in a late July 2004 public survey, 61.4 percent of respondents backed a rectification of South Korea's "wronged history," with 33.7 percent opposed for its negative effect on national identity.[110] The response changed dramatically, however, when the respondents were asked to identify their priorities. In a mid-September poll, 88.1 percent of respondents chose economic recovery and only 8 percent historical rectification.[111] Entrapped in a stagnating economy and a bewildering political war over national identity between Uri and Hannara, 65.7 percent thought South Korea was confronting a crisis.[112]

As much as the campaign of historical rectification helped consolidate Roh Moo Hyun's rise as leader and spokesperson of the progressives, it also unified South Korea's conservatives by triggering a sense of crisis over national identity. The lines of conflict emerged over his four action programs: (1) replacing the NSL with newly amended criminal laws, as part of an effort to protect human rights; (2) dismantling the three conservative newspapers' monopoly power over opinion making and agenda setting through a legal restriction on market shares; (3) making South Korea's private educational institutions transparent by enabling teachers and parents to elect a third of their board members; and (4) investigating human rights abuses committed by state authorities since 1948 to rectify the history. The conservatives exploded in a rage, characterizing his proposal to abrogate the NSL as an act of irresponsibility within the context of continued national division. The media bill received an equally negative verdict; it was portrayed as an attempt to silence conservative voices while keeping South Korea's TV networks under state (that is, progressive) control. The conservatives opposed his school bill as well, because with cohesively organized NTU teachers dominating school politics, it could open school boardrooms and classrooms to progressive ideas. The issue of state-orchestrated white terror committed since South Korea's founding days of 1945–53, by contrast, made the conservatives counter with their own proposal for investigating red terror.

Society also polarized and split, depriving it of any "judiciary" role it could play between the progressives and conservatives. To encourage Hannara, a solid majority opposed replacing the NSL with newly amended criminal laws (58.6 percent), as well as restraining monopoly newspapers through a regulation of market shares (52 percent). However, the supporters were sizable (respectively, 35.9 and 38.2 percent), thus keeping alive Roh Moo Hyun's hope of transforming public opinion through political persuasion and organization. Society split even more evenly on his school bill, by

44.5 : 44.9. The issue of investigating white terror also won as many friends as enemies (47.9 : 46.4).[113] Such a sharp polarization of public opinion offered Uri and Hannara an opportunity to carve out their separate ghettos of unswerving supporters in society. The two political parties were in a hostile but symbiotic relationship, with both using public distrust of its rival as a basis for mobilizing votes in elections. Selling oneself as a lesser evil of South Korea's two main parties worked, making both Hannara and Uri—especially their hawks—welcome Roh Moo Hyun's historical rectification campaign in spite of a spread of discontent and alienation among more centrist forces in society. Consequently, the ideological conflict rose and fell but never disappeared, given the two political parties' interest in keeping South Korea's identity issue alive.

The Uri Party's moderate leadership did prepare a compromise on all four issues, only to step down under its radical factions' accusation of betrayal on 3 January 2005. This was a third turnover of party leadership since its establishment only a year earlier. Two more leadership changes awaited the Uri Party before a second round of ideological conflict exploded a half-year later, making its chairman's average tenure only four months. After Lee Bu Young's aborted compromise of January 2005, Uri and Hannara adopted a strategy of deadlock on both the school board and NSL issues, threatening each other with a showdown but without actually crossing a red line with a legislative motion. The strategy profoundly fractured society but also aligned social groups with partisan cleavages even more closely. By September 2005, both NTU teachers and school board directors were locked in protest, while the Catholic Church was calling for a postponement of school reform.[114] The hitherto unorganized conservative wing of the intelligentsia rapidly and extensively began assembling into a "New Right,"[115] thus giving Hannara its own 386 activists and ideologues. They zeroed in on North Korean human rights issues in an effort to defeat Roh Moo Hyun's Peace and Prosperity policy as well as the historical rectification campaign.

By contrast, Uri and Hannara compromised on both media and historical rectification bills, but that did not keep them from periodically reigniting ideological conflict. In March 2004, trying to distance from its past and forge a new image fit for South Korea's democratic era, Hannara reluctantly agreed on legislating a "Truth Law on Collaborators and Traitors during Japanese Rule-by-Force," only to see the Uri Party's radical wing demand its revision. After a long fight, the Hannara Party conceded in expanding the scope of investigation in December 2004. Then, in May 2005, again after a long tug-of-war, Hannara agreed on passing a "Basic Law on Truth Finding and Reconciliation," which opened a way for investigation into human rights abuses and state crimes since 1905. That was not likely to end partisan conflict, however. Because the Uri Party's original bill was toned down through interparty negotiation, much of the legislative support for the bill came from Hannara (92 yeas, 9 nays, 6 abstentions) rather than its architect the Uri Party (59 : 51 : 12), placing the basic law under pressure of a revision as soon as it was legislated. The National Intelligence Service, police, and military, meanwhile, organized a truth-finding commission for investigating into their past acts of human rights abuses and violence.

The media bill also had a spoiler—this time, Hannara. The two parties reached a compromise on 31 December 2004 by respecting each other's central interests.[116] To accommodate Hannara's core constituency of conservative national dailies, Uri agreed on including in its calculation of newspaper market size not only ten national dailies (as its original bill intended), but also 128 other papers distributed nationwide. That formula saved South Korea's three major dailies from fair trade regulation by bringing down their market shares. In return, Uri won Hannara's acquiescence in making the printed media an object of antimonopoly regulation. Additionally, Hannara conceded in establishing a publicly subsidized Newspaper Development Fund, with which Uri hoped to support its constituency of minor dailies, Internet news media, and progressive papers. The revised bill was legislated on a bipartisan basis, but with a strong show of dissent in both parties (133 : 99 : 12). The issue was rekindled when a minor newspaper petitioned South Korea's increasingly activist Constitutional Court on 18 February 2005 for a constitutional review of the bill's key provisions. *Donga Ilbo* followed suit in March and *Chosun Ilbo* in June.[117] Hannara drew up a revised bill in July that deleted its constitutionally contested provision of monopoly and fair trade regulation. The opposition also proposed removing the bill's mandatory provision for establishing a joint editing committee of managers and workers to oversee reporting.[118] Enraged over Hannara's backtracking, a group of Uri legislators sought revisions, as well, with three radical provisions: an upper ceiling on stock ownership, a mandatory wealth-reporting system for publishers and chief editors, and an advisory committee of outsiders established within each of the newspapers to look after subscriber rights.[119]

The consolidation of core constituencies, however, came at a high cost, especially for Roh Moo Hyun's coalition. Hannara saw its public rating hit a plateau after Uri engaged in historical rectification in September 2004 (see Figure 3), neither falling precipitously nor rising steeply (23.5–31.5 percent), whereas the Uri Party's rating began a downward slide in April 2005, hitting 13.9 percent a half-year later. Before then, the party's ratings fluctuated between 23.2 and 29.4 percent for seven months. The presidential rating followed a similar trajectory, except it increased more during good times and fell less during bad times than Uri's level of popular support. There were two good times for Roh Moo Hyun. When he pledged to focus on economic recovery, away from his campaign of historical rectification, his approval rating rose by 4.5 points to 30.7

percent in January 2005. The launching of what he called a "diplomatic war" against Japan's revisionist history textbooks and aggression on Tokdo Island even put his rating at 37.5 percent in April 2005. Conversely, the toning down of economic pragmatism and diplomatic war led to a plummeting of his approval rating to 23.8 percent by October 2005. By then, he was proposing a grand coalition with the Hannara Party, again bewildering not only his core supporters but also his primary foes. With only a fifth of South Korea's electorate positively evaluating presidential performance, he said he was prepared to turn over his power in its "entirety" if Hannara joined him in launching a coalition cabinet.[120]

Roh Moo Hyun was responsible for his own loss of support. He launched his campaign of historical rectification because he knew there was a huge generational divide on history issues and identity questions in South Korea. In this sense, he was a genius of South Korean politics, not only grasping the profound ideological implications of generational change before anyone else, but also bravely acting on his understanding in spite of myriad risks and dangers. By traversing a path no one before him had walked, he awakened South Korea's latent divide and personified the next generation's incoherently articulated but ardently felt hope for change. But he also sowed the seeds of crisis when he answered the question of national identity negatively rather than positively, going backward into South Korea's history rather than forward into a different future. That choice ironically made his era an extension of the Cold War. Roh Moo Hyun claimed he was going beyond the Cold War conflict in constructing a new national identity for South Korea, but his historical rectification campaign was as much based on Cold War dichotomies as his conservative foes' political ideas, values, and strategies. Rather than developing a new set of symbols, rituals, and myths acceptable to the greatest number of South Koreans, he actively polarized society in search for a sturdy constituency. However, to believe that he could govern with a third of society (that is, an overwhelming majority of its powerful 5060 group) up in arms in defense of their national identity was utter political naïveté.

Equally if not more damaging was the huge gap in priorities separating Uri from society. High-tech, *chaebol*-led export growth coexisted with a stagnation of domestic markets, causing a serious wage gap between South Korea's labor aristocracy and underprivileged workers, and threatening job security for the middle class. With the economy in distress, public opinion identified economic recovery as its top priority (88.1 percent in September 2004), while splitting over history issues.[121] Thus, support for historical rectification did not necessarily translate into a positive presidential rating. As economic growth slowed down, job security deteriorated, and inequality worsened throughout most of 2005, public support for Uri fell, even if society solidly backed state policy on identity issues. But society did not decisively support Roh Moo Hyun's historical rectification. To drive an even sharper wedge between society and the party, two of Uri's ideologues—Sin Gi Nam and Kim Hee Seon—saw conservative newspapers, NGO activists, and politicians dig up the record of their fathers' collaboration with Japan before 1945, while Uri continued to lash out against Park Geun Hae for her father's act of collaboration.[122] The investigation of state crime also went wrong in July 2005, when a prosecutorial investigation of illegal wiretapping inadvertently exposed the NIS's effort of political surveillance during Kim Dae Jung's presidency. As part of its program of historical rectification, NIS admitted illegal wiretapping before March 2002, thus making all of Kim Dae Jung's four NIS directors legally vulnerable. The prosecutors even talked of investigating Kim Dae Jung through a written questionnaire on October 9.[123] That triggered an exodus of Cholla regional voters from the Uri Party. In a public poll conducted two days later, NMDP (26.2 percent) secured more support from Cholla Provinces than Uri (25.4 percent), for the first time since January 2004. Only two weeks earlier, Uri's Cholla regional rating (36.8 percent) was twice that of NMDP (18.4 percent).[124]

Table 3   **By-Election Results of 2005, Compared with General Election Results of April 2005**

Province	District	Uri '04	'05	Hannara '04	'05	DLP '04	'05	NMDP '04	'05	Independent '04	'05
Kyong'gi	Seongnam Jungwon[1]	38.9	21.6	24.6	34.7	20.6	27.4	10.1	11.6	3.7	
	Pocheon Youngcheon[1]	42.8	26.1	40.2	64.6			4.8	2.9		
	Bucheon Wonmi Gap[2]	46.7	33.4	33.8	50.5	8.4	3.4	11.1	8.3		3.0
	Gwangju[2]	43.7	17.6	44.5	33.2		3.7	10.9	14.2		30.8
Chungcheong	Gongju Yeon'gi[1]	45.8	35.7	8.7	6.5			4.0	8.8	34.9[3]	43.3[4]
	Asan[1]	37.0	25.3	15.4	42.4	7.2	8.1		3.0	33.9[3]	11.5[3]
Kyongsang	Youngcheon[1]	27.9	48.7	42.0	51.3					15.5	
	Gimhae Gap[1]	47.0	35.4	43.8	61.3				1.6	4.8	3.4
	Daegu Dong'gu Ul[2]	21.3	44.0	55.1	52.0		2.0		0.8	21.0	1.6
	Ulsan Bukgu[2]	17.7	5.4	34.4	49.1	46.9	45.5				

1. By-election of 30 April 2005.

2. By-election of 26 October 2005.

3. ULD candidate.

4. The ULD candidate of the April 2004 national assembly election ran as an independent in the by-election of 26 October 2004.

The by-elections of 30 April and 26 October 2005 were set off by a series of prosecution on violations of election laws, making Roh Moo Hyun a lame duck in his third year of rule. Among six National Assembly seats under contest on 30 April, five were previously Uri seats and only one a Hannara slot. As shown in Table 3, however, Uri lost all six districts, five to Hannara and one to an independent with a conservative

ULD color. To trigger a deep sense of crisis among Uri legislators, moreover, their defeat subsumed three strategic target groups identified by Roh Moo Hyun as core constituencies of his presidency: (1) Chungcheong regional voters, drawn in by his electoral pledge of relocating South Korea's capital city south (Gongju Yeon'gi and Asan in Table 3); 2) lower-class voters of urbanized Kyong'gi Province, presumably free from South Korea's regionalist power rivalry centered on Cholla and Kyongsang natives, and maybe even yearning for a welfare state (Seongnam Jungwon); and (3) industrialized South Kyongsang Province, known for its historic distrust of North Kyongsang Province, Hannara's most unswerving supporter, and housing Roh Moo Hyun's home (Kimhae Gap). The by-election of 26 October only reconfirmed this trend of coalition breakdown. The Hannara Party won all four seats under contest, two of which were previously held by Uri and the DLP. The rightward shift of public mood was apparently contagious. Hit by a series of newspaper reports on corruption scandals involving progressive KCTU as well as conservative KFTU union leaders and publicly viewed as an ideological cousin of the Uri Party for having actively backed and even coauthored several of its initiatives for historical rectification, the DLP failed in defending its Ulsan Bukgu, a proletariat district known for labor militancy. On 28 October the Uri leadership resigned for the fifth time in its 21 months of existence.

CONCLUSION

In 2004 the political parties of South Korea escalated a long-simmering war over national identity, with the war moderating only slightly in 2005. But neither party contested what South Koreans are as an "ethnie" and how they differ from others along primordial boundaries of inclusion and exclusion, including territory, ethnic-racial origins, and common historical, linguistic, and cultural roots. They are Tangun's daughters and sons, bound together by "consanguineous" ties, acculturated in a unique language, and yearning for a common homeland. Rather, what was at stake was the "synthetic" definition of national identity, which is a set of abstract principles identifying a particular nation with a particular state. The South Korean crisis of national identity involved the legitimacy of its state, understood as an "ensemble of symbols collected to represent the principles on which the group was founded and on the basis of which its members have contracted to live together."[125] It is over these principles that intense conflict arose in South Korea. The *guksi* of anticommunism—an ensemble of symbols on which the "separate" state was founded in 1948[126]—began collapsing under the triple successes of modernization, political democratization, and Cold War victory, all evident well before Roh Moo Hyun won power in 2002. But Roh became a spokesperson for South Korea's younger generations, who were profoundly disillusioned by and alienated from its *guksi* of 1948.

The questioning of South Korea's 1948 *guksi* had thus unleashed a profound soul-searching in both internal and external affairs. Without it, South Korea could not explain why a huge discrepancy existed between what South Korea formally stood for and what it actually practiced. In 1948, to justify its declaration of separate statehood, South Korea defined itself as North Korea's polar opposite—both *positively,* in terms of liberal democracy and market capitalism, and *negatively,* in terms of anticommunism—but it failed to deliver on the former part of its promise until after 1987. The existing state was anticommunist, but not liberal. The economy was capitalist, but driven by a powerful dirigiste state. The crisis of legitimacy resulting from such an ideological gap lent a generic instability to the political regime. However, despite the political crises of 1960, 1961, 1979, and 1980, most people refrained from translating their sense of alienation and betrayal into political action, lest North Korea seize on such moments of division and weakness as an opportunity for armed invasion. The state lived off its people's sense of vulnerability, raising a McCarthyite fear of communist infiltration and instigation to deter South Korea's general public from joining dissidents and activists in political protest. The strategy succeeded in containing most protests, but it did not weed out South Korea's internally inconsistent and even contradictory national identity. The strategy, in fact, made national identity only more contradictory. Repression sold as a defense of liberal democracy grossly violated liberal norms. The unequal alliance with America underwrote South Korea's survival as a sovereign state but weakened its principle of sovereignty. The developmental state never shied away from infringing upon labor and even private property rights whenever it thought necessary to catch up with North Korea. By doing so, South Korea surpassed its northern rival in capability but failed to live up to the ideals of market capitalism and liberal democracy.

These internal contradictions in national identity began to implode when the South Korean people celebrated victory in their Cold War rivalry after 1992. The change in public perception of North Korea from a formidable military threat to a decaying rogue state dethroned anticommunism from its *guksi* role. The demise of anticommunism unleashed a search for a new identity, understood as a set of norms and values identifying the divided nation with its separatist state. Kim Young Sam and Kim Dae Jung made its identity internally less contradictory by taking on liberal democracy and market capitalism as its true *guksi,* thus ushering in an era of political and economic reform[127] and putting into momentum the drive to reduce gross inequalities in South Korea's alliance with America.[128] The presidency of Roh Moo Hyun was on the path of giving life to a positively defined national identity for South Korea, but it descended into a negative campaign by looking not forward but backward into South Korea's troubled history. He initiated what his conservative foes called a witch hunt, with a ready-made list of villains and traitors. Top on his list was Park Chung Hee, whose daughter led Hannara. The conservative newspapers also became a primary target. Moreover, the negative campaign was extremely contagious once Roh Moo Hyun began it. Uri condemned South Korea's conservative forces as collaborators with Japanese rule before 1945 and accused them of causing gross human rights abuse after 1945.

In essence, Roh Moo Hyun had turned South Korea's political identity on its head. With the public's threat perception of North Korea dramatically lowered, the progressives succeeded in making anticommunism a bad word by 2004, a synonym of authoritarian rule and human rights abuse. From here, it took only a step or two to fundamentally question both the internal and external dimensions of national identity. As shown in Figure 7, once anticommunism was judged unfit and illegitimate for an economically prosperous, militarily secure, and democratically vibrant South Korea, many of its Cold War beliefs no longer looked obvious. Was North Korea an enemy or a brother? Who constituted South Korea's natural ally, democratic America or authoritarian China? Should South Korea continue its role as a frontline base of U.S. troops when George W. Bush's war on terror looked as threatening as North Korea's nuclear brinkmanship?

Questions of South Korea's international friends and foes, moreover, were soon followed by equally troubling questions on its internal order. Why should South Korea keep its NSL when it was building a Kaesong industrial complex and running a

Figure 7   Ideological Chain Reactions under South Korea's Triple Successes

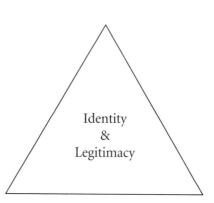

Anticommunism?

Identity
&
Legitimacy

Repeal National Security Law?   Reduce USFK Military Troops?
Rewrite Colonial and Postwar History?   Ally with China?

Keumkang Mountain tour in North Korea? Should it keep its Cold War history text-books or endorse revisionist writers? How could Rhee Syngman be a patriot when he constructed an alliance with collaborators of Japanese rule? These were troubling questions. Roh Moo Hyun believed that South Korea had to raise issues of history and confront the past to build a new future of liberal democracy and a market economy. Unlike Kim Young Sam, who embraced South Korea's Cold War past as laying an infra-structure for its democracy, or Kim Dae Jung, who maintained ideological ambiguity on history issues out of his persecution for unorthodox ideas on unification, Roh Moo Hyun took a negative stand on all questions. He provided a radical reinterpretation of South Korea's Cold War state as an essentially reactionary force led by traitors and col-laborators of Japanese colonial rule and grossly violating human rights in defending its illegitimate separatist system of governance. Moreover, until he made a U-turn in March 2003, Roh Moo Hyun publicly disparaged South Korea's alliance system as unequal and unfair.

The *guksi* of 1948 was dead long before Roh Moo Hyun assumed presidential power. He simply confirmed its death. No one, including Park Geun Hae, saw anticommu-nism as South Korea's "national essence." However, by taking his 386 supporters' radi-cal generational identity as the basis for establishing a new national identity, Roh Moo Hyun brought back South Korea's Cold War past from its grave and triggered a thor-oughly negative war over national identity. The conservatives accused his NGO allies of being North Korea sympathizers, while his Uri leaders condemned Hannara as the inheritor of South Korea's disgraceful history of repression and national betrayal. The organized political forces crossed a bridge of no-return in July 2004, treating the polit-ical struggle as a zero-sum game with clear winners and losers. The game they actually played, however, was more likely to have only losers. With only 8 percent of South Korea's general public identifying the "history issue" as among the most urgent items on the national agenda,[129] Uri lost supporters, whereas Hannara saw its ratings plateau at the level of 30 percent in spite of (or because of) ideological struggles (see Figure 3). The rating of 30 percent assured Hannara of victories in multiparty national assembly elec-tions, but not the presidential elections. The voters were turned off by the two parties' negative war on national identity, which replayed South Korea's Cold War images and myths rather than constructing a new, positive identity out of the triple successes of the last forty years.

The top-down campaign of historical rectification was unlikely to achieve the goal of triggering a realignment of party politics around Roh Moo Hyun's Uri Party. By nega-tively rather than positively redefining South Korea's self as the opposite of its past, Roh ironically brought back to life its Cold War culture of hatred and mistrust and lost a window of opportunity to build a new consensus. South Koreans fight over what they hate, not what they stand for. The certain failure of his campaign, however, did not persuade Roh Moo Hyun into reconsidering his options. The conservatives had their own ideologues, who saw his campaign as a carefully calculated populist act of remolding national identity into a progressive image by condemning the conservatives as an immoral force of traitors, compradors, and torturers even as his actions hurt international economic competitiveness by dragging South Korea into another internal Cold War. Without cleansing South Korea of its past injustice, he declared, "it will have no future. Nor is it possible to construct an economy with a per capita GNP of thirty thousand dollars. Even if it were possible, it would not be worth much."[130] These two opposite images of Roh Moo Hyun, as a man of incompetence or of a Machiavellian mind, were damaging his personal reputation as well as aggravating uncertainty in South Korean politics. With its next presidential and general elections still several years away, South Korea was trapped in a crisis without an exit.[131]

NOTES

This research was supported in 2005 by the Brain Korea 21 Project.

1. The "Jusapa" refers to a radical left wing of South Korea's student activists of the 1980s who embraced North Korea's *Juche* Ideology in their struggle against Chun Doo Hwan's authoritarian Fifth Republic.

2. *Chosun Ilbo*, 1 July 2004.

3. *Chosun Ilbo*, 15 July 2004.

4. *Chosun Ilbo*, 31 July 2004.

5. Consult www.truthfinder.go.kr/info/sub3.html for the mission of the Truth Commission as established by a "Law on the Recovery of Honor and Compensation for Peoples Engaged in Struggles for Democratization," 15 January 2000.

6. *Chosun Ilbo*, 14 July 2004.

7. See Han'gyorae's interview with Kim Huiseon, a key member of a revisionist "National Assembly Members' Congregation for National Spirit." *Han'gyorae*, 15 January 2004.

8. *Chosun Ilbo*, 22 July 2004.

9. *Chosun Ilbo*, 11 and 14 July and 5 August 2004.

10. *Chosun Ilbo*, 10 August 2004.

11. The 386 generation refers to South Korea's radical political activists. The number "3" refers to their age (30–39 years old), the number "8" to their years of college entrance (1981–1990), and the number "6" to their decade of birth (1961–1970).

12. *Chosun Ilbo*, 23 July and 10 August 2004.

13. *Joongang Ilbo*, 28 April 2004.

14. *Chosun Ilbo*, 22 July 2004.

15. See Robert S. Ross, "The U.S.-China Peace: Great Power Politics, Spheres of Influence, and the Peace of East Asia," *Journal of East Asian Studies* 3, no. 3 (September–December 2003), pp. 365–66.

16. Anthony D. Smith, *National Identity* (Reno: University of Nevada Press, 1991), p. 14; and idem., *The Ethnic Origins of Nations* (Oxford: Blackwell, 1986), pp. 21–44, 137–38, 141.

17. Roh Tae Don, "Hankuk minjokui hyongseong sikiae daehan geomto" (A Review on the Formative Period of the Korean Minjok), *Yoksa bipyong* 19 (Winter 1992), pp. 1–24.

18. The Korean mythology traces the historical root of Koreans to Chosun, established in

2333 BC by Tan'gun, a grandson of the Creator Hwan'in.

19. Consult Walker Conner, "Nation-Building or Nation-Destroying?" *World Politics* 24, no. 3 (April 1972), pp. 319–55, and Consuelo Cruz, "Identity and Persuasion: How Nations Remember Their Pasts and Make Their Futures," *World Politics* 42, no. 3 (April 2000), pp. 275–312 for an analysis of relationship between primordial identity and nation building.

20. See Park Myung Rim, "Hankukui gukka hyongseong, 1945–1948" (State Building in Korea, 1945–1948), *Hankuk jeongchi hakheobo* 29, no. 1 (1995), pp. 196–220.

21. The crisis of identity and legitimacy was nowhere more visible than in the South Korean conservatives' identification with Kim Ku as one of their historical roots. Assassinated after his failed meeting with North Korea's Kim Il Sung for national unification in 1949, Kim Ku became a symbol of the "Third Way" that tried to transcend East-West ideological conflict by putting the minjok (ethnie) before and above the guk'ka (state) to prevent the separation of the two Koreas. Kim Ku was a loser in both domestic and international realpolitik of the post-liberation years, but became a winner in South Korea's world of *myongbun* (moral duty and obligation), revered by the left and right alike for his ethnic nationalism. Kim Ku grew even bigger in political mythology after his defeat in 1948 in South Korea. Korea Gallup reported Kim Ku as the fourth most frequently cited (7.9 percent) in its August 2002 poll on Korea's most revered historical figure. The top on the list was Park Chung Hee (20.1 percent). The next two were from the Chosun dynasty: King Sejong (16 percent), whose royal court invented the Korean alphabet, and Admiral Yi Sunsin (15.3 percent), who defeated Hideyoshi's invading Japanese navy. See *Chosun Ilbo*, 25 August 2002.

22. See Chang Miseung, "Bukhanui namhan jeomryong jeongchaek" (The Occupation Policy of North Korea during the Korean War), in *Hankuk jeonjaengui ihae* (Understanding the Korean War), ed. Hankuk jeongchi yon'guhwae jeongchisa bun'gwa (Seoul: Yoksa bipyongsa, 1990), pp. 170–203; Kim Hakjun, "Haebangkwa bundanui jeongchi munhwa" (Political Culture of Liberation and National Division), in *Hankuk sahwaeui jeontongkwa byonhwa* (Tradition

and Change in the Korean Society) (Seoul: Beommunsa, 1983), p. 307.

23. Consult Seymour M. Lipset and Stein Rokkan, "Cleavage Structures, Party Systems and Voter Alignments," in *Party System and Voter Alignment*, ed. Lipset and Rokkan (Boston: Free Press, 1967), pp. 1–56, for the concept of ideological freezing. See Son Ho Cheol, "Hankuk jeonjaengkwa odeorogi jihyong: gukka, jibaeyonhap, ideorogi" (The Korean War and the Ideological Terrain: The State, Ruling Coalition, and Ideology), in *Hankuk jeonjaengkwa nambukhan sahwaeui gujojeok byonhwa* (The Korean War and the Structural Change in North and South Korea), ed. Son et al. (Seoul: Geukdong munjae yon'guso, 1991), pp. 1–27, for a similar idea on the Korean War.

24. See endnote 21 for the ideological position of Kim Ku in post-liberation South Korea. Also consult Joungwon A. Kim, *Divided Korea: The Politics of Development, 1945–1972* (Cambridge: Harvard University Press, 1975), and Se-Jin Kim, *The Politics of Military Revolution in Korea* (Chapel Hill: The University of North Carolina Press, 1971), for Rhee Syngman's strategy to coalesce with the colonial elites to consolidate his political grip over society.

25. See Kwan Bong Kim, *The Korea-Japan Treaty Crisis and the Instability of the Korean Political System* (New York, Praeger, 1971).

26. Pak Taekyun, *Cho bongam yeon'gu* (A Study on Cho Bongam) (Seoul: Changjakkwa bipyongsa, 1995).

27. Committee of Human Rights, National Council of Churches in Korea, *Chilsip nyondae minjuhwa undong 3* (Democratization Movement of the 1970s Volume III) (Seoul: The National Council of Churches in Korea, 1987), pp. 2064–2065.

28. See Minister of Unification Lim Dong Won's statement at a National Assembly hearing. *Donga Ilbo*, 19 April 2001.

29. This generation came to be called the "5060 Generation" because they were in their fifties and sixties. The name also has a pejorative meaning as the generation of Chun Doo Hwan's authoritarian Fifth Republic (1980–1988) and Roh Tae-woo's Sixth Republic (1988–1993), which are respectively called "ogong" and yukgong," the same in pronunciation as "50" and "60" in Korean.

30. See Sung-joo Han, *The Failure of Democracy in South Korea* (Berkeley: University of California Press, 1974).

31. EASI called for a three-stage reduction of forward deployed American troops in East Asia, reflecting

a sharply reduced threat of war in the post–Cold War era. See U.S. Department of Defense, *A Strategic Framework for the Asia Pacific Rim: Looking Toward the 21st Century* (Washington, D.C.: U.S. Government Printing Office, April 1990), and also U.S. Department of Defense, *A Strategic Framework for the Asia Pacific Rim: Report to Congress 1992* (Washington, D.C.: U.S. Department of Defense, May 1992).

32. The Global Posture Review envisioned a transformation of U.S. military forces into a military with "greater mobility, precision, speed, stealth, and strike range," in order to "detect, identify, and track far greater numbers of targets over a larger area for a longer time than ever before" in the war on terror. See National Defense Panel, "Transforming Defense: National Security in the 21st Century," (December 1997), p. iii., www.dtic.mil/ndp/FullDoc2.pdf, for an early discussion of military transformation.

33. For an analysis of events in 1980, including the Kwangju Massacre, see Chong-Sik Lee, "South Korea in 1980: The Emergence of a New Authoritarian Order," *Asian Survey* 21, no. 1 (January 1981), pp. 125–43.

34. Consult Cho Huiyeon, "Sahwae gusongchae nonjaengui bansongkwa gusipnyondae nonjaengui chulbaljom" (A Critical Review of Ideological Polemics on Social Community and a New Beginning of Debates for the 1990s), *Gil* (December 1992), p. 187.

35. Siminui sinmun, *Han'guk min'gan danchae chongram* (Annual on South Korea's NGOs) (Seoul: Siminui sinmun, 2000).

36. The European Union countries lagged behind considerably, having on average only 0.8 Internet users per hundred people. The United States was better networked, but not by a large margin: 3.2 users per hundred residents. See Ministry of Information and Communication, "Gukminui jeongbu sanyon: jeongbo tongsin seonggwa" (The achievement in the area of information and communication during the first four years of the "government of the people") December 2001, www.mic.go.kr/jsp/ mic_b/b100-0001-1.jsp.

37. *Chosun Ilbo,* 27 March 2002.

38. *Chosun Ilbo,* 18 April 2002.

39. *Chosun Ilbo,* 12 September 2002.

40. "Every president of South Korea," Roh Moo Hyun argued, "risked his life for one or another reason. Rhee Syngman did so in his anticolonial struggles. Park Chung Hee endangered his life, too, when he crossed Han River with his troops. Chun Doo-hwan and Roh Tae-woo were not different.

There is no free ride. Kim Young-sam and Kim Dae Jung also almost died in struggle against authoritarian rule." See *Chosun Ilbo,* 27 May 2004.

41. *Chosun Ilbo,* 10 October 2003.

42. *Naeil Sinmun,* 10 October 2003.

43. *Chosun Ilbo,* 15 December 2003.

44. *Chosun Ilbo,* 27 November 2003.

45. *Chosun Ilbo,* 21 May 2004.

46. The Status of Forces Agreement enumerates U.S. military and GIs' legal rights and responsibilities over a diverse range of issues, including facility and land grant, tax and custom duties, and criminal jurisdiction. The agreement was signed in 1966 when its NGO critics believed South Korea was economically too poor and militarily too weak to demand an equal arrangement. To secure the U.S. military commitment, South Korea compromised its people's basic rights as well as sovereign rights. Now, after almost forty years of an uninterrupted economic growth, many NGOs argued, South Korea was on a par with major trading powers and deserved a more "equal" military alliance system. The call for its revision grew louder especially after the U.S. military court judged Sergeant Fernando Nino and Mark Walker not guilty of negligent homicide at Hyochonli. See www.korea.army.mil/sofa/sofa1966_ui1991 .pdf and www.korea.army.mil/sofa/2001sofa _english%20text.pdf for "Basic Agreement," "Agreed Minutes," and other related documents of South Korea's 2001 revised Status of Forces Agreement. Consult *Joongang Ilbo,* 26 June, 24 July, 5 August, 1 October 2002 and 13 December 2002, for reports on South Korea's demand for a revision of its Status of Forces Agreement.

47. Roh Moo Hyun's conversation with United States Assistant Secretary of State for East Asian and Pacific Affairs James A. Kelly, as reported by *Chosun Ilbo,* 14 January 2003.

48. *Joongang Ilbo,* 9 December 2002.

49. *Joongang Ilbo,* 9 December 2002.

50. *Jugan Chosun,* 9 January 2003.

51. *Chosun Ilbo,* 2 January 2003.

52. *Chosun Ilbo,* 19 January and 20 February 2003.

53. *Chosun Ilbo,* 2 January 2003.

54. See *New York Times,* 16 January 2003, former U.S. National Security Advisor Richard V. Allen's critique on Roh Moo Hyun's North

Korea policy. Allen depicted South Korea as having walked into a politically neutral zone and warned South Korea had only two options: either stand with its American ally on war against terrorism or "take another path."

55. *Chosun Ilbo*, 7, 8, and 9 February 2003.

56. *Chosun Ilbo*, 4 and 20 March 2003 and 4 and 9 April 2003.

57. *Chosun Ilbo*, various issues, January and February 2003.

58. Moody's Investor Service warned against another credit downgrading on 15 March 2003, if South Korea failed to move toward resolution of the nuclear crisis. See *Chosun Ilbo*, 11 February 2003 and 15 March 2003.

59. *Chosun Ilbo*, 9 January, 17, 22–26 February, and 23 March 2003.

60. *The Korea Times*, 7 May 2003.

61. See www.kse.or.kr/webkor/tong/tong_index.jsp.

62. National Security Advisor Ra Jong Il publicly acknowledged Bush's request for war support on 10 March. The president convened a newly strengthened National Security Council on 20 March to draw up South Korea's response, then secured a cabinet approval for noncombat troop dispatch on 21 March and finally spoke before National Assembly Members on 2 April in order to pass his troop dispatch bill on a bipartisan basis. See *Chosun Ilbo*, 11, 21 March 2003 and 4 April 2003.

63. *Chosun Ilbo*, 5, 19, and 21 April 2003.

64. *Chosun Ilbo*, 4 April 2003.

65. *Joongang Ilbo*, 2 May 2003.

66. *Chosun Ilbo*, 24 June 2003.

67. *Chosun Ilbo*, 12, 15 May 2003.

68. *Chosun Ilbo*, 6 March 2003 and 13 and 28 May 2003.

69. *Chosun Ilbo*, 25, 29, and 30 June 2003 and 2 July 2003.

70. *Chosun Ilbo*, 6, 11, and 16 July 2003.

71. *Chosun Ilbo*, 15, 21, and 29 August 2003.

72. *Chosun Ilbo*, 15 May 2003.

73. *Chosun Ilbo*, 13 May 2003.

74. *Chosun Ilbo*, 23 June 2003.

75. *Chosun Ilbo*, 19 June 2003.

76. *Chosun Ilbo*, 30 June 2003.

77. *Chosun Ilbo*, 27 June 2003.

78. *Chosun Ilbo*, 27 August 2003.

79. *Chosun Ilbo*, 22 August 2003.

80. A telephone survey conducted by the East Asia Institute in collaboration with *Joongang Ilbo* on 19 August 2003, with a randomly selected national sample of 834 adults. The respondents were asked to evaluate Roh Moo Hyun's performance as either "very good," "good on balance," "bad on balance," or "very bad." The approval ratings are calculated by adding up those respondents who gave an appraisal of "very good" or "good on balance." The margin of error is plus or minus 3.1 percentage points at the 95 percent confidence interval.

81. The February approval ratings were reported in *Munhwa Ilbo*, February 2003.

82. The telephone survey was conducted by the East Asia Institute in collaboration with *Joongang Ilbo* on 2–3 February 2004, with a randomly selected national sample of 1,006 adults. The survey respondents were asked to evaluate Roh Moo Hyun's presidential performance as either "very good," "good on balance," "mediocre," "bad on balance," or "very bad." The margin of error is plus or minus 3.1 percentage points at the 95 percent confidence interval.

83. The expert survey was conducted by the East Asia Institute in collaboration with *Joongang Ilbo* on 26 January–9 February 2004, through both Internet and telephone. The survey targeted 1,178 professors, researchers, corporate executives, and NGO leaders who worked as advisors for 22 state ministries. Two hundred fifty-three experts, or 21.4 percent of the total, responded.

84. The appraisals of "very good," "good on balance," "mediocre," "bad on balance," and "very bad" were weighted 100, 75, 50, 25 and 0, respectively. So, if 8 percent of the respondents answered "do not know" and 10 percent of those answering chose "very bad," their weighted appraisal was (10 x 0) / (100 - 8) = 0. Likewise, if 43 percent gave an evaluation of "bad on balance," their weighted appraisal was calculated as (43 x 25) / (100 - 8) = 11.7. The simple average evaluation is the sum of the five weighted appraisals.

85. *Chosun Ilbo*, 11 November 2003.

86. *Jugan Chosun*, 15 January 2004.

87. *Chosun Ilbo*, 8, 11 January 2004 and 29 March 2004.

88. See public survey results reported by *Chosun Ilbo* on 2, 14, and 27 January 2004, 15 February 2004, and 22 February 2004.

89. *Chosun Ilbo*, 6 February 2004.

90. *Chosun Ilbo,* 9 March 2004.

91. See *Chosun Ilbo,* 11 March 2004, for the full text of Roh Moo Hyun's televised press conference.

92. A postelection survey by Korea Gallup, as reported by *Chosun Ilbo* on 19 April 2004.

93. The last time South Korea's left had won a National Assembly seat was in 1960.

94. Two hundred thirty seven National Assembly Members, or 87.8 percent of the total, responded in 2002. The survey of 2004 also had a high response rate of 76.6 percent.

95. The survey of February 2002 asked for views on ten highly contested issues, including foreign affairs and security, regulations on *chaebol* conglomerates, welfare spending, high school education, National Security Law, economic aid to North Korea, a legal reform to allow class action, household registration, death penalty, and environmental protection. The survey of August 2004 included all ten issues plus two questions on South Korea's dispatch of military troops to Iraq and its workers' right to participate in company management. See *Joongang Ilbo,* 1 February 2002, and 31 August 2004.

96. Each survey question had four possible answers, which were later numerically coded as "10" (very conservative), "6.7" (moderately conservative), "3.3" (moderately progressive), or "0" (very conservative). The overall ideological index was calculated by averaging out a respondent's answers to all survey questions.

97. The two public polls each consisted of the ten questions asked to National Assembly Members in February 2002. Consequently, directly comparing the 2004 public and National Assembly surveys requires a caution. The public survey of 2004 excludes two of the twelve questions included in the National Assembly survey of the same year. The public survey of 2002 and 2004 was a randomly selected national sample of 1,063 and 1,026 people, respectively. The margin of error was plus or minus 3.1 percentage points at the 95 percent confidence interval.

98. Calculated from *Joongang Ilbo's* survey data of February 2002 and August 2004.

99. There were only four legislators who leaned farther left than Roh Moo Hyun in Sim Jeyeon's survey of February 2002. The NMDP legislators of 2002 had an average ideological index of 3.7. The Uri legislators of 2004 showed an average index of 3.5. The general public, by contrast, had a more centrist ideology, with an index of 4.7 in 2002 and 4.6 in 2004. The average indexes are calculated in Figures 4, 5, and 6.

100. The Department of Central Investigation indicted a total of 23 incumbent National Assembly Members for illegal political fundraising during South Korea's presidential election of 2002 under An Daehui's leadership (March 2003–May 2004) alone. The Department of Public Security also indicted a total of 30 newly elected National Assembly Members for violating the election laws by 31 August 2004. See *Chosun Ilbo,* 28 May 2004 and 1 September 2004.

101. The National Intelligence Service secured from the court a total of 5,424 permits to wiretap telephones, cellular phones, and even emails in 2003, an increase of 3,190 permits since 2002. The wiretapping activities continued expanding, reaching 5,033 in the first six months of 2004. Consult *Chosun Ilbo,* 24 September 2004.

102. See *Chosun Ilbo,* 22, 26 July and 22 September 2004 for reports of "harsher" court rulings on Roh Moo Hyun's political foes and "lighter" rulings on his confidantes, including An Huijeong and Yi Gwangjae. Whether legally accurate or inaccurate, such media reports made Uri legislators think twice before challenging Roh Moo Hyun.

103. See *Chosun Ilbo,* 2–25 June 2004.

104. See *Chosun Ilbo,* 1, 9, 14, and 23 July 2004.

105. See *Chosun Ilbo,* 22 July 2004.

106. *Chosun Ilbo,* 22 July 2004.

107. *Chosun Ilbo,* 20 August 2004.

108. *Chosun Ilbo,* 27 July and 14–15 September 2004.

109. *Chosun Ilbo,* 14 July 2004.

110. *Yeonhap News,* 20 July 2004.

111. *Donga Ilbo,* 13 September 2004. The survey was conducted with a randomly selected national sample of 1,004 adults. The margin of error was plus or minus 3.1 percentage points at the 95 percent confidence interval.

112. *Donga Ilbo,* 13 September 2004.

113. Results of a survey jointly conducted by *Moonhwa Ilbo* and Taylor Nelson Sofres on 27 October 2004.

114. *Chosun Ilbo,* 5 September 2005.

115. *Chosun Ilbo,* 19 November, 3 December 2004; 25 January, 23 March, 30 June, and 18 October 2005.

116. *Chosun Ilbo,* 1 January 2005.

117. *Chosun Ilbo,* 23 March and 9 June 2005.

118. *Chosun Ilbo,* 27 July 2005.

119. *Chosun Ilbo,* 28 July 2005.

120. *Chosun Ilbo,* 5 July and 25 August 2005.

121. See endnotes 110–11.

122. *Chosun Ilbo,* 16–19 August, 16 September 2004, and 20 July 2005.

123. *Chosun Ilbo,* 26 July, 5 August, and 9 October 2005.

124. *Chosun Ilbo,* 13 October 2005.

125. Consult Lowell Dittmer and Samuel S. Kim, "In Search of a Theory of National Identity," in *China's Quest for National Identity,* ed. Dittmer and Kim (Ithaca: Cornell University Press, 1993), pp. 6–10, 12–13.

126. The *guksi* is *guocui* in Chinese and *kokutai* in Japanese, meaning national essence. See Dittmer and Kim, pp. 17–18.

127. See Jin-Young Suh and Byung-Kook Kim, "The Politics of Reform in Korea; Dilemma, Choice and Crisis," in *The World after the Cold War,* ed. Suh and Changrok Soh (Seoul: Graduate School of International Studies, Korea University, 1999), pp. 17–53; Larry Diamond and Byung-Kook Kim, eds., *Consolidating Democracy in South Korea* (Boulder: Lynne Rienner Publishers, 2000); Byung-Kook Kim, "The Politics of Crisis and a Crisis of Politics: The Presidency of Kim Dae Jung,"
in *Korea Briefing, 1997–1999: Challenges and Change at the Turn of the Century,* ed. Kongdan Oh (Armonk: M. E. Sharpe, 2000), pp. 35–74; and Byung-Kook Kim, "The Politics of Financial Reform in Korea, Malaysia, and Thailand: When, Why and How Democracy Matters," *Journal of East Asian Studies* 2, no.1 (February 2002), pp. 185–240.

128. See Byung-Kook Kim, "The U.S.-South Korean Alliance: Anti-American Challenges," *Journal of East Asian Studies* 3, no. 2 (May–August 2003), especially pp. 241–46. Also consult Byung-Kook Kim, "To Have a Cake and Eat It, Too," in *Between Conflict and Compliance: New Pax Americana in East Asia and Latin America,* ed. Jorge I. Dominguez and Kim (London: Routledge, forthcoming 2005).

129. *Donga Ilbo,* 13 September 2004. The survey was conducted with a randomly selected national sample of 1,004 adults. The margin of error was plus or minus 3.1 percentage points at the 95 percent confidence interval.

130. *Han'gyorae,* 25 August 2004.

131. In a public poll by *Donga Ilbo,* 65.7 percent thought South Korea was confronting a crisis. *See Donga Ilbo,* 13 September 2004. The survey was conducted with a randomly selected national sample of 1,004 adults. The margin of error was plus or minus 3.1 percentage points at the 95 percent confidence interval.

PART THREE

Peninsular Economic Futures

6

Korea's Economic Dynamics
Scenarios and Implications

Marcus Noland

Over the past four decades economic performance in the Republic of Korea (ROK), or South Korea, has been nothing short of spectacular. Between 1963, when a wide-ranging economic reform program was initiated, and 1997, when the country experienced a financial crisis, real per capita income growth averaged more than 6 percent annually in purchasing power–adjusted terms, and per capita income stood at more than eight times its level when reforms began. According to the Penn World Tables, at the start of that period the country's income level was lower than that of Bolivia and Mozambique; by the end it was higher than that of Greece and Portugal.

In marked contrast, over a period of eight years during the 1990s, the Democratic People's Republic of Korea (DPRK), or North Korea, experienced a cumulative decline of 33 percent in real per capita income.[1] A famine during the 1990s resulted in the deaths of perhaps 600,000 to 1 million people, out of a prefamine population of roughly 22 million.[2] Since then, a combination of humanitarian food aid and development assistance has ameliorated the situation, but grain production remains below its level in 1990; the provision of assistance is highly politicized, revolving around the North Korean nuclear weapons program; and a significant share of the population remains food insecure. In 2005, the World Food Program (WFP) began to warn that the country could slip back into famine if there were a major interruption in aid.

The origins of the North Korean economic crisis extend at least as far back as the mid-1980s. In 1987, frustrated by North Korean unwillingness to repay accumulated debts, the Soviets withdrew support. (Despite its *juche*-inspired declarations of self-reliance,

North Korea has been dependent on outside assistance throughout its entire history, with first the Soviet Union, later China, and most recently South Korea in the role of chief benefactor or patron.) According to Central Intelligence Agency figures, the net flow of resources turned negative, though Nicholas Eberstadt argues that these figures understate implicit Soviet fuel and military assistance subsidies. That same year, the North Koreans initiated possibly conflicting policies in the agricultural sector, including the expansion of state farms, tolerance of private garden plots, expansion of grain-sown areas, transformation of crop composition in favor of high-yield items, maximization of industrial inputs subject to availability, and the intensification of double-cropping and dense planting. Continuous cropping led to soil depletion, and the overuse of chemical fertilizers contributed to acidification of the soil and eventually a reduction in yields. It is unclear whether these policy changes were undertaken in response to the reduction in Soviet support or were merely coincident with it.

The economy was hit by massive trade shocks beginning in 1990, as the Soviet Union disintegrated and the Eastern bloc collapsed. Trade with the Soviet Union had accounted for more than half of North Korean two-way trade, including most of its fuel imports. The fall in imports from Russia in 1991 was equivalent to 40 percent of all imports; by 1993 imports from Russia were only 10 percent of their 1987–90 average, and North Korea proved incapable of reorienting its commercial relations.[3] Imported fuel was used to power irrigation systems and agricultural machinery and as the feedstock for the production of chemical fertilizers. The North Korean industrial economy imploded as it was progressively deprived of industrial inputs, and agricultural output plummeted. Isolation from the outside world reduced the genetic diversity of the North Korean seed stock, making plants more vulnerable to disease. As yields declined, hillsides were denuded to bring more and more marginal land into production. This contributed to soil erosion, river silting, and, ultimately, catastrophic flooding. China initially stepped into the breach, offsetting some of the fall in trade with the Soviet Union and emerging as North Korea's primary supplier of imported food, most of it reportedly on concessional terms. But in 1994 and 1995, a disillusioned China reduced its exports to North Korea. If there was a single proximate trigger to the North Korean famine, this was it. The floods of 1995 and 1996, though a contributory factor, were not a primary cause of the famine.

At the same time that it was entering a famine, North Korea stumbled into a nuclear confrontation with the United States. The two events became inextricably linked as the provision of aid was highly politicized, reflecting the interests of the main donors, and was often used to induce North Korean participation in diplomatic negotiations. North Korea subsequently emerged as the largest Asian recipient of U.S.

aid in the 1990s, receiving more than $1 billion in food and energy assistance between 1995 and 2002.[4]

Famine relief is one leg of North Korea's three-legged engagement with the outside world. Its nuclear weapons program is another, which gave rise to the Agreed Framework and the Korean Peninsula Energy Development Organization (KEDO).

The third leg of North Korea's engagement with the outside world has been the effective shift, over the decade of the 1990s, from reliance on Soviet patronage to a more diversified multilateral set of supporters. The most important enabler of this transformation has been the ideological and strategic shifts in South Korea manifested in the presidential elections of 1997 and 2002. Nevertheless, this coping behavior proved inadequate to pull the country out of its decline, and in 2002 North Korea arguably attempted its first strategic reorientation in half a century toward a policy of peaceful coexistence built around a three-part strategy of deterrence, conventional forces demobilization, and economic policy changes.

Since its founding, North Korea has adhered to a doctrine of imposing its communist dogma on its southern neighbor, forcibly if need be. To that end, it maintains the world's most militarized society, with the bulk of its million-strong army deployed in an offensive posture along the demilitarized zone separating it from South Korea. More than a decade of economic decline in the North and the South's growing prosperity and alliance with the United States have rendered that dream of unification on Pyongyang's terms an anachronism. Under such circumstances, the North Koreans have two basic options: to play for time, hoping that the strategic environment changes favorably; or throw in the towel, recognizing that they are on the wrong side of history, and redefine the strategic goals of the regime. In the second case, one such goal could be self-enrichment. The North Korean elite's one card is its control over the levers of power, from which it is able to appropriate the lion's share of economic gains generated by economic reform.

From this perspective, a certain investment in weapons of mass destruction and delivery systems capable of striking targets beyond the Korean peninsula is probably warranted to maintain double-sided deterrence. However, once deterrence is secured, the mass deployment of conventional forces would be a counterproductive impediment to its rapprochement with the South, a prospective provider of capital, technology, and commercial and diplomatic entrée around the world. If a nuclear-armed North Korea were to forswear aggression toward South Korea, then its huge conventional forces would be redundant, and its million-man army, an albatross around the economy's neck, could be demobilized. North Korea signaled in 2002 that it was contemplating cutting its armed forces by as many as 500,000 soldiers, which, perhaps more than co-incidentally, would have reduced them to roughly the same size as South Korea's armed forces. Such demobilization can work only if the troops have somewhere to go.

North Korea has huge infrastructure needs that can be met using labor-intensive techniques. Its sectors of comparative advantage—apart from missiles—tend to be labor intensive, too. With economic reform, demobilization could yield a sizable peace dividend.[5] It is pure speculation whether the North Koreans actually had this goal in mind. Nevertheless, North Korea's actions and statements in 2002 were consistent with this interpretation. The October 2002 public revelation of a second nuclear weapons program based on highly enriched uranium (HEU) made this gambit diplomatically unsustainable, and the regime is left with the legacy of the July 2002 economic reforms but without the politically derived complementary parts of the package.

The remainder of this chapter focuses on four topics: the current state of the economy; the possibility of political regime change; the character of possible successor regimes; and the implications for South Korea.

THE JULY 2002 REFORMS

In July 2002, North Korea announced changes in economic policy comprising four components: microeconomic policy changes; macroeconomic policy changes; special economic zones; and aid seeking. These initiatives followed moves begun in 1998 to encourage administrative decentralization.[6] Some observers interpreted a September 2003 cabinet reshuffle as signaling the rise of a younger, more technocratic leadership. However, despite these changes, there has been no mention of the military's privileged position within the economy, and indeed, the "military-first" campaign has intensified.

To some analysts, the microeconomic reforms are an attempt to increase the importance of material incentives, though opinions vary widely about what the North Koreans are trying to accomplish.[7] In the industrial sector, the government was attempting to adopt a dual-price strategy similar to what the Chinese first implemented in the industrial sphere. The Chinese instructed their state-owned enterprises to continue to fulfill the plan, but once planned production obligations were fulfilled, the enterprises were free to employ capital and labor and produce goods for sale on the open market.[8] The plan was therefore frozen in time, and marginal growth occurred according to market dictates. Yet the North Korean planning apparatus may have been in such acute decline that the conditions for such an approach were no longer viable.[9]

North Korean enterprises have been instructed that they are responsible for covering their own costs—that is, they will no longer receive state subsidies. But at the same time, the state has administratively raised wage levels, with certain favored groups such as military personnel, party officials, scientists, and coal miners receiving supernormal increases.[10] This alteration of real wages across occupational groups could be an attempt to enhance the role of material incentives in labor allocation or, alternatively, simply an attempt to reward favored constituencies. Likewise, the state continues to maintain an administered price structure, though by fiat the state prices are being brought in line with prices observed in the markets. However, the North Koreans have not announced any mechanism for periodically adjusting prices, so over time disequilibria, some possibly severe, will develop.

In essence, enterprise managers are being told to meet hard budget constraints, but they are being given little scope to manage. Managers have been authorized to make limited purchases of intermediate inputs and to make autonomous investments out of retained earnings. They are also permitted to engage in international trade. Yet it is unclear to what extent managers have been sanctioned to hire, fire, and promote workers, or to what extent the market will determine remuneration. This is problematic (as it has proven to be in other transitional economies): the state has told the enterprises that they must cover costs, yet it continues to administer prices, and in the absence of any formal bankruptcy or other "exit" mechanism, there is no prescribed method for enterprises that cannot cover costs to cease operations; nor, in the absence of a social safety net, is there a provision for aiding workers from closed enterprises with survival.

Anecdotal evidence suggests that North Korean enterprises are exhibiting a variety of responses: some have set up side businesses, either as a legitimate coping mechanism, or as a dodge to shed unwanted labor; some have cut wages (despite the official wage increases); some have kept afloat by procuring loans from the Central Bank. (The North Koreans have sent officials to China to study the Chinese banking system, which may well make sense, but it is also the primary mechanism through which money-losing state-owned firms are kept alive.) Some enterprises have closed.[11] It is likely that some enterprises will be kept in operation, supported by implicit subsidies, either through national or local government budgets.

In the agricultural sector, the government has implemented a policy of increasing the procurement prices for grains—to increase the volume of food entering the public distribution system (PDS), the state-run rationing system that historically provided necessities to roughly two-thirds of the population—along with a dramatic increase in PDS prices to consumers, with the retail prices of grains rising from 40,000 to 60,000 percent in the space of six months.[12] The increase in the procurement price for grain was motivated, in part, to counter the supply response of the farmers, who, in the face of derisory procurement prices, were diverting acreage away from grain to tobacco and using grain to produce liquor for sale.

The maintenance of the PDS as a mechanism for distributing food is presumably an attempt to guarantee a minimum survival ration while narrowing the disequilibrium between the market and plan prices. Residents are still issued monthly ration cards; if they do not have sufficient funds to purchase the monthly allotment, it is automatically carried over to the next month. Wealthier households are not allowed to purchase quantities in excess of the monthly allotment through the PDS. The system is organized to prevent arbitrage in ration coupons between rich and poor households.[13]

Some have questioned the extent to which this is a real policy change and how much this is simply a ratification of system fraying that had already occurred. There is considerable evidence that most food was already being distributed through markets, not the PDS. But this may indeed be precisely the motivation behind the increases in producer prices. With little supply entering the PDS, people increasingly obtained their food from nonstate sources, and by bringing more supply into state-controlled channels, the government can try to reduce the extent to which food is allocated purely on the basis of purchasing power. Yet another motivation may be to reduce the fiscal strain imposed by the implicit subsidy provided to urban consumers.

The WFP reports that since the July 2002 price changes, prices for grain in the farmers' markets have risen "significantly" while the PDS prices have remained largely unchanged.[14] Despite the increase in procurement prices, anecdotal accounts suggest that the policy has not been successful in coaxing domestic supply (as distinct from international aid) back into the PDS system. Although daily rations through the PDS have been raised, the practical importance of these measures remains unclear, other than perhaps to alter the maximum allocation per household when food is available. The system no longer appears to be the primary source of food, and scattered reports indicate that the system is not operating in all areas of the country.

When China began its reforms in 1979, more than 70 percent of the population was in the agricultural sector; this was also the case in Vietnam when that country initiated reforms the following decade.[15] Debureaucratization of agriculture under these conditions permitted rapid increases in productivity and the release of labor into the nascent non-state-owned manufacturing sector. The key in this situation is that change is likely to produce few losers: farmers' incomes go up as marginal and average value products in the agricultural sector increase; the incomes of those leaving the farms rise as they receive higher-wage jobs in the manufacturing sector; and urban workers in the state-owned heavy-industry sector see their real wages rise as a result of lower food prices associated with expanded supply. The efficiency gains in agriculture essentially finance an economy-wide Pareto improvement (i.e., no one is made worse off). This dynamic was understood by Chinese policy makers, who used a combination of the dual-price system (allowing the market to surround the plan, to use a Maoist metaphor) and side payments to state-owned enterprises, their associated government ministries, and allied local politicians to suppress political opposition to the reforms. The existence of a large, labor-intensive agricultural sector is one of the few robust explanations of relative success in the transition from central planning to the market.[16]

In contrast, North Korea has perhaps half that share employed in agriculture. As a consequence, the absolute magnitude of the supply response is likely to be smaller and the population share directly benefiting from the increase in producer prices for agricultural goods is roughly half as large as in China and Vietnam. This means that reform in North Korea is less likely to be Pareto-improving than in the cases of China or Vietnam. Instead, reform in North Korea is more likely to create losers, and with them the possibility of unrest, as discussed in the next section. In sum, there is little, if any, evidence of resurgence in industrial activity, and the consensus among most outside observers is that marketization has not delivered as hoped. The fall 2003 and 2004 harvests were fairly large, but it is unclear how much was due to favorable weather, provision of fertilizer aid by South Korea, or incentive changes. Even with these increases, the output remains below its 1990 level.

At the same time that the government announced the marketization initiatives, it also announced massive administered increases in wages and prices. The magnitude of these price changes is truly staggering. When China raised the price of grains at the start of its reforms in November 1979, the increase was on the order of 25 percent. In comparison, North Korea has raised the prices of corn and rice by more than 40,000 percent. In the absence of huge supply responses, the result has been an enormous jump in the price level and ongoing inflation abetted by central bank loans to uncompetitive state-owned enterprises (SOEs).[17] Fragmentary data on the price of foreign exchange indicates that since August 2002, the black market exchange rate of the North Korean won has been depreciating against the U.S. dollar at a relatively steady rate of 7–9 percent *monthly*, or at an *annualized* rate of 130–140 percent. Since inflation in the United States over this period has been trivial in comparison, this indicator suggests that North Korea has been experiencing ongoing inflation in excess of 100 percent a year since the introduction of the July 2002 policy changes. Unfortunately, macroeconomic stability at the time reforms are initiated is the second robust predictor of relative success in transition from a planned to a market economy.[18] High rates of inflation do not bode well for North Korea.

Under these conditions, access to foreign currency may act as insurance against inflation, and those, such as senior party officials, with access to foreign exchange will be relatively insulated from its effects. Agricultural workers may benefit from "automatic" pay increases as the price of grain rises, but salaried workers without access to foreign exchange will fall behind. In other words, the process of marketization and inflation will contribute to the exacerbation of existing social differences in North Korea.

The government continues to insist that foreign-invested enterprises pay wages in hard currencies (at wage rates that exceed those of China and Vietnam). For a labor-abundant economy, this curious policy would seem to be the very definition of a contractionary devaluation, blunting the competitiveness-boosting impact of the devaluation by aborting the adjustment of relative labor costs while raising the domestic resource costs of imported intermediate inputs.

In yet another wheeze to extract resources from the population, in March 2003 the government announced the issuance of People's Life Bonds, which despite their name would seem to more closely resemble lottery tickets than bonds as conventionally understood. These instruments have a ten-year maturity, with principal repaid in annual installments beginning in year five (there does not appear to be any provision for interest payments, and no money for such payments has been budgeted). There would be semiannual drawings for the first two years of the program, and annually thereafter, with winners to receive their principal plus prizes. No information has been provided on the expected odds or prize values other than that the drawings are to be based on an "open and objective" principle. The government's announcement states, without a hint of irony, that "the bonds are backed by the full faith and credit of the DPRK government." Committees have been established in every province, city, county, institute, factory, village, and town to promote the scheme—citizens purchasing these "bonds" will be performing a "patriotic deed."[19] Both the characteristics of the instrument and the mass campaign to sell it suggest that politics, not personal finance, will be its main selling point.[20] According to Pyung Joo Kim, when the government has resorted to lottery-like instruments in the past to deal with monetary overhang problems, they have been unpopular.[21]

The third component of the North Korean economic policy change is the formation of various special economic zones (SEZs).[22] In September 2002, the North Korean government announced the establishment of a special administrative region (SAR) at Sinuiju. In certain respects, the location of the new zone was not surprising: the North Koreans had been talking about such a project in the Sinuiju area since 1998. Yet in other respects the announcement was extraordinary. The North Koreans announced that the zone would exist completely outside North Korea's usual legal structures, that it would have its own flag and issue its own passports, and that land could be leased for fifty years. To top off these bizarre arrangements, a Chinese-born entrepreneur with Dutch citizenship named Yang Bin was to run the SAR, but he was promptly arrested by Chinese authorities for tax evasion and subsequently convicted. Press reports over the next two years serially touted a Hong Kong businessman-philanthropist, Kim Jong Il's brother-in-law, and a female ethnic Korean Republican mayor of a small town in California (?!) as slated to succeed Yang. In October 2004, it was reported that North Korea was abandoning the project.

Ultimately, the industrial park at Kaesong, oriented toward South Korea, may have a greater impact on the economy than either the Rajin-Sonbong or Sinuiju zones. In the long run, South Korean small- and medium-sized enterprises (SMEs) will be a natural source of investment and transfer of appropriate technology to the North. However, in the absence of physical or legal infrastructure, South Korean firms are unlikely to invest appreciable resources. The signing of four economic cooperation agreements between the North and South on issues such as taxation and foreign exchange transactions could be regarded as providing the legal infrastructure for economic activity by the SMEs of negligible political influence. However, the North Koreans inexplicably delayed the opening of the planned rail transport links to South Korea on their side of the DMZ and snubbed South Korean officials during the ceremonial opening of the park. Nevertheless, restricted trans-DMZ road links have been established, and limited production in the zone began in December 2004.[23]

The fourth component of the economic plan consists of passing the hat. In September 2002, during the first-ever meeting between the heads of government of Japan and North Korea, Chairman Kim Jong Il managed to extract from Prime Minister Junichiro Koizumi a commitment to provide a large financial transfer to North Korea as part of the diplomatic normalization process to settle post-colonial claims, despite the shaky state of Japanese public finances.[24] Both leaders then expressed regrets for their countries' respective transgressions and agreed to pursue diplomatic normalization. However, Kim's bald admission that North Korean agents had indeed kidnapped 12 Japanese citizens and that most of the abductees were dead set off a political firestorm in Japan. This revelation, together with the April 2003 claim that North Korea possessed a "nuclear deterrent capability," put the diplomatic rapprochement on hold, and with it the prospects of a large capital infusion from Japan, as well lessening the already-dim prospects of admission to international financial institutions such as the World Bank and the Asian Development Bank. A second visit to Pyongyang by Prime Minister Koizumi in July 2004 generated a resumption of Japanese aid, but not a fundamental breakthrough.

IMPLICATIONS FOR POLITICAL STABILITY

The policy changes in the North have exacerbated preexisting social inequality and created a new group of food-insecure households among the urban nonelite. According to a WFP survey, most urban households are food insecure, spending more than 80 percent of their incomes on food. In December 2003, Masood Hyder, the United Nations (UN) humanitarian relief coordinator in North Korea, told the world press that the food problem was concentrated among up to one million urban workers, a view echoed by Rick Corsino, head of the WFP's local operation, who claimed that "some people are having to spend all their income on food."[25] According to the Food and Agricultural Organization,[26] for the period 1999–2001, 34 percent of North Korea's population was malnourished—though it is unclear on what basis the organization reached such a precise figure, especially in light of the problematic nature of the survey evidence.[27]

Yet there is less room to doubt the rupture of the traditional social compact, necessitating a reinterpretation of the North Korean doctrine of *juche*, or self-reliance, to legitimate the reforms and justify the departure from the country's socialist tradition. The response has been to intensify the "military-first" campaign, elevating the military above the proletariat in the North Korean political pantheon.[28] The effect has been to overturn the traditional paths to power and status: captains and entrepreneurs have now replaced party cadres and bureaucrats as preferred sons-in-law. As the military waxes while the commitment to socialism wanes, North Korea appears to be evolving toward some kind of unique postcommunist totalitarian state—not the sort of classically fascist regime that its propaganda excoriates, but a strange revival of dynastic feudalism in the form of a nonsocialist, patrimonial state, though with a more efficient state apparatus than Iraq under Saddam Hussein. The central issue is whether the regime can manage this internal change while confronting economic stress, the implicit legitimization challenge posed by prosperous, democratic South Korea, and diplomatic tensions emanating from its nuclear weapons program.

These developments, while daunting, may not signal the imminent demise of the regime. There is no clear mapping between economic distress and political change, and while the degree of economic distress experienced in North Korea has been great, it is not historically unique.[29] Furthermore, the socialist model did deliver industrialization and development, at least in its initial stages. Most estimates suggest that per capita income in the South did not surpass that of the North until the 1970s. Thus, while North Korea did experience systemic macroeconomic problems at least as early as 1990, if not earlier, this should be judged in the context of a political-economic system that had some track record of delivering the goods. Presumably this conveyed some legitimacy to the regime. Moreover, the amount of external support necessary to keep North Korea on "survival rations" was (and remains) relatively small (perhaps $2 billion annually) and easily within the scope of its neighbors to provide—each of whom for their own reasons would prefer to forestall collapse.[30]

Second, with the possible exception of the Korean People's Army, there is a complete absence of institutions capable of channeling mass discontent into effective political action. There is no Solidarity trade union as in Poland, or Civic Forum as in Czechoslovakia. Indeed, there are not even alternative sources of moral authority capable of legitimating dissent, such as played by the Roman Catholic church in the uprising against the martial law regime in Poland or the "People's Power" revolt against the dictatorship of Ferdinand Marcos in the Philippines.

Externally, North Korea's neighbors have not provided sanctuary to anti-Kim political forces. There is little or no evidence of anti-Kim political organizing among the refugees in the Chinese border region, and there are no marauding guerrilla insurgencies on North Korea's borders. If anything, North Korea's neighbors might be expected to actively cooperate with North Korean security services to crack down on such activity if it were to develop. Indeed, the absence of antiregime organizing, together with people voluntarily crossing back into North Korea, suggests a more complicated politics of deprivation.

I have separately undertaken an examination of the likelihood of political instability, or (more precisely) regime change, based on formal statistical analysis.[31] The models are estimated from three separate cross-national data sets on political developments worldwide since 1960.[32] Several dozen explanatory variables, generally falling into three categories, were considered. The first category consists of political, legal, and cultural variables that tend to change slowly, if at all. These would include variables such as the origin of the country's legal system, whether it originated that system, adopted it, or had it imposed by a colonial power; and proxies relating to the quality of domestic political institutions. A second group of variables involves demographic and social indicators that also tend to change slowly. These include factors like the level of urbanization and the degree of ethnic or religious heterogeneity within a country. Economic policy and performance indicators make up the final category. These measures tend to exhibit the greatest temporal variability. As a consequence, the more slowly changing political and social variables tend to determine whether a particular country is generally prone to instability, while the more rapidly changing economic variables tend to affect whether the likelihood of regime change is rising or falling.

These models were estimated and then used to generate the probability of regime change in North Korea. The results from one such model are displayed in Figure 1. In this particular model, the hazard of political regime change is a function of per capita income, per capita income growth, openness to international trade, inflation, the share of trade taxes in total tax revenue, aid receipts per capita, and whether the country has a tropical climate, a proxy of institutional quality. (Stability is a positive function of income level and growth, trade openness, and aid, and a negative function of inflation, trade taxes, and institutional quality.)

According to this particular model, the probability of regime change peaked at nearly 10 percent in 1992, declined, peaked again in the late 1990s, and has since declined to

Figure 1   **Hazard of Regime Change under Three Scenarios**

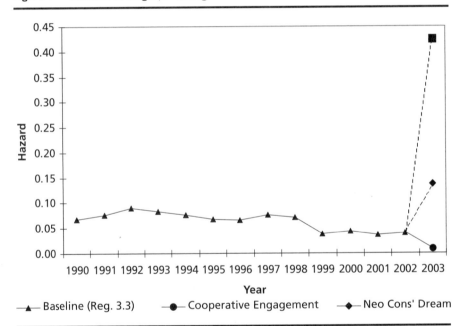

approximately 4 percent in 2002, the most recent year in the simulation. Other models reported generally yield higher probabilities, though a similar time-series pattern.[33] Statistically speaking, those observers who, during the 1990s, predicted North Korea's collapse probably were not making such a bad bet; the cumulative likelihood of regime change in all of these models rises above 50 percent over the course of the decade.

Another implication is that economic performance critically influences regime stability and that the North's external relations play a crucial role in this regard. To explore this theme, the models were simulated under three alternative scenarios. Under one scenario, which might be labeled "cooperative engagement," diplomatic tensions are eased, and North Korea successfully globalizes in a diplomatically supportive environment. North Korea receives higher levels of aid from South Korea, China, the United States, and other countries as compared to the status quo. It normalizes diplomatic relations with Japan and begins to receive postcolonial claim settlement payments. It joins the multilateral development banks and begins receiving aid from them as well. Total aid reaches $3 billion annually. Under the less threatening environment, it liberalizes its economy. The share of trade in national income rises to 71 percent—i.e., what it would exhibit if it were as integrated into the world economy as a "normal" country with its characteristics—and trade taxes are cut to the South Korean level.[34] The rate of economic growth rebounds to its 1999 peak of 6 percent. All other variables stay at their 2002 values.

In the "neocon's dream" scenario, the global community puts the squeeze on the Kim Jong Il regime: aid is cut off; growth falls to its previous low of -6 percent; and the inexpertly enacted July 2002 economic policy changes drive inflation up to 300 percent, reportedly its rate during the first year following the introduction of the reforms.

In the "international embargo" scenario, North Korea's relations with the rest of the world deteriorate precipitously, perhaps under suspicion of exportation of nuclear weapons, and all international trade is cut off. Admittedly, this scenario is a stretch for the underlying statistical model, which does not distinguish between food, oil, and video games in the maintenance of a society, and some might object that a total embargo is politically unrealistic as well. It may not be without some utility, however, revealing something about the nature of regime dynamics, at least in a cross-country sample.

For heuristic purposes, the predicted hazard rates associated with each of these alternatives are appended to the graph as "2003," although there is nothing unique in the scenarios to link it to that date, and indeed, some of the changes envisioned in the "cooperative engagement" scenario would probably take more than one year to realize. Nevertheless, the simulations may be revealing in terms of how outside forces might affect regime survival in North Korea. According to these results, under the "cooperative engagement" scenario, the likelihood of regime change falls to less than 1 percent. Kim Jong Il dies in his sleep, and one of his sons dons his grandfather Kim Il Sung's mantle. In the "neocon's dream" the likelihood of regime change rises to about a one-in-seven probability, growing thereafter, and in all probability, Kim Jong Il is out of power before George W. Bush. In the final scenario, "international embargo," the likelihood of regime change is over 40 percent in the first year, and the Kim Jong Il regime probably collapses within two years. Hufbauer, Schott, and Elliott find that sanctions aimed at destabilization succeed about half the time.[35] In comparing the results obtained in this simulation and the historical track record, the scenario modeled involves a comprehensive and successful embargo. An embargo that was less complete by design (i.e., allowing exceptions for certain categories of exchange) or less thoroughly implemented (i.e., there was cheating) would have an attenuated impact on regime stability.

One caveat should be underlined: there may be psychopolitical phenomena that are not well captured by these models. In particular, foreign pressure may provide the regime with a rationale for poor performance, while a lack of foreign pressure (i.e., an absence of enemies) may conversely deprive the regime of an excuse. This is simply to say that the models may overstate the impact of these alternative scenarios on regime stability. The good scenario may not be quite as good and the bad scenario not quite as bad as depicted in Figure 1, regardless of how one defines "good" and "bad" outcomes. Given the complexity of the underlying conceptual issues, and the poor quality of the data used in the analysis, these estimates encompass very wide confidence intervals. Caveat emptor.

POTENTIAL SUCCESSOR REGIMES

Suppose the current regime is unable to manage this transition. Regime change—at least the internally generated variety—would not necessarily imply the disappearance of the North Korean state, though this is surely one possibility. The key issues would be the viability and character of the successor regime. Would any non–Kim Il Sungist North Korean regime be viable? Would it be able to legitimate itself, or would this simply be a transitional state toward unification? Is a post-*juche* North Korean state possible? The current "military-first" ideological campaign, which at first blush would appear to signal the ascendance of the most reactionary element of the polity, may actually be the mechanism through which a broad-ranging top-down modernization of a society subject to external threat is justified.[36] By elevating the military to the vanguard, the "military-first" ideology justifies all manner of departures from past practice (including the jettisoning of socialism in practice, if not as a teleological ideal) in pursuit of military modernization.

There is historical precedent for this outcome. In the Meiji Restoration and the founding of modern Turkey under Mustafa Kemal, revolutionary changes were justified as responses to external threats and legitimated in terms of restoring past historical glory. Yet in this North Korean production, Kim Jong Il would be playing the roles of both the Tokugawa Shogun and the Emperor Meiji. Perhaps this is consistent with the fact that, in an exchange with former U.S. Secretary of State Madeleine Albright, he expressed his interest in the "Thai model," in which he would reign but not rule.[37]

In a positive sense, top-down military-centered modernization may be a successful political development strategy. From a normative perspective, the results of that strategy—a nuclear-armed, and possibly proliferating, North Korea—would be hugely antithetical to American interests. Moreover, there is no guarantee that a military modernizer would be the Park Chung Hee or Augusto Pinochet of North Korea, and not its Alexander Kerensky or Lothar de Maizière. The legitimization challenges for a post-*juche* North Korea would be profound, and there is no certainty of success, even if the regime were supported by a South Korea fearful of the implications of collapse and absorption.

South Korea would be key, not only because of the resources it could provide to a new North Korean regime, but also because of the challenge the ROK's very existence would pose for the legitimization of any successor regime in North Korea. Ironically, one can imagine a situation in which the most radical forces in North Korea would be revolutionary nationalist unifiers, who might well be opposed by a South Korean government that, fearing a collapse and absorption scenario, might try to prop up the North Korean state. Indeed, there is talk in some quarters that under the proper political conditions, the South might make "reconciliation transfers" to the North of 1 percent of GDP, or about $6 billion, multiples of the $2-billion-a-year "survival rations" estimated by Mitchell.[38] Whether the existence of this South Korean 911 line would be sufficient to guarantee the political survival of the Kim Jong Il regime is an existential question, though it suggests that the reality we may be headed toward lies somewhere between "cooperative engagement" and "the neocon's dream."

IMPLICATIONS FOR SOUTH KOREA

This discussion will start with the apocalyptic and work backward. In a collapse-and-absorption scenario, the "costs" of unification, defined as capital transfers to North Korea, might be on the order of $600 billion over the course of a decade.[39] "Costs" is a bit of a misnomer in this context. This process would also generate benefits, and the incidence of these costs and benefits would be a function of policy—for example, the degree to which the transfers took the form of public grants, as distinct from private investments yielding a stream of remitted profits to their South Korean owners. Although remaining positive, economic growth in the South would slow relative to a no-unification baseline, and unless compensatory policies were undertaken, the process of economic integration with the North would lead to an increase in income and wealth inequality.[40]

Yet even less apocalyptic gradual-integration scenarios pose significant challenges for South Korea. These considerations could be conceptualized in terms of "real," "institutional," and "risk" channels. Suppose North and South Korea experience a gradual process of consensual economic integration that does not involve significant cross-border movement of labor. There would still be a "real" impact on the South Korean economy through an impact on relative product prices, and possibly through a slowing of capital accumulation due to investment diversion. Yet the impact would be highly attenuated relative to the collapse-and-absorption scenario, and might be thought of as something akin to the economic impact on the United States of deeper integration with Mexico through NAFTA: considerable to some individuals, firms, and communities, but of little macroeconomic importance.

Institutionally, South Korea has considerable problems with nontransparent and corrupt government-business relations. In the North, there is no real difference between the state and the economy. Large-scale economic integration between the North and the South will be a highly politicized process and will in all likelihood retard progress in cleaning up business-government relations in the South. The corruption scandals involving the Blue House and the Korean Development Bank with respect to Hyundai Asan's activities in the North under the Kim Dae Jung administration are emblematic in this regard.

Finally, regardless of its policy stance, South Korea remains exposed to the vagaries of North Korean behavior. Financially, South Korea is increasingly integrated into the world economy, creating new vulnerabilities. While it is true that the South Korean stock market actually rose during the 1994 nuclear crisis, the expanded role of foreign participants and the increased complexity of the financial transactions, including the extensive use of derivatives and off-balance-sheet instruments by South Korean financial institutions, mean that the market today is far less susceptible to political intervention than it was a decade ago.

In this context, three policy recommendations for South Korea can be made:

- First, commit to the principle of efficient, transparent engagement. Adopt a tax-based approach to engagement to minimize the scope for selective political intervention.

- Second, while engaging, prepare for the possibility of collapse in the North by strengthening the South Korean economy, improving its internal mechanisms of resource mobilization, allocation, and management.

- Third, accumulate fiscal reserves in anticipation of a possible collapse in the North. This means maintaining a cyclically adjusted bias toward fiscal surplus.

NOTES

I would like to thank Paul Karner for his research assistance in preparation of this chapter.

1. The quality of the data for North Korea is poor. The South Korean Bank of Korea (BOK) estimate of North Korean national income is reportedly constructed by applying South Korean value-added weights to physical estimates of North Korean output derived through classified sources and methods, and reputedly subject to prerelease interagency discussion within the South Korean government. This raises a variety of concerns: that the reliance on physical indicators may augur an overemphasis on the industrial sector (where output is relatively easy to count) relative to the service sector; that prerelease discussions may imply interagency bargaining and a politicization of the estimate; and that the methods through which the figures are derived are not subject to independent verification. The use of South Korean value-added weights is surely inappropriate. It is rumored that a classified mock North Korean input-output table exists, though what role this might play in the BOK's calculations are obviously speculative. For all these reasons, outside analysts have at times questioned the reliability, if not the veracity, of the BOK figures.

2. Marcus Noland, "North Korea: Famine and Reform," *Asian Economic Papers* 3, no. 2 (2004).

3. Nicholas Eberstadt, Marc Rubin, and Albina Tretyakova, "The Collapse of Soviet and Russian Trade with the DPRK, 1989–1993," *The Korean Journal of National Unification*, no. 4 (1995), pp. 87–104.

4. Marcus Noland, *Avoiding the Apocalypse: The Future of the Two Koreas* (Washington, D.C.: Institute for International Economics, 2000), Table 5.2, provides nine examples of "food for talks." A recent example is the February 2003 U.S. government announcement, in the run-up to diplomatic talks over the North Korean nuclear weapons program, that it would provide 40,000 metric tons of grain to North Korea. This was despite the fact that the North Koreans had not fulfilled the June 2002 aid transparency and monitoring conditions, which had been reaffirmed the previous month, January 2003, by USAID Administrator Andrew S. Natsios. China implicitly linked donations to political behavior continued in the diplomatic maneuvering around the Six-Party Talks over the North Korean nuclear program in 2003 and 2004. The termination of support by Japan in 2002 and its resumption in 2004 were explicitly linked to diplomatic developments. See Mark Manyin, "U.S. Assistance to North Korea," *CRS Report for Congress* (Washington, D.C.: Congressional Research Service, updated 26 April 2005), and Mark Manyin, "Foreign Assistance to North Korea," *CRS Report for Congress* (Washington, D.C.: Congressional Research Service, updated 26 May 2005), for further details.

5. Noland, *Avoiding the Apocalypse.*

6. Seung-yul Oh, "Changes in the North Korean Economy: New Policies and Limitations," *Korea's Economy 2003,* vol. 19 (Washington, D.C.: Korea Economic Institute of America, 2003).

7. See Jung-chul Lee, "The Implications of North Korea's Reform Program and Its Effects on State Capacity," *Korea and World Affairs* 26, no. 3 (2002), pp. 357–64; Yun Ho Chung, "The Prospects of Economic Reform in North Korea and the Direction of Its Economic Development," *Vantage Point* 26, no. 5 (May 2003), pp. 43–53; Ruediger Frank, "A Socialist Market Economy in North Korea? Systemic Restrictions and a Quantitative Analysis," unpublished paper (New York, Columbia University, 2003); Sung-wook Nam, "Moves Toward Economic Reforms," *Vantage Point* 26, no. 10 (2003) pp. 18–22; William Newcomb, "Reflections on North Korea's Economic Reform," *Korea's Economy 2003,* vol. 19 (Washington, D.C.: Korea Economic Institute of America, 2003); Seung-yul Oh, "Changes in the North Korean Economy"; and Peter Gey, "North Korea: Soviet-style Reform and the Erosion of the State Economy," *Internationale Politik und Gesellschaft,* Heft 1/2004, S. 115–133, www.fes.de/ipg/ONLINE1 _2004/ARTGEY.HTM (in German); English version, *Dialogue and Cooperation,* Singapore, no. 1/2004.

8. Lawrence J. Lau, Yingi Qian, and Girard Roland, "Reform without Losers: An Interpretation of China's Dual-Track Approach to Transition," *Journal of Political Economy* 108, no.1 (2000), pp. 120–43.

9. Bradley O. Babson and William J. Newcomb, "Economic Perspectives on Demise Scenarios for DPRK," 2004, processed.

10. Gey, "North Korea: Soviet-style Reform," Table 2.

11. One result of these changes has been a noticeable upsurge in small-scale retail activity

with Gey ("North Korea: Soviet-style Reform") estimating that 6 to 8 percent of the workforce is engaged in informal trading activities. Although this is usually interpreted as household-level entrepreneurial activity, Han Shik Park, a frequent visitor to North Korea, argues that most of this activity is sponsored by SOEs, which own capital such as the carts used by the peddlers. According to Park, SOEs partly deprived of state subsidies have entered small-scale retailing as a means of generating revenue.

12. Noland, "Famine and Reform," Table 4.

13. Oh ("Changes in the North Korean Economy") claims that the rationing coupons have been abolished, and in theory, wealthy households can buy unlimited supplies through the PDS.

14. World Food Programme, "Public Distribution System (PDS) in DPRK," DPR Korea Country Office, 21 May 2003.

15. Noland, *Avoiding the Apocalypse*, Table 3.7.

16. Anders Aslund, Peter Boone, and Simon Johnson, "How to Stabilize: Lessons from Post-Communist Countries," *Brookings Papers on Economic Activity* 1 (1996), pp. 217–313.

17. See Frank ("A Socialist Market Economy in North Korea?"), Oh ("Changes in the North Korean Economy"), and Noland ("Famine and Reform") for recitations of other, nonagricultural, price increases.

18. Aslund et al., "How to Stabilize."

19. The discussion in Chung (2003) suggests that purchases of the bonds may be compulsory. According to another account, while purchases are not mandatory, the authorities use purchases as "a barometer of the buyers' loyalty and support for the party and the state" (*Itar-Tass*, 23 May 2003, KOTRA translation).

20. Frank ("A Socialist Market Economy in North Korea?") argues that the issuance of these instruments is a response to the large expansion in expenditures associated with the increased procurement price for grains, and indeed, North Korean government expenditures appeared to increase by double digits in 2003. However, the rise in outlays associated with the increase in the procurement price for grain ought to be offset by a similar increase in revenues from the expanded PDS sales. Some have claimed that these instruments could ultimately serve as a basis for privatizing state-owned enterprises.

21. Pyung Joo Kim, "Monetary Integration and Stabilization in the Unified Korea," in *Policy Priorities for the Unified Korean Economy*, ed. Il SaKong and Kwang Suk Kim (Seoul: Institute for Global Economics, 1998).

22. The first such zone was established in the Rajin-Sonbong region in the extreme northeast of the country in 1991. It has proved to be a failure for a variety of reasons, including its geographic isolation, poor infrastructure, onerous rules, and interference in enterprise management by party officials. The one major investment has been the establishment of a combination hotel/casino/bank. Given the obvious scope for illicit activity associated with such a horizontally integrated endeavor, the result has been less Hong Kong than Macau North. For an appraisal of the North Korean SEZ policy, see Eliot Jung, Young-soo Kim, and Takayuki Kobayashi, "North Korea's Special Economic Zones: Obstacles and Opportunities," in *Confrontation and Innovation on the Korean Peninsula* (Washington, D.C.: Korea Economic Institute, 2003).

23. Although foreign invested enterprises will continue to be subject to the hard currency minimum wage, in principle firms in the Kaesong industrial park will be able to hire and fire workers directly, bypassing the usual state hiring combine.

24. Japanese officials did not deny formulas reported in the press that would put the total value of a multiyear package in the form of grants, subsidized loans, and trade credits at approximately $10 billion. This magnitude is consistent with the size of Japan's 1965 postcolonial settlement with South Korea adjusted for population, inflation, exchange rate changes, and interest forgone. Given the puny size of the North Korean economy, this is a gigantic sum. For further discussion, see Mark E. Manyin, "Japan-North Korea Relations: Selected Issues" (Washington, D.C.: Library of Congress Congressional Research Service, 26 November 2003).

25. Jonathon Watts, "How North Korea Is Embracing Capitalism," *The Guardian,* 3 December 2003. See also Sungwoo Kim, "North Korea's Unofficial Market Economy and Its Implications," *International Journal of Korean Studies* 7, no. 1 (2003), pp. 14–64; Amnesty International, "Starved of Rights: Human Rights and the Food Crisis in the Democratic People's Republic of Korea (North Korea)," 2004, web.amnesty.org/library/index/engasa240032004; and Seongji Woo, "North Korea's Food Crisis," *Korea Focus* 12, no. 3 (2004), pp. 63–80, for an analysis of food insecurity issues.

26. Food and Agricultural Organization (FAO), *The State of Food Insecurity in the World 2003* (FAO: Rome, 2003), Table 1.

27. Noland, "Famine and Reform."

28. Frank ("A Socialist Market Economy in North Korea?"); Marcus Noland, *Korea After Kim Jong-il* (Washington, D.C.: Institute for International Economics, 2004).

29. Noland, *Korea After Kim Jong-il*, Table 2.1.

30. Anthony Michell, "The Current North Korean Economy," in *Economic Integration on the Korean Peninsula,* ed. Marcus Noland (Washington, D.C.: Institute for International Economics, 1998).

31. Noland, *Korea After Kim Jong-il.*

32. The underlying sample consisted of 71 countries. In some applications, the sample size was reduced due to missing data on the explanatory variables. See the appendix to Noland, *Korea After Kim Jong-il,* for a more complete description of the data used in this analysis.

33. Noland, *Korea After Kim Jong-il.*

34. Noland, "Avoiding the Apocalypse," Table 7.2.

35. Gary C. Hufbauer, Jeffrey J. Schott, and Kimberly Ann Elliott, *Economic Sanctions Reconsidered* (2nd edition), (Washington, D.C.: Institute for International Economics, 1990).

36. It could also be the mechanism through which a skeptical military is reassured that the primacy of its status will not be challenged in the reform process.

37. Madeleine Albright, *Madame Secretary* (New York: Miramax, 2003).

38. Michell, "The Current North Korean Economy."

39. Noland, "Avoiding the Apocalypse."

40. These results were derived from a dynamic, computable, general equilibrium model incorporating a variety of North Korea–specific distortions. Qualitatively similar results are obtained by Bradford and Phillips using a somewhat different model and assumptions. See Scott C. Bradford and Kerk L. Phillips, *The Economic Reunification of Korea: A Dynamic General Equilibrium Model* (Provo, Utah: Brigham Young University, 17 April 2004, processed).

7

Why Hasn't the DPRK Collapsed?

Nicholas Eberstadt

Can the Democratic People's Republic of Korea (the DPRK, or North Korea) survive—as a distinct regime, an autonomous state, a specific political-economic system, and a sovereign country? Can it continue to function in the manner that it has since the final collapse of the Soviet empire? Is North Korea doomed to join the Warsaw Pact's failed Communist experiments in the dustbin of history? Might it, instead, adapt and evolve—"surviving" in the sense of maintaining its political authority and power to rule, but transforming its defining functional characteristics and systemic identity?

In 1995, I would not have expected to pose these questions in a paper written a decade later. My work on the North Korean economy has been characterized as part of the "collapsist"[1] school of thought, and not unfairly. As far back as June 1990, I published an essay entitled "The Coming Collapse of North Korea"; since then, my analyses have recurrently questioned the viability of the DPRK economy and political system.[2] How has the North Korean system managed to survive for another decade and a half? This essay offers an explanation. The first section discusses the epistemology of state collapse, focusing on a historical example of potential relevance. The second section analyzes some of the factors that may have abetted state survival in the DPRK case in recent years. The third section considers the sustainability of North Korea's current economic modus operandi. The final section examines questions pertaining to a DPRK transition to a more pragmatic variant of a planned socialist economy.

THE EPISTEMOLOGY OF STATE COLLAPSE: A CAUTIONARY OTTOMAN TALE

Although major efforts have been undertaken in the hope of systematizing the study of state failure,[3] the modern world lacks a corpus of scientific writings that offer robust predictions about impending social revolution, systemic breakdown, or state collapse. At the very best, the anticipation of such dramatic political events might aspire to art rather than science[4]—just as the technique of successful stock-picking (or short-selling) has always been, and still remains, an art and not a science.[5] A common set of factors, furthermore, consigns both of these endeavors to the realm of art: the extraordinary complexity of the phenomena under consideration, the independent and unpredictable nature of the human agency at their center, and the ultimately irresolvable problem of asymmetries of information. Hence, there is no reason that students and analysts should be able to predict the breakdown of political-economic systems with any degree of accuracy on the basis of a regular and methodical model. Indeed, predicting breakdown for Communist systems is arguably even more difficult than for open societies, insofar as the asymmetries of information are much more extreme.[6]

If anticipating state collapse is at best a matter of art, the most obvious failures fall into two categories of error. First, there are the failures to predict events that did actually take place. The 1989–91 collapse of the Warsaw Pact states—an upheaval that caught almost all informed Western observers unawares[7]—is the most memorable recent example of this type of error. Second, there is the error of predicting upheaval and abrupt demise for states or systems that do not end up suffering from such paroxysms. This category of error would encompass, inter alia, Marxist-Leninist prognoses for Western Europe over the past century; the apocalyptic assessments from the 1970s and 1980s on the future of South Africa;[8] the premature predictions of the fall of Soviet Communism[9]—and, at least to date, the presentiments of the collapse of the DPRK.

These particular types of mistakes can be likened to "Type I" and "Type II" errors in statistical inference. For our purposes, however, the family of analytical errors in assessments of state failure or collapse is not dichotomous. Other types of errors can also occur, especially the failure to recognize imminent, but averted, collapse. This is not a fanciful hypothetical category. History is replete with examples of this phenomenon. One particularly relevant example involves the collapse of the Ottoman Empire and the battle of Gallipoli.

As early as 1853,[10] the Ottoman Empire had been dubbed "the sick man of Europe" by other great powers engaged in the struggle for mastery of the continent. With a sclerotic and corrupt Byzantine administrative system and an overtaxed, underinnovating economy,[11] Constantinople was set on a course of steady relative decline.[12] However, the Ottoman invalid survived for almost 70 years after this diplomatic diagnosis of its poor political health. The Empire was finally laid to rest in 1922–23, with Mustapha Kemal/Ataturk's revolution and the founding of the modern Turkish state. What is less well known, however, is that the Ottoman Empire very nearly came to an end in 1915, in the World War I campaign of Gallipoli.

The Gallipoli campaign of 1915–16 is remembered as a military debacle for France and, more particularly, the British Empire. In a bold and risky bid to capture Constantinople by naval attack and amphibious invasion, the Allied troops were instead trapped on their own beachheads on the Gallipoli peninsula, unable to displace the Ottoman forces from their fortified positions on the high ground. For months the soldiers of the British Commonwealth—quite a few of them Australian and New Zealand regulars—were slaughtered in futile attempts to break the Ottoman line. At the end of 1915, the British began a total evacuation of the surviving combatants, a total of over one hundred thousand Commonwealth casualties having been sustained in the campaign. In the course of the Gallipoli campaign, Ottoman General Mustapha Kemal secured his reputation as a brilliant and heroic military leader, while Winston Churchill, the then young Lord Admiral of the British Navy, was obliged to resign his post in humiliation. Gallipoli is now widely deemed a textbook case of military blunder. The campaign was included in an influential treatise on great military mistakes;[13] for decades the campaign has been studied in military academies around the world. Unbeknownst to most, however, the Franco-British naval assault very nearly did succeed—and indeed nearly toppled the Ottoman Empire.

In early March 1915, a Franco-British flotilla that included sixteen battleships, cruisers, and destroyers commenced Churchill's plan to "force" the Dardanelles Strait. Artillery fire from the Turkish gun emplacements proved ineffectual against these mighty warships. On 18 March, the flotilla prepared to advance through the Dardanelles Strait into the Sea of Marmora—whence it would steam on to Constantinople. Over the course of a daylong battle between big guns, the Allied fleet slowly moved forward against the Ottoman emplacements. In the late afternoon, three British ships—one of them a battleship—unexpectedly struck mines and suddenly sank. The British commander of the operation, Rear Admiral John de Roebeck, was severely shaken by this setback, feeling certain he would be sacked for the loss of those ships.[14] But the Allied fleet regrouped, though it did not pursue its assault the next day, or in the weeks that followed. As David Fromkin notes, "only a few hundred casualties had been suffered, but the Admiralty's Dardanelles campaign was over."[15]

De Roebeck could not have known about the circumstances on the other side of the barricades. With the benefit of Ottoman and German records and memoirs, historians have since described these conditions: the Ottoman administration and its German military advisers were grimly convinced the Allied assault would spell doom for Constantinople—for they had no hope of putting up a successful resistance. As Alan Moorehead recounts, the Ottoman Minister of the Interior Talaat himself was utterly despondent. As early as January he had called a conference (with the top German military allies and advisers), and all agreed that when the Allied Fleet attacked it would get through.[16] In the days before the attempt to "force" the Dardanelles, Constantinople had begun to take on the smell of a defeated capital. As described by David Fromkin:

> Morale in Constantinople disintegrated. Amidst rumors and panic, the evacuation of the city commenced. The state archives and the gold reserves of the banks were sent to safety. Special trains were prepared for the Sultan and for the foreign diplomatic colony. Talaat, the Minister of the Interior, requisitioned a powerful Mercedes for his personal use, and equipped it with extra petrol tanks for the long drive to a distant place of refuge. Placards denouncing the government began to appear in the streets of the city. . . . The [German ship] *Goeben* made ready to escape to the Black Sea. . . . [Ottoman War Minister] Enver bravely planned to remain and defend the city, but his military dispositions were so incompetent that—as [German military adviser General Otto] Liman von Sanders later recalled—any Turkish attempt at opposing an Allied landing at Constantinople would have been rendered impossible.[17]

Among the disadvantages weighing on the beleaguered Turks was the fact—unappreciated by de Roebeck—that the defenders were virtually out of artillery shells. As Moorehead observes, "[Nothing] could alter the fact that they had so much ammunition and no more . . . .[I]f the battle went on and no unforeseen reinforcements arrived it was obvious to the commanders that the moment would come when they would be bound to order their men to fire off the last round and then to retire. After that they could do no more."[18] As a historian who fought in Gallipoli would later note, the official records of Minister Enver's German advisers jotted the following entry on the fateful day of 18 March 1915:

> Most of the Turkish ammunition has been expended; the medium howitzers and mine fields have fired more than half their supply. Particularly serious is the fact that the long range high explosive shells, which alone are effective against British Ship's armor are all used up. We stress the point that Fort Hamidieh has only seventeen shells and Kalid Bahr Fort only ten: there is also no reserve of mines; what will happen when the battle is resumed.[19]

The Ottoman government and its German advisers could not believe their good fortune when the Allied naval assault inexplicably (from their perspective) halted. Looking back later, Enver reportedly commented: "If the English had only had the courage to rush more ships through the Dardanelles, they could have got to Constantinople; but their delay enabled us thoroughly to fortify the Peninsula, and in six weeks' time we had taken down there over 200 Austrian Skoda guns."[20]

General Liman von Sanders later commented tersely that the evacuation procedures underway in Constantinople "were justified. . . . Had the [Allied landing] orders been carried out. . . . the course of the world war would have been given such a turn in the spring of 1915 that Germany and Austria would have had to continue without Turkey."[21] Fromkin stated the matter more plainly: "The Ottoman Empire, which had been sentenced to death, received an unexpected last-minute reprieve."[22] By the same logic, a state might be on the verge of collapse without interested outsiders fully understanding that these circumstances were not merely an abstract theoretical possibility. The example of Gallipoli offers us an "existence proof" that such things do indeed happen, sometimes with great historical consequence.[23]

From this Turkish parable, let us return to North Korea. The DPRK continues to function as a sovereign and independent state. But is the North Korean state's recent survival a modern-day variant of the Gallipoli phenomenon—in other words, a case of imminent but averted collapse? And to address this question fully, what information would we require that we presently lack?

FINANCING THE SURVIVAL OF THE NORTH KOREAN STATE

These speculative questions unfortunately remain unanswerable—and for now, quite untestable. We will probably have to await the eventual opening of the Pyongyang state archives to delve into those issues with any precision—assuming that the DPRK's official files and data offer a sufficiently coherent and faithful record of events. Available data does, however, cast light on one aspect of the DPRK's struggle to avoid collapse in the wake of the Soviet bloc's demise. This is the international data on North Korean trade patterns as reported by the DPRK's trade partners, also known as "mirror statistics." Mirror statistics cannot tell us how close North Korea may have come to collapse in recent years, but they can help us explain how North Korea has managed to finance state survival.

It is incontestable that the DPRK national economy was in the grip of stagnation—or incipient decline—in the 1980s. It then began to spiral downward once aid and subsidized trade from the Soviet bloc suddenly ceased at the start of the 1990s. The steep and apparently unbroken decline in the North Korean economic performance in the first half of the 1990s led to the outbreak of famine in the DPRK by the mid-1990s. This is the only known instance of such mass hunger in an industrialized and literate society during peacetime. North Korea's patent economic dysfunction and the leadership's seeming unwillingness or incapability to address and correct it raised the possibility of one very particular kind of systemic collapse: economic collapse. I discuss this prospect in some detail in my 1999 book, *The End of North Korea*.[24]

The prospect of economic collapse did not encompass judgments about the possibility of a dramatic political event that might bring the North Korean regime to an end, such as a coup at the top or a revolt from below. Then, as now, the information that might permit such a judgment was unavailable to outside observers, especially to those with no access to sources of intelligence. "Economic collapse" seemed an exceedingly elastic term, but I attempted to use it with some conceptual precision. In my earlier study, "economic collapse" was not defined as an economic shock, an economic dislocation, or a severe depression, or even a famine. It instead described the breakdown of the division of labor in the national economy—the process through which ordinary people in complex productive societies trade their labor for food. (This conception of "economic collapse" was first developed and defined by Jack Hirshleifer.[25])

North Korea in the mid- and late 1990s seemed set on a trajectory for economic collapse. Its domestic economy was incapable of producing the requisite goods necessary for the maintenance of a division of labor, and the regime seemed utterly unable to finance their purchase from abroad. Although it was impossible to determine from the outside the precise breaking point at which the division of labor would unravel, events were bringing the DPRK system progressively closer to that point. The present situation looks somewhat different. The ordinary North Korean today does not exactly live in the lap of luxury. However, by most accounts the typical North Korean no longer suffers from the desperate privation that characterized the mid- to late 1990s. As best as can be determined, the North Korean famine—which almost certainly claimed hundreds of thousands of victims, and may well have killed a million people between 1995 and 1998[26]—subsided by the late 1990s. The North Korean leadership indicated a new confidence in the DPRK's staying power in September 1998, at the Supreme People's Assembly that formally elevated Kim Jong Il to "the highest position of state." The convocation publicly declared that the "Arduous March" of the previous several years was completed and announced that the DPRK was now on the road to becoming a "powerful and prosperous state" (Kangsong Taeguk).[27]

It is debatable whether the North Korean economy has enjoyed actual growth since 1998. However, the economic situation has in a meaningful sense stabilized and improved since the grim days of the Arduous March. Mirror statistics provide some clues to how this was accomplished. We can begin by looking at reconstructions of North Korea's overall trends for merchandise imports.[28] (See Figure 1.) In 1990, the reported value of imports was nearly $3 billion (in current U.S. dollars). By 1998, the reported level had dropped below $1.2 billion, a catastrophic fall of over 60 percent. After 1998, however, North Korea's imports rebounded markedly. By 2001, the reported level exceeded $2 billion—and it appears to have risen still further in 2002, 2003, and 2004. To

Figure 1   **North Korean Merchandise Imports, 1989–2003**

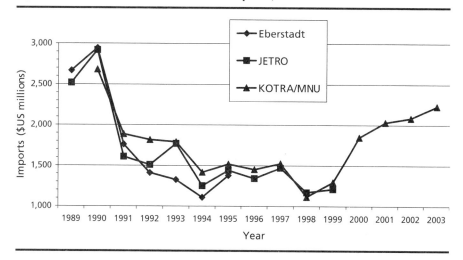

Source: Nicholas Eberstadt, "Economic Recovery in the DPRK: Status and Prospect," *International Journal of Korean Studies* IV, no. 1 (Fall/Winter 2000); JETRO; KOTRA; ROK Ministry of Unification (MNU).

judge by these numbers, North Korea was obtaining almost twice as much in the way of supplies of goods from abroad in 2003 than it had in 1998. In 2004, the dollar volume of North Korean merchandise imports was at the highest level registered since the collapse of the Soviet Union.

How did North Korea pay for this upsurge in imports? To judge by the mirror statistics, it did so not through any corresponding jump in export revenues. (See Figure 2.) Between 1990 and 1998, North Korea's reported merchandise exports collapsed, plummeting from about $2 billion to under $600 million. By 2004, these had recovered to a reported level of just under $1 billion. Nevertheless, by any absolute measure, the DPRK's reported export level remained remarkably low in 2004—less than half as high as it had been in 1990, and even lower than it had been in the bitter Arduous March year of 1997.

In a purely arithmetic sense, North Korea substantially increased its merchandise imports despite only modest improvements in its almost negligible levels of reported merchandise exports by appreciably increasing its reported balance of trade deficit. (See Figure 3.) In the Arduous March period—the famine years of 1995–98—North Korea's reported surfeit of imports over exports averaged under $600 million a year. By contrast, in the years 2000–2003—the Kangsong Taeguk era—the DPRK's reported trade deficit was over twice that high, averaging about $1.2 billion annually.

Figure 2 **North Korean Merchandise Exports, 1989–2002**

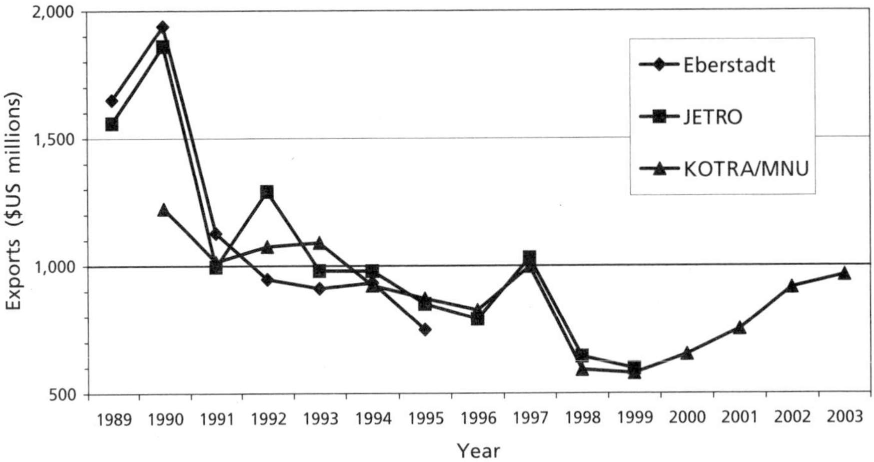

Source: Nicholas Eberstadt, "Economic Recovery in the DPRK: Status and Prospect," *International Journal of Korean Studies* IV, no. 1 (Fall/Winter 2000); JETRO; KOTRA; ROK Ministry of Unification (MNU).

How was this reported trade deficit financed? The answer is not self-evident. North Korea is a state with a commercial creditworthiness rating of approximately zero, having maintained for a generation its posture of defiant de facto default on the Western loans it contracted in the 1970s. Historically, the DPRK relied upon aid from its Communist allies—principally, the Soviet Union and China—to augment its imports. After the collapse of the USSR, China perforce emerged immediately as North Korea's principal foreign patron. Beijing's largesse extended beyond its officially and episodically announced subventions for Pyongyang. The DPRK's seemingly permanent merchandise trade deficit with China actually constitutes a broader and perhaps more accurate measure of Beijing's true aid levels for Pyongyang (insofar as neither party seems to think the sums accumulated in that imbalance will ever be corrected or repaid).

Implicit Chinese aid, however, cannot account for North Korea's import upsurge of 1998–2004. To the contrary: China's implicit aid to North Korea—i.e., its reported balance of trade deficit—fell during these years, dropping from about $340 million in 1998 to about $270 million in 2002. (In 2003, implicit Chinese aid rose to about $340 million, meaning that it again attained its nominal 1998 level.) North Korea's non-Chinese balance of trade deficit, by contrast, apparently soared upward. (See Figure 4.) Whereas in 1997 the DPRK reportedly managed to obtain a net of $50 million more of merchandise from abroad than its commercial exports would have paid for—after factoring out China—by 2003 the corresponding total was well over $900 million. Indeed, if China is removed from the picture, the line describing North Korea's net imports of

Figure 3   **North Korean Merchandise Trade Deficit, 1989–2002**

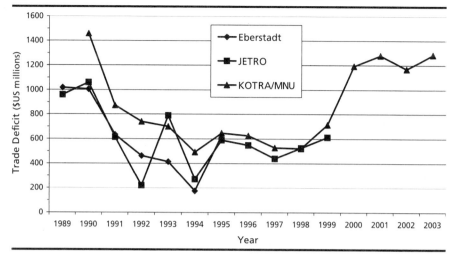

Source: Figures 1 and 2

supplies from abroad rises steadily upward between 1997 and 2003. It is this graphic that captures the economic essence of North Korea's shift from its Arduous March period to its Kangsong Taeguk epoch.

How was this jump in non-Chinese net imports financed? Unfortunately, we cannot be precise about this, since many of the sources of funds involve illicit transactions. North Korea's international counterfeiting, drug trafficking, and weapons/weapon technology sales all figure here, although the sums raised from those activities are a matter of some dispute. Nor do we yet know exactly how much of the South Korean taxpayers' money was furtively channeled from Seoul to Pyongyang during this period. One set of prosecutorial investigations has convicted former President Kim Dae Jung's national security adviser and several other aides of illegally transferring up to $500 million to Kim Jong Il's "Bureau 39" on the eve of the historic June 2000 Pyongyang summit.[29] The possibility of other unreported Seoul-to-Pyongyang payoffs during the 1998–2004 period cannot be ruled out—nor can the potential volume of any such attendant funds be determined.

Broadly speaking, the timing and the magnitude of the upswing in North Korea's non-Chinese net imports can be explained by the North Korean policies that were embraced during those years by the United States and its Northeast Asian allies. The year 1998 heralded the inauguration of ROK President Kim Dae Jung and the advent of South Korea's Sunshine Policy for détente and reconciliation with the North. In 1999, the United States followed suit with the unveiling of the "Perry Process" (i.e., the

Figure 4   **North Korea's Merchandise Trade Deficit, 1990–2003, Excluding Trade with China**

Source: Figures 1 and 2; PRC General Administration of Customs, *China's Customs Statistics*, various volumes.

"grand bargain" approach to dispute resolution with the DPRK that was hailed by the ROK Foreign Minister in 2000 as "based on our engagement policy toward North Korea"[30]). Between 1998 and mid-year 2004, according to one estimate from the U.S. Congressional Research Service, Seoul spent over $3 billion on legally approved "engagement" activities for North Korea.[31] Japan and the European Union (EU) both joined in the pursuit of "engagement" with North Korea during these years as well, although in differing degrees.

In their strict performance specifications—that is, in their defining actions, as opposed to their official rationales or stated intentions—the Sunshine Policy and the policy of peace and prosperity continue to mean organized activity by Western governments to mobilize transfers of public resources to the North Korean state. (Though this formulation may sound provocative, the particulars of those multilateral policies include the Hyundai/ROK National Tourism Office payments for vacations to Mt. Kumgang; the U.S. "inspection fee"[32] of 500,000 tons of food aid granted in 1999 for permission to visit a suspect underground North Korean facility at Kumchang-ri; the continuing food and fertilizer shipments from Seoul and the occasional food transfers from Japan; the secret payment for the historic June 2000 Pyongyang summit; and the new, albeit modest, flows of aid from EU countries in the wake of the flurry of diplomatic normalizations between Pyongyang and EU states in 2000–2001.) Thus it is perhaps not surprising that North Korea's financial fortunes should have improved so markedly since 1998.

It may sound perplexing and counterintuitive to hear the United States—the DPRK's longtime principal antagonist in the international arena—described as a major contemporary backer of the North Korean state. Yet this is in fact the case. Figures compiled by Mark Manyin of the Congressional Research Service provide the details. (See Table 1.) In the 1996–2002 period, Washington provided Pyongyang with just over $1 billion in food aid, concessional fuel oil, and medical supplies. (Interestingly enough, nearly $350 million of these resources were transferred in the years 2001 and 2002, under the aegis of the George W. Bush administration.)

Table 1 **U.S. Assistance to North Korea, 1995–2004**

Calendar or Fiscal Year	Food Aid (per FY)		KEDO Assistance (per CY*)	Medical Supplies (per FY*)	Total*
	Metric Tons	Commodity Value*			
1995	0	$ 0.00	$ 9.50	$ 0.20	$ 9.70
1996	19,500	8.30	22.00	0.00	30.30
1997	177,000	52.40	25.00	5.00	82.40
1998	200,000	72.90	50.00	0.00	122.90
1999	695,194	222.10	65.10	0.00	287.20
2000	265,000	74.30	64.40	0.00	138.70
2001	350,000	102.80	74.90	0.00	177.60
2002	207,000	82.40	90.50	0.00	172.90
2003	40,170	33.60	2.30	0.00	35.90
2004	60,000	n.a.	0.00	0.00	n.a.
Total	1,953,864	$ 648.80	$ 403.70	$ 5.20	$1,057.60

Sources: Figures for food aid and medical supplies from USAID and U.S. Department of Agriculture; KEDO (Korean Peninsula Energy Development Organization) figures from KEDO. Courtesy of Mark Manyin, Congressional Research Service.

* $ million

By the second half of the 1990s, North Korea's reliance on U.S. aid for financing its international purchases and supplies of goods was more pronounced than that of almost any other recipient of military, economic, or humanitarian assistance programs from the United States. This may be seen from Table 2. Total American aid allocations to key recipients Israel and Egypt for the five years 1996–2000, for example, amounted to 34 percent and 67 percent of those states' respective export earnings for the year 2000. U.S. 1996–2000 assistance to North Korea, by contrast, actually exceeded the DPRK's reported year-2000 commercial export revenues. (Since most American aid resources in Table 1 were not tallied in the international commercial ledgers upon which mirror statistics rely,[33] the DPRK's actual level of reliance upon non-Chinese net supplies from abroad was consistently higher for the years 1998–2003 than the graphic in Figure 4 suggests.) When considered in relation to the economy's evident capability to finance its international needs from its own regular commercial exports, Washington's aid lifeline for the DPRK in recent years looks more consequential than any of the bilateral assistance relationships that Washington arranged for treaty allies or friendly states in any spot on the globe.

Table 2 **U.S. Military and Economic Aid**

U.S. Foreign Aid Recipients, 1996–2000

	Total Military and Economic Aid, 1996–2000	Exports of Goods and Services, 2000	Total Aid as Percentage of Exports
Pakistan	$ 253,300,000	$ 9,575,000,064	2.65%
Ukraine	$ 743,400,000	$19,522,000,896	3.81%
El Salvador	$ 234,700,000	$ 3,645,691,392	6.44%
Nicaragua	$ 206,600,000	$ 962,200,000	21.47%
Jordan	$ 1,221,000,000	$ 3,534,132,736	34.55%
Israel	$14,880,000,000	$44,146,860,032	33.71%
Egypt	$10,595,200,000	$15,931,033,600	66.51%
Haiti	$ 485,000,000	$ 506,236,864	95.80%
DPRK	$ 661,500,000	$ 653,100,000	101.29%

Sources: Manyin (DPRK Total Aid, 1995–2002); KOTRA/Korean Ministry of Unification (DPRK Exports, 2002); USAID (Total Military and Economic Aid); World Development Indicators Database, 2002 (Export Revenues)

Historical Comparison to Taiwan and the ROK

	Total Military and Economic Aid[1]	Total Exports[2]	Total Aid as Percentage of Exports
DPRK	$ 1,021,800,000	$ 751,100,000	136.04%
Taiwan	$ 2,512,100,000	$ 220,750,000	1137.98%
ROK	$ 4,346,200,000	$ 56,000,000	7761.07%

Sources: Manyin (DPRK Total Aid, 1995–2002); KOTRA/Korean Ministry of Unification (DPRK Exports, 2002); USAID (Total Military and Economic Aid); and IMF International Financial Statistics (ROK and Taiwan Exports, 1962)

1. For DPRK, figures represent Total Aid for 1995–2002; for Taiwan and ROK, Total Aid for 1955–1962

2. For DPRK, Total Exports for 2002; for Taiwan and ROK, Total Exports for 1962

This is not the first time that American aid has helped a Korean state survive. After the 1953 Korean Armistice, Washington devoted tremendous resources to propping up and strengthening the Rhee Syngman government in Seoul—a regime fascinated with "aid-maximizing stratagems"[34] and manifestly disinterested in improving its then-miserable export performance. Judged by the metric of U.S. aid to recipient-country exports, the American Cold War project for preserving the ROK was vastly more intensive than Washington's post–Cold War programs sustaining the North Korean state. (See Table 2.) In the late 1950s, however, U.S. bilateral aid was the only "game in town" for states seeking Western largesse. If we were able to consider all the aid packages—overt, covert, or semiformal—that were extended to the DPRK by Western governments in the Kangsong Taeguk period, the ratio of such outside assistance to local commercial earnings would very likely begin to approach the scale of disproportion earlier witnessed in the late-1950s U.S. project to preserve the independence of the Republic of China (Taiwan).[35]

We will never know what would have happened if the United States and its allies in Asia and Europe had refrained from underwriting the survival of the North Korean state in the late 1990s and the early years of the present decade. (Such exercises in counterfactual speculation—"imaginary history," as their modern-day devotees know them[36]—can make for fascinating reading but are ultimately inconclusive.) We do not know, furthermore, how close North Korea came to the critical breaking point of an "economic collapse" during the Arduous March period between Kim Il Sung's death and Kim Jong Il's formal anointment. But the DPRK was failing economically in the mid-1990s—moving closer to the notional point of an economic collapse. In the late 1990s and the early years of the current decade, the prospect of economic collapse was diminished materially by an upsurge in provisions of goods from abroad—goods, in turn, that were financed in considerable measure by new flows of Western foreign aid.

Whether Western aid flows were the indispensable or instrumental factor in averting a North Korean collapse cannot yet be discussed with the historical knowledge and texture of the averted collapse of the Ottoman Empire in March 1915. However, the upsurge of Western aid for the DPRK under the Sunshine and Peace and Prosperity policies played a role—possibly a very important role—in reducing the risk of economic collapse and increasing the odds of survival for the North Korean state.

FINANCING STATE SURVIVAL IN THE DPRK: IDEOLOGICAL AND CULTURAL INFILTRATION AND MILITARY-FIRST POLITICS

Although North Korea's flirtation with economic collapse did not commence until after the disintegration of the Soviet bloc, the DPRK's relative (and perhaps its absolute) economic decline has been a long-term process and by some indicators was already well underway in the latter years of the Cold War. The DPRK's long-term trade performance vividly describes this record of economic decline. International trade bears directly upon the state's risk of economic collapse (and on systemic survival prospects as well). From an early 21st-century vantage point, we may not recall how steep and steady this long decline has been. The DPRK was not always known as an international trade basket case. In 1970, the levels of per capita exports in North and South Korea were roughly comparable ($21 vs. $27, in then-much-more-valuable dollars).[37] As late as 1980, North Korea's export profile, though hardly robust, was also not manifestly disfigured. In 1980, for example, the DPRK's level of reported per capita exports was just slightly higher than Turkey's, and over five times higher than India's. That same year North Korea's reported imports exceeded reported export revenues, but by a margin that was in keeping with the performance of other developing economies, including quite successful ones. The DPRK's 1980 ratio of exports to imports, for example, was just slightly higher than Chile's—but it was a bit lower than either Thailand's or South Korea's.

By 1990, the picture had worsened considerably. Despite a politically determined surge in exports to the USSR under the terms of the 1985–1990 Soviet-DPRK economic co-operation accord, per capita exports ranked in the lowest quartile of the world's econo-mies—in a league with Equatorial Guinea and Kenya. The ratio of exports to imports had risen, so that North Korea was among the quartile of states where this imbalance was greatest. By 1990, North Korea's disproportion between import and export revenues al-ready ranked next to such heavily aid-dependent economies as Jordan and Ghana.

By 2000, the DPRK was an outlier within the world system. That year, the DPRK's re-ported per capita export level would have ranked 158th among the 168 countries tracked by the World Bank's World Development Indicators: below Chad and at less than half of India's level. Reported per capita exports in Turkey were now nearly twenty-five times as high as in the DPRK. Although the nominal level of per capita ex-ports for the world was nearly 2.5 times higher in 2000 than in 1980,[38] North Korea's nominal reported per capita export level fell by almost two-thirds over those years. At the same time, North Korea's imbalance between reported imports and export earn-ings (with the former nearly three times as great as the latter) ranked among the ten most extreme cases recorded that year. A glaring discrepancy between imports and ex-ports did not automatically betoken aid dependence. Several outliers, Lesotho and West Bank/Gaza among them, highlight the importance of remittances in the local balance of payments. But North Korea's ratio of reported commercial export revenues to reported imports was even lower in 2000 than in such all-but-permanent wards of the ODA community as Haiti and Burkina Faso.

In terms of trade performance and patterns of international finance, North Korea's downward trajectory and its current straits (that is, its structural descent from Turkey to Haiti in just one generation) represents, in part, the misfortune of circumstance. Clearly, the sudden and unexpected downfall of the Soviet bloc was a disaster for the North Korean economic system: a disaster, indeed, from which the DPRK economy has not yet recovered. But North Korea's aberrant and seemingly dysfunctional trade regimen is also a result of a conscious purpose, deliberate design, and considered offi-cial effort. There is deeply embedded regime logic in the DPRK's tangential and pre-carious relationship with the world economy. Far from being irrational, it is based on careful and cool-headed calculations about regime survival.

Consider the DPRK's trade performance over the past generation with the twenty-nine countries the IMF terms the "advanced economies."[39] Between 1980 and 2000 the total size of the import market for this collectivity grew from about $1.8 trillion to about $6.1 trillion. The DPRK is precluded from exporting any appreciable volume of goods to the United States by Washington's thicket of sanctions and restrictions against U.S.-DPRK commerce, and America offers the world's single largest import market. But if we exclude the United States from the picture, the remaining "advanced economy" market for foreign imports is vast and (at least in nominal terms) rapidly expanding—growing from about $1.5 billion in 1980 to $4.6 billion in 2000. DPRK exports to this group, however, remained negligible and stagnant over these decades, even after the loss of Soviet bloc markets added some urgency to cultivating new sources of commercial export revenue. In 1980 and 1990, North Korea's reported sales to this grouping totaled roughly $430 million and roughly $470 million, respectively. In 2000, the reported aggregate was about $560 million, but that total may have been inflated somewhat by an unusual and perhaps questionable $60 million in North Korean imports recorded that year by Spain. Even accepting that year's exceptional Spanish data, the real level of North Korean exports to these "capitalist" countries would have been substantially lower in 2000 than it had been two decades earlier.[40]

Pyongyang's remarkably poor long-term performance in the advanced economies' huge markets is no accident. Instead it is a direct consequence of official DPRK policy and doctrine—most particularly, Pyongyang's concept of "ideological and cultural infiltration." Official North Korean pronouncements relentlessly decry the dangers of this phenomenon, which is said to be a technique by which outsiders attempt to undermine the foundations of established Communist states. A recent declamation gives the flavor of the general argument:

> It is the imperialists' old trick to carry out ideological and cultural infiltration prior to their launching of an aggression openly. Their bourgeois ideology and culture are reactionary toxins to paralyze people's ideological consciousness. Through such infiltration, they try to paralyze the independent consciousness of other nations and make them spineless. At the same time, they work to create illusions about capitalism and promote lifestyles among them based on the law of the jungle, in an attempt to induce the collapse of socialist and progressive nations. The ideological and cultural infiltration is their silent, crafty and villainous method of aggression, intervention and domination. . . .
>
> Through "economic exchange" and personnel interchange programs too, the imperialists are pushing their infiltration. . . . Exchange and cooperation activities in the economic and cultural fields have been on the rise since the beginning of the new century. The imperialists are making use of these activities as an important lever to push the infiltration of bourgeois ideology and culture. . . .
>
> The imperialists' ideological and cultural infiltration, if tolerated, will lead to the collapse and degeneration of society, to disorder and chaos, and even to the loss of the gains of the revolution. The collapse of socialism in the 20th century—and the revival of capitalism in its place—in some countries gave us the serious lesson that social deterioration begins with ideological degeneration and confusion on the ideological front, throws every other front of society into chaos and, consequently, all the gains of the revolution go down the drain eventually.[41]

DPRK party lecture notes published in South Korea late in 2002 put the point more succinctly:

> The capitalists' ideological and cultural infiltration will never cease, and the struggle against it will continue, as long as the imperialists continue to exist in the world. . . . The great leader, Kim Jong Il, pointed out the following: "Today, the imperialists and reactionaries are tenaciously scheming to blow the wind of bourgeois liberalism into us." . . . Under these circumstances, if we turn away from reality and we regard it as someone else's problem, what will happen? People will ideologically degenerate and weaken; cracks will develop in our socialist ideological position; and, in the end, our socialism will helplessly collapse. A case in point is the bitter lesson drawn from the miserable situations of the former Soviet Union and Eastern European countries.[42]

Economic exchange with the "capitalist" world is thus explicitly and officially regarded by Pyongyang as a process that unleashes powerful, unpredictable, and subversive forces—forces that ultimately erode the authority of socialist states. Viewed from this perspective, North Korea's record of trade performance vis-à-vis the advanced market economies is not a record of failure—that is, failure to integrate into the world economy—but rather a mark of success—effective containment of a potentially lethal security threat.

Moreover, the DPRK's public misgivings about "ideological and cultural infiltration" are longstanding, almost precisely paralleling the state's record of minimal export outreach to advanced market economies over the past generation. Although DPRK pronouncements about ideological and cultural infiltration have attracted some attention abroad since the downfall of Soviet bloc socialism, the slogan itself was not a response to that defining historical event. To the contrary, the North Korean leadership had been highlighting the dangers of that tendency for at least a decade before the final collapse of the Soviet Union. At the Sixth Congress of the Korean Workers' Party in 1980, for example, Kim Il Sung inveighed against the dangers of "cultural infiltration." And by 1981, he was urging North Korea's "workers and trade union members" to "combat the ideological and cultural infiltration of the imperialists and their subversive moves and sabotage."[43]

It is true that official directives from Pyongyang have from time to time discussed the desirability of significantly increasing the DPRK's volume of international trade. Against such comments, North Korea's extraordinary and continuing weakness in export performance may seem especially curious. But Pyongyang's conspicuous neglect of the revenue potential from trade with advanced market economies is not to be explained away as a prolonged fit of absent-mindedness. Instead, it speaks to fundamental and abiding calculations in Pyongyang's strategy for state survival.

If staying out of the poisonous embrace of the world economy is viewed by DPRK leadership as an imperative for state survival, a corollary question inevitably arises: how can North Korea generate sufficient international resources to forestall economic collapse? To date, Pyongyang's answer has been through nonmarket transactions. The DPRK has always pursued an "aid-seeking" international economic strategy—but in the post–Soviet bloc era, the particulars of that approach have mutated. In the Kangsong Taeguk era, North Korea's main tactics for generating international resources are viewed through the prism of the current state campaign for "Military-First Politics" (Songun Chongchi).

Like the concept of ideological and cultural infiltration, the theory and recommended practice of Military-First Politics have received a tremendous amount of airtime in the North Korean media over the past five years. As a long official analysis in March 2003 instructed, it was a renewed emphasis on military development that enabled North Korea to conclude its Arduous March and to step onto the pathway to power and prosperity:

> Today, the peoples' struggle for their nations' independent development and prosperity is waged in an environment different from that of the last century. . . . In building a state in our era, it is essential to beef up the main force of the nation and fortify the revolutionary base, and, in this regard, it is most important to build up powerful military might. In today's world, without powerful military might, no country can . . . achieve development and prosperity.

> During . . . "the Arduous March" in our history, great Comrade Kim Jong Il firmly believed that the destiny of the people and the future of the revolution hinged on the barrel of a gun, and that we could break through the difficulties and lead the revolution to victory only by depending on the Army. . . . Through the arduous practice in which the Army was put to the fore and the unheard-of trials were overcome, the revolutionary philosophy that the barrel of a gun was precisely the revolution and the barrel of a gun was precisely the victory of socialism was originated. . . .

> Our theory on the construction of a powerful state . . . is the embodiment of the profound truth that the base of national strength is military might, and the dignity and might of a country hinges on the barrel of a gun. . . . In a powerful state, the defense industry takes a leading and key position in the economy. . . . Today, by firmly adhering to the principle of putting prime effort into the defense industry and, based on this, by developing the overall economy ceaselessly, our party is brilliantly resolving the issue of consolidating the national strength of a powerful state.[44]

How exactly does military power conduce to prosperity? A statement the following month hinted at the answer:

> A country's development and the placement of importance on the military are linked as one. . . . *Once we lay the foundations for a powerful self-sustaining national defense industry, we will be able to rejuvenate all economic fields, to include light industry and agriculture and enhance the quality of the people's lives.*[45]

This is a fascinating, and revealing, formulation. For most states, a country's defense outlays are regarded as a weight that the value-adding sectors of the national economy must shoulder (thus the phrase "military burden"). The North Korean leadership, however, evidently entertains the concept of a "self-sustaining" defense sector—implying that Pyongyang views its military activities as generating resources, and not simply absorbing them. In the enunciated view of North Korean leadership, the DPRK's military sector is the key not only to unlocking the resources necessary to finance its own considerable needs, but to financing the recovery of the national economy as a whole.

The operational details of this approach seem straightforward. While forswearing any appreciable export revenues from legitimate commerce with advanced market economies, North Korean policy today seems to be banking on the possibility of financing state survival by exporting strategic insecurity to the rest of the world. In part, such dividends are derived from exports of merchandise (e.g., missile sales or potential transfer of WMD technology). But these revenues also depend heavily on what might be described as an export of services: in this case, military extortion services (what we might better call "revenue-sensitive threat reduction services") based upon Pyongyang's nuclear development and ballistic missile programs.

The export of strategic insecurity, in its different components, helps account for much of the upsurge in North Korea's unexplained surfeit of imports over commercial export revenues since 1998, especially when Western aid policies in recent years can be described as appeasement-motivated.[46] In an important tactical sense, that approach has enjoyed a success, since it has facilitated state survival under imposing constraints. But the territory demarcated by ideological and cultural infiltration on one side and Military-First Politics on the other is also a no-man's land: an inherently unstable niche in which survival is utterly contingent and sustained development utterly unlikely. North Korea's current strategic policy, in short, may be deferring the question of economic collapse, but it has not yet answered it.

AVOIDING ECONOMIC COLLAPSE THROUGH ECONOMIC REFORM?

If the DPRK is currently sustaining its system through aid-seeking stratagems grounded in military menace, it has settled upon a particularly meager and highly uncertain mode of state finance. It is not clear that it generates sufficient funding to maintain (much less improve) the nation's aging and badly decayed industrial and transport infrastructure. Moreover, the stratagem may fail at any time for any number of reasons (for example, donor "aid fatigue," DPRK miscalculation, or an external push for "regime change" in Pyongyang). Under these circumstances, a more secure and ultimately satisfactory path for avoiding economic collapse and preserving the sovereignty of the North Korean state might be a pragmatic reorientation of policy, a reorientation in the name of promoting sustained growth. In some variants of this argument, China and Vietnam have already demonstrated that it is feasible for Marxist-Leninist governments in Asia to execute a shift to an outward-oriented economic regimen, to achieve rapid economic growth, and to maintain leadership authority and political stability.

Whether "reform" and "outward orientation" could be consonant with the preservation of unquestioned power for North Korea's leadership is a question that will not detain us here.[47] Nor will we be diverted by a discussion of the potential problems and preconditions of any reform worthy of the name under contemporary North Korean conditions. Instead we will briefly address two practical and subsidiary questions. First, how far have North Korea's much-discussed reforms progressed to date? Second, if the DPRK were truly moving in the direction of reform and self-sustaining growth, how would we tell and what would we see?

North Korea's Economic Reforms to Date

Predictions that the DPRK would soon be embracing economic reform come from a family tree that is, if anything, even more prolific and older in lineage than predictions about imminent or eventual DPRK collapse. Scholars and analysts have been detecting quiet signs of reform and opening in the North Korean system since at least the 1980s.[48] The intensity of these premonitions typically waxed and waned according to the current temperatures in Pyongyang's relations with Washington and Seoul.[49]

In July 2002, however, Pyongyang enacted a package of macroeconomic policy changes that marked a notable departure from DPRK practices over the previous generation. Moreover, North Korea sometimes describes these measures as "economic reform"[50]— a term the DPRK had vigorously rejected heretofore, on the understanding that no reforms were needed for the existing DPRK system. Some observers see these changes as evidence that far-reaching or even systemic economic reforms are now under way in North Korea. These examples include the emergence (or reemergence) of small markets for food and consumer goods in many urban and rural localities; construction of a number of commercial billboards in Pyongyang and environs; an announcement that North Korea will soon open a large-scale supermarket; and an indication in North Korean media in June 2004 that the Dear Leader made a positive reference to "the principle of profitability."[51]

Unfortunately, the meaning of this trickle of anecdotes is a matter very much in the eye of the beholder. In July 2004, for example, news reports from South Korea claimed that the DPRK had been caught selling a bogus knockoff of Viagra overseas[52]—should this, too, be taken as proof of a new spirit of entrepreneurship and market awareness and profit orientation? Rather than descend into the swamp of semiotics, it is more fruitful to attempt a more structural assessment of North Korea's recent program of deliberately induced economic change.

The specifics of the July 2002 measures have been described in detail elsewhere.[53] Scholars and analysts have offered some initial assessments of the significance and portent of these policy changes.[54] By comparison with North Korea's economic policy adjustments since the late 1960s, these measures may indeed seem quite bold. Yet this only attests to how impoverished our expectations for DPRK policy have become over the decades. The July 2002 package of economic changes are rather modest, either by comparison with economic reforms undertaken in other troubled economies, or by comparison with the job that needs doing in the DPRK.

In practical terms, the July 2002 package—consumer price increases, wage hikes, currency devaluation, and ration system devolution—accomplished one important function: it re-monetized a limited portion of the DPRK domestic economy. By the late 1980s, the DPRK was already shockingly demonetized. Back-of-the-envelope calculations for 1987 suggest that the wage bill in that year would have amounted to less than a third of North Korea's official net material product. Over the following decade and a half, the role of the national currency in domestic economic activity was progressively diminished. By the turn of the century, North Korea was perhaps the modern world's most completely demonetized economy—excepting only Khmer Rouge Cambodia, where for a time, by decree, money was abolished altogether.

The reemergence of money in North Korean economic life—and with it, the re-emergence of a limited measure of open-market activity—mark an incontestable and important improvement for the DPRK's tiny consumer sector. But it is important to recognize that the July 2002 package does not represent an unambiguous move toward market principles. To the contrary: remonetization of the domestic economy is a sine qua non for resurrecting the DPRK's badly broken central planning mechanism ("a planned economy without planning," in Mitsuhiko Kimura's apt phrase[55])—which has not managed to launch another multiyear national plan since 1993.

Limited remonetization of the domestic economy, furthermore, does not signify transformation of the DPRK's badly distorted production structure. To the contrary: the manifestly limited supply-response of the DPRK economy to the July 2002 measures is indicated, on one hand, by the subsequent steep drop in the black market exchange rate for the DPRK won,[56] and on the other by Pyongyang's hurried introduction, barely ten months after the July 2002 package, of new "people's life bonds"—worthless, utterly illiquid, and involuntarily assigned—in lieu of wages for workers or payments for enterprises.[57]

To be sure, the limited reintroduction of money in the DPRK domestic economy may elicit some supply response—for example, a Leibenstein-style increase in "x-efficiency."[58] But without the possibility of a reallocation of state resources in accordance with new demand conditions, the supply response must perforce be tepid and superficial. Thus, the World Food Program (WFP) has warned prospective donors that North Korea faces an imminent return to mass hunger barring an influx of new food aid into the relief pipeline[59]—heartening signs of newly sprouted "people's markets" notwithstanding. The contrast is not a contradiction, but rather a faithful reflection of the scope and limits of the July 2002 reforms.

Thus, the July 2002 reforms do not necessarily stave off the specter of DPRK economic collapse. Nor do they have any obvious or direct bearing on the prospects for a shift to China-style or Vietnam-style export-led growth. Contrasting North Korea's patterns of trade performance over the past generation with those of China and Vietnam illustrates this consideration. (See Figures 5 and 6.) Vietnam began its push for export orientation when its Soviet subsidies abruptly ended, whereas North Korea's export performance markedly worsened, and its aid dependence increased, after 1991. Though still predominantly agrarian societies, Vietnam and China both manage to export far more merchandise on a per capita basis today than does the ostensibly industrialized DPRK (precisely because of the linkages and supply-response mechanisms that the DPRK has assiduously prevented from taking root). The DPRK has not even begun to tinker with the macro-policies, or to promote the micro-institutions, that would permit a China- or Vietnam-style export response.[60] Thus, for the time being, economic survival through export orientation is simply not in the cards for North Korea.

Figure 5 **Per Capita Exports, 1977–2002**

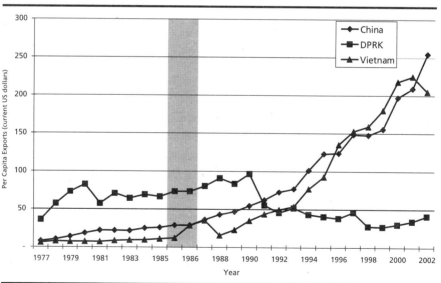

What Would a Genuine Reform and Opening Look Like?

Instead of sketching the full contours of a DPRK transition to sustainable export-led growth, we will focus on three essential and inextricably linked features: the outward opening itself; military demobilization; and normalization of relations with the ROK.[61]

Figure 6   **Per Capita Exports, 1977–2002**

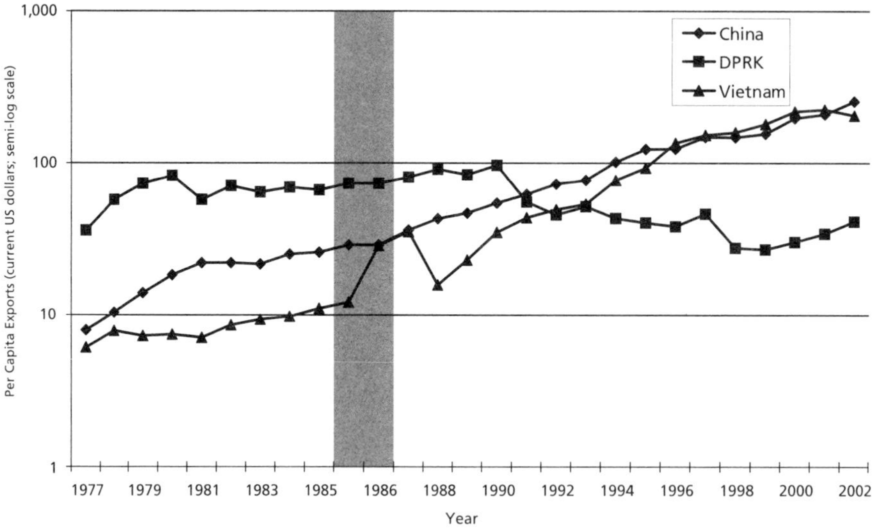

Economic Opening

If Pyongyang were to embark upon a genuine move toward an economic opening, what initial signs would outsiders be able to see? Some of these might include: (1) meaningful departure from old "economic" themes, and new dialogue about economic issues, in DPRK propaganda and guidance organs; (2) doctrinal reorientation regarding the treatment of profit-generating transactions in official DPRK pronouncements, especially profits involving transactions with foreign concerns; (3) an attempt by the DPRK to settle its longstanding international "debt default" problems;[62] (4) a move toward greater economic transparency, that is, the publication of economic and social statistics describing the North Korean domestic situation; and (5) serious attempts to promulgate a legal framework for potential foreign investors that might assist in attracting profit-seeking overseas entrepreneurs to North Korean soil. Although some observers may see glimmers of conditions (1) and (2), none of these "blinker lights" are yet flashing brightly and consistently.

Military Demobilization

Military demobilization would represent a critical aspect of a North Korean program of "reform" and "opening." A dismantling of Pyongyang's WMD programs would indicate that North Korean leadership was committed to earning its living from activities other than international military extortion, and reallocation of resources from the hypertrophied military to the civilian sectors would permit much more potentially productive economic activity in the DPRK. To date, there is little evidence that North Korea has ever voluntarily abjured any new instrument of military force that might possibly lie within its grasp. Indeed, such a renunciation today would seem fundamentally inconsistent with the state's established policies of Kangsong Taeguk and Military-First politics. Moreover, North Korea's commitment to developing weapons of mass destruction was implicitly reaffirmed in the exhortation that "We should hold fast to the military-first politics and *build up our military strength in every possible way*"[63][emphasis added].

If North Korea were to head on a different road regarding proliferation, the first clear sign of a change in attitude would be a new stance toward outside verification of North Korean WMD activities. However, Pyongyang maintains that U.S. calls for verification conceal "a dark ulterior motive to thoroughly investigate our national defense and military bases . . . [a plot to] completely dig out our interior organs [sic]"[64] and that "the issue [of verification] can never be on the agenda for DPRK-U.S. talks."[65]

Normalization of DPRK-ROK Relations

The DPRK cannot execute a successful economic opening unless it demobilizes, and it cannot demobilize unless it comes to terms with the right of the Republic of Korea to coexist with it on the Korean Peninsula. Consequently, an indispensable marker of movement toward reform and opening would be a change in North Korea's official stance concerning the legitimacy of the ROK. If North Korea displayed a new attitude toward the legitimacy of the ROK, the indications of this change would be direct and unmistakable: its highest figures and its official media would simply disclose that they were prepared to accept the existence of the South Korean state, that they recognized the ROK's right to conduct its own foreign policy, and that they respected (while respectfully disagreeing with) Seoul's decision to maintain a military alliance with the United States. No such disclosures have been offered to date.

In sum: There is little evidence that North Korea has yet embarked upon a path to "reform" and "opening," with all the transformations in polity this path would foreshadow. That oft-discussed strategy for economic survival appears, as yet, to be an option not chosen by the DPRK's own leadership. How long the DPRK can survive on its current trajectory is anyone's guess. My personal guesses on this score have admittedly been off the mark. But if our analysis is correct, the specter of an economic collapse is a ghost that haunts the DPRK to this very day—and one that will not be exorcised unless or until North Korea's leadership agrees to undertake what, in a very different context, they have called "a bold switch-over." Whether Pyongyang accepts such a challenge remains to be seen.

NOTES

This is an extended and revised version of a paper first prepared for an American Enterprise Institute for Public Policy (AEI)–Korean Economic Institute (KEI)–Korea Institute for International Economic Policy (KIEP) conference in February 2004.

1. Cf. Marcus Noland, *Korea After Kim Jong-il* (Washington, D.C.: IIE Policy Analyses in International Economics no. 71, January 2004), pp. 12–19.

2. Perhaps most memorably, including this quote from my 1995 study, *Korea Approaches Reunification*: "There is no reason at present to expect a reign by Kim Jong Il to be either stable or long."

3. Cf. the large interdisciplinary State Failure Task Force, the U.S. government–funded undertaking that spent six years attempting to devise econometric formulae by which to predict political upheaval or breakdown. (The report from this project can be accessed electronically from the University of Maryland's Center for International Development and Conflict Management, at www.cidcm.umd .edu/inscr/stfail.)

4. The distinction between art and science is elucidated in many places, but perhaps nowhere better and more clearly than in the writings of Michael Oakeshott. Cf. Michael Oakeshott, *Rationalism in Politics and Other Essays* (Indianapolis, Ind.: Liberty, 1991).

5. This is not to gainsay the utility of particular new mathematical or quantitative techniques used by particular contemporary stock-pickers and investors (e.g., Black-Sholes option pricing models, etc.). Some principals have enjoyed fantastic success with these tools and have amassed enormous personal wealth as a result. The point is that these successes are not *generalizable*, as scientific knowledge in principle always is. George Soros and Warren Buffett are practitioners of art, not science (as they themselves have said).

6. One scholar who has explored aspects of this asymmetry is Timur Kuran. See in particular Timur Kuran, "Sparks and Prairie Fires: A Theory of Unanticipated Political Revolution," *Public Choice* 61, nos. 1–2 (April 1989), pp. 41–78; idem, "The East European Revolution of 1989: Is It Surprising That We Were Surprised?" *American Economic Review* 81, no. 1, pp. 121–25; idem, "Now or Never: The Element of Surprise in the East European Revolutions of 1989," *World Politics* 44, no. 1 (October 1991), pp. 7–48; and idem, "The Inevitability of Future Revolutionary Surprises," *American Journal of Sociology* 100, no. 4 (May 1995), pp. 1528–51).

7. For an inventory and analysis, see Seymour Martin Lipset and Georgy Bence, "Anticipations of the Failure of Communism," *Theory and Society* 23, no. 2 (April 1994), pp. 169–210.

8. For example, R.W. Johnson, *Can South Africa Survive?* (New York: Oxford University Press, 1977). Seventeen years before the RSA peace transition to pan-racial democracy, Johnson explained why this occurrence was an impossibility.

9. Cf. Andrei Amalrik, *Will the Soviet Union Survive to 1984?* (New York: Harper & Row, 1970). In a bitter historical irony, the USSR *did* last to 1984—but Amalrik did not.

10. Christopher de Bellaigue, "Turkey's Hidden Past," *New York Review of Books*, 8 March 2001.

11. For some background on the long relative decline of the Ottoman economy, see Suraiya Faroqhi, Bruce McGowan, Donald Quataert and Sevket Pamuk, *An Economic and Social History of the Ottoman Empire: Volume Two, 1600–1914* (New York: Cambridge University Press, 1994).

12. An indication of that decline may be gleaned from estimates by the economic historian Angus Maddison. In 1870, by his reckoning, per capita GDP for modern-day Turkey would have been $825 (in 1990 international dollars)—or about 39 percent the contemporary level for western Europe. By 1913—on the eve of World War I—Turkey's per capita GDP had risen to an estimated $1213: but its relative standing had dropped to just 34 percent of the western Europe level. [Derived from Angus Maddison, *The World Economy: Historical Statistics* (Paris: OECD Development Research Centre, 2003), pp. 61, 156.]

13. Elliot Cohen and John Gooch, *Military Misfortunes: The Anatomy of Failure in War* (New York: Vintage Press, 1990).

14. Stephens has surmised that de Roebeck's "naval timidity" can be explained in part by "the high regard for battleships at that time. The loss of even one battleship was considered a national tragedy, more so than the loss of several thousand troops." Lt. Col. Cortez D. Stephens, "Gallipoli—What Went Right?" *Marine Corps Gazette* 77, no. 10 (October 1993), pp. 73–77, citation at 74.

15. David Fromkin, *A Peace to End All Peace: Creating the Modern Middle East 1914–1922* (New York: Henry Holt and Company, 1989), p. 154.

16. Alan Moorehead, *Gallipoli* (London: Hamish Hamilton, 1956), p. 72.

17. David Fromkin, *A Peace to End All Peace*, p. 152.

18. Moorehead, *Gallipoli*, p. 77. In recent years a revisionist literature has challenged the notion that the Turkish and German defenders were critically short of ammunition. See, for example, Edward J. Erickson, "One More Push: Forcing the Dardanelles in March 1915," *Journal of Strategic Studies* 24, no. 3 (September 2001), pp. 158–76. The literature does not account for, or explain, Ottoman and German military officers' own contemporary reports—and subsequent reminiscences—to the contrary.

19. Lieutenant Colonel S. H. Watson, "The Gallipoli Blunder," *The Army Quarterly and Defence Journal* 112, no. 2 (April 1982), pp. 178–83, citation at p. 179.

20. Cited in Henry W. Nevinson, *The Dardanelles Campaign* (London: Nisbet & Co., 1929), p. 62.

21. Moorehead, *Gallipoli*, p. 74.

22. Fromkin, *A Peace to End All Peace*, p. 154.

23. Here again, we note the role of asymmetries of information in the outsider's analytical failure—circumstances that tend to be most acute in times of hostility, with little regular communication between the actors in question, and with strategic deception being actively practiced in the quest for state survival.

24. Nicholas Eberstadt, *The End of North Korea* (Washington, D.C.: AEI Press, 1999).

25. Cf. Jack Hirshleifer, *Economic Behavior in Adversity* (Chicago: University of Chicago Press, 1987).

26. See Daniel Goodkind and Loraine West, "The North Korean Famine and Its Demographic Impact," *Population and Development Review* 27, no. 2 (June 2001), pp. 219–38. Goodkind and West's modeling conjectures center on a range of 600,000 to 1,000,000 deaths for the late 1990s.

27. Not too long thereafter, the ROK Bank of Korea (BOK) declared that North Korea's economy had resumed economic growth. BOK reports have suggested positive growth in the DPRK for 1999 and every subsequent year. Whether the BOK analysis can withstand scrutiny is another question. For a skeptical look, see Nicholas Eberstadt, "Prospects for Economic Recovery: Perceptions and Evidence," in the 2001 edition of the Korea Economic Institute's *Joint U.S.-Korean Academic Studies*, pp. 1–25.

28. The methods used here in reconstructing North Korea's patterns of merchandise trade are outlined in Eberstadt, "Prospects for Economic Recovery."

29. For some of the details, see Andrew Ward, "Six Convicted for Korea Payments," 27 September 2003, p. 9; Samuel Lem, "Seoul Court Convicts Six over Summit Funds," *International Herald Tribune*, 27 September 2003, p. 2. U.S. government researchers place these surreptitious payments to Pyongyang at a "mere" $200 million: see footnote 32 below.

30. "Seoul Firmly Backs 'Perry Process,'" *Korea Times*, 7 February 2000.

31. Mark E. Manyin, "Foreign Assistance to North Korea," Congressional Research Service, CRS-RL31785, 26 May 2005, Appendix A, p. 38. Note that this number, for a variety of reasons, is not a measure of *actual economic support* for North Korea. It does, however, suggest the scale of the subsidies in question.

32. Pyongyang's description of the transaction.

33. In theory, none of these American assistance resources should be included in "mirror statistics"—but real-world practice is more haphazard. U.S. heavy fuel oil shipped to the DPRK in South Korean vessels, for example, has often been registered as "North-South trade" in the ROK Ministry of National Unification's inter-Korean trade statistics.

34. In the felicitous phrase of David C. Cole and Princeton Lyman, *Korean Development: The Interplay of Politics and Economics* (Cambridge, Mass.: Harvard University Press, 1971).

35. To be clear here: the earlier Taiwan effort would have undoubtedly been the more aid-intensive by our selected metric; while lower, however, the aid intensity of the recent DPRK arrangements would perhaps fall within the same approximate order of magnitude.

36. Interestingly enough, a growing number of eminent historians and respected social scientists seem to be engaging in this pastime. See, for example, Nelson W. Polsby, ed., *What If? Explorations in Social-science Fiction* (Lexington, Mass.: Lewis, 1982); Niall Ferguson, ed., *Virtual History: Alternatives and Counterfactuals* (London: Picador, 1997); and Robert Cowley, *What Ifs? Of American History: Eminent Historians Imagine What Might Have Been* (New York: G.P. Putnam, 2003).

37. Nicholas Eberstadt, *Korea Approaches Reunification* (Armonk, N.Y.: M.E. Sharpe, 1995), chap. 1.

38. Global calculations derived from IMF World Economic Outlook Database (September 2003), www.imf.org/external/pubs/ft/2003/02/data/index.htm; and UN Population Division World Population Prospects Database, esa.un.org/unpp.

39. This grouping includes twenty-four of the current thirty OECD members (omitting Czech Republic, Hungary, Mexico, Poland, Slovak Republic, and Turkey) and five others: Cyprus, Hong Kong, Israel, Singapore, and Taiwan.

40. Between 1980 and 2000 the U.S. producer price index—the more appropriate deflator for international tradables—rose by 51 percent. Using that deflator, North Korea's inflation-adjusted export volume to this grouping of countries would have declined by about 16 percent between 1980 and 2000. Note that the grouping includes South Korea and figures in inter-Korean trade.

41. *Nodong Sinmun,* 20 April 2003, translated as "DPRK Organ Scores 'Imperialists' for Ideological, Cultural Infiltration Schemes," U.S. Foreign Broadcast Information Service (hereafter, FBIS), AFS Document Number KPP20030429000057.

42. *Chosun Ilbo,* 20 December 2002; translated as "'Full Text' of DPRK Lecture Program in Capitalists' 'Ideological and Cultural Infiltration,'" *FBIS,* AFS Document Number KPP20021222000016.

43. *KCNA,* 30 November 1981, reprinted as "Kim Il-sung's Speech to Trade Union Congress," *BBC Summary of World Broadcasts,* FE/6896/B/1, 3 December 1981.

44. *Nodong Sinmun,* 21 March 2003; translated text available on Nautilus Institute's website at www.nautilus.org/pub/ftp/napsnet/special _reports/MilitaryFirstDPRK.txt.

45. *Nodong Sinmun,* 3 April 2003; translated text available on Nautilus website at www.nautilus.org/pub/ftp/napsnet/special_reports/MilitaryFirstDPRK.txt. Emphasis added.

46. Even ostensibly humanitarian food aid transfers to North Korea are informed by the reality of military extortion: think in particular of Kumchang-ri, and more generally whether the opaque rules under which food relief is administered in the DPRK would be tolerated by the international donor community in any other setting.

47. However, both Robert Scalapino and Ezra Vogel have suggested that North Korea might plausibly evolve from today's hermetic *juche* totalitarian system to a more familiar, Park Chung Hee-type authoritarian state—and the judgment of these two leading American authorities on modern Asia should be respectfully weighed in this consideration. Robert Scalapino, *The Last Leninists: The Uncertain Future of Asia's Communist States* (Washington, D.C.: CSIS, 1992); Ezra Vogel, personal communications with the author, 1994–2004.

48. See, for example, Hy-sang Lee, "North Korea's Closed Economy: The Hidden Opening," *Asian Survey* 28, no. 12 (December 1988), pp. 1264–1279; Kongdan Oh, "North Korea's Response to the World: Is the Door Ajar?" *RAND Paper Series* P-7616 (1990); and John Merrill, "North Korea's Halting Efforts at Economic Reform," in *North Korea in Transition,* ed. Chong-Sik Lee and Se-Hee Yoo (Berkeley, Calif.: Institute of East Asian Studies, 1991), pp. 139–53. Each of these papers was written and initially presented in the 1980s.

49. The announcement of the Pyongyang North-South Summit occasioned an especially vigorous pulsation of such premonitions. Thus, for example, Marcus Noland in June 2000: "The secret visit to Beijing last month by Kim Jong Il supports the argument that this is the real deal and that the North Koreans are serious about opening to the outside world." [Marcus Noland, "The Meaning in the Meeting of the Two Koreas: Out of Isolation," *Washington Post,* 12 June 2000, p. A21.] This was before the "outside world" had learned the true details of the "real deal" underpinning that historic summit.

50. Thus SPA President Kim Yong Nam in August 2002, in a conversation with UN officials: "We are reactivating the whole field of the national economy. . . . We are reforming the economic system on the principle of profitability." [Cited in United Nations, *Consolidated Inter-Agency Appeal 2003: Democratic People's Republic of Korea* (November 2002), p. 127, available electronically at www .reliefweb.nt/appeals/2003/files/dprk03.dpf.] Note, however, that the term "reform" has not yet been embraced by the DPRK media, which still treats the concept as anathema. This March 2003 formulation from *Minju Chosun* remains representative: "Even though the imperialists are trying to stifle our economy by inducing it to 'reform' and 'opening,' our economic management is being improved without deviating even an inch from socialist principles." [*Minju Chosun,* 6 March 2003, translated as "DPRK Cabinet Organ Discusses Improving Economic Management," *FBIS,* AFS Document Number KPP 20030313000122.]

51. See, among many such items, "North Korea's Largest Supermarket Will Open at the End of 2004" (KOTRA North Korean Team, 27 April 2004, available electronically at crm.kotra.or.kr/main/common_bbs/notice_read_nk.php3?board_id=21&pnum=899711&cnum=0); Bertil Lintner, "North Korea; Shop Till You Drop," *Far Eastern Economic Review*, 13 May 2004; and James Brooke, "Kim Jong Il Now Extols the Virtues of Profit," *International Herald Tribune*, 4 June 2004.

52. Andrew Ward, "Pyongyang May Have Potent New Cash Raiser: Fake Viagra," *Financial Times*, 3 July 2004.

53. See, for example, United Nations, *Consolidated Inter-Agency Appeal 2003: Democratic People's Republic of Korea* (November 2002), pp. 127–32, available electronically at www.reliefweb.nt/appeals/2003/files/dprk03.dpf.

54. For cautiously optimistic analyses, see Marcus Noland, "West-Bound Train Leaving the Station: Pyongyang on the Reform Track," October 2002, available electronically at www.iie.com/publications/papers/noland1002.htm; Ruediger Frank, "A Socialist Market Economy in North Korea? Systemic Restrictions and a Quantitative Analysis" (unpublished paper, Columbia University, 2003), and idem, "North Korea: 'Gigantic Chance' and a Systemic Change," *NAPSNET Policy Forum Online PFO 3–31*, 9 May 2003, available electronically at www.nautilus.org/fora/security/0331_Frank.html. For a more cautiously skeptical assessment, see William J. Newcomb, "Economic Development in North Korea: Reflections on North Korea's Economic Reform," in *2003 Korea's Economy*, (Washington, D.C.: Korea Economic Institute, May 2003), pp. 57–60.

55. Mitsuhiko Kimura, "A Planned Economy Without Planning: *Su-ryong*'s North Korea," *Discussion Paper F-081*, Faculty of Economics, Tezukayama University, March 1994.

56. The initial July 2002 exchange rate was set at 153 won to the U.S. dollar. By October 2003, DPRK government foreign exchange booths in Pyongyang were paying 900 won per dollar. *Yonhap* (Seoul), "N. Korea Depreciate (sic) Its Currency. Adopts Floating Rates: Asahi," 4 October 2003. By July 2004—two years into the July 2002 measures—the unofficial rate for the DPRK won was reportedly about 1600 to the U.S. dollar. *Chosun Ilbo*, 27 July 2004; translated as "South Korea Reports Defections Rising despite North Efforts to Tighten Border," *BBC Worldwide Monitoring*, 29 July 2004. By those numbers, the pace of depreciation against the dollar (a serviceable proxy for the implied pace of domestic price inflation)

averaged 10 percent per month since the advent of the new economic measures. And the decline continues: in August 2004 the director of the World Food Programme office in Pyongyang stated that prices in local North Korean markets had risen 10–15 percent during the previous two months. Cindy Sui, "No Turning Back for North Korea's Reforms: UN Official," *Agence France Presse*, 18 August 2004. If that estimate is roughly correct, the rate of inflation in these markets is running at an annualized rate of 75 to 130 percent per annum—fairly compelling testimony that too much currency is still chasing too few goods in the DPRK domestic market.

57. *KCNA*, 8 May 2003, reprinted as "North Korea Reports 'Brisk' Sale of Public Bonds," *BBC Worldwide Monitoring*, 8 May 2003.

58. Harvey Leibenstein, "Allocative Efficiency versus 'X-Efficiency,'" *American Economic Review* 56, no. 3 (June 1966), pp. 392–415.

59. Kim So-young, "WFP Warns of N.K. Food Crisis," *Korea Herald*, 11 February 2004; Joe McDonald, "WFP Makes Emergency Food Appeal for North Korea, Saying Supplies Nearly Exhausted," *Associated Press*, 9 February 2004. The WFP's own institutional interests, to be sure, comport with an alarmist reading of the North Korean food situation—but that does not mean the WFP's recent warnings are wrong.

60. To date the only appreciable movement in these general areas would seem to be the events that found their denouement in the September–October 2002 Yang Bin fiasco.

61. The following paragraphs draw on Nicholas Eberstadt, "If North Korea Were Really Reforming, How Could We Tell—And What Would We Be Able to See?" *Korea and World Affairs* 26, no. 2 (Spring 2002), pp. 20–46.

62. For the past quarter century, the DPRK has been in effective default on roughly $1 billion in European, Japanese, and Australian loans contracted in the early 1970s. For more detail, see Nicholas Eberstadt, *Korea Approaches Reunification* (Armonk, N.Y.: M.E. Sharpe, 1995), chap. 1.

63. *Nodong Sinmun*, 1 June 2001, translated as "DPRK Daily Full Front-Page Article Discusses 'National Pride,'" *FBIS-EAS-2001-0629*, 3 July 2001.

64. *Pyongyang Central Broadcasting Station*, 8 July 2001, translated as "North Korea Demands Compensation from USA for Delay to

Reactor Project," *BBC Monitoring Asia Pacific—Political Supplied by BC Worldwide Monitoring,* 8 July 2001.

65. *Yonhap* News Service, 1 August 2001, reprinted as "ROK's Yonhap: N.K. Says U.S. Demands for Verification Ruse to Disarm It," *FBIS*-EAS-2001-0801, 2 August 2001.

8

North Korea's Economic Futures
Internal and External Dimensions

Phillip Wonhyuk Lim

Since the death of North Korea's paramount leader Kim Il Sung in 1994, many out-side observers have speculated about North Korea's impending collapse. Some even attempted to estimate its probability.[1] In 1999, Nicholas Eberstadt felt so confident about North Korea's bleak prospects that he even wrote a book entitled *The End of North Korea*. Much like Mark Twain's premature obituary, however, the rumors of North Korea's demise have proven greatly exaggerated. Over the past decade, Pyong-yang has demonstrated its ability to respond to crisis and ensure the survival of the re-gime. Moreover, in recent years, North Korea has attempted to go beyond stop-gap measures and explore more fundamental changes in economic policy, producing re-markable images that defy conventional wisdom. "Stitch by Stitch to a Different World," proclaimed an *Economist* article in July 2002, showing a photo of a garment factory in North Korea. "Shop Till You Drop" was the title of a May 2004 *Far Eastern Economic Review* article on economic changes in Pyongyang, with a smiling image of Kim Jong Il on the cover with the caption "Capitalist Kim." Although some North Korea watchers continue to express ample skepticism about the economic reforms under-taken by Pyongyang, the changes have the potential of transforming North Korea, es-pecially if a peaceful resolution of the nuclear crisis enables North Korea to attract a significant amount of outside capital in the form of economic assistance and invest-ment. In light of these developments, it is useful to examine a wider range of alterna-tive futures for North Korea, instead of focusing exclusively on the possibility of a regime collapse.

COLLAPSE OF COLLAPSE SCENARIOS?

This chapter assesses the economic reforms undertaken by North Korea and examines North Korea's alternative futures, using a policy decision forecasting model and a scenario-planning framework as analytic tools. I posit two key drivers for North Korea's future: (1) the extent of economic reform it chooses to undertake; and (2) the degree of external cooperation it is able to attain. The policy outcomes obtained on both fronts will result from the interaction among actors within the system with different preferences and variable amounts of power. Four prototypical economic futures for North Korea are presented: (1) Outward-Oriented Developmental Dictatorship; (2) Half Full, Half Empty; (3) Arduous March; and (4) Neither a Rogue nor a Tiger.

CRISIS AND RESPONSE: NORTH KOREA'S ECONOMIC REFORM IN CONTEXT

Economic Shocks and Initial Responses

In the late 1980s and 1990s, a series of external and internal shocks rocked the North Korean economy, forcing Pyongyang to explore nontraditional measures to cope with the crisis and ensure regime survival. In the late 1980s, the breakdown of the Soviet trading bloc made it extremely difficult for North Korea to import essential food and energy inputs, with serious repercussions for the economy as a whole. In 1993–94, North Korea's nuclear standoff with the United States greatly raised tension on the Korean peninsula, aggravating North Korea's economic difficulties. In 1994, the death of Kim Il Sung, who had ruled North Korea since the state was first established in the 1940s, fueled speculation about impending collapse from political as well as economic instability. In 1995–96, heavy floods devastated an agricultural sector already weakened by unsustainable farming methods. Although North Korea managed to survive these shocks, they left an indelible imprint on its economy. North Korea's economic reforms in recent years should be understood within this context.

North Korea's foreign trade suffered a catastrophic decline after the collapse of the socialist bloc. (See Figure 1.) The former Soviet Union not only accounted for 60 percent of North Korea's total trade in the late 1980s, but was also providing de facto aid of hundreds of millions of dollars by running a chronic trade surplus with North Korea. With the disintegration of the Soviet Union, this trade all but vanished. As a consequence, North Korea's trade volume declined by more than 50 percent, from $4.8 billion in 1989 to $2.1 billion in 1995. In addition, North Korea no longer could conduct trade on "friendly terms" with China, which now insisted on commercial terms. This drove up the prices of energy and food imports, delivering a crushing blow to the economy as a whole. Crude oil imports plummeted from 18.5 million barrels in 1990

Figure 1   **Economic Trends in North Korea, 1990–2000**

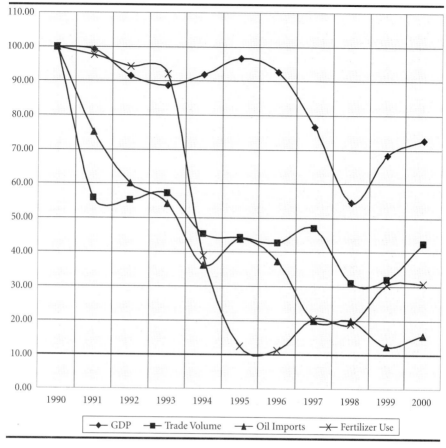

Source: North Korea's GDP, trade volume, oil imports, and fertilizer use estimates are provided by the Bank of Korea, Kotra, Korea Energy Economics Institute, and FAO, respectively.

Note: Level values are converted to index numbers and normalized at 100 in base year 1990. Base-year values are as follows: GDP, $23.1 billion; trade volume, $4.6 billion; oil imports, 18.5 million barrels; and fertilizer use, 832,000 tons.

to 8.1 million barrels in 1995 and 2.9 million barrels in 2000, a whopping 84 percent decline. Although North Korea tried to maximize the use of domestic energy resources such as coal, its primary energy supply declined from the equivalent of 24.0 million tons of oil in 1990 to 17.3 million in 1995 and 15.7 million in 2000.[2] Food imports, which used to account for as much as 20 percent of total food consumption in 1990, also plummeted; domestic food production suffered a significant decline as well, due primarily to the lack of critical inputs such as fertilizers.[3] According to estimates by the Food and Agriculture Organization (FAO), North Korea's fertilizer use declined from 832,000 tons in 1990 to 104,000 tons in 1995.[4]

Unable to generate a sufficient amount of hard currency to finance the imports of raw materials and critical inputs, the North Korean command economy broke down. Local plant managers and workers could no longer rely on central authorities and had to fend for themselves. The public distribution system, the very symbol of the socialist economy, could no longer provide food on a consistent basis, and many citizens had to engage in various "illegal" activities to obtain food. These activities included cultivating private plots and crossing the border to China to obtain food. Economic activities outside the plan increased, and these unsystematic improvisations on the part of individuals served as both a complement and a threat to the dysfunctional command economy.[5]

Pyongyang was clearly aware that it faced a severe economic crisis. Kim Il Sung's last policy speech, on 6 July 1994, was filled with references to North Korea's economic troubles, especially in the area of infrastructure and basic industries. He made three policy suggestions: (1) expand trade with any country that is willing to engage in economic exchanges with North Korea; (2) devise ways to sell manufactured goods overseas instead of exporting labor; and (3) eradicate bureaucratism and learn from the people. He seemed to understand that North Korea needed to expand economic exchanges with the outside world in order to fill the vacuum left by the collapse of the socialist bloc.

However, actual policy measures adopted by Pyongyang in the first half of the 1990s were halting and tentative, producing largely disappointing results. For example, Pyongyang established a free trade zone in the Rajin-Sonbong area in December 1991, one of several such zones it planned to open. However, other free trade zones with a more promising location and business environment did not materialize. Far removed from major cities in the northeastern corner of North Korea, with inadequate infrastructure for an industrial park, the Rajin-Sonbong free trade zone indicated that Pyongyang was still more interested in isolating the effects of economic experiments than in ensuring their success.

Disillusioned by Pyongyang's half-hearted measures, North Korea watchers began to doubt if Pyongyang had the political will to undertake major economic reforms. More skeptical observers, such as Nicholas Eberstadt, saw Pyongyang's efforts as little more than "tactical and opportunistic improvisations." Eberstadt argued that fundamental reforms would require Pyongyang to embrace "bold new answers" to three enduring issues that defined the character of the state: the problem of "ideological and cultural infiltration"; the problem of weapons of mass destruction (WMD) and regime survival; and the problem of South Korea's legitimacy.[6] As suggested by the title of his subsequent book, Eberstadt argued that North Korea would have to stop being North

Korea to undertake major reforms.[7] The hereditary succession of power in Pyongyang appeared to make it even more difficult for North Korea to adopt major reforms. Many North Korea watchers argued that Kim Jong Il, as the eldest son of Kim Il Sung and a top decision maker in his own right for more than two decades, would not be able to repudiate the policies that he and his father had long advocated.

North Korea's Policy Challenges

By the late 1990s, it had become clear that half-hearted measures would not end North Korea's economic troubles. The old command economy had broken down, and the regime had to condone informal economic activities and allow ordinary citizens to do whatever they could to obtain food. The informal sector began to play an increasingly important role in the food distribution chain. Although only vegetables and minor nongrain agricultural products were supposed to be bought and sold in farmers' markets, corn and rice produced on private plots or obtained through illegal channels were increasingly traded in these markets. According to an estimate by South Korea's Ministry of Unification, ordinary citizens in North Korea obtained as much as 60 percent of their food in the informal sector in the late 1990s.[8] Farmers' markets also began to play an increasingly important role in the distribution of consumer goods.

Although the growth of the informal sector helped to alleviate economic difficulties for ordinary citizens, it created serious financial problems for the state because of the increasing gap between informal and formal prices. In the informal sector, prices were largely set by market mechanisms. By contrast, prices in the formal sector were fixed by fiat. Although there were serious shortages in the formal sector, prices did not adjust to balance supply and demand. As a result, the increasing gap between prices in the formal and informal sectors created arbitrage opportunities. For instance, rice was supposed to be procured at 0.80 won and sold at 0.08 won per kilogram in the formal sector, whereas the price of rice was around 40 to 50 won per kilogram in the informal sector in 2002. If farmers siphoned off rice from the formal sector to the informal sector, they could profit handsomely. As shown in Table 1, the situation was similar for other "basic necessities" for which generous public subsidies were provided. The result was a financial hollowing out of the state.[9]

Central planners in Pyongyang were faced with a serious dilemma. To arrest the deterioration of public finance and rehabilitate the formal sector, planners had to either crack down on the informal sector or accommodate changed economic realities and transform the formal sector; otherwise, there was little alternative but to throw in the towel and give up any semblance of a planned economy. Yet each of the policy choices carried significant risks. Cracking down on the informal sector could cause serious

Table 1   **North Korea's Price Reform Official Prices before and after 1 July 2002**

Item	Before (B)	After (A)	A/B
Rice (kg)	(Buy) 0.80	(Buy) 40	50
	(Sell) 0.08	(Sell) 44	550
Corn (kg)	(Buy) 0.49	(Buy) 20	41
	(Sell) 0.06	(Sell) 24	400
Peas (kg)	-	(Buy) 40	-
Pork (kg)	(Buy) 7	(Buy) 170	24
Chicken (kg)	-	(Buy) 180	-
Pyongyang-Chongjin Rail Fare	16	590	37
Bus, Subway Fare	0.10	2	20
Tram Fare	0.10	1	10
Coal (ton)	34	1,500	44
Electricity (thousand kWh)	35	2,100	60
Coking Coal, Light Bulbs, Steel Plate, Rubber	-	-	45
Petroleum (ton)	923	64,600	70
Sneakers	18	180	10
Facial Soap	3	20	6.7
Laundry Soap	0.50	15	30
Soybean Paste (kg)	-	17	-
Soybean Sauce (kg)	-	16	-
Vegetable Oil (kg)	-	180	-
Food Additive (kg)	-	300	-
Soju	-	43	-
Fish (kg)	-	100	-
House Rent (Monthly/60 m^2)	-	78	-
Heating Bill (Monthly/m^2)	-	175	-
Songdowon Beach Entrance Fee	3	50	17
Chosun Literature (Magazine)	1.2	35	29

Source: Ministry of Unification, "Analysis of Price Trends in North Korea," various years [in Korean].

disruptions, because it was no longer a negligible part of the economy. Ordinary citizens had come to rely on farmers' markets for much of their food, and closing these markets might cause a policy-induced food crisis. Transforming the formal sector by adopting market-oriented measures also carried its share of risks. Measures taken to transform the formal sector could create a number of adjustment problems without producing tangible benefits, at least in the short term. Closing the formal-informal price gap could lead to dangerous inflation. Finally, throwing in the towel was not a realistic option when it was unclear what would replace the old economic order.

In seeking new directions for economic policy, Pyongyang also faced three interrelated challenges. First, Pyongyang had to provide ideological and political justifications for any major departure from "the one and only system." Second, Pyongyang had to decide how to strike a balance between the formal and informal sectors, whose relative importance had increased significantly during the crisis years. In theory, policy makers could crack down on informal economic activities or accommodate changes that had occurred, perhaps even giving up on central planning. In practice, Pyongyang had to condone informal economic activities to a certain extent to compensate for the woeful performance of the formal sector, but it had to limit arbitrage opportunities that existed between the formal and informal sectors. Third, faced with limited domestic resources, Pyongyang had to create an investor-friendly environment at least in some special zones to attract capital and technology from the outside world; at the same time, however, it had to manage risks associated with "foreign infiltration" and economic inequality.

Ideological and Institutional Groundwork for Economic Reform

Pyongyang used a number of ideological and institutional innovations to justify changes in its economic policy. When Kim Jong Il officially assumed leadership in 1998, he presented the vision of "a strong and prosperous nation" as his blueprint for the twenty-first century. While this slogan apparently gave equal weight to military strength and economic prosperity, official explanations made it clear that the emphasis was on the latter task. Kim proclaimed military-first politics as the cornerstone of North Korea's security, but the weakening of the Korean Workers' Party and the depoliticization of economic decision making in the cabinet were more decisive than the provocative rhetoric of military-first politics.

In exploring alternative economic policy, Pyongyang put forth pragmatism and "new thinking" as guiding principles.[10] Kim Jong Il personally endorsed these principles on many occasions, including on his January 2001 visit to the Pudong area in Shanghai, which he said had been transformed beyond recognition in a decade. On 4 January 2001, in a striking pronouncement in *Rodong Sinmun*, the official newspaper declared: "Things are not what they used to be in the 1960s. . . . We should bring about technical modernization by boldly doing away with what needs to be abolished, instead of being shackled by ready-made ideas or hanging on to the old and outdated conceptions."[11] Although the same newspaper had frequently warned against the dangers of "the imperialists' ideological and cultural infiltration," it no longer defended old practices as eternal truths. It acknowledged that new times would call for new ideas, as long as they did not belong to the domain of the imperialists.

Several ideological innovations were offered to support these guiding principles. One was to stretch the definition of socialism. Another was to implement substantive changes without explicitly repudiating what the Kim family had done in the past, by simply declaring that times had changed. Major economic reforms were introduced as measures to "improve and perfect socialism," rather than dismantle and repudiate socialism.[12] Performance-based rewards were declared to be the essence of the socialist distribution principle, and rampant "average-ism" by which everyone was paid equally regardless of the quantity and quality of work was condemned as an anti-socialist principle. By redefining socialism in line with market principles, Pyongyang cleared an ideological hurdle. Also, by implementing changes without rejecting the past, Pyongyang ensured that the hereditary succession of power would not get in the way of reform.

These ideological innovations were accompanied by institutional and generational changes designed to facilitate economic reform. For instance, a constitutional amendment in September 1998 freed technocrats from the oversight of the Central People's Committee, a body dominated by conservative party ideologues. Subsequently, Pyongyang reduced the number of salaried Workers' Party members by 20 to 30 percent and redeployed these members in various industries. Pyongyang also promoted a number of managers in their 30s and 40s to top posts.[13] In addition, Pyongyang introduced or amended major economic laws to allow more flexibility in the drafting of the central economic plan, promote small workteams in agriculture, and recognize the inheritance of personal property such as houses, automobiles, and savings.[14]

Price and Incentive Reform, Decentralization, and Marketization

With the ideological and institutional groundwork undertaken, Pyongyang turned to striking a balance between the formal and informal sectors. By adopting measures to improve economic management on 1 July 2002, Pyongyang appears to have chosen the middle road. Instead of cracking down on "underground" market activities or "throwing in the towel," Pyongyang chose to transform *and* rehabilitate the formal sector by accommodating changes that had taken place in the informal sector.[15] (See Table 2.) The July 2002 reform package consisted of three components: reduction of double-distortions in prices, increase in and differentiation of wages based on performance, and decentralization of enterprise management.

To recover the costs of production and prevent a further financial hollowing out of the state, Pyongyang adopted far-reaching price reforms. It reduced distortions in relative prices among goods in the formal sector by raising the prices of "basic necessities" that had been heavily subsidized. The price of pork was increased from 7 won to 180 won per kilogram, and the price of electricity was raised from 0.03 won to 2.1 won per kilowatt-hour. Pyongyang also reduced the price gap between the formal and informal sectors so that undue arbitrage opportunities would not be created. For example, as Table 1 shows, the sales price of rice per kilogram in the formal sector was raised from 0.08 won to 44 won, and the procurement price was increased from 0.80 won to 40 won so that the state would no longer have to incur losses on rice transactions. Even in principle, the public distribution system no longer provided the most essential of goods nearly free of charge. All transactions would be monetized. Moreover, the new procurement price was to be set close to the market price.

To give workers sufficient purchasing power to buy goods at new prices in the formal sector, their wages were raised. On average, workers' wages were increased by 18 times to 2,000 won per month. This wage increase was based on the assumption that two people in a typical four-member household would work and monthly living expenses of 4,000 won would be needed. Perhaps more significant than the wage raise was the increase in income differentiation based on skill level and performance. The wage gap between highly skilled and unskilled labor was doubled. Performance-based incentives were strengthened as well.

Finally, Pyongyang gave greater autonomy to local plant managers. Pyongyang depoliticized economic decision making at the local level by transferring managerial rights from party cadres to plant managers. The scope of central planning was reduced to major indicators such as total industrial output, construction investment, and electricity and steel production; and the authority to formulate detailed production plans (including labor management) was decentralized. Pyongyang sought to strike a balance between the plan and market, reminiscent of the "dual-track" strategy adopted by China in its early reform years.[16] Enterprises were now allowed to produce and dispose of their products in markets, so long as they met general production targets. In other words, as long as enterprises satisfied their production obligations, they were allowed to produce and sell what they wanted. Enterprises could also start new businesses. For example, an enterprise operating hotels, restaurants, and shops set up a new company producing buttons. Before the reform, enterprises could not freely procure inputs and dispose of their products outside the plan, but now they could legally engage in market transactions. As long as enterprises had cash reserves (i.e., retained earnings), they no longer had to worry about running out of raw materials and inputs, unlike under the extensive command-and-control system. Some enterprises even took loans from merchants and other more moneyed individuals to expand their business.[17] In addition, Pyongyang also allowed local enterprises to engage in external trade under the guidance of the Ministry of Trade, instead of giving exclusive rights to specialized agencies.

The July 2002 economic reforms were initially accompanied by an official attempt to crack down on the informal sector. The authorities in Pyongyang apparently wanted to phase out farmers' markets and force commercial transactions to take place in the "transformed and rehabilitated" formal sector. When disruptions proved to be significant, however, the authorities changed their approach in March 2003. Instead of cracking down on the informal sector, they decided to expand farmers' markets into general markets and collect taxes and fees on transactions. In other words, Pyongyang decided to bolster public finance in return for the legalization and expansion of farmers' markets.

Cabinet Resolutions No. 24 and No. 27, dated 5 May 2003, officially recognized existing markets and stipulated the establishment of new markets as well, with a view toward setting up more than 300 general markets around the country. The Cabinet Resolutions also allowed state-run enterprises and cooperatives to make use of general markets. While the authorities are supposed to set price ceilings in general markets, these price ceilings are updated regularly to reflect changing demand and supply conditions. The authorities collect "market user fees" from merchants and "contributions" (income tax) based on their earnings.[18]

Economic Opening

Although the July 2002 reform package was hailed as a groundbreaking initiative at the time of its introduction, it did not deliver spectacular results. As shown in Table 2, the combination of price and wage increases produced some inflation. However, it would be an exaggeration to claim that the July 2002 reform package triggered "hyperinflation." Pyongyang opted for limited monetary accommodation, avoiding a price-wage spiral. The limited supply response was perhaps more disappointing than the price trend. While the July 2002 reform package provided incentives largely based on market principles, its effectiveness was limited because of the shortage of raw materials and critical inputs. A simple growth accounting exercise could show that there was only so much North Korea could achieve in the absence of resource inflows from the outside. North Korea's labor was stretched thin, and its division of labor had broken down. Due to the lack of hard currency and previous defaults on foreign loans, North Korea had only limited access to capital. Productivity improvement from embodied technology was limited as a result.

North Korea did try to address this problem by attracting outside investment. In August 2002, to make the prices of domestic goods reflect economic realities, Pyongyang drastically raised the official exchange rate from 2.2 to 153 won to the dollar. Subsequently, the authorities set up currency exchange booths in general markets applying the market-determined exchange rate. North Korea also tried to create an investor-friendly environment, at least in some special zones, to attract capital and technology from the outside world, targeting South Korea in particular. In September 2002 Pyongyang announced the establishment of the Sinuiju Special Administration Zone,[19] and two months later, it promulgated the Kaesong Industrial Zone Law in addition to the Mt. Kumgang Tourist Zone Law. Also, it created an umbrella body under the cabinet to oversee the development of special economic zones.

Table 2   **North Korea's Price Reform Price Trends in Farmers' Markets (North Korean won)**

Group	Item	Unit	1998	1999	2000	2001	2002	2003
Grain	Rice	kg	77.0	64.0	46.6	49.5	52.5	156.1
	Corn	kg	39.6	32.6	27.2	31.8	35.0	115.6
	Peas	kg	77.5	48.1	43.4	42.0	44.0	160.0
	Wheat Flour	kg	61.0	44.5	43.1	42.4	47.5	175.6
Meat and Fish	Pork	kg	181.0	160.0	130.1	138.4	165.0	538.9
	Chicken	-	240.0	478.6	404.7	369.3	325.7	1100.0
	Sausages	-	25.0	18.4	26.2	24.0	24.3	92.2
	Eggs	-	16.0	13.0	11.8	10.0	10.0	46.3
	Fish	-	32.0	40.9	35.0	82.6	25.0	198.9
Vegetables and Fruits	Cabbage	-	9.0	20.0	24.6	14.1	27.5	75.0
	Dried Seaweed	kg	31.0	30.6	67.1	70.0	200.0	225.6
	Apples	-	23.0	33.1	22.9	31.6	50.0	94.3
Food Additives	Salt	kg	19.3	14.6	19.3	13.8	21.3	93.3
	Cooking Oil	500g	136.0	147.6	126.0	120.8	75.0	622.2
	Taste Enhancer	Pack	199.0	242.9	206.7	261.9	200.0	911.1
	Vegetable Oil	kg	255.0	163.1	194.6	202.6	200	475.0
	Red Pepper Powder	kg	273.8	239.4	273.8	240.6	190	1083.3
Other Food Items	Bread	-	19.0	15.0	11.7	17.1	18.8	88.9
	Rice and Soup	Bowl	162.0	142.5	150.0	94.0	80.0	411.1
	Wonton	-	10.0	22.9	10.1	11.9	13.3	60.0
	Spring Water	Bottle	3.0	17.5	30.9	13.3	25.0	134.3
	Beer	Bottle	78.0	68.2	52.5	35	51.4	197.1
Nonfood Items	Dress Shoes	-	1489.0	900.0	1180.0	700.0	316.7	6000.0
	Soap	-	92.0	66.3	64.4	82.5	60.0	394.4
	Toothpaste	-	50.0	55.0	38.4	50.6	28.3	66.0
	Shirt	-	400.0	472.3	613.8	394.9	275.0	861.1

Source: Ministry of Unification, "Analysis of Price Trends in North Korea," various years [in Korean].

Among North Korea's economic opening measures, the Kaesong Industrial Zone generated the greatest amount of interest. It was regarded as a project that would not only accelerate North Korea's economic reform but also push inter-Korean economic cooperation to the next stage. Pyongyang made serious efforts to ensure the success of the project. As shown in Table 3, wage and tax rates in Kaesong were set at competitive levels in comparison with China. According to the Bank of Korea's estimate, for North Korea the annual output from the Kaesong Industrial Complex is expected to contribute 0.3 percent of North Korea's 2003 gross national income (GNI) in four years and as much as 12.4 percent of North Korea's 2003 GNI in 17 years. For South Korea, its contribution is estimated to increase from 0.4 percent of South Korea's 2003 GNI in

Table 3 **Comparative Factor Prices in Kaesong, China, and South Korea**

	Unit	Kaesong	China	South Korea	A/B	A/C
(Minimum)Monthly Wage	USD	57.5	100–200	423	0.29–0.58	0.12
Working Hours per Week	hours	48	44	44	1.1	1.1
Corporate Income Tax Rate	percent	10–14	15	23–28	-	-
Land Price per Pyong (36 sq. ft.)	KRW	150,000	50,000	407,550	3	0.37

Source: Bank of Korea
Note: A = Kaesong; B = China; C = South Korea

four years to 3.1 percent in 17 years.[20] Due to the eruption of the second nuclear crisis in October 2002, however, the progress of the Kaesong Industrial Complex has been slower than originally expected.

ALTERNATIVE SCENARIOS

Although North Korea has adopted a number of economic reform measures over the past several years, there is a great deal of uncertainty regarding its economic prospects. Will North Korea remain on the reform path? Will the external environment faced by North Korea improve or deteriorate, especially in regard to the nuclear issue? These questions go to the heart of the problem. The method of scenario planning allows the systematic consideration of alternative futures. There may be many factors, or drivers, that shape the future; however, for visual purposes, two axes representing two key drivers are typically drawn in a scenario-planning exercise. If there are M possibilities for the first key driver and N possibilities for the second key driver, there would be M x N outcomes. Again, for simplicity, the various possibilities are presented in a 2 x 2 framework, producing four prototypical outcomes.[21]

As noted previously, two key drivers for North Korea's future are the extent of economic reform it chooses to undertake and the degree of external cooperation it manages to attain. Conceptually, the extent of economic reform can vary from retrogression (i.e., reversion to a closed command economy) to full-fledged market-oriented reform based on private property rights; the degree of external cooperation can range from military conflict to complete normalization of relations. I posit that the policy outcomes related to economic reform and external cooperation are obtained as a result of interaction among actors with different preferences. A policy decision forecasting model is outlined in the sidebar "Policy Decision Forecasting Model." It is assumed that actors within North Korea largely determine the extent of economic reform, whereas external actors and the North Korean leadership determine the degree of external cooperation jointly.

Driver I: Economic Reform

The extent of economic reform is only a proximate cause of economic change in North Korea. It is shaped in turn by a political mediation process involving North Korea's policy makers but also participants in the informal sector, as well as external actors. To what extent can economic reform be realistically implemented in North Korea? To answer this question, it is necessary to extend the framework of Bueno de Mesquita and Mo and combine a policy decision forecasting approach with economic analysis (see the sidebar "Policy Decision Forecasting Model").[22] Under this extended framework, major players in North Korea and the outside world are specified. The framework also includes "the real world" as a player in order to account for the feedback mechanism between policy decisions and outcomes. Major players in North Korea would include those in the formal sector (e.g., Kim Jong Il, ideologues, military, technocrats, etc.), but also producers and merchants in the informal sector. Significant players in the outside world would include national governments as well as corporations. Analysis would then hypothesize the policy position and political clout of these players. A "real world" policy position, for example, might maximize social welfare and minimize the probability of regime collapse, depending on the ultimate objective of the North Korean leadership. Its level of influence would largely depend on the sensitivity of the leadership to social welfare and the political implications of policy decisions. Instead of bringing in "the real world" as an actor, an alternative approach might account for possible changes in the policy position of major players as they adapt to the effects of previous policy decisions on the economy and regime stability.

North Korea's economic policy since the collapse of the socialist bloc shows that in policy decisions economic realities matter as much as ideological inclinations. Concerned with potentially adverse political implications of economic changes, Pyongyang's official propaganda channels, as well as Kim Jong Il himself, strongly denounced market-oriented reform and vowed to defend socialism in the early 1990s. However, when North Korea was faced with a serious famine in the mid-1990s, Pyongyang had to condone, if not encourage, informal economic activities and explore various reform measures, including far-reaching price reform. If the ultimate goal of the North Korean leadership is to maintain its grip on power, it would be unwise for them to risk regime collapse just for the sake of ideological purity. As illustrated by North Korea's ideological innovations in recent years, *juche* may not be as serious a stumbling block as initially feared.

However, once reform is launched, it may not be easy to apply the brakes, even if improved economic conditions no longer require "change-to-survive" measures. Reform may benefit not only the general population but also the ruling elite, many of whom are

Policy Decision Forecasting Model

The policy decision forecasting model is based on the premise that a policy outcome is obtained as a result of competition among interest groups with different preferences. The model predicts policy outcomes based on three variables: the *potential power* and *policy position* (preference) of each actor on each issue examined and the *salience* each actor associates with those is-sues.* Although this model is powerful in predicting the (short-run) policy outcome as a political bargaining process, it is largely silent on the issue of the stability of this outcome. In a sense, the model overlooks the feedback pro-cess through which policy decisions impact the real world and vice versa.

For the case of economic reform in North Korea, Bueno de Mesquita and Mo identify major players in the North Korean policymaking circle (e.g., Kim Jong Il, ideologues, military, economic planners, diplomats, etc.) and surmise their positions on economic reform (ranging from reversion to a closed command economy to privatization). For example, even when Kim Jong Il is assumed to prefer Chinese-style reform, the forecasting model predicts that the policy outcome will be close to the status quo, as hard-liners build coalitions to gain the upper hand. Kim Jong Il is forced to side with these hard-liners lest he be reduced to a figurehead.

It is unclear, therefore, whether this policy outcome is stable given North Korea's economic conditions. Without serious reform, North Korea's eco-nomic conditions will almost certainly deteriorate and force policy makers to propose an alternative policy decision. Depending on how policy makers re-spond in this subsequent round of political bargaining, North Korea may be headed toward an economic recovery, a palace coup, or a popular revolt. Hard-liners may win the immediate political battle, but if they cannot improve the economy, they cannot win the war. Consequently, the long-run policy-making dynamics may be very different from the short-run outcome. Changes in economic fundamentals affect the policy position and political clout of in-terest groups and ultimately the outcome of the political bargaining process. In short, it seems clear that political forecasting should be complemented by an analysis of the fundamentals if it is to predict accurately the evolution of policy outcomes.

---

* The term *salience* refers to the degree of importance or relevance that each actor attaches to a particular issue. Note that the importance of a particular issue (e.g., eco-nomic reform, abortion, foreign policy, etc.) is not uniform across all interest groups. In policy decision forecasting models, the index number associated with the *power* of an actor is multiplied by the index number for the issue *salience* to measure the influence of the actor over that issue.

---

likely to enjoy access to profit opportunities arising from increased exchanges with the outside world. While more ideologically rigid members of the elite may prefer reform with a satiation point, others may opt for further reform. There is also a possibility that conservatives may change their minds if they can receive benefits from economic reform. For example, the military may be asked to undertake important economic functions. This political process is likely to be played out in North Korea over the next decade.

Driver II: External Cooperation

The degree of external cooperation is the other key driver of change. Unlike economic reform, which is largely determined by actors within North Korea, external cooperation is shaped by interaction between the North Korean leadership and external actors. Understanding the motives of major players would be essential to accurate policy decision forecasting. As the nuclear problem on the Korean Peninsula has had a great influence on international relations in Northeast Asia, it may be useful to look at this issue from the perspective of each of the major players. The stance of different actors on the North Korea nuclear crisis reflects their thinking on the larger issue of creating a new order in Northeast Asia.

The DPRK's nuclear program seems to serve three major policy goals: a deterrent against security threats; a useful bargaining chip in diplomatic negotiations; and an important element of indigenous energy development utilizing 26 million tons of natural uranium available within the country. In 1994, Pyongyang 's nuclear program was mainly used as a bargaining chip, but the Bush administration's tough policy toward the North has brought about a significant change. Perhaps believing North Korea's threat to "demonstrate" the existence of nuclear weapons is not credible given the potential reactions by neighboring states, the Bush administration first sought to ignore Pyongyang 's attempt to use its nuclear program as a bargaining chip.[23] Although the DPRK's long-range artillery serves as an effective deterrent against South Korea, the North increasingly seems to regard nuclear weapons as a possible deterrent against the United States, especially in light of the Iraq War. Unless the United States credibly abandons what North Korea believes is its "hostile policy" toward it, there is very little chance that Pyongyang will give up its nuclear program. More specifically, the DPRK may try to improve relations with the outside world without completely dismantling its nuclear program, instead offering to safeguard nuclear materials within its borders and cease production of nuclear weapons or fissile material. Unless the United States is willing to engage and test North Korea through serious negotiations, it is impossible to know how Pyongyang will respond. This is the challenge that Washington confronts in relation to the Six-Party Talks.

Why was the United States so long unwilling to engage North Korea and improve relations with it? First, Pyongyang's track record does not make it a trustworthy partner, and despite the pledge to improve bilateral relations contained in the Agreed Framework, there is a natural inclination to proceed slowly. Moreover, many Americans seem to have a serious problem with the DPRK's tough negotiating style. For the United States, the thought of the world's only superpower getting "jerked around" by what they regard as a "rogue state" is too much to accept. More hawkish policy makers may even prefer regime change in Pyongyang. Other U.S. policy makers, however, may see a strategic value in keeping North Korea as a rogue state. The United States can use an "irredeemable" North Korea not only as a convenient justification for weapons programs such as ballistic missile defense (BMD), but also as a useful tool to keep Japan and South Korea from pursuing a more independent foreign policy.[24] Instead of seeking a new order in Northeast Asia after the end of the Cold War, some policy makers may be content to prolong the status quo. As long as Pyongyang faithfully plays the role of a rogue state, this policy of "malign neglect" might prove effective. However, if the United States, not the DPRK, is perceived as the stumbling block in the resolution of the nuclear problem, such a policy might lead to a nationalist backlash against Washington.[25]

Other players in Northeast Asia have different perspectives on the issue, depending on their perceived national interests. China's priority is to continue its rapid economic growth and its "peaceful rise" as a global power. Until very recently, China has acted in a cautious manner in international affairs, so as not to attract unnecessary scrutiny from its neighbors as well as the United States. China does not want a rapid escalation of hostilities on the Korean Peninsula that may disrupt its economic growth and threaten its position in Northeast Asia. Building on the strength of its rapid economic growth, China is engaging in proactive economic diplomacy on all fronts.

Japan is interested in becoming a more "normal country," freeing itself from the legacies of World War II. However, there is some debate on the best means to achieve this objective. Many Japanese conservatives seem to be content to go along as "junior partner" of the United States, at least for the foreseeable future, and use the North Korean threat as a justification for remilitarizing Japan. By contrast, more liberal-minded Japanese call for a tighter integration with Northeast Asia on the basis of historical reconciliation. To them, normalizing relations with North Korea is an integral component of this strategy.[26]

Russia's priority in Northeast Asia is to reestablish its influence in the region and develop the Russian Far East. Russia believes that multilateral diplomacy on the North Korean nuclear issue will enable Moscow to take a more proactive role in Northeast Asia. A comprehensive solution to the problem is likely to involve energy assistance to North Korea, supporting Russia's plans to develop energy resources and promote economic development in the Russian Far East.

A divided land bridge in Northeast Asia, South Korea has much to gain from ending North Korea's isolation and building energy and transportation networks that connect different parts of Northeast Asia. To resolve North Korea's nuclear problem and to promote peace and security in Northeast Asia, South Korea is pushing for the construction of infrastructure networks in the region, facilitating economic development not only in North Korea but also in China's northeastern provinces and the Russian Far East. Such investment projects will also create business opportunities for firms from this region, as well as from the outside, and allow them to share in the benefits of increased regional integration. Ultimately, to achieve reunification, South Korea must maintain good relations with all its neighbors as well as the United States, and build an "optimal" level of national strength so that a unified Korea would be viewed as neither a pushover nor a threat.

To South Korea, inter-Korean economic cooperation is a particularly useful tool in this regard. Such cooperation would create mutually beneficial business opportunities for involved companies, but it would also have even more significant political implications. First, it would help the DPRK to see a way out its current predicament as a rogue state. Through economic exchanges, Pyongyang would be able to earn money the old-fashioned way rather than through questionable transactions involving narcotics or weapons. Also, by helping North Korea to get accustomed to market principles, inter-Korean economic cooperation would have the effect of facilitating and consolidating the North's economic reform. Second, it would help South Korea to undertake industrial restructuring in a less painful manner. In particular, labor-intensive small and medium-size enterprises (SMEs) faced with increasing competition from China and other late-developing countries have welcomed Pyongyang's economic opening. Third, inter-Korean economic cooperation would have the strategic significance of counterbalancing China's increasing influence in North Korea. As Table 4 shows, China's share in North Korea's trade volume has exceeded 30 percent in recent years.

While North Korea's neighbors have somewhat different policy priorities in Northeast Asia, they share some very important common interests. One is to prevent the outbreak of war on the Korean Peninsula. The other is to prevent any one of the DPRK's neighbors from dominating it in such a way as to cause a significant change in the regional balance. A U.S. surgical strike against North Korea is flatly unacceptable to all of

Table 4   Composition of North Korea's Trade (billions of dollars)

	1990	1995	2000	2001	2002	2003
Total	4.17	2.05	1.97	2.27	2.26	2.34
North Korea–China	0.48 (11.5%)	0.55 (23.5%)	0.49 (20.4%)	0.74 (27.6%)	0.74 (25.4%)	1.02 (33.4%)
North Korea–Japan	0.48 (11.4%)	0.60 (25.4%)	0.46 (19.4%)	0.48 (17.8%)	0.37 (12.7%)	0.27 (8.6%)
North Korea–South Korea	0.01 (0.3%)	0.29 (2.2%)	0.43 (17.8%)	0.40 (15.1%)	0.64 (22.1%)	0.72 (23.6%)

Source: Kotra (www.kotra.or.kr).
Note: Figures in parentheses represent percentage shares in North Korea's total trade volume.

Pyongyang's neighbors. First, as the location of the alleged highly enriched uranium (HEU) program is not known, the target of a surgical strike is not clear. Second, a limited surgical strike would not be construed in these terms by the North Korean leadership. For Pyongyang, there is certainly no guarantee that a U.S. surgical strike would not be followed by a decapitation campaign. The DPRK will almost certainly retaliate against an initial strike in a "use it or lose it" mode, and South Korea and Japan would suffer devastating losses as a result. China and Russia, for their part, will not find it in their interest to see the United States dictating the course of the war and postwar settlement on the Korean Peninsula.

North Korea's strategic location enables it to play its neighbors off against one another. South Korea cannot afford to allow the North to become overly dependent on China, especially in light of the 2004 controversy over the Koguryo dynasty.[27] Russia, seeking to correct its shortsighted disengagement from the Korean Peninsula during the Yeltsin era, has made serious efforts to strengthen relations with Pyongyang in recent years. Japan has also made diplomatic overtures to the DPRK, influenced by traditional geopolitical thinking that sees the Korean Peninsula as a dagger aimed at Japan and a bridge connecting to the Asian heartland. Given the small amount of money required to keep North Korea afloat, its neighbors appear to be willing to provide aid to Pyongyang to maintain their influence. As a result, imposing multilateral sanctions on the DPRK is a very difficult proposition.

Against this background, the outline of a solution to the nuclear problem should be reasonably clear. The United States and North Korea should address each other's security concerns. The United States should end what North Korea regards as its hostile policy toward it. Pyongyang should freeze and then dismantle its nuclear program under inspection. Through various programs to assist North Korean economic development, the international community should convince the DPRK that a nonnuclear future would be better than a nuclear one. As the United States and North Korea have both been criticized for their failure to uphold the Agreed Framework, top leaders from both sides, joined by other concerned parties, should make personal commitments and take a series of steps to show that they are implementing the agreement in good faith. Whether the Six-Party Talks can reach such a settlement remains to be seen.

PROSPECTIVE OUTCOMES

As demonstrated in Figure 2, combining different levels of economic reform and external cooperation produces four prototypical outcomes or scenarios. The northeast quadrant shows the "outward-looking developmental dictatorship" scenario, in which North Korea adopts fundamental market-oriented reform and normalizes its relations

Figure 2   **North Korea's Alternative Futures**

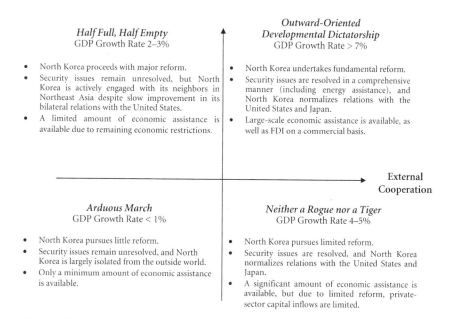

Economic Reform

Half Full, Half Empty
GDP Growth Rate 2–3%

- North Korea proceeds with major reform.
- Security issues remain unresolved, but North Korea is actively engaged with its neighbors in Northeast Asia despite slow improvement in its bilateral relations with the United States.
- A limited amount of economic assistance is available due to remaining economic restrictions.

*Outward-Oriented
Developmental Dictatorship*
GDP Growth Rate > 7%

- North Korea undertakes fundamental reform.
- Security issues are resolved in a comprehensive manner (including energy assistance), and North Korea normalizes relations with the United States and Japan.
- Large-scale economic assistance is available, as well as FDI on a commercial basis.

External
Cooperation

Arduous March
GDP Growth Rate < 1%

- North Korea pursues little reform.
- Security issues remain unresolved, and North Korea is largely isolated from the outside world.
- Only a minimum amount of economic assistance is available.

Neither a Rogue nor a Tiger
GDP Growth Rate 4–5%

- North Korea pursues limited reform.
- Security issues are resolved, and North Korea normalizes relations with the United States and Japan.
- A significant amount of economic assistance is available, but due to limited reform, private-sector capital inflows are limited.

with the United States and Japan. In this outcome, the DPRK is supposed to follow a path similar to China's and Vietnam's, with an annual economic growth rate of well over 7 percent. The southeast quadrant shows the "neither a rogue nor a tiger" scenario. Here, after a comprehensive resolution of security issues at the Six-Party Talks, Pyongyang is no longer regarded as a rogue state, but it pursues only limited reform and fails to transform itself into another East Asian tiger. The "half full, half empty" scenario in the northwest quadrant closely resembles the current situation in Pyongyang. In this outcome, the North embarks on major reform to modernize its economy, but due to a stalemate over security issues there is only limited improvement in its external environment, especially in its bilateral relations with the United States. The "arduous march" scenario in the southwest quadrant is the worst possible outcome short of war. Here North Korea does not actively pursue internal reform or external engagement, perhaps due to concerns about regime stability. The economy is likely to contract, as it indeed did in the mid-1990s.

None of the four potential scenarios is based on the extreme case of military conflict or renewed Sovietization. International relations in Northeast Asia and economic conditions in the North seem to make these extreme policy choices unrealistic unless major actors are willing to stake their political as well as personal lives for a potential catastrophe in the form of war or famine. The possibilities for economic reform and external cooperation are bound by a realistic consideration of alternatives, informed by what has transpired in and around the DPRK over the past decade. A more detailed description of each of the four hypothesized outcomes follows.

Outward-Oriented Developmental Dictatorship

This is the best possible outcome for Pyongyang in this scenario-planning exercise. While maintaining its monopoly on political power, the North Korean regime undertakes fundamental reform, building on economic management improvement measures it adopted in July 2002. Not content to depend indefinitely on foreign aid, the DPRK tries to enhance its economic independence by adopting market-oriented reform and engaging actively with the outside world. The key is that Pyongyang escapes from the so-called mendicant mentality, much as South Korea did in the 1960s.[28]

The United States realizes that it risks becoming isolated in Northeast Asia if it takes an uncompromising position on the nuclear issue. In this scenario, Washington decides to address North Korea's security concerns in return for the dismantlement of North Korea's nuclear program. Based on a credible program of mutual threat reduction between the United States and North Korea and backed by Pyongyang's neighbors, a comprehensive solution to security issues leads the North to give up its nuclear program in exchange for the normalization of relations with the United States and Japan, as well as economic assistance from the international community. Energy provision is a key component of the economic package. A significant amount of foreign direct investment (FDI) also becomes available.

This settlement enables North Korea to expand the scope of economic reform and reap tangible benefits from an outward-oriented development strategy. The ruling elite, many members of which have personally benefited from economic opportunities, gains popular support for further reform as outward-oriented industrialization brings "rapid shared growth," as in the case of tiger economies in East Asia. In line with the previous experiences of tiger economies, the DPRK is projected to record an annual GDP growth rate of well above 7 percent. Benchmarks for this outcome include South Korea in the 1960s, China in the 1970s, and Vietnam in the 1980s. Determined to enhance economic independence, South Korea launched major economic reform in the 1960s and took full advantage of the rapidly expanding global market. The normalization of relations with Japan in 1965 helped South Korea to have better access to foreign capital and technology. China in the 1980s also secured a favorable external environment and launched fundamental economic reform.

Vietnam is a particularly illuminating case, because not long ago Vietnam was considered both an economic basket case and a military threat to its neighbors, much like North Korea. After achieving unification by force in 1975, Hanoi sovietized the former South Vietnam and invaded Cambodia three years later, provoking hostile reaction from China and the United States. Due to the ensuing economic embargo and policy failures, food shortages and rampant inflation were threatening to destroy the very fabric of the society. Recognizing the grave consequences of their actions, the Vietnamese launched comprehensive economic reform at the end of 1986. After taking measures to liberalize trade and encourage joint ventures with foreign companies, the Vietnamese Communist Party dissolved collective farms, freed food prices, and cut off subsidies to state enterprises in 1988. When Vietnam withdrew its main forces from Cambodia in 1989, foreign investment began to flow into the country, albeit slowly at first. Although Vietnam lost large-scale Soviet aid, it was able to expand trade with market economies and record an average growth rate of around 10 percent per year during the 1990s. Thus, it took less than 10 years of systematic reform for Vietnam to make a leap from the depths of economic troubles and become one of the rising stars among late-developing countries.

Neither a Rogue nor a Tiger

In this scenario, the North Korean leadership has undertaken partial reform by incorporating into the formal sector many of the changes first introduced in the informal sector. For fear of causing major disruptions in the economy, Pyongyang refrains from rolling back such measures as price liberalization and marketization. At the same time, however, concerned with political instability, Pyongyang chooses not to go further with reform. Externally, the Six-Party Talks reach a comprehensive settlement. The DPRK agrees to freeze and then eventually dismantle its nuclear program in return for multilateral security assurances and the end of enmity between North Korea and the United States.

The combination of limited economic reform and improved external relations produces an outcome somewhat inferior to the outward-looking development dictatorship scenario. Although the comprehensive settlement of the nuclear issue and subsequent normalization of relations with Japan and the United States would bring economic assistance to North Korea, private-sector capital inflows are limited due to Pyongyang's half-hearted reform.[29] Economic assistance available after the resolution of security issues provides "a shot in the arm," but economic growth is constrained by limited reform and inadequate private-sector capital inflows. As a result, the DPRK's economic growth under this scenario is likely to be slower, perhaps around 4 to 5 percent per year. However, the North Korean leadership may not be disappointed with this outcome, because it may well feel that the combination of moderate growth and limited exposure to foreign capital is more conducive to stability.

Half Full, Half Empty

In this scenario, although Pyongyang embarks on economic reform, external cooperation is limited because of a continuing impasse over the nuclear issue. The North Korean leadership is reluctant to explore solutions to the nuclear problem unless there is a signal from the United States that it is committed to normalizing relations. At the same time, to avoid total isolation and to secure valuable economic assistance, Pyongyang tries to play its neighbors against each other. The United States, for its part, is content to keep North Korea as a rogue state as long as it does not cross the red line of transferring nuclear materials to the outside world or testing a nuclear weapon.

This impasse limits the effectiveness of reform: A shortage of capital and limited access to foreign markets constrain economic growth. Capital-strapped, with only a limited amount of economic assistance available, North Korea finds its efforts to modernize its economy inadequate to produce rapid economic growth. With little increase in the available amount of labor and capital, growth has to come almost entirely from productivity improvement, but productivity improvement itself is limited due to a lack of capital goods imports (embodied technology). This outcome roughly corresponds to North Korea's current situation. Annual economic growth cannot be much more than 2 or 3 percent per year.

Arduous March

This outcome is more in the past than in the future. In this scenario, North Korea does not undertake internal reform, since it is convinced that it confronts a serious risk of political instability and faces a hostile external environment. Contraction of the economy creates a great deal of suffering among unprivileged people. Pyongyang found itself in this position in the mid- to late 1990s. In many ways, North Korea's recent reform is in response to this costly experience. The DPRK is unlikely to revert to the policy choices that led to the arduous march, but this outcome cannot be wholly precluded.

Over the past decade, North Korea has moved from the arduous march to the "half full, half empty" situation. Pyongyang is unlikely to revert to the traditional planned economy, but its commitment to far-reaching market-oriented reform remains to be seen.

On the external front, unless the United States decides to truly move beyond the Cold War in Northeast Asia and craft a new order, it is likely to maintain its policy of malign neglect toward Pyongyang. In turn, North Korea is likely to engage in a series of provocative actions to escalate the crisis to the boiling point and draw attention from the United States. If and when the nuclear crisis is resolved, North Korea will then have to decide whether it is prepared to move toward full pursuit of economic integration with the outside world.

NOTES

1. See, for example, Marcus Noland, *Korea after Kim Jong Il* (Washington, D.C.: Institute for International Economics, 2003).

2. Northeast Asia Energy Database, Korea Energy Economics Institute, www.neasiaenergy.net/nea/stat/statview.nsf/Mainpage?OpenPage.

3. See Phillip Wonhyuk Lim, "North Korea's Food Crisis," *Korea and World Affairs* (Winter 1997), pp. 568–85.

4. FAOSTAT data, updated February 2005, faostat.fao.org.

5. On the growth of the informal sector in North Korea in the 1990s, see Hong-Tack Chun, "The Second Economy in North Korea," *Seoul Journal of Economics* (Summer 1999), pp. 173–94.

6. See Nicholas Eberstadt, "If North Korea Were Really 'Reforming,' How Could We Tell—And What Would We Be Able to See?" *Korea and World Affairs* (Spring 2002), pp. 20–46.

7. See Nicholas Eberstadt, *The End of North Korea* (Washington, D.C.: American Enterprise Institute Press, 1999). By contrast, Aidan Foster-Carter has argued that one of the possible modes of North Korea's "collapse" could take the form of North Korea's peaceful transformation. See Aidan Foster-Carter, "All Roads Lead to Collapse: All the More Reason to Engage Pyongyang," in *The Economic Integration of the Korean Peninsula,* ed. Marcus Noland (Washington, D.C.: Institute for International Economics, 1998), pp. 27–38.

8. This is from an unpublished Ministry of Unification survey of defectors from North to South Korea and visitors to North Korea (cross-border merchants, etc.). The 500-person survey was conducted in January 1999.

9. According to an internal document circulated in October 2001, Kim Jong Il talked about these problems as follows: "Because official prices set by the state are lower than farmers' market prices, there aren't enough goods in the formal sector, but individuals have stocked up goods ranging from rice to automotive parts. . . . The state is producing goods, but most goods and money end up in the hands of individuals. . . . Frankly, the state has no money, but individuals have two years' budget worth. . . . There was too much average-ism in distribution. Socially there were too many freebies. In providing food to residents, billions of won were spent annually at the expense of the state. . . . Because the socialist distribution principle was not properly observed and because there was socially an excess of freebies and average-ism, it had the effect of promoting hoodlums and discouraging workers' efforts."

10. See Chae-Ki Sung, "An Evaluation and Forecast of New Economic Policy Directions in the Kim Jong Il Era," *KDI Review of the North Korean Economy* (October 2002), pp. 11–30 [in Korean].

11. The title of the article in *Rodong Sinmun* may be roughly translated as follows: "The 21st century is a century of grand transformation, a century of creation."

12. See note 9. For example, Kim Jong Il's talk on economic reform on 3 October 2001 was titled "On Improving and Perfecting Socialist Economic Management in Line with Requirements for Building a Strong and Prosperous Nation."

13. For instance, the chairman of the External Economic Cooperation Promotion Committee is 47 years old, the governor of the External Trade Bank is 44, and the chief executive officer of the Chollima Steelmaking Company is 40. The recruiting procedure for public officials was also changed from a recommendation and interview system to an examination system in January 2004. For details, see Kim Young Yoon and Soo Young Choi, "North Korea's Economic Reform Trends" (Seoul: Korea Institute for National Unification, 2005), p. 12 [in Korean].

14. For details, ibid., p. 11.

15. In assessing the significance of the July 2002 reforms, some have tended to focus on the "transformation" aspect, while others have emphasized the "rehabilitation" aspect of the policy package. For an example of the former, see Yeon-Chul Kim, "The Nature and Outlook of North Korea's Economic Management Reform," in *A Study on North Korea's Economic Reform*, ed. Yeon-Chul Kim and Sun Song Park (Seoul: Humanitas, 2002) [in Korean]. For a more conservative interpretation emphasizing the rehabilitation of the formal sector, see Dongho Jo, *Prospects for Changes in North Korea's Economic Policy and the Role of Inter-Korean Economic Cooperation* (Seoul: Korea Development Institute, 2003) [in Korean].

16. For details on China's dual-track strategy, see Lawrence J. Lau, Yingyi Qian, and Gerard Roland, "Pareto-Improving Economic Reforms Through Dual-Track Liberalization," *Economics Letters* (1997), pp. 285–92. See also Justin Yifu Lin, Fang Cai, and Zhou Li, *The China Miracle: Development Strategy and Economic Reform*, revised edition (Peking: Chinese University Press, 2003).

17. See Moon-Soo Yang, "North Korea's General Markets: Realities, Repercussions, Character and Significance," *KDI Review of the North Korean Economy* (February 2005) [in Korean], pp. 19–21.

18. For details, see Yang, "North Korea's General Markets."

19. Although the Sinuiju venture was quite remarkable in that Pyongyang ceded administrative authority in the zone to a foreign businessman, it failed mainly due to China's concerns about the border city's plans to set up casinos.

20. For details, see Bank of Korea, "An Analysis of the Economic Impact of Establishing the Kaesong Industrial Complex" (July 2004) [in Korean].

21. On the fundamentals of scenario planning, see Peter Schwartz, *The Art of the Long View: Planning for the Future in an Uncertain World* (New York: Doubleday, 1991), and Liam Fahey and Robert M. Randall, *Learning from the Future* (New York: Wiley, 1998). For an applied example of scenario planning in a geopolitical context, see National Intelligence Council, *Mapping the Global Future: Report of the National Intelligence Council 2020 Project* (Washington, D.C.: Government Printing Office, 2005).

22. Bruce Bueno de Mesquita and Jongryn Mo, "Prospects for Economic Reform and Political Stability," in *North Korea after Kim Il Sung: Continuity or Change?* ed. Thomas Henriksen and Jongryn Mo (Stanford, Calif.: Hoover Institution Press, 1997), pp. 13–31.

23. Responding to North Korea's bargaining tactics, George W. Bush allegedly once said: "You're hungry and you can't eat plutonium."

24. Jonathan Pollack notes that faced with South Korean and Japanese moves to improve relations with North Korea in 2002, the Bush administration might have seen "a real possibility that its options on the [Korean] peninsula would be increasingly driven by the policy agendas of others." See Jonathan D. Pollack, "The United States, North Korea, and the End of the Agreed Framework," *Naval War College Review* 56, no. 3 (Summer 2003), pp. 10–49.

25. On this point, see Desaix Anderson, "Who Is Losing Asia?" mimeo, 2004. Also, Desaix Anderson gave a similar speech on 20 March 2003 at the Croft Institute of International Studies, University of Mississippi, Oxford, which was later published as a Policy Forum Online piece (PFO 03-25) on Nautilus (www.nautilus.org). The title of the speech is "Crisis in North Korea: the U.S. Strategic Future in East Asia."

26. See, for example, Haruki Wada, *A Northeast Asian Common House,* translated from Japanese to Korean by Won-Duk Lee (Seoul: Ilchogak, 2004).

27. Given China's efforts to present itself as a benign and nonhegemonic power, its handling of the Koguryo controversy was something of a surprise. With its territory extending from the northern half of the Korean Peninsula to Manchuria, the ancient kingdom of Koguryo had the potential to develop into a contentious issue between Korea and China for some time. A major controversy erupted in 2004 when the Chinese Foreign Ministry decided to remove Koguryo from the ancient history of Korea in the country profile section on its website. When South Korea protested, China responded by deleting the entire pre-1948 history of Korea. The only consolation to Koreans was that China was at least fair enough to do the same to Japan. Given North Korea's dependence on China, some Koreans interpreted these Chinese actions as an attempt to do the historical groundwork to expand its influence into the Korean Peninsula. The Chinese could have said that Koguryo was a multiethnic ancient kingdom whose rulers were Korean but whose cultural heritage was

shared by China and Korea, but the Chinese Foreign Ministry decided to go well beyond that. The Koguryo controversy led many Koreans to take a second look at China.

28. On South Korea's political and economic transition in the 1960s, see Wonhyuk Lim, *The Origin and Evolution of the Korean Economic System* (Seoul: Korea Development Institute, 2000).

29. While the Marshall Plan provided "seed money" in the postwar reconstruction of western Europe, it was private-sector capital that accounted for the lion's share of new investment. On this point, see J. Bradford De Long and Barry Eichengreen, "The Marshall Plan: History's Most Successful Structural Adjustment Program," in *Postwar Economic Reconstruction and Lessons for the East Today,* ed. Rudiger Dornbusch, Wilhelm Nolling, and Richard Layard (Cambridge: MIT Press, 1993).

PART FOUR

Strategic Horizons and Military
Futures, North and South

9

North Korea's Military Buildup and Strategic Outlook

Seung Joo Baek

As the North Korean economy has suffered major deterioration even as North-South relations have improved, the future prospects and directions of DPRK military strategy against South Korea assume crucial importance. Can the Pyongyang regime continue its traditional policy of maintaining superior military forces and devising military strategies to undermine and ultimately defeat South Korea? Or is this long-standing policy approaching its end? What signs, if any, exist of major changes in North Korean strategy?

Since the Korean armistice agreement of 1953, the DPRK has continuously pursued a strategy of military superiority against the ROK. North Korea managed to maintain the upper hand in military force levels over South Korea throughout the Cold War era. However, the economic crisis in the North since the collapse of the Soviet Union has posed very severe challenges for the DPRK in sustaining its long-standing military superiority.[1] It seems almost impossible for North Korea to maintain the necessary defense expenditures for its military buildup, making an adjustment of North Korea's defense policy virtually inevitable. In addition, North Korea's acceptance of simultaneous entry into the United Nations alongside South Korea in 1991, its adoption of the Agreed Framework in 1994, and the North-South summit in 2000 all seemed to reflect Pyongyang's effort to reduce outside military threats by political means.

However, since the onset of the second nuclear crisis in 2002, North Korean efforts to decrease military tension on the peninsula have taken a sudden U-turn. In particular, as the North witnessed American military precision attacks in the second Iraq war, its threat perception level was elevated. North Korea's military strategy remains based on fielding superior armed forces against the South, enabling "surprise attack, short-term blitz tactics, and the integration of conventional and unconventional warfare" to achieve rapid conquest of the southern half of the peninsula. Pyongyang has increased its military forces and deployed troops in precise accordance with this southward invasion strategy.

Nevertheless, with the near collapse of the DPRK's economy, modernizing the equipment necessary for conducting Pyongyang's southward blitzkrieg has become an enormous burden. North Korea's past military alliances are also of dubious operational value. The Russia-DPRK military alliance was abrogated at the request of the Kremlin in 1996. In addition, enhanced PRC-ROK military relations mean that the North can no longer count on China to uphold the terms of the China-DPRK mutual defense treaty.

This chapter has two principal objectives. The first objective is to project the possible directions of North Korea's force buildup. I intend to differentiate various components of the traditional DPRK policy into those that can continue and those that must be changed. The second objective is to anticipate how North Korea's military strategy will be maintained or developed.

NORTH KOREA'S FORCE BUILDUP: HISTORY AND THE POTENTIAL FOR CHANGE

Military Policy in the Kim Il Sung Era

The North's military force buildup was launched at the fifth plenary meeting of the fourth Korean Workers' Party (KWP) Central Committee in December 1962. This meeting "plac[ed] the build-up of the military as the first priority, despite the possibility of impeding the development of the people's economy," with the leadership adopting the principle of a completely independent national self-defense.[2] This principle was embodied in the Four-Point Military Guidelines. They were designed specifically to implement the independent national self-defense doctrine: (1) equipping all the people with arms; (2) transforming the whole country into an impregnable fortress; (3) converting the whole army into an army of cadres; and (4) modernizing the military establishment.

Under these precepts, North Korea emphasized domestic production of basic military equipment, construction of underground military facilities, establishment of Red Labor Civilian Forces, and other armed civilian groups. At the Fifth KWP Congress in November 1970, Kim Il Sung personally evaluated the implementation of the four principles as a success:

As a result of implementing the four military principles, the entire population possesses and can fire a rifle. An ironclad bastion of defense structures has been built all around the country and even vital production sites have been fortified. The establishment of self-reliant military equipment production facilities has empowered us to manufacture necessary modern weaponry and combat hardware.[3]

Table 1   North Korea's Four-Point Military Guidelines

Guideline	Contents
Equipping all the people with arms.	Laborers, farmers, and other rank-and-file workers shall be "armed" with political ideology and military expertise, along with the Korean People's Army (KPA)
Transforming the whole country into an impregnable fortress.	By constructing enormous defensive structures all over the country, the territory shall be formed as an impregnable military fortress.
Converting the whole army into an army of cadres.	To render the possibility of performing a one-higher level task in case of a conflict, the ranks of the KPA shall be trained with intensive political ideology and military expertise.
Modernizing the military establishment.	The KPA shall be armed with modernized weapons according to the needs in fighting a modern warfare.

In the 1970s, North Korea attained absolute quantitative force superiority vis-à-vis South Korea thanks to its indigenous military production capabilities built during the 1960s. The DPRK began producing tanks, self-propelled artillery, and armored vehicles for the ground forces, and small submarines and combat vessels for the navy. Pyongyang undertook manufacture of Chinese T-59 tanks with assistance from the Soviet Union; by duplicating Soviet and Chinese models, the North also mass-produced large field artillery and self-propelled artillery. With a major improvement of its shipbuilding skills, the North began to manufacture various types of patrol boats, Soviet KOMAR-class guided-missile frigates, 1,500-ton cruisers, and Romeo-class submarines. At the Sixth KWP Congress in October 1980, Kim Il Sung stated that "accomplishment of the self-reliant military principle has provided a formidable defensive capability."[4]

In the 1980s, North Korea focused on the development of more technologically advanced hardware, including a potential nuclear weapons capability and ballistic missiles. The North also improved the conventional weapons in its inventory, manufacturing Mi-2 helicopters, MiG-21 fighters, and YAK-18 trainers. The DPRK was also able to import advanced military hardware from the Soviet Union. In the 1990s, the North noticeably accelerated its development of strategic weaponry over additional conventional weapons development. The North pursued strategic offensive capabilities through nuclear weapons development, enhanced pursuit of asymmetric warfare capabilities with the development of MRBMs and IRBMs, and acceleration of chemical weapons and biological weapons programs.[5]

Military Policy during the Kim Jong Il Era

It is likely that Kim Jong Il seeks to maintain superior military forces against the South, placing first priority on flaunting the North's strengthened capabilities and denying any potential weakness. By extolling its military might (which it believes to be superior), the North hopes to reinvigorate its frail economy and also strengthen its international standing. This course of action is not surprising. Kim Jong Il has emphasized that the strong military might of the North has established and protected the North Korean socialist system as a "Great and Powerful State":

> Regardless of how much a state pretends to be a superpower, the absence of accurate leadership ideology, independent political philosophy, ideological conflicts, and a strong military presence makes the state's assertion of superpower status unfounded.

> Beginning with erecting an ideologically formidable state, constructing a strong military that is built upon firm columns of the revolutionary might, and then concentrating on the economic prosperity with the momentum gained from the military, are the teachings of our General's construction method of a superpower state through *juche*. When the party is strong and the people's ideological resolve and enthusiasm are at the fever pitch, achieving economic prosperity becomes an easy task; and by having a formidable army, we need not fear even an enemy of 10 million strong; thus, Chosun has proven that it can proudly demonstrate the dignity and preeminence of the Korean race to the world.[6]

Thus, Kim Jong Il and his inner circle believe that military might affords the best means to enhance the power and security of the DPRK. For example, Hwang Jang Yop, the senior North Korean official who defected to South Korea in February 1997, believes that North Korean military might is far superior to that of the South. As he subsequently testified, "I overheard the military personnel of North Korea boasting about their possession of a weapon that has enough capability to turn South Korea into 'ashes' three times." He also referred to "unimaginably strong military capacity and a mysterious new weapon" that officials in the North bragged about in private. What might these capabilities be?

On 5 April 1996, around the time Hwang Jang Yop decided to flee North Korea, a former editor of *People's Korea,* Kim Myung Chol, discussed four distinctive characteristics of North Korea's military capability, in an article entitled "Supreme Leader Kim Jong Il's War Plan."[7] First, Kim asserted that fortification of the entire country had been completed to prepare for war. All of the military necessities, such as airfields, army bases, submarine docks, and missile launch sites, had been placed in granite shelters and deep underground bunkers, enabling North Korea to defend itself either in a conventional or nuclear conflict. Second, Kim argued that the North's military forces were superior in size to those of the South. According to Kim, if a conflict were to break out, the North's available military reserves totaled 250 operational divisions.

Third, Kim claimed that North Korea was preparing to develop new weapons especially suitable for its war plans. North Korea's ballistic missiles could cover the entirety
of South Korea, most of Japan, and American military installations in the West Pacific;
he further asserted that North Korean missiles had the capability to reach the west
coast of the United States. The North Korean navy's large number of diesel submarines
was designed to deploy and operate in the shallow waters of the Yellow Sea and in the
deeper waters of the East Sea. Moreover, domestically produced antitank missiles
would supposedly counter the American M1A1 tank, and KPA infantry purportedly
carried specially engineered antiaircraft rifles that can bring down aircraft and helicopters. According to Kim, North Korea's frontline defense force used this rifle against
an American helicopter in December 1994, supposedly downing it with only one shot.
Kim further described North Korea's vast air-defense network, centered on surface-to-
air missiles and shoulder-launched Stinger missiles; this system could supposedly detect and shoot down any type of aircraft flying over North Korean airspace.

Fourth, Kim claimed that the North had the ability to build nuclear weapons at a time
of its choosing, enabling it to carry out a nuclear war scenario against the United
States. According to Kim, "if Kim Jong Il feels the need to produce nuclear weapons,
the North could acquire a few nuclear weapons in a short period of time, and it employs numerous nuclear physicists and experts related to the weaponization process."
In addition, Kim claimed that the DPRK "possess[ed] a tactical ability to generate the
same effects of nuclear weapon usage by exploding nuclear generators and other nuclear facilities in its controlled territory."

The claims of Kim Myung Chul and defectors like Hwang Jang Yop cannot be accepted
uncritically.[8] For example, Kim's claims may be intended to exaggerate North Korea's
capabilities for psychological and political purposes. But these accounts suggest that
Pyongyang believes it has achieved absolute force superiority vis-à-vis South Korea.[9]
To paraphrase, the North Korean regime appears to underestimate the military capabilities of the South while overrating its own. Pyongyang's overconfidence in its military capabilities is reflected in its offensive military policy toward South Korea. North
Korea's test-firing of a long-range missile on 31 August 1998, was an additional attempt to flaunt its supposed military supremacy. The repeated infiltration of spy vessels (even during a period of closer relations with the South during the late 1990s)
highlights a persistent strain of hostility directed against the ROK, as well as the
North's continued reliance on military capabilities for political purposes. However, the
potential effects of these policies on North Korean behavior in an acute crisis are more
difficult to judge.

Evaluating the North's Capabilities

In terms of quantity, North Korea's military force ranks as the fifth-largest in the world. As shown in the table below, the KPA consists of approximately 1,106,000 soldiers. The army has about 3,500 tanks and roughly 950,000 personnel; the navy has 313 combat vessels and about 46,000 personnel; and the air force possesses 504 fighters and about 110,000 personnel. Such large forces reveal North Korea's immense military might.

Table 2   North Korea's Military Forces

Forces		Numbers
Total Number of Troops		1,106,000
Army	Troops	950,000
	Units	Corps: 20; Reserve Divisions: 40; Brigades: 18
	Tanks	3,500
	Armored Vehicles	2,500
	Artillery	10,400
	Antitank Weapons	AT-1/3/4/5
	Guided Missiles	1 SCUD brigade, 1 Frog brigade
Navy	Sailors	46,000
	Vessels	313 combat vessels
Air Force	Troops	110,000
	Aircraft	504 fighters, 80 bombers, 306 helicopters.

Source: IISS, The Military Balance 2004–2005. London: Oxford University Press, 2004, pp. 178–79.

Defense policy makers in Seoul believe that the North continues to increase its military force despite its extreme economic stagnation. South Korea judges that the North has continued its policy of attaining WMD capabilities, including nuclear and chemical weapons, as summarized below.[10]

Table 3   North Korea's WMD Capabilities and Potential

Nuclear	Chemical	Biological
10–14 kilograms of weapons-grade plutonium, which can produce 1–2 bombs, and necessary weaponization expertise.	2,500–5,000 metric tons of chemical agents.	Presumed to have various strands of biological agents, such as smallpox.

Source: Ministry of National Defense, Defense White Paper 2004, pp. 44–45.

The most important evaluation, however, is to compare North Korea's military forces with those of the South, rather than in absolute terms. There are two sharply contrasting opinions on this issue. One view asserts that the North still maintains its force superiority over the South, and a separate view claims that the North has lost such superiority.[11] The Ministry of National Defense holds the former view. South Korean defense officials and conservative military analysts base their judgments about the military superiority of the North on several major factors. First, although the reinforcement rate of the North's major weapons systems has been stalled, the North's quantitative advantage over the South has been maintained. Second, the North has absolute superiority in strategic weapons over the South. Third, the command structure and the deployment have been tailored to implement Pyongyang's version of blitzkrieg. In addition, the ground force's high mobility and the rapid invasion capability of the navy and the air force would allow Kim to carry out a blitzkrieg strategy.

In contrast to South Korean defense circles, certain nongovernment researchers believe that the North Korean military has lost its superiority over the South. First, the continued deterioration of the North's equipment has rendered their quantitative advantage meaningless. Second, most North Korean hardware is heavily reliant on Soviet design and expertise, which has been proven inferior to that of the United States in one military conflict after another. Third, the North Korean military's preparedness and training are increasingly unsound because of the nation's economic crisis. Fourth, given the wide gap between the economies of the North and the South, Pyongyang is at an absolute disadvantage in fighting a protracted war. Fifth, North Korea's overall spending on operations and defense procurement since the late 1980s has lagged far behind that of the South. Sixth, Pyongyang's military alliance status has been weakened due to the abrogation of its alliance with Russia and also due to the development of friendly relations between the South and the PRC.

The North Korean regime also assesses the North-South military balance in relation to the continued presence of U.S. forces. Hwang Jang Yop and other defectors from the North have testified that the North Korean regime believes it would have a military advantage over the South if the USFK withdraws from the peninsula. Hwang further suggests that Pyongyang believes that possession of nuclear weapons confers particular military advantage to the DPRK.

Outlook for the Future

Over the past five decades, the North Korean regime has tried to maximize its military advantage, believing that military superiority would guarantee its security and political-military dominance. However, it is probable that Pyongyang will shift its primary objective to the ability to cause damage.[12] For the next several years, the North is likely to seek ways to maintain and extend its buildup of military capacity. The question is how the North can undertake such steps in a far less favorable political and economic environment.

First, the DPRK will try to extend the operational life span of its conventional weapons. Although North Korea enjoys a quantitative advantage over South Korea in conventional weapons, most of these weapons are outdated and of questionable value. Even with the North's clear advantage in strategic capabilities, maintaining its conventional forces is unquestionably part of the North's strategy. Pyongyang will most likely lean toward extending the operational life span of outdated weapons, a far more economical option than procuring new conventional weapons. Second, the North will continue its efforts to build an asymmetric force. Although the North might temporarily suspend or deemphasize the development of strategic weapons for the sake of improved relations with various major powers (including the United States), such political breakthroughs will not eliminate Pyongyang's continued desire to acquire such weapons. With regard to missile development, North Korea will likely comply with restrictions on exporting or transferring of technology to other nations, but it will continue to claim a sovereign right to produce and deploy these missiles for its own security. Third, in order to counter South Korea's pursuit of the revolution in military affairs (RMA), it is highly likely that the North will pursue its own RMA by building cyberforces and enhanced intelligence capabilities, so as to neutralize the advanced technologies of the South.

Fourth, the North will attempt to limit the ROK's own military buildup. Pyongyang would seek to meet its objectives by seeking: (1) withdrawal of USFK; (2) suspension of ROK-U.S. joint military exercises; (3) dissolution of the Combined Forces Command (CFC); and (4) slowing of the South Korean military's arms procurement efforts. Under the difficult circumstances that the North faces, it is more than likely that the North will try to limit the enemy's force buildup by political means. The North recognizes that the most cost-effective means to neutralize the South Korean military's ability to challenge the KPA is through political negotiations with the United States and the ROK. Thus, the above objectives would all be main agenda items in prospective talks on the normalization of U.S.-DPRK and ROK-DPRK relations.

EVALUATING THE DPRK'S MILITARY STRATEGY

Kim Il Sung's Military Strategy

The basic tenets of the military strategy formulated by the Kim Il Sung regime consist of surprise attack, blitzkrieg, and the integration of conventional and unconventional warfare (i.e., launching of simultaneous surprise attacks in the forward and rear areas). To understand this approach, we need first to examine the ideological factors behind the North's strategy and the feasibility of executing the strategy, given the current military capabilities of the North.

Surprise Attack

The term "surprise" is defined as "striking the enemy at a time and place and through means that the enemy did not anticipate." The guideline states that "attacking the enemy in an unaware state is important; however, it is more important to make certain that the enemy believes it is already too late to effectively counter the attack, even if the enemy has become aware of the attack." Generally, surprise would mean that "a defender would miscalculate first, whether or not the enemy would attack, and if so, misjudge at least one element of when, where, and how the enemy would attack, and thus would be unable to effectively defend itself." Tactical surprise occurs when the defending state is unable to acquire intelligence regarding the enemy's intent to invade, or regarding determining the timing, direction, and means of attack before the conflict arises.

There are three ways to detect signs of an enemy's intent to attack: political, strategic, and tactical. At a political level, a forewarning of war is evident when political tension between two states crosses the threshold of sustaining peace. At the strategic level, the enemy's mobilization of forces, infiltration of forces, or execution of an invasion plan are the critical indicators. Forewarning at a tactical level would involve detection of the enemy's movement plan before the start of the conflict. In assessing the effects of surprise at the strategic level, the advantage of having specific forces and equipment is multiplicative, and the expected effect of a successful all-out surprise attack is like a geometric progression. It is impossible to precisely gauge the effect of a surprise attack in terms of quantity. However, some research suggests a force attrition rate for the defense in case of a surprise attack to be 1 to 5 in favor of the attacker, whereas in the case of a nonsurprise attack the ratio is 1 to 1, favoring neither side. For the instigator, the importance of establishing the element of surprise is inversely proportional to its strategic inferiority or the expected reciprocation from the enemy.[13]

North Korea's strategic objective would be to isolate and neutralize the greater Seoul metropolitan region, hindering the operation of South Korean military forces. The focus of the North Korean attack would be on neutralization or destruction of command and control posts, neutralization or annihilation of major field forces in the northern metropolitan area, and obliteration of the South's capability to continue the war. In executing the surprise attack strategy, the first strike, conducted by the North's strategic bombers, would target air force bases, antiaircraft and radar sites, and communication systems, as well as artillery and mechanized divisions. In addition, the strategy would focus upon infiltrating/striking the North's unconventional forces into the greater Seoul metropolitan region, suppressing South Korean resistance, and inducing potential chaos.

The secondary strike would consist of breaking through the frontline South Korean forces, possibly using chemical attacks, which would be followed by an attempt by mechanized forces to widen the invasion corridors and intensify the conflict. The critical region would be a target or area that is directly related to a state's ability to continue the war. It would include water networks, military command headquarters, key littoral waters, and concentrated military infrastructure; the next priority would be regional areas and target cities that would directly influence the conduct of the war and serve as transportation hubs, command and control posts, and key navy and air force bases.

To execute a surprise attack, the North has forward-deployed its ground troops and naval vessels; occupied several forward air bases; maintained a disproportionately high number of special forces and equipment for their infiltration; and increased the number of self-propelled artillery while extending their range. In considering capability, deployment, and the distinctive nature of modern warfare, the North is believed to be capable of limited strategic attack as well.

The North Korean Blitzkrieg

The North Korean version of blitzkrieg focuses on rapid and concentrated force, obliterating the main ground force of the enemy before the arrival of reinforcement troops in the theater, thereby destroying the enemy's will to fight. The core components of this strategy are rapid strategy and execution capability and a massive attrition rate achieved in the early stages of a war, most likely utilizing chemical weapons. North Korea also possesses seven rapid movement forces (four mechanized divisions, two artillery divisions, and one tank division), with these divisions deployed far to the south, near the invasion corridors. Pyongyang would insert two mechanized divisions, a tank division, and an artillery division in the forward area at an early stage of the conflict, and would utilize two mechanized divisions and an artillery division as a follow-on force.

With regard to chemical warfare, the North can produce 4,500 tons of chemical agents at its eight chemical factories, and it already has 1,000 tons of agents in storage; furthermore, it has diversified delivery mechanisms for the chemical agents, such as artillery shells, missiles, and aircraft. Chemical warfare would play a critical role in the rapid strategy execution capability to be employed against frontline South Korean troops. North Korea's surprise tactics would be focused mainly on attaining the conditions favorable to mobility warfare; thus Pyongyang's forces would first move to destroy roadblocks and other impediments to the operation of its mobile forces. By utilizing its special forces to neutralize the fence line, penetrate through assault, or infiltrate underground or from the air into the Forward Edge of the Battle Area (FEBA) "A" defensive belt and other key sites, the North plans to capture invasion corridors, disable the command structure of the South Korean military, and cause massive chaos. The tactical environment of the Korean Peninsula and the invasion corridors do pose problems for the success of the North's blitz tactics; however, Pyongyang would stick to its plan and do its best to achieve its strategic goals.

INTEGRATING CONVENTIONAL AND UNCONVENTIONAL WARFARE

An integrated conventional and unconventional strategy would seek to compel South Korean forces to form a second front in a rear area, using unconventional tactics while continuing the fight at the first front by conventional means. This would disrupt Seoul's supply lines or compel ROK forces to shift to multiple fronts, which would undermine Seoul's resolve by instituting the "simultaneous front and rear battle effect." This approach is the conceptualization of *juche* strategy contained in the "Kim Il Sung Anthology," a collection of Kim's writings. Former Chief of the General Staff Han Ik Soo of North Korea describes this strategy as "concentration and separation, vigilant defense and causing disturbance in the rear, forming of a second front in the enemy's rear, and effective deployment of snipers and mobile artillery." Kim Il Sung asserted that his tactical strategy of *juche* is the accurate reflection of modern and revolutionary warfare's merging point, finalizing the KPA's strategic concept.[14]

The integration of modern and diversionary warfare calls for integration of conventional and unconventional warfare methods, incorporating the operations of large and small fighting units. Fortification of all regions, all people's resistance, blitz tactics, effective use of troops, and sensible command are core principles of the integration tactics, and they are divided into tactical, operational, and strategic considerations, according to the command echelon.[15] The special infiltration forces are formed into brigades, light infantry, land support, air, and naval brigades, as well as snipers. Numerous light infantry and reconnaissance units are configured at the battalion level. Landing Craft Air Cushioned (LCAC) ships, submarines, and high-speed landing craft can be used to infiltrate along both the eastern and western coasts. The North also has helicopters, transport aircraft, AN-2s, and other low-altitude air infiltration assets.[16] To carry out such a combined strategy without distinguishing the front or the rear, the North would plan on destroying metropolitan areas or regions where South Korean military bases are concentrated, simultaneously attacking other strategic sites with special forces and WMD capabilities to cause chaos, seeking to reap maximum benefits from the element of surprise.

KPA deployments reflect the larger strategy. North Korea has forward-deployed 60 percent of its ground forces below the Pyongyang-Wonsan Line, which allows the army to conduct a surprise attack without repositioning itself. By using its quantitative advantage of patrol boats, landing craft, and small submarines, the KPA Navy has the capability to rapidly transport and infiltrate conventional and unconventional forces into the South. The numerous LCACs in its inventory can be operated over tidal flats, efficiently carrying out infiltration and landing operations. By using its quantitative advantage and employing its numerous AN-2s, the North can conduct massive air in-filtrations. North Korea has a relatively high number of strategic sites, and these are spread across its territory. The North can deploy large numbers of aircraft even under severe time constraints; the aircraft can be positioned deep and spread across its terri-tory. The command structure of the KPA is designed to give the General Staff Depart-ment control of the ground force's command center and that of the navy and the air force, hence providing a combined command structure. The Ministry of People's Armed Forces (MPAF) exercises administrative and command authority under the overall control of the Military Committee of the Central Party and the National De-fense Committee (NDC).

KIM JONG IL'S MILITARY-STRATEGIC GOALS

North Korea confronts major challenges to successfully executing its blitzkrieg strat-egy. If the North could acquire additional resources for its military forces, it could in-crease the effectiveness of its already quite formidable blitz tactics.[17] It would seek to increase the mobility of the ground forces by procuring more hardware for the tank and mechanized divisions. It would also try to acquire an army aviation support group (such as attack helicopters) to increase the mobility of its forces. Furthermore, it would enhance its outdated armored and mechanized forces. In order to fix the flaws of its naval forces, which were exposed during the Yeun-pyung naval engagement in 1999, the North would strive to modernize and acquire larger vessels. Although it has retained a quantitative advantage in naval forces, small vessels dominate the navy, and this has significantly limited the force's operational range.[18] To increase the utilization rates in its air force, it would construct additional airfields, enabling more rapid distri-bution of its air assets. Finally, to decrease the effectiveness of the South's precision-strike-capable and qualitatively superior air force, the North would diversify its target list. Pyongyang could also construct numerous decoy bases; the Kosovo conflict dem-onstrated the effectiveness of such deception tactics.

Pyongyang clearly recognizes the disadvantages of trying to conduct a protracted war against the South, and the growing gap in economic resources cannot be overcome in a short time. Despite these constraints, Pyongyang will likely stick to its blitz tactics and prepare its forces according to current war doctrine. Logically, it would also continue its efforts to frustrate South Korea's ability to fight a protracted war. It would step up its psychological warfare, seeking to hinder effective execution of the ROK's war plans and possibly intensifying a terror-based strategy to undermine the South's continued reliance on foreign support. It will not lightly set aside a strategy it has developed and refined for decades, but it clearly seeks all available means to compensate for the potential limitations of this approach to warfare.

Nuclear Weapons Development

In his article "The War Plan of Marshal Kim Jong Il," Kim Myung Chol highlights Kim Jong Il's reputed perspectives on war and nuclear weapons.[19] According to Kim, there are six situations that Kim Jong Il has described as war-prone conditions on the Korean Peninsula:[20]

- The United States and the ROK initiate a war due to the sudden rise in political dangers faced by the South Korean government.
- The United States and the ROK seek to destroy Pyongyang's socialist system and forcefully reunify Korea, all the while underestimating the North's military, political, economic, and social capability.
- Economic sanctions are placed on North Korea, after which the North accelerates its nuclear weapons development.
- Miscalculation on the part of the United States and South Korea.
- The United States and ROK militaries instigate a limited conflict. For instance, an American aircraft could intrude into North Korean airspace and be shot down, or an American naval vessel could enter North Korean territorial waters and be sunk, triggering major hostilities.
- The United States and the ROK preemptively attack the North based on a miscalculation that the demise of North Korean socialism is imminent.

All six of these situations could be used domestically and internationally by Kim Jong Il to place responsibility on the United States and South Korea in the case of a conflict. According to Kim Myung Chol, Kim Jong Il has stated that "North Korea would not sit idly while the U.S. and South Korea show signs of preemption against her, and the KPA is well trained for this type of defensive–initial attack to protect itself," thereby laying out a scenario in which the North would initiate a war.[21]

How would the North conduct such a war? Kim Myung Chol claims that Kim Jong Il has disclosed the following commands that he would give in the case of war with the United States:

> First, kill tens of thousands of American soldiers. Second, shoot down hundreds of American planes. Third, sink the U.S. 7th Fleet, such as a nuclear-powered aircraft carrier or a nuclear submarine. Fourth, completely demolish the American nuclear bases. Fifth, let the inhumane conditions of the war be broadcast to the American mainland. Sixth, launch long-range missiles loaded with highly effective warheads to Japanese and American strategic targets, such as nuclear power plants, along with the metropolitan areas of New York and Washington, D.C.[22]

These purported instructions seem almost beyond comprehension, and well beyond the realm of what is remotely feasible in operational terms. Can they possibly reflect real guidance to North Korean forces? This seems hugely doubtful, but they may be intended to avoid lapses into extreme pessimism on the part of North Korea.

Kim Myung Chol also asserts that Kim Jong Il recognizes the major constraints imposed on any state employing nuclear weapons, with the United States inhibited for multiple reasons from again employing such weapons in war. But he further states that even without nuclear weapons and with its preexisting conventional forces, North Korea can conduct a war with nuclear implications. Kim asserts that, in response to an American attack, the North Korean military might attack nuclear-armed American forces or bases, nuclear-powered naval vessels, and nuclear power plants near American bases, deriving the same effect as using its own nuclear weapons against these targets. According to Kim Myung Chol, these targets could include

- Nuclear power plants in South Korea, Japan, and the United States;
- Nuclear-powered U.S. naval vessels;
- Nuclear weapons deployed at American bases;
- Nuclear-armed American weapons systems (i.e., bombers, submarines, and missiles).

Does Kim Jong Il believe that developing nuclear weapons is a realistic goal? In 1994, the North's acceptance of the Agreed Framework suggested that Pyongyang would forgo such capabilities. However, Kim sought to emphasize that signing the agreement was not submitting to American demands, but relinquishing only one of the means to conduct warfare with nuclear implications. Although he appeared to give up pursuit of nuclear weapons, Kim must have wanted to demonstrate the North's ability to cause massive damage to American forces, even by conventional means.

But North Korea now claims to possess nuclear weapons. Assuming that Pyongyang has such capabilities, how does Kim Jong Il perceive their strategic value? At the very least, he would have discarded the "notion of uselessness" he seemed to accept after signing the Agreed Framework. He could also attempt to blackmail South Korea by identifying the potential circumstances in which he might be forced to use nuclear weapons. The first is if the United States initiates war with North Korea. He would caution the South that he would respond with nuclear weapons if the United States conducts surgical air strikes against suspected nuclear weapons sites. The second situation is if the United States and South Korea attempt to overthrow the Pyongyang regime and militarily reunify the North. The third situation is if the United States and South Korea militarily respond in full force against a limited conflict initiated by the North. Fourth, should the Pyongyang leadership fall into chaos and foreign forces intervene in the internal politics of the North, Kim might threaten to use nuclear weapons to fend off such an intervention. To defend itself against challenges from the outside, a nuclear-armed North Korea would send a simple and clear message: North Korea will never die alone.

These claims highlight the profound changes in North Korea's strategic situation. The economic hardship experienced by North Korea has adversely affected its defense spending, and hence its military buildup. If the North Korean leader chooses to shift course in response to these new circumstances, he will still seek to retain the military advantage while trying to decrease the burden of defense spending on the nation's economic recovery.[23] The North Korean regime will seek to maintain its policy of military superiority over the South because it believes that a weakened military puts the survival of the regime at risk. Therefore, to minimize the negative effects of its outdated forces, it will try to develop a strategy that enhances the role of strategic weapons. This will be especially relevant if the North ever concedes that it has lost its conventional force superiority. It will pursue a policy that tries to demonstrate its superiority over the South by flaunting the strategic capabilities in its hands, rather than concede that its military buildup can no longer protect the fundamental interests of the North Korean regime.

NOTES

1. Chae Ki Sung et al., *Ten Years of Economic Crisis and North Korea's Capacity to Increase Military Spending* (Seoul: KIDA, 2003), pp. 54–103.

2. Ministry of Unification [hereafter MOU], *North Korea Guide* (Seoul: Ministry of Unification, 2000), available at unibook.unkkorea.go.kr/bukhandb_01_view.jsp.

3. MOU, *North Korea Guide*, available at unibook .unikorea.go.kr/bukhandb/bukhandb_06 _09.jsp.

4. Kang Seok-seung, "DPRK Military Trend and ROK Security," *National Defense Journal*, November 2001.

5. Ryu Dae-bum, "North Korea at the Brink of Regime Crisis," *National Defense Journal*, July 2003.

6. *Nodong Sinmun*, 22 August 1998.

7. Kim Myung Chol, "Marshal Kim Jong Il's War Plan," www.kimsoft.com/kim-war.htm, pp. 4–8.

8. Hwang Jang Yop, "Grand Strategy to Seize DPRK Regime," *North Korea Democratization Forum*, 29 March 2005; Hwang Jang Yop, "Special Report: Future of Korean Peninsula," *Daily NK*, 11 May 2005, available at www.dailynk.com/korean/read.php?catald=nk02200&num=5391; Kim Duk-hong, "Kim Jong Il, National Enemy," paper presented at the 13th Defense Security Seminar, hosted by the Korea National Defense University, 28 April 2004.

9. Kim Myung Chol, "Last Round of DPRK-US Nuclear Confrontation," *Minjok Tongsin*, 27 March 2003.

10. Ministry of National Defense, ROK, *The ROK's Defense Expenditure in Preparation for the Future, 2003* (Seoul: MND, 2003), p. 10.

11. Representatives from several civil groups and individual participants presented two different views at the discussion on the *Defense White Paper—2004*, held in the National Assembly on 30 May 2005.

12. The buildup of military superiority over the South denotes the force superiority of the North Korean military over the combined forces of South Korea and the United States. Bruce Bennett, "The Dynamics of The North Korean Threat: The Erosion of North Korean Military Capabilities, Real or Imagined?" *The Changing Dynamics of Korean Security*, presented at the Joint Conference, Korea National Defense University, 1998, pp. 187–88.

13. Yun Kwang-sup, "Characteristics of DPRK Military," *National Defense Journal* 332, August 2001.

14. KPA, *Korean People's Army* (Pyongyang: KPA Military Press, 1987), pp. 43–47.

15. Ministry of Unification, *North Korea Guide 2004* (Seoul: Ministry of Unification, 2004).

16. *Defense White Paper—1999*, (Seoul: Ministry of National Defense, 1999), Chapter 3.

17. Ibid., p. 37.

18. At the hearing at the National Assembly, the ROK Defense Minister said that North Korea increased the frequency and level of training after the June naval clash. The Air Force Chief of Staff said that North Korea had increased efforts to build up its military preparations in October 1999.

19. Kim Myung Chol, "Marshal Kim Jong Il's War Plan," www.kimsoft.com/kim-war.htm, pp. 4–8.

20. Ibid., p. 9.

21. Ibid.

22. Ibid.

23. Sung, "Ten Years of Economic Crisis," pp. 131–32. Sung and four other KIDA researchers predict that Pyongyang in the future will (1) begin troop reductions; (2) restructure the economy, which is still heavily concentrated on military hardware production; (3) reorganize the military to cut defense spending; (4) focus on improving the performance of its key equipment; and (5) continue the production of more cost-effective weapons.

10

South Korea's Military Capabilities and Strategy

Yong Sup Han

Since the end of the Korean War, South Korea has focused its conventional military capabilities on deterring and defending against the military threats posed by North Korea. The United States has played an essential role in deterrence as well as defense, because of the North's persistent threats and its numerical and strategic advantage. Seoul's primary emphasis has been on maintaining and strengthening the alliance relationship with the United States. In recent years, however, the alliance has faced increased challenges, as both countries have experienced major changes in their perceptions of international security. As a result, South Korean policy makers have sought to develop a future-oriented strategy that ensures national security while retaining core alliance ties with the United States.

Despite the decreasing possibility of armed conflict, the Korean Peninsula remains the most dangerous flash point in Northeast Asia and perhaps in the world. Korea is still divided, and the two Koreas continue to engage in a sustained arms competition, with massive forces arrayed on both sides. The North seeks to maintain its military advantage at the risk of regime failure; it has also renewed development of nuclear weapons. Although Pyongyang argues that the purpose of its nuclear weapons capability is to deter the threats posed by the United States, the North's claims of nuclear weapons possession undermine security on the Korean Peninsula and in Northeast Asia as a whole. Thus, even as the South's economic and political situation continues to improve relative to the North, it faces new security challenges, all at a time of increased uncertainty about the longer-term U.S. role on the peninsula.

Over the decades, South Korea's role in the U.S.-ROK alliance has undergone major changes, from sole dependence to combined defense, and, prospectively, to a self-reliant defense. But Seoul's recent advocacy of self-reliant defense is not entirely new. In the early 1970s, then-President Park Chung Hee first proclaimed this goal, hoping to dispel abandonment fears triggered by President Nixon's unilateral withdrawal of U.S. forces from the peninsula. The incumbent South Korean president, Roh Moo Hyun, has renewed calls for a self-reliant defense in response to the Bush administration's implementation of its Global Posture Review, which is realigning the worldwide distribution of U.S. military forces. These changes require security planners and decision makers in both countries to rethink South Korea's defense objectives, to assess North Korean threats, and to redesign military strategy and force planning goals in the alliance. This chapter reviews South Korea's military capabilities and strategy, with particular attention to South Korea's defense objectives and future national security requirements.

SOUTH KOREA'S DEFENSE OBJECTIVES

South Korea's official national security goals were established in 1973 and were largely unchanged until the advent of the Roh Moo Hyun government. The goals were: (1) to protect the nation under the ideology of liberal democracy and preserve permanent independence through peaceful unification of the peninsula; (2) to protect people's rights, freedom, and social welfare through enhanced living standards; and (3) to enhance national pride and prestige and contribute to world peace.[1] From these national goals, South Korea's defense leadership inferred security objectives, including defending the nation from external military threats and invasion, upholding peaceful unification, and contributing to regional stability and world peace.[2]

However, South Korea's official national goals have been redefined by the Roh Moo Hyun government. They include the following: to preserve the nation and uphold sovereignty; to safeguard the nation under a liberal democracy and promote human rights; to achieve and promote economic growth and people's welfare; to establish peaceful coexistence between South and North leading to national unification; and to contribute to world peace and prosperity.[3] National security goals now include maintenance of peace and stability on the Korean Peninsula, pursuit of common prosperity for South and North and in Northeast Asia, and assurance of public safety. Defense goals had not directly been linked to higher national goals until the advent of the Roh presidency.

The Roh government has defined South Korea's principal defense objective as realization of a self-reliant and advanced defense posture.[4] This encompasses four guiding principles: to establish a firm national defense posture, to build future-oriented defense capabilities, to reform the defense system continuously, and to improve the welfare and living conditions of the military. South Korea also intends to contribute to global peace and security by expanding the roles and missions of its armed forces. The ROK government has actively participated in international peacekeeping operations and has pursued confidence-building measures on the peninsula and in the Northeast Asian region.

South Korea has also maintained an exclusively defensive strategy and doctrine against possible attacks by North Korea, in part by not undertaking retaliatory actions against North Korea's military provocations. South Korea has also maintained its commitment to a nonnuclear policy, thereby hoping to contribute to the resolution of the North Korean nuclear issue through dialogue and by peaceful means. South Korea also advocates the goals of cooperative security and common economic prosperity. This environment-shaping policy goal is worth highlighting, because until 2003 South Korea's defense goals were limited to deterrence and defense.

THE NORTH KOREAN MILITARY THREAT TO SOUTH KOREA

North Korea's offensive strategy and posture represent the gravest military threat that South Korea continues to face. North Korea's long-standing military strategy has been to launch a surprise attack intended to sweep the entire peninsula before the arrival of U.S. reinforcements. In this context, North Korea's nuclear weapons development is very disturbing, because nuclear weapons could be used to deter the United States from introducing reinforcements in the Korean theater. It is assumed that the North Koreans will strike the front and rear at the same time with a mix of mechanized troops, armored vehicles, self-propelled artillery and missiles, and special forces. Although this is a worst-case scenario, it has become less likely because the military balance on the peninsula no longer clearly favors Pyongyang.

The shifting estimates of the North Korean threat have been a major factor in national policy debate. This has included whether the South should continue to designate the North as the main enemy. This issue first arose following the first North-South summit of June 2000 and the signing of a Joint Statement by former President Kim Dae Jung and North Korean leader Kim Jong Il. North Korea used the Joint Statement and subsequent events to split South Korea and the United States. North Korean propaganda attempted to pit the Korean race against a foreign country, an obvious ploy to expel the United States from the peninsula while simultaneously advocating national cooperation between North and South. The Bush administration's labeling of North Korea as part of the "axis of evil" added more fuel to the fire, thus enabling South

Korean progressives to join the North in its propaganda war against the United States. In 2001 the ROK Ministry of Defense also suspended publication of its annual Defense White Paper, which until then had consistently termed North Korea the main enemy. The principal enemy issue aside, most South Koreans still acknowledge that North Korea's military threat remains substantial.[5]

Despite economic constraints, North Korea has maintained a military buildup emphasizing heavily mechanized forces, massive forward-deployed forces, and strengthened firepower with long-range artillery and missiles. North Korea has also sought qualitative improvement of its conventional forces, and it has resumed military exercises that it had halted because of the major economic downturns of the 1990s. In addition to its traditional Four Point Military Guidelines (fortification of the entire nation, armament of the entire populace, modernization of military equipment, and conversion of all servicemen into cadres), North Korea in 1992 revised its constitution to reiterate the importance of short-time surprise attack and breakthrough warfare. North Korea has continued to field long-range heavy artillery units equipped with 170-mm self-propelled artillery and 240-mm multiple rocket launchers, combined with the full-fledged development of long-range missiles, while periodically undertaking provocative actions against South Korea.

Despite South Korea's efforts to match North Korea's military force levels, the South is still far behind the North in numerical terms. The North has also retained its numerical advantage in most categories of conventional weapons. Although some experts maintain that the technological edge of the South can compensate for the numerical advantage of the North, other analyses of the conventional balance indicate that the South would not be able to maintain forward defense under a war scenario, should the North achieve the strategic surprise that underlies its military plans of the past four decades.[6] Some analysts perceive a growing danger that North Korea might initiate a war out of desperation. In particular, some U.S. experts warn that the North might initiate the use of chemical warfare based on a belief that this is the only way for the North to win the war before U.S. reinforcements are mobilized to counterattack.

North Korea is estimated to possess approximately 2,500 to 5,000 tons of chemical weapons and agents, while maintaining eight chemical plants to produce more chemical agents.[7] It also possesses delivery systems for chemical weapons such as mortars, field artillery, multiple rocket launchers, and Frog-5, Frog-7, and Scud missiles. In addition to chemical weapons, North Korea's missiles constitute a major threat to South Korea as well as Japan. The North is estimated to have more than 600 Scud-B and C missiles and to have developed and deployed one hundred No Dong-1 missiles with ranges over 1,000 km. If the North starts a chemical campaign against U.S. forces in

Korea and the South's major military bases, especially air bases, the North will be able to inflict acute damage on the ROK-U.S. Combined Forces. Therefore, chemical and biological attacks are considered increasingly worrisome as the conventional balance approaches parity, provided that South Korea and the United States adhere to a defense-only strategy and posture. If the North Koreans experience initial success with their air suppression and ground surprise attack, this may tempt them to use chemical weapons with missile delivery systems, which could seriously undermine U.S. and South Korean defenses.

There are also other dangers associated with crises and conflicts short of war, in particular associated with North Korea's possible threats to employ nuclear weapons. For example, the North Koreans might turn their internal crisis into an external conflict either by deploying weapons against South Korea in an effort to receive assurances of regime survival, or by launching suicidal attacks that would end their regime.

SOUTH KOREA'S MILITARY STRATEGY AND DOCTRINE

South Korea's military strategy is designed to meet two simultaneous defense objectives: deterring military threats in peacetime and defending in wartime. These two objectives are the centerpiece of South Korean defense goals. The possibility of a North Korean surprise attack is the most obvious threat to South Korea's security. Seoul has relied on the bilateral alliance with the United States to deter North Korea's military threats. Nuclear and conventional deterrence through the bilateral alliance has been the core of South Korean strategy. The nuclear equation on the peninsula could therefore significantly affect future deterrence. If North Korea somehow retained nuclear weapons, it could greatly complicate U.S. nuclear deterrence commitments to South Korea. Thus, if the Six-Party Talks do not succeed, the situation on the Korean Peninsula will become far more unstable.

South Korea has also relied upon the combined ROK-U.S. deterrence strategy. Although South Korea is far stronger than North Korea in comprehensive national power, South Korea has not made maximal use of its economic and technological capabilities to develop a strong conventional weapons arsenal, because of competing budgetary demands from other sectors of society. Instead, the South has maintained self-imposed restraints on military manpower and has adopted a defensive strategy requiring smaller numbers of military personnel and weapons than the North.

Following the Korean War, South Korea strengthened fortifications and chose a linear and forward defense, so as not to allow North Korea even an inch of South Korea's territory. The U.S. role was indispensable to these efforts. Together with U.S. forward presence in the South, the deterrence strategy has long served the security objectives of both South Korea and the United States, although it has not prevented periodic North Korean terrorist and infiltration activities. However, it is questionable whether South Korea can quickly fill the security vacuum as forward-deployed U.S. forces in Korea relocate to rear areas or withdraw outright from the peninsula. It is also questionable whether South Korean ground forces can deal effectively with a major firepower attack initiated by the North. This is a priority area where South Korea needs to invest as the U.S. moves away from its tripwire mission.

What types of operational concepts and guiding principles of war would the South use in the case of a North Korean attack? South Korea's countermeasures against all-out war initiated by North Korea consist of three parts: (1) responding to North Korea's surprise attack as quickly as possible; (2) defending the capital and rear areas; and (3) defending territorial sea and air space at the same time. To minimize damage and casualties in the initial phase of the war, South Korean forces are well trained to immediately counter a North Korean attack. This includes performing blocking maneuvers with tank barriers and artillery counterattack, directed against North Korea's first-echelon forces (including highly mobile and mechanized forces), while cutting off logistical support for invading forces by executing an air-ground attack on the first echelon. However, South Korean forces' ability to quickly restore a coherent defense hinges on their overcoming any panic that might result from artillery and missile attacks on Seoul at the beginning of the war. In 2004, South Korea released war-game results indicating that even in an armed conflict limited to conventional weapons only, there might be two million casualties within 24 hours after the outbreak of war.[8]

South Korea is also establishing an integrated operational command system to implement joint operations at the initial stage of combat with ground, air, and sea forces. Enhanced information warfare capabilities would undoubtedly shorten Seoul's response time. To minimize initial damage or panic, automated and integrated warning systems are crucial, thereby leading Seoul to operate a 24-hour-a-day early-warning system. Since it is South Korea's responsibility to defend Korea before the arrival of U.S. reinforcements, South Korea needs to enhance its air-defense capabilities together with its own surveillance and early-warning capabilities. South Korea's improvements in battlefield surveillance and early warning systems; command, control, communications, computers, and intelligence (C4I); and air defense missiles can improve the balance, but these projects will require major budgetary outlays, including plans to acquire an AWACS system from the United States.

Should the security environment around the Korean Peninsula and North Korea's long-term prospects become even more unstable and uncertain, new threats that

South Koreans have not previously considered will likely draw increased attention. Debates on the utility of a blue-water navy and the use of deterrence by denial in the form of augmented air power have surfaced periodically, only to be halted because of budgetary constraints faced by the ROK government. South Korea hopes that the United States will draw down its forces from South Korea gradually, so as not to create a major vacuum in defense capabilities on the peninsula, but this remains to be seen.

To accomplish a successful defense of the capital and rear areas, South Korea is emphasizing defense against long-range artillery and missile attack on Seoul and improving the readiness of reserve forces in the rear. Rear-area defense is required to prevent North Korea from simultaneously making front and rear attacks by relying on its special forces. Thus, early mobilization of reserve forces and training becomes very important. But South Korea must also defend the territorial sea and air from a North Korean attack. South Korea has established a twelve-mile territorial sea zone and has upgraded sea patrols to protect the territorial sea and sea lanes of communication. For air defense, the ROK Air Force is continuously keeping air control over Korean air space by quickly intercepting enemy aircraft. In addition to holding the North Korean attack at the front, a counterattack doctrine is necessary to strengthen deterrence and defense. In this connection, South Korea has adopted an active defense doctrine. New operational measures are being taken at the Combined Forces level between South Korean and U.S. forces. Active defense is under increased consideration to shorten the time between holding operations and a counterattack mission.

SOUTH KOREA'S DEFENSE PLANNING AND FORCE STRUCTURE

South Korea's defense planning centers around three specific goals: (1) fostering an advanced self-reliant defense posture through a technology-intensive force modernization; (2) maintaining and strengthening the ROK-U.S. security alliance; and (3) improving security relations with neighboring countries. To foster a more self-reliant defense posture, the South has continuously pursued its Force Improvement Program, both to address North Korean military threats and to look beyond the immediate security requirements toward potential threats arising beyond the Korean Peninsula. This last point is related to a notable increase in naval and air modernization in recent years. However, South Korea's economic crisis in 1997 and competing demands on budgetary resources from other sectors of the nation have reduced the defense budget's share of the GNP over time: 3.2 percent of Korea's GNP was spent on defense before the economic crisis in 1997, with this figure declining to 2.7 percent in 2002, though it experienced a modest increase in 2003 and 2004 in pursuit of a self-reliant defense policy.

Table I   **Ratio of Defense Expenditures to GDP and Government Budget (in percentage terms)**

	1999	2000	2001	2002	2003	2004
Share of GDP	3.1	2.8	2.8	2.7	2.8	2.8
Share of Budget	16.4	16.3	15.5	14.9	15.6	15.8

Source: The Republic of Korea Ministry of National Defense, *Defense White Paper 2004*, p. 215.

As shown in the table, modest increases in the share of GNP devoted to national defense are insufficient to fulfill President Roh Moo Hyun's goal of self-reliant defense. The five-year plan to accomplish a self-reliant military force envisions that South Korea will possess multipurpose satellites, AWACS and tactical command and control systems, ground force capabilities able to conduct mobile and deep strikes, and next-generation destroyers for the navy and next-generation fighters for the air force, while simultaneously filling the capability gap created by the withdrawal or redeployment of U.S. forces.[9]

In the early 1990s, South Korea and the United States had agreed that South Korea would assume the lead role in the alliance, with the United States in the supporting role.[10] The two countries further materialized the division of labor in 1994 with the transfer of peacetime operational control authority from the Commander-in-Chief, Combined Forces Command, to the South Korean Armed Forces. However, planned reductions of USFK force levels and discussions over possible transfer of wartime operational control to South Korea halted during the nuclear crisis of 1993–94. The Clinton administration subsequently decided to maintain a 100,000-troop level in the west Pacific, including 37,000 troops in Korea. These U.S. decisions reduced South Korea's willingness to fulfill its commitment to assume the lead role in the alliance. It was not until June 2004, when the United States notified South Korea of its plan to withdraw 12,500 troops from the peninsula and to move troops from the Yongsan area to the Pyongtaek area by 2008, that the ROK was compelled to rethink its budgetary commitments.

Modernization of national defense capabilities has been achieved through a combination of domestic production and foreign acquisitions, mainly from the United States. In 1973, Seoul began to produce basic defense equipment and weapons with U.S. technical assistance in the name of self-reliance, principally because the Nixon administration withdrew the 7th Army Division from the peninsula. During the 1980s, defense production declined significantly because the ROK government changed its arms procurement policy from domestic production to overseas procurement in order to acquire more high-tech weapons, once again from the United States. At that time, South Korea imported F-16 fighters and other advanced weaponry from the United States.

Seoul is currently reforming its defense system with an emphasis on the creation of forces suitable for the knowledge-based information age. It is transforming its force structure from a labor-intensive force into one that will become more technology intensive, thereby meeting future requirements stemming from information warfare. A self-reliant defense will also require a more balanced force structure among three military services. Traditionally, the ground forces have dominated the South Korean armed forces. However, South Korea faces a major dilemma in force structure changes because the United States is removing its ground forces from South Korea, thereby transferring to South Korean forces missions previously assumed by U.S. personnel. At the same time, South Korea recognizes the need of its armed forces to integrate ground, naval, and air forces to execute joint war plans effectively. The Korean ground forces are stressing the importance of improved strategic and tactical intelligence to secure high-speed air-land battle capabilities and joint warfighting capabilities. The navy is focusing on improving joint operation capabilities and enhanced naval power. The air force is concentrating on improving combat capabilities for multiple purposes and early warning. However, changes in force structure are difficult because of bureaucratic inertia and interservice rivalry.

Since the Korean War, almost all of Seoul's defense efforts have been devoted to maintaining and developing the ROK-U.S. alliance. Currently, the ROK-U.S. alliance is supported by three pillars: the ROK-U.S. Mutual Defense Treaty, signed in 1953; the ROK-U.S. Combined Forces Command, established in 1978; and the annual Security Consultative Meetings, started in 1968. Until very recently, U.S. forces in Korea were mainly responsible for holding a North Korean attack in the front, with later counterattack against North Korean forces. However, with the United States forgoing its tripwire mission, the traditional alliance is undergoing drastic change. It is also expected that the size and speed of U.S. reinforcements on Korean soil will change as the United States undertakes major shifts in its military strategy. In this regard, wartime reserve stocks for allies, prepositioning, and wartime host-nation support will assume increased importance.

South Korea and the United States have been consulting to devise mutually acceptable solutions to changes in alliance relations. Through the Future of the ROK-U.S. Alliance Policy Initiative (FAPI) talks, the two allies have sought to address U.S. force reduction and base relocation issues. However, it is not yet certain that these discussions will produce an outcome that is satisfactory to both sides. The outcome of these deliberations will have major implications for future South Korean defense strategy. The ROK-U.S. security alliance has profoundly influenced all aspects of South Korean strategy, doctrine, defense planning, and training and exercises. Indeed, Seoul cannot think of its defense without the United States, and South Korea wants the United States to pay increased attention to ensuring a successful transition.

With the end of the Cold War, South Korea has sought to broaden ties with countries in Asia and the Pacific through military exchanges and cooperation. In an effort to stabilize the Korean Peninsula, South Korea has increased military-to-military contacts with neighboring countries, including Japan, Russia, and China. South Korea has also tried to diversify defense procurement and defense technology cooperation, especially with European countries, although it acknowledges the importance of interoperability with U.S. forces. As long as North Korea remains the major military threat, South Korea realizes that there will be inherent limitations to efforts to enlarge military ties with Asia-Pacific countries. Multilateral cooperation cannot guarantee security. Nevertheless, broadening and deepening policy consultations with surrounding countries can contribute to the creation of a more peaceful and cooperative security environment in Northeast Asia.

ALLIANCE TRANSFORMATION UNDER TENSION

The ROK-U.S. alliance has long been deemed a major success story in bilateral security cooperation. However, this history has hardly been free of conflict or tension. Two major changes have been attributable to U.S. initiatives and South Korea's resultant responses. In 1971, in response to the U.S. decision to withdraw the 7th Army Division, President Park Chung Hee proposed the goal of self-reliant defense. After the end of the Cold War, the Nunn-Warner Act authorized a three-stage troop withdrawal from South Korea. The latter case entailed a more productive, forward-looking response, because it linked phased changes in the U.S. presence and the alliance structure to developments in the North-South relationship.

The third and biggest change is currently under way, with the United States initiating major shifts in strategy and deployment under the banner of alliance transformation.[11] The USFK is undergoing fundamental change through relocation of military bases and reduction of forces but also in defense strategy. According to U.S. Secretary of Defense Donald Rumsfeld,[12] the tripwire function has been rendered obsolete, replaced by rapidly deployable forces; the United States describes this as a shift to capability-based force planning, instead of the threat-based force planning of the past.

However, South Korea is also proposing major changes in the alliance. With the improvement of inter-Korean relations, Sunshine Policy proponents began to argue that the United States was a hindrance to peninsular reconciliation and cooperation, rather than a facilitator of the peaceful coexistence of the two Koreas and ultimate unification. Growing nationalistic assertiveness within South Korea led to calls for a more equitable bilateral relationship. A number of serious security issues are challenging the future of the alliance, including the rise of China; Japan's growing nationalism and territorial claims; North Korea's nuclear weapons program; and terrorism and potential proliferation of weapons of mass destruction.

Many in Seoul and Washington are voicing increased concern about the future of the alliance. But sharp debate continues in both capitals over North Korea's resumed pursuit of nuclear weapons and over U.S. strategy to deal with this renewed challenge. Numerous South Korean leaders and public opinion supporting reconciliation toward North Korea have expressed discontent with the Bush administration, with some even questioning the continued need for the alliance. After the South Korean government decided to send troops to Iraq and reiterated the importance of the ROK-U.S. alliance, hostility toward the United States somewhat diminished, but tension continues to flare intermittently. However, future prospects for the alliance remain highly uncertain. There are three major challenges to the future alliance, as discussed below. Differences between Korea and the United States could become bigger unless properly managed by policy makers in both systems.

Perception Gaps Regarding the North Korean Threat

Inside South Korea, there are widely divergent views about the North Korean threat. Those who regard all Koreans as "one people" or see North Korea as "a partner in cooperation" have greatly increased in strength, compared with those who still regard the North as the enemy. "One people" advocates argue that the United States and the South Korean defense community have exaggerated the North Korean threat, so that a lasting reduction of tensions can happen only if South Korea more actively aids Pyongyang, ends its military alliance with the United States, and predicates its unification policies on an independent stance.[13] Pyongyang has manipulated this view in an effort to separate South Korea from the United States, demanding that South Korea should choose between "national unity" and "cooperation with external forces."

Some South Koreans also believe that North Korea's conventional weapons have become so degraded and obsolete that Pyongyang's nuclear weapons may represent the only real threat.[14] Some civic groups have accused South Korea's Ministry of Defense of exaggerating North Korean military strength and dwelling on South Korea's supposed military weakness.[15] Former President Kim Dae Jung's belief that a war on the Korean Peninsula was a virtual impossibility led some in the South to conclude that the North Korean threat had disappeared. Even those concerned about the North's renewed nuclear activities tend to regard North Korea's threat as overestimated by U.S. intelligence.

By contrast, U.S. officials assert that the North Korean threat has neither diminished nor disappeared, especially in the context of Pyongyang's nuclear weapons development.[16] The Pentagon has asserted that there had been no tangible reduction of the North Korean threat despite the June 2000 inter-Korean summit. In early 2002, North Korea was designated as part of the "axis of evil" by President Bush; subsequently, the United States labeled North Korea an "outpost of tyranny."[17] The United States believes that the North's nuclear weapons claims reinforce these judgments.

In late 2004, the South Korean government sought to end the internal debate on whether to still deem North Korea the main enemy. After suspending publication for several years, a new Defense White Paper was released at the end of the year. It did not employ the term "enemy" but did describe North Korea as a direct threat to South Korea with respect to its conventional military forces, its weapons of mass destruction, and its forward-deployed forces.[18] Therefore, South Korea is trying to bridge the differences in threat assessment without triggering hostile reactions by the North. However, there is a growing gap in Korean and American perceptions of the North Korean military threat that makes a coordinated strategy toward the North increasingly difficult to achieve.

Self-Reliant Defense versus Alliance

The Roh Moo Hyun administration has renewed calls for a self-reliant defense. The government argues that South Koreans cannot live in anxiety whenever the United States decides to pull out troops from Korea. The concept of a self-reliant national defense policy has drawn attention from conservatives in Korea as well as America. Korean progressives claim that the ROK-U.S. alliance has prolonged South Korea's subservience to the United States.[19] They have criticized conservatives for viewing the goal of self-reliance as harmful to South Korea's security and to the alliance. Indeed, the debate over defense strategy parallels the earlier debate over the Sunshine Policy.

The present debate represents a domestic reaction to the U.S. cutback of troops in Korea and to the realization that the alliance with the United States has put limits on South Korea's autonomy in security and defense policy. South Korea has voiced entrapment fears that it might be dragged unintentionally into a war if the United States makes a surgical strike on North Korean nuclear facilities. The U.S. attack on Iraq not only reinforced North Korea's resolve to pursue its nuclear weapons program but also reaffirmed the goal of South Korean progressives to pursue a more independent stance. North Korea exploited this situation, claiming that North Korea's nuclear question arose not because of North Korea's nuclear weapons program but because of the U.S. "hostile policy" toward North Korea.[20] Pyongyang's strategy to split Seoul and Washington partly succeeded.

The South Korean government asserts that self-reliant defense and a strengthened alliance with the United States can go hand-in-hand, calling its objective a cooperative and self-reliant defense policy.[21] South Korea intends to build up self-reliant defense capabilities to be able, within a decade, to deter and defend against North Korean attack on its own. The South Korean armed forces will be strengthened to the extent that they can acquire full command and control within a decade. By then, USFK would assume primary responsibility for maintaining regional stability, while South Korea would take charge of defense on the Korean Peninsula. But huge questions persist about South Korea's new strategic direction and how it could affect the future of the alliance.

Regional Security and Strategic Flexibility

As South Korea deliberates its longer-term approaches to peace and security, the role of the ROK-U.S. alliance is undergoing increased domestic scrutiny. South Korea's increasing political and economic tilt toward China and renewed tensions with Japan have been central to these deliberations. Japan's growing nationalism and territorial claims have aroused anti-Japanese sentiment in Seoul that parallels anti-Japanese views in China. Before these rifts and fissures vis-à-vis Japan erupted, South Korea showed more affinity with Japan. Some Korean experts advocated a southern triangular relationship, which the United States also sought to encourage.[22] But disputes over territory and history textbooks again triggered bitter memories of the Japanese colonial period. Japan's efforts to become a normal state were seen by South Koreans and Chinese as encouraging a strengthened U.S.-Japan alliance. This included mounting criticism of the United States for allowing Japan to become overly assertive in its defense and foreign policy.

The United States needs to remain fully aware of Koreans' memory of Japan's colonial rule and deeply rooted distrust of further Japanese rearmament. South Korea remains uneasy about being included in enhanced U.S.-Japan alliance arrangements. South Korean political leaders and predominant public opinion criticize any suggestion that strengthening the trilateral relationship would provide immunity to Japan for its past wrongdoings. South Koreans are unwilling to enhance trilateral security cooperation that could antagonize China.

Korean views of the U.S. pursuit of strategic flexibility are equally critical in this context. According to this concept, U.S. forces deployed in one location can redeploy to another region and do not require an ally's explicit approval to do so. This concept connects all U.S. forces abroad (including those assigned to Korea) to a broader set of missions. Such an approach is readily understandable from the perspective of U.S. military planners, since strategic flexibility is indispensable to U.S. global military strategy. The implementation of the Global Posture Review is meant to utilize lighter, speedily deployable military capabilities by making maximum use of the U.S. superiority in command, control, communications, computers, intelligence, surveillance, and reconnaissance (C4ISR); precision-guided munitions (PGMs); and computer networks.[23] As the United States is transforming its alliances by connecting all military assets across national borders, it is inevitable that strategic flexibility will affect the sovereignty and security of traditional allies. To different degrees, Japan, Australia, and various members of NATO are supporting this concept, and the United States hopes to persuade South Korea to do so as well.

However, the South Korean government and significant portions of the Korean public believe that the ROK-U.S. alliance should remain focused principally on Korean security. The perceived linkage between the alliance and regional stability appeared to weaken in the 1990s as support for a U.S. military presence in Korea after unification diminished.[24] Korean civic groups expressed increased concern about the possibility that South Korea might be drawn into a war either on the peninsula or in the Taiwan Strait. President Roh strongly argued that South Koreans will never allow themselves to be involved in any conflict in Northeast Asia against their will.[25] This statement was made several times during March 2005 in support of South Korea's pursuit of a "balancer role" in Northeast Asian security. President Roh thus argued that strategic flexibility should not allow any possibility of South Korea's involvement in a regional conflict against its interests and preferences.

There is obvious potential for a major dispute between South Korea and the United States in this area. If South Korea stands firm on not allowing flexibility to USFK, will USFK remain limited to the Korean peninsula, or will USFK leave the peninsula altogether? Will USFK be shrunken to a small-scale force for a purely peninsular role? Or will South Korea consent to increased flexibility for USFK in a future crisis? None of the answers to these questions are yet clear.

CONCLUSION

The U.S. influence on South Korea's defense planning, force structure, crisis management, military strategy, and doctrine has been dominant for so long that many observers cannot imagine South Korea's defense without the alliance. However, the alliance is changing rapidly, as the United States applies its military transformation and new global posture to the Korean Peninsula. As South Korea endeavors to take a primary role in defending against North Korea, the command structure of the ROK-U.S. combined forces and the force mix of the two countries need to change accordingly. As most South Koreans begin to believe that military parity with the North has been achieved and that a smaller U.S. force will remain in Korea, demands for a reconfigured alliance will increase within South Korea. During this transition period, therefore, Seoul and Washington need to pay more attention to the maintenance and development of the alliance.

For more than a half-century, the ROK-U.S. security alliance has been successful in achieving its basic objectives. But past accomplishments do not guarantee future success. New challenges and increased distrust are overloading the old alliance. Younger generations, new political elites, and different policy rationales have already begun to undermine the robust security relationship. These circumstances suggest an imperative need for a new vision and new values in the alliance, ones that can address the emergent challenges of peace and stability on the peninsula and beyond. Deterrence and defense need to be supplemented by a vision of peaceful coexistence and peaceful unification of the Korean Peninsula. Devaluing and mistrusting the relationship with the United States needs to end in Seoul, while impatience and anger about the new South Korean elite needs to end in Washington.

Now is also the time to rebuild and enhance trust through joint actions, not by words. So far, Washington has failed to fully recognize the growing national pride in South Korea, resulting both from the country's economic and political achievements and from the change of generations in Korea. The United States should avoid unilateral notification to South Korea of its redeployment decisions regarding U.S. forces on the peninsula. The "shock therapy" directed against South Korea should be avoided, if the two allies want to sustain a healthy two-way alliance. Security consultation talks also need to include issues of how to deal with an emerging China and other countries in the Northeast Asian region, enabling both leaderships to plan for the long-term future.

In attempting to develop a self-reliant defense posture, South Korea needs to be more responsible for increasing defense expenditure and to prepare to assume command and control of the ROK-U.S. Combined Forces. With South Korea more self-reliant, the defense policy–making process will become more mature and accountable and the force structure will become more balanced. South Korea also needs to manage the alliance relationship more prudently and skillfully. Therefore, a policy of strengthening a self-reliant defense posture for South Korea is desirable for both countries. South Korea will need more U.S. advice and mature consultation for the future success of its long-term defense goals.

NOTES

1. The Republic of Korea, Office of the National Security Council, *Official Memorandum 911-18*, 26 March 1973.

2. ROK Ministry of National Defense [hereafter MND], *The Defense White Paper 1994*, May 1994.

3. The National Security Council of the Republic of Korea, *Peace, Prosperity, and National Security: Security Policy Framework of the Participatory Government* (Seoul: NSC, 2004), p. 20.

4. MND, *Participatory Government Defense Policy 2003* (Seoul: MND, 2003), p. 30.

5. In the nationwide opinion poll taken in 2003, 60.2 percent of South Korean respondents agreed that North Korea's military is stronger than South Korea's military if U.S. forces in Korea are not taken into consideration, whereas 19.7 percent of the respondents said the reverse was true.

6. The Korea Institute for Defense Analysis conducted a military balance assessment in 2004 and submitted the report to the National Security Council. According to the KIDA report, South Korean ground forces amount to 80 percent of North Korea's, South Korean naval forces amount to 90 percent of North Korea's, and South Korean air forces amount to 103 percent of North Korea's. This analysis was based on the WEI/WUV (Weapons Effectiveness Index/Weighted Unit Values) method. However, war sustainability was not taken into account. See *Joongang Ilbo*, 30 August 2004.

7. *Defense White Paper*, p. 45.

8. *Kukmin Ilbo*, 20 August 2004, A-2.

9. ROK MND, *Defense White Paper 2004*, December 2004, p. 210.

10. U.S. Department of Defense, *A Strategic Framework for the Asia Pacific Rim: Looking Toward the 21st Century* (Washington, D.C.: 1992), p. 15.

11. Director of Force Transformation, Office of the Secretary of Defense, *Military Transformation: A Strategic Approach* (Washington, D.C.: Fall 2003).

12. Secretary of Defense Donald Rumsfeld, speech at the Shangri-La Dialogue, *Straits Times*, 5 June 2004.

13. Norman Levin and Yong-Sup Han, *Sunshine in Korea: The South Korean Debate over Policies Toward North Korea* (Santa Monica, Calif.: RAND, 2002), p. 50. At the peak of the South-North relationship (especially after the inter-Korean summit), the "one people" viewpoint amounted to 40 percent of respondents, a "partner to cooperate with" reached 50 percent of respondents, and "enemy" view holders declined to 5 percent of respondents. *Joongang Ilbo*, 3–6 August 2000. This rate sharply changed to 22 percent of respondents indicating North Korea as enemy in January 2001. *Joongang Ilbo*, 3 January 2001.

14. Korea Institute for Defense Analysis, *Strategic Outlook 2004* (Seoul: KIDA, 2004).

15. Kang Jung Koo, et al., *Reorganizing the Korea-U.S. Relationship in Transition Period* (Junhwangi Hanmigwangei ui Saepanjjagi) (Seoul: Hanul Publishers, 2005).

16. Assistant Chief of Staff, Resource Management, HQ U.S. Forces in Korea, *US Forces Korea Resource Management Fact Book*, 2002, pp. 10–12.

17. U.S. President George W. Bush, Inauguration Speech, 20 January 2005.

18. ROK Ministry of National Defense, *Defense White Paper 2004*, December 2004.

19. Kang, et al., *Reorganizing the Korea-U.S. Relationship*, Chapter 1.

20. DPRK News Agency, New Year's Address of Kim Jong Il, 1 January 2004.

21. ROK National Security Council, *Peace, Prosperity and National Security*.

22. Sung Han Kim, "Challenges and Visions of ROK-U.S. Alliance: A Korean Perspective," paper presented at the International Conference hosted by the Korean Association of International Studies for Fifty Years' Alliance: Reflections and Future Vision on the ROK-US Security Cooperation, 25–26 September 2003.

23. U.S. Under Secretary of Defense for Policy Douglas J. Feith, *Prepared Statement before the House Armed Services Committee*, 23 June 2004, www.pentagon.mil/speeches/2004/sp20040623-0522.html.

24. Norman Levin, *The Shape of Korea's Future: South Korean Attitudes Toward Unification and Long-Term Security Issues* (Santa Monica, Calif.: RAND, 1999), p. 44.

25. President Roh Moo Hyun, speech at the Korea Air Force Academy, 8 March 2005.

PART FIVE

Korea in Northeast Asia

Korea as Viewed from China

Phillip C. Saunders

The Korean Peninsula constitutes an enduring focus of Chinese political, economic, and security interests. Concerns about foreign influence in Korea have prompted Chinese involvement in two major wars, the Sino-Japanese war in 1895 and the Korean War in 1950, with significant long-term consequences for China's territorial integrity and internal political development. Defeat in the Sino-Japanese war cost China control of Taiwan and influence in Korea, as both territories eventually became Japanese colonies. China's involvement in the Korean War strengthened the U.S. commitment to the Republic of China and resulted in the continued separation of the island of Taiwan from mainland China.

These historical interests are still relevant today. Instability in Korea has the potential to damage the security environment in Northeast Asia, with significant implications for China's security and economic development. North Korea's nuclear weapons development could prompt a military conflict or proliferation of nuclear weapons in Northeast Asia that would directly affect China's security. Even if the current nuclear crisis is managed successfully, a collapse of the North Korean regime could produce a flood of refugees and local instability that would affect the stability and economies of China's northeastern provinces. Although North Korea is a net drain on China's economy, South Korea plays an increasingly important positive role in China's economic development. This includes not only robust bilateral trade relations but also contributions from South Korean investment and technology. In addition, Korea plays an important role in Sino-U.S. relations, giving China's Korea policy a global dimension.

To assess Chinese policy priorities and calculations regarding the Korean Peninsula, I will first examine changing Chinese assessments of North and South Korea over the last twenty years. These assessments illuminate the range of Chinese interests at stake on the peninsula and illustrate how broader changes in Chinese domestic and foreign policy have influenced Chinese thinking about Korea. The next section reviews Chinese short-term interests in Korea, with particular attention to China's efforts to avoid worst-case outcomes such as an overtly nuclear North Korea, a North Korean collapse, or a military conflict. The chapter concludes by exploring China's long-term interests on the Korean Peninsula and how Korean reunification might affect those interests. There is significant divergence among Chinese analysts on these issues, partly because the nature and intensity of Chinese interests in Korea depend heavily on analytical assumptions about the timing and process of reunification, the future security environment in Asia, and the state of Sino-U.S. relations. Although cooperation between the United States and China in managing the nuclear crisis has been relatively successful to date, over the long run many Chinese analysts expect Korea and the U.S. military presence in Asia to become a source of conflict in Sino-U.S. relations.

RELATIVE VALUE OF NORTH AND SOUTH KOREA

Chinese assessments of the relative value of North and South Korea have shifted significantly in South Korea's favor over the last twenty years. A major reason is the impact of Deng Xiaoping's policy of *gaige kaifang* (reform and opening up). Market-oriented economic reforms not only sparked China's remarkable period of sustained economic growth but also moved China away from Marxist-Leninist orthodoxy. The high priority that Chinese leaders placed on economic development had significant foreign policy implications. Deng's assessment that the international situation was basically peaceful supported improved relations with capitalist neighbors and an emphasis on maintaining a stable regional environment that would assist Chinese economic development. The shift away from ideological solidarity toward a more pragmatic foreign policy reduced barriers to establishing relations with South Korea and raised South Korea's potential value as an economic partner.

Nevertheless, moving from recognition of North Korea as the sole legitimate government of Korea to dual recognition of "two Koreas" was a delicate matter for the Chinese government. The DPRK was China's only formal ally. Its ideological importance as a fellow socialist country increased after Chinese leaders used force to suppress the Tiananmen protests in June 1989 and as communism collapsed in Eastern Europe later that year. North Korea was the only country to provide public support for China's Tiananmen crackdown. In response to these conflicting considerations, Beijing adopted a cautious policy that followed the Soviet Union's lead in supporting the admission of both Koreas into the United Nations in 1991. After making efforts to cushion the negative impact on relations with Pyongyang, China established formal diplomatic relations with Seoul in 1992.[1]

The priority placed on stability and economic development in Chinese foreign policy eased this delicate transition, but Chinese leaders were also concerned with two important ideological issues: (1) whether joint recognition of North Korea and South Korea would have negative implications for Chinese reunification with Taiwan; and (2) the perceived link between North Korea's survival as a communist country and the legitimacy of the Chinese Communist Party. In contrast to the competition between the People's Republic of China (PRC) and the Republic of China (ROC) for diplomatic recognition by other governments, both North and South Korea had permitted dual recognition by other countries. The governments (and people) in both Koreas strongly supported the goal of reunification. China's efforts to delink Korea from the China-Taiwan case were strengthened by its success in the immediate post–Cold War period in establishing relations with the former Soviet states and in persuading countries such as South Africa to accept the "one-China principle" and to switch diplomatic recognition to the PRC. China has largely achieved its desired objective. Successful Korean reunification would boost China's efforts to achieve peaceful reunification with Taiwan, but the status quo on the Korean Peninsula is not viewed as a precedent for dual recognition or for Taiwan's admission into the United Nations.[2]

Similarly, while North Korea's survival as a communist state mattered very much to Beijing in the early 1990s, China's economic success and gradual political evolution have greatly reduced North Korea's relevance to the Chinese regime's domestic and international legitimacy. The result has been a reduction of North Korea's ideological importance to China.[3]

In recent years, China's diplomatic strategy has increased the emphasis placed on China's neighbors in Asia. South Korea has played an important role in regional initiatives such as ASEAN + 3, while North Korea's inability to make contributions to regional initiatives has reduced its importance in China's regional diplomacy. China's emphasis on a positive international image and its desired role as a "responsible great power" have also made its ties with a North Korean regime that regularly violates international norms (for example, via ballistic missile sales and counterfeiting and drug-smuggling activities) something of an embarrassment. North Korea's nuclear and missile programs also serve as continued, if unwanted, reminders of the legacy of China's past proliferation behavior, which contributed significantly to North Korea's ballistic missile program and supported Pakistan's development of nuclear weapons.

Revelations that Pakistani scientists were involved in a covert proliferation network supplying uranium enrichment technology to a number of countries (including North Korea) were embarrassing, because the Pakistani network was also supplying countries with a nuclear weapons design of Chinese origin.[4] These revelations undercut China's significant efforts over the last decade to improve its compliance with nonproliferation norms and to promote an image as a responsible great power on proliferation issues.

Changing Chinese priorities are the principal cause of shifts in the relative value of North and South Korea, but the pattern of China's relations with the two Koreas also matters. North Korea has been a difficult and demanding diplomatic partner,[5] while Beijing's relations with Seoul have strengthened remarkably in the economic, political, and security realms. Providing economic assistance to keep the North Korean regime afloat has clearly become a drain upon the Chinese economy. Although it is difficult to estimate the precise value of Chinese assistance, China reportedly provides about 40 percent of North Korea's food imports and 90 percent of North Korea's imported oil. Moreover, to keep North Korea engaged in the Six-Party-Talk process, China has increased its economic assistance.[6] Chinese officials express frustration at North Korea's reluctance to adopt economic reforms modeled on China's successful experience. During official visits, they have made a point of taking Kim Jong Il and other North Korean officials to sites they visited years ago, to demonstrate the extent of China's economic success. Yet even as North Korea has moved forward with market-oriented economic reforms, it has stressed that it is following its own path rather than the Chinese model. Chinese analysts also regard North Korea as unappreciative of the considerable sacrifices China has made on Pyongyang's behalf. One expert has noted that Chinese military officers who visited North Korea to commemorate the fiftieth anniversary of China's intervention in Korea were shocked by how little recognition China's military actions received in Korean memorials.

In private discussions, Chinese officials and analysts are highly critical of North Korea's use of threatening and provocative behavior that exacerbates regional security tensions. Although many feel that this behavior stems largely from North Korea's weakness and profound sense of insecurity, North Korean actions have had negative consequences for China's security. Besides creating regional instability and the possibility of a military conflict on China's border, North Korea's provocative behavior has strengthened the U.S.-Japan security alliance and has prompted efforts to loosen restrictions on the Japanese military. North Korea's 1998 Taepo-dong 1 test caused Japan to increase security cooperation with the United States on ballistic missile defense, and North Korea's nuclear weapons programs have prompted discussion in

Japan and South Korea about developing offensive weapons to deter or respond to North Korean attacks.

North Korea's behavior contrasts markedly with improvements in PRC relations with South Korea.[7] High-level visits between South Korean and Chinese leaders have become routine; in 1999 the two militaries began an ongoing series of visits by senior military officers and defense officials.[8] The economic relationship has deepened to the point where China is now South Korea's top trading partner and the leading site for South Korean foreign direct investment. Although PRC officials have expressed concerns about China's bilateral trade deficit with South Korea, they are generally happy with the economic relationship. Moreover, cultural and tourism ties are also expanding, as Seoul becomes a destination for Chinese tourists and an increasing number of South Korean students come to China to learn Chinese and to enroll in Chinese universities. Chinese professors report that about 80 percent of their foreign students now come from South Korea.[9] Although disputes over the Koguryo dynasty have the potential to dampen positive South Korean attitudes toward China,[10] overall relations are running smoothly in most areas. Chinese analysts boast privately that South Korea now has better relations with China than it does with the United States.[11]

A convergence in South Korean and Chinese preferences on reunification and on strategies for dealing with North Korea has also contributed to China's tilt toward Seoul. As South Korean assessments on the impact of German unification on the West German economy appeared in the early 1990s, South Korean elite preferences shifted from seeking a speedy collapse of the North Korean regime toward an extended reunification process to ease the transition costs. This partly reflected concerns about the high economic costs of reunification, which would be aggravated by North Korea's economic backwardness and the lower level of the South Korean economy compared to West Germany. It also reflected increasing South Korean concerns about the social impact of North Korean refugees who might head south in the event of a regime collapse.[12] This change in elite preferences has underpinned the efforts of former South Korean President Kim Dae Jung's Sunshine Policy and incumbent President Roh Moo Hyun's Policy of Peace and Prosperity toward the North. Generational changes that are giving the 386 generation increasing influence also support efforts to engage North Korea economically and politically.[13] These shifts in the South Korean polity and in South Korean policy toward the North have brought Chinese and South Korean preferences about the reunification process into closer alignment. South Korea has taken advantage of opportunities to strengthen relations with China to pursue its economic interests and advance its reunification agenda. In contrast, these changes have increased tensions in South Korea's relations with the United States.

SHORT-TERM CHINESE POLICIES TOWARD KOREA

There have been repeated political and diplomatic efforts to stabilize the Korean Peninsula and achieve reconciliation between Pyongyang and Seoul over the past fifteen years, but all have proven false starts. These include the agreements between North and South Korea in the early 1990s (including an agreement on the denuclearization of the Korean Peninsula); the Agreed Framework signed by North Korea and the United States in 1994; the Four-Party Talks undertaken in the late 1990s; and Kim Dae Jung's summit meeting with Kim Jong Il in Pyongyang in 2000. (Japanese Prime Minister Koizumi's visits to Pyongyang in 2002 and 2004 also belong on this list of abortive efforts.) All these initiatives eventually fizzled, often due to North Korean reluctance to implement agreements or reciprocate positive gestures.[14]

Chinese analysts have regularly expressed hope that diplomatic efforts could stabilize the peninsula and help the two Koreas achieve normal relations, while usually also expressing concerns about the implications of various diplomatic possibilities for China's long-term interests.[15] Yet in the words of Ralph Cossa, North Korea has never failed to miss an opportunity to miss an opportunity. This dismal history and North Korea's track record of diplomatic brinkmanship color Chinese perceptions of the present nuclear crisis. But Chinese analysts also blame the United States for the failure of diplomacy to achieve a major breakthrough, with some analysts suggesting that continued tensions on the Korean Peninsula serve U.S. strategic interests by providing a justification for U.S. bases in South Korea and Japan.[16]

Since North Korea's reported October 2002 admission to U.S. diplomats that it possessed a secret highly enriched uranium program, the North Korean nuclear crisis has been the focal point of Chinese diplomacy toward the Korean Peninsula. North Korea's admission (which Pyongyang subsequently denied) and its actions to escalate the nuclear crisis forced China to deal directly with the issue of nuclear weapons on the Korean Peninsula.[17] Most Chinese activity focused on the short-term task of managing the nuclear crisis to prevent damage to Chinese interests. Beijing thus has both a major substantive interest in the outcome and a procedural interest in managing the crisis.

China's short-term concerns about the Korean nuclear issue have focused mainly on outcomes to be avoided. The worst scenario would be a nuclear domino effect, where an overt North Korean nuclear weapons capability compels Japan, South Korea, and perhaps even Taiwan to go nuclear. This would profoundly alter the security environment in Northeast Asia and likely prompt the United States to accelerate deployment of ballistic-missile defenses in the region. From China's perspective, a North Korean collapse would be almost as bad. China would lose a security buffer, have only a limited ability to influence future security arrangements on the peninsula, and be forced to deal with the economic burden of refugees fleeing a collapsing North Korean regime. In a worst-case scenario, South Korea might inherit the North's nuclear arsenal, and U.S. forces based in a reunified Korea could have direct access to China's border.

China also worries that the United States might use force to try to resolve the nuclear crisis. A major war on the peninsula would have profound strategic, economic, environmental, and humanitarian consequences for China. Even if weapons of mass destruction were not used, the economic damage would be tremendous, and the potential for serious environmental degradation would be equally great. A limited U.S. strike against North Korean nuclear facilities would also set troubling precedents in terms both of the U.S. use of force without authorization from the United Nations Security Council and of the U.S. use of force along China's borders. This point highlights Beijing's preferences for a peaceful outcome, avoidance of the use of force, and a process that gives China a larger voice in future security arrangements on the Korean Peninsula.

The nuclear crisis has persisted for over three years, but it appears to be moving more toward China's preferred approach to addressing the crisis. However, China's activism on this issue raises the stakes for Beijing if diplomacy should ultimately fail. China's initial response to the nuclear crisis followed a familiar pattern, with Foreign Ministry statements calling for a nuclear-free Korean Peninsula, maintaining peace and stability, solving the problem through dialogue, and preserving the Agreed Framework. Beijing's statements adopted an even-handed tone toward the United States and North Korea, expressing concern about the North Korean nuclear program but also calling on the two sides to normalize their relations through "constructive and equal" dialogue. China also supported North Korea's position that a solution required direct talks between the United States and North Korea.

However, as the crisis intensified, Beijing was forced to play a more active diplomatic role. North Korea escalated its confrontation with the United States by withdrawing from the Nuclear Nonproliferation Treaty (NPT), expelling International Atomic Energy Agency (IAEA) inspectors, restarting a mothballed nuclear reactor, and reprocessing eight thousand spent nuclear fuel rods to produce plutonium that could be used to build additional nuclear weapons. In response to these developments, Chinese statements about the importance of a nuclear-free Korean Peninsula became more insistent. There were numerous meetings between Chinese leaders and senior U.S., North Korean, Japanese, and Russian officials; actions to limit the United Nations Security Council's deliberations on the nuclear crisis (in particular, to prevent imposition of economic sanctions); and active efforts to encourage the United States and North Korea to begin direct negotiations.

China initially offered to host bilateral talks in Beijing. When the two sides deadlocked over the format of the talks (with Pyongyang insisting on bilateral talks and Washington insisting on a multilateral format), China brokered a compromise trilateral format and actively participated in the April 2003 talks in Beijing. China also temporarily cut off the flow of oil to North Korea and sent a senior envoy to urge Pyongyang to compromise on the format of the talks, while steadfastly refusing to endorse multilateral economic sanctions against Pyongyang. China's diplomatic efforts led to a series of six-party talks in Beijing. Three rounds were held in August 2003, February 2004, and June 2004. A fourth round was initially scheduled for September 2004, but Pyongyang refused to return to the talks. In February 2005, the DPRK declared that it possessed an unspecified number of nuclear weapons. Following repeated Chinese importuning, North Korea rejoined the talks in July 2005, and a follow-on round in September 2005 produced a declaration of principles (based on a Chinese draft agreement) obligating all six parties to pursue denuclearization of the peninsula (this included North Korea's return to the NPT and IAEA) and normalization of U.S.-DPRK and Japan-DPRK relations. A primary Chinese objective was to establish a diplomatic process that would avert negative outcomes and prevent the situation from spinning out of control. Chinese diplomats believe they have accomplished this minimal goal by creating and sustaining the Six-Party Talks.

Although China initially accommodated U.S. demands for a multilateral process, Chinese officials and analysts believe that the fundamental conflict remains between the United States and North Korea. In private conversations during 2003 and 2004, Chinese officials expressed frustration with both Washington and Pyongyang and noted that they had made considerable efforts to get North Korea to participate in the Six-Party Talks and to keep Pyongyang at the negotiating table.[18] Many remain sympathetic to North Korea's security concerns and view Pyongyang's nuclear weapons program as a rational response to its weak and insecure position. They contend that North Korea's security concerns must be meaningfully addressed if Pyongyang is to be persuaded to give up its nuclear weapons. Chinese officials and analysts claim that Beijing does not have a good understanding of North Korean nuclear capabilities and have expressed doubts about the existence and extent of a North Korean uranium enrichment program. Most Chinese officials and analysts agree that Kim Jong Il's primary objective is regime survival and note that U.S. statements about regime change are viewed as serious threats in Pyongyang. Chinese officials emphasize their belief that pressure and military threats will only cause Pyongyang to become more stubborn and might even cause North Korea to lash out militarily.

Most Chinese analysts believe North Korea must eventually adopt economic reforms if the regime is to survive. Although reforms will trigger new pressures on the North Korean system, Chinese analysts are more optimistic than most Western observers that economic reforms are possible without bringing down the regime. Chinese observers have long argued that the North Korean regime is unlikely to collapse because Kim Jong Il is in firm control and the population is able to endure tremendous suffering.[19] Some recent assessments are slightly more pessimistic about the regime's long-term prospects, but most Chinese analysts do not expect North Korea to collapse any time soon. Unlike the United States, both the South Korean and Chinese governments want to avoid this outcome if possible. Chinese concerns center around the domestic economic and social impact of refugee flows, but analysts also worry that a sudden collapse would limit Beijing's ability to influence future security arrangements on the Korean Peninsula.

Although a few Chinese analysts have argued that Beijing should abandon Pyongyang, the Chinese government has continued to emphasize the need for a diplomatic solution that avoids the use of force and that does not cause the North Korean regime to collapse. Some Chinese officials view Washington's previous unwillingness to engage in bilateral negotiations with Pyongyang as a sign that Washington was not really serious about a diplomatic solution. But evidence of increased U.S. flexibility (including extensive bilateral meetings between American and North Korean officials at the resumed Six-Party Talks of 2005) have validated Beijing's policy stance. As noted previously, the declaration signed in the September 2005 round of the Six-Party Talks was prepared by Chinese representatives. Chinese officials reportedly told American negotiators that there was no possibility of gaining North Korean concurrence with a statement of principles if the United States did not commit to explicit security assurances and prospective energy and economic assistance to Pyongyang, with the United States ultimately deciding that an imperfect agreement was preferable to none at all.[20] The declaration can best be described as skeletal, leaving a host of hugely contentious issues still unresolved.

Chinese officials acknowledge that the negotiations will be protracted and very difficult, but Beijing sees increased possibilities of a diplomatic solution along the lines that it has consistently proposed to both Washington and Pyongyang. As viewed by China, the Bush administration has diverged significantly from its previous hints on the need for regime change in Pyongyang, including earlier intimations that North Korea could be the next target for U.S. military action after Iraq.[21] These shifts in U.S.

policy, in turn, have enabled Beijing to induce North Korea both to resume its participation in the talks and assent (at least on paper) to ultimately yielding its nuclear
weapons capabilities. Chinese officials believe that a diplomatic solution will ultimately require the United States to address Pyongyang's legitimate security concerns.
For Beijing, reassuring Pyongyang is a necessary part of any settlement of the crisis.

Despite the close communication between Chinese and American officials, the essence
of Washington's diplomatic strategy still diverges significantly from China's expressed
preferences. The United States has tried to focus international attention on North Korea's
actions in order to pressure Pyongyang to give up its nuclear programs. The U.S. emphasis on "not rewarding bad behavior" and "not giving in to blackmail" has allowed
various factions in the administration to agree on a common tactical approach. For
those who believe a negotiated solution may be possible, downplaying the urgency of
the situation and exhibiting patience are important means of reducing North Korea's
leverage. By insisting on a multilateral forum for talks and extensive North Korean
concessions before the United States and others will provide major compensation to
the DPRK. American officials believe that the United States can increase its own negotiating leverage. In this view, international economic, political, and military pressure
will eventually make Pyongyang realize it has no alternative to giving up its nuclear
weapons. For those who believe regime change in North Korea is necessary, maximizing international pressure against Pyongyang and setting an extremely high bar for the
start of serious negotiations provides a means to frustrate what they believe would
likely be an inherently flawed agreement and advance their larger goals.[22] The increased negotiating flexibility given to Assistant Secretary of State Christopher Hill in
the additional rounds of talks in July and September 2005 suggests a greater U.S. emphasis on trying to reach a negotiated settlement of the issue.[23]

China has played the unfamiliar role of mediator and facilitator at the Six-Party Talks,
pressing both the United States and North Korea to make the concessions necessary
for a negotiated solution. At times, this has involved Chinese pressure on both countries to participate in the talks and to put a serious offer on the table. At other times, it
has involved side payments to Pyongyang, in the form of additional food and energy
aid, to continue participation in the talks. Despite impatience with Pyongyang's negotiating tactics, Chinese officials appear to believe that China must reassure North Korean
leaders that they can maintain regime and national security even if they give up their
nuclear weapons. China has taken various actions to demonstrate that it will protect
North Korean interests and not force Pyongyang to sign a deal that damages its security. These include preventing strong UN Security Council actions in response to
Pyongyang's withdrawal from the NPT, commitments to continue providing food and

energy assistance, statements acknowledging the legitimacy of North Korea's desire for a security guarantee, and a willingness to press the United States to respond to North Korean concerns.

Despite these efforts to reinforce China's pivotal role at the talks, Chinese officials and analysts emphasize that the United States and China share the common goal of a Korean Peninsula free of nuclear weapons. But China does not attach the same degree of urgency to this objective as the United States. Beijing wants to eliminate North Korea's nuclear weapons, but Chinese officials want to achieve this objective while maintaining stability on the Korean Peninsula and by providing North Korea clear indications of what it would gain by forgoing the nuclear option. This makes Beijing reluctant to adopt measures to unduly pressure Pyongyang, a position shared by South Korea. Chinese officials argue that the Six-Party Talks represent the best hope of resolving the issue, in that they involve the relevant parties in an ongoing process that avoids worst-case outcomes. However, China deems the United States and North Korea as the key players, with Washington and Pyongyang ultimately needing to address each other's concerns if there is to be a negotiated settlement.

Some Chinese analysts argue that the Bush administration's need to keep the North Korean nuclear issue under control gives China leverage to push the United States for concessions on Taiwan. While China has clearly used cooperation in managing the nuclear crisis as a tool to improve relations with the United States, it has refrained from demanding explicit quid pro quos. Instead, Chinese diplomats typically employ more subtle arguments that U.S. actions such as arms sales cast doubt on U.S. sincerity on the Taiwan issue and reduce Chinese incentives to work hard to resolve the North Korean nuclear issue.

Although some Chinese analysts hope the Six-Party Talks will evolve into an enduring security arrangement, Chinese government officials are more focused on the operational issues involved in getting an agreement. A security structure based on the Six-Party Talks might (or might not) be useful in implementing and protecting a nuclear agreement. Such a structure's potential value for this purpose would be the main consideration. One official has noted that ASEAN countries had concerns about an Asian security framework that did not include them. When asked about China's response if diplomatic efforts to resolve the nuclear crisis failed, Chinese officials and analysts essentially replied that failure was not an option. Conversations with Chinese analysts suggest that China will try to keep the talks going, even if this requires a lengthy recess, so that a breakdown in the six-party process does not provide the United States or North Korea an opportunity to withdraw from the diplomatic process.[24]

Four outcomes of the Six-Party Talks seem possible: (1) a diplomatic settlement that permanently resolves the North Korea nuclear issue; (2) a partial settlement that contains the issue by limiting North Korean nuclear capability; (3) an interim settlement (such as a nuclear freeze) that postpones the issue; or (4) a breakdown of talks without an agreement. China would prefer a settlement that permanently removes North Korea's nuclear weapons capability, improves North Korean relations with the United States and Japan, and supports North Korean economic reforms.[25] However, China appears willing to live with a more limited agreement that resolves the immediate crisis without fully eliminating North Korea's nuclear potential.[26] Chinese officials privately indicate that once the right deal is on the table, China is willing to press North Korea to accept an agreement to resolve the crisis.

If the talks ultimately break down without an agreement, China would likely seek to contain the situation and avoid potential worst-case outcomes. One component of this policy would involve efforts to prevent the United States from toppling the North Korean regime or using force against North Korean nuclear facilities. China would appeal to South Korea and Japan to oppose an aggressive U.S. policy and would probably be willing to use its Security Council veto to prevent a resolution authorizing sanctions or the use of force. While this would inevitably create tension in Sino-U.S. relations, China would try to persuade the United States that its best course of action would be to deter North Korea from using nuclear weapons rather than taking risky actions to try to eliminate North Korean nuclear capabilities.

The other leg of Chinese policy would involve efforts to keep any North Korean nuclear weapons capability limited and ambiguous. China would likely discourage North Korea from operationally deploying nuclear weapons or conducting a nuclear test to demonstrate its weapons capability. China might also press North Korea for formal statements or commitments that it would not export fissile material or nuclear technology. Beijing's objective would be to limit the proliferation consequences of a nuclear North Korea in Japan and South Korea.[27] In this scenario, China would be operating in damage-control mode, with the objective of preventing Japan and South Korea from developing nuclear weapons of their own. China would probably reluctantly accept U.S. efforts to strengthen alliance relations with Japan and South Korea if it concluded that the alternative was for those countries to go nuclear. If South Korea or Japan acquired nuclear weapons, this would be regarded in Beijing as a dramatic deterioration in China's security environment and might prompt a fundamental reevaluation of Chinese security policy.

While Beijing may have been forced to become more actively involved in the Korean nuclear crisis to avoid worst-case outcomes, Chinese leaders have played their cards shrewdly. China's position on how to deal with North Korea is closely aligned with South Korea's, which has helped China strengthen relations with Seoul. China has positioned itself as a diplomatic middleman in the negotiations between Washington and Pyongyang and has shown a willingness to pressure each side to come to the negotiating table prepared to address the other's concerns.

If a negotiated settlement is ultimately reached, Beijing will receive much of the credit (including from U.S. allies South Korea and Japan). Conversely, if talks break down, Washington will be blamed for its intransigence and Beijing will be excused for having made a good-faith effort to broker an agreement. But it is equally possible that U.S. officials would hold China at least partly responsible for a failed negotiation, given Beijing's evident unwillingness to heighten pressure on Pyongyang or to limit its economic assistance to the DPRK. Despite the clear political risks for China if the talks should ultimately fail, Beijing sees few credible alternatives to diligent, patient diplomacy. China's fundamental interests are still best served by an agreement that eliminates North Korea's nuclear weapons and places North Korea on a reformist path. Otherwise, North Korea will remain a country on the edge, with the potential to trigger a destabilizing crisis in Northeast Asia at any time.

CHINESE LONG-TERM INTERESTS IN KOREA

Most Chinese analysts believe that an active role in promoting the Six-Party Talks serves China's immediate interests. However, there is less agreement about the best way to pursue longer-term Chinese interests on the Korean Peninsula. Analysts have a range of views on how the timing of Korean reunification; the future U.S. military presence in Asia; and a unified Korea's regional, political, and security role might affect Chinese interests. This is partly because views on these issues depend heavily on assumptions about key variables, such as the timing and manner of Korean unification, how a unified Korea would behave, China's future role within Asia, and the nature of Sino-U.S. relations.

One crucial uncertainty is the timing and manner of Korean unification. China's official position is that reunification is a matter for North and South Korea to decide between themselves. Given the strong national identity of Korean people on both sides of the DMZ, Chinese analysts increasingly regard Korean unification as inevitable. The timing, however, is much less certain. Many analysts expect unification to occur in the next ten to fifteen years.[28] Chinese analysts appear to believe that a gradual process of unification will reduce the risks of transition and give Beijing more opportunity to protect China's territorial integrity, remove weapons of mass destruction from the Korean Peninsula, and influence future security arrangements in Korea. They expect China to play a constructive role in Korean reunification and to have a significant voice in the security alignment and political orientation of a reunified Korea.[29] But uncertainty about the "when" and "how" of Korean unification creates uncertainty about China's ability to advance its long-term interests during the unification process.

These long-term interests include concerns about the impact of developments in Korea on China's internal and external security. One set of internal security concerns focuses on the impact of North Korean refugees on China's northeastern provinces of Jilin, Liaoning, and Heilongjiang. Estimates of the number of North Korean refugees that have fled across the border range from one hundred to two hundred thousand. Some press reports also suggest that North Korea is using refugees as cover for intelligence operations in China.[30] Famine or collapse of the regime could prompt hundreds of thousands of additional refugees to flee across the border, posing a difficult economic and security burden for China. In 2003, to better prepare for future contingencies, China replaced its existing border guards with People's Liberation Army (PLA) units to improve its ability to control the border.[31]

Another set of internal security issues involves China's ethnic Korean minority. An estimated two million ethnic Koreans live in China, mainly in the Yanbian Korean Autonomous Prefecture in Jilin Province.[32] Chinese officials worry about the loyalty of these citizens and remain concerned about the potential for ethnic Koreans to engage in separatist activities. China has complained about South Korean laws that seek to give special status to ethnic Koreans living outside Korea.[33] These concerns prompted China to delay permission for a South Korean consulate in Shenyang for seven years. Chinese analysts worry that a nationalistic Korea that no longer needs Chinese goodwill to achieve unification might eventually assert claims to Chinese territory in Manchuria. These concerns are an underlying factor in the dispute between China and South Korea over whether the Koguryo Dynasty belongs to Chinese or Korean history.

China will continue to be concerned about threats to its external security and about how events on the Korean Peninsula could affect regional stability. So long as North Korea has hostile relations with its neighbors and with the United States, there is always the potential for a major military conflict on China's borders. Korean reunification is likely to create some new security concerns for China, but it will also remove a major source of regional instability. Another long-term external security issue involves physical threats to Chinese territory through Korea. Although some Chinese analysts believe North Korea still has strategic value as a buffer, most appear to view a North Korean buffer state as an outmoded concept, given China's excellent relations with South Korea.[34] However, this geopolitical concern has more salience when Chinese analysts consider the possibility of U.S. troops being based in a unified Korea, especially if they were based close to the Chinese border.

Another external security issue involves efforts to remove all weapons of mass destruction from the Korean Peninsula, a task that extends far beyond the current nuclear crisis. In addition to its nuclear weapons programs, North Korea is believed to have extensive chemical and biological weapon stockpiles.[35] In the event of a North Korean collapse, China (like the United States) would have a strong interest in ensuring that North Korean WMD stocks were secured and destroyed. Even if reunification occurs in a more gradual manner, China will likely seek to ensure that a reunified Korea will give up its nuclear weapons capability and allow international inspections to verify that the program is completely dismantled.

As China strives for increased regional influence within Asia, one concern will be the orientation and foreign policy behavior of a unified Korea. Chinese analysts have explored a variety of possible futures for a reunified Korea, including the idea of a "neutralized" Korea that would not take sides between the United States and China.[36] China's ability to limit the future sovereignty of a unified Korea in unification diplomacy is questionable, as is the relevance of "neutrality" in the post–Cold War era. In any case, reunification is likely to cause Korean leaders to focus on internal issues for at least ten to fifteen years. Improvements in Chinese relations with Seoul (and recent difficulties in U.S.-Korean relations) have given China increased confidence that a unified Korea is likely to be friendly to Beijing. China's regional ambitions, and the demands that those ambitions place on Korea, are likely to be an equally important determinant of the state of future Sino-Korean relations.

One of the key uncertainties in Chinese thinking about a future Korea is the mixture of cooperation and competition in future Chinese relations with the United States. Unexpected improvements in Sino-U.S. relations over the last four years have not eased Chinese concerns about the future.[37] Chinese analysts hope that the United States will accept China's "peaceful rise," but their realist orientation leads many to expect increasingly conflictual relations with the United States as China's power increases.[38] In particular, many expect China and the United States to compete for influence in Asia. The potential for the United States and China to become strategic rivals colors Chinese concerns about the U.S. military presence in Asia and about future U.S. relations with Korea. As a result, many Chinese analysts see Korea as a future competition ground between the United States and China.[39]

The "North Korean threat" has played an important role as a geopolitical buffer that has muted concerns in Japan and the United States about rising Chinese power and about China's future strategic role. Japanese military reforms and modernization programs use the threat from North Korea as a planning tool that is less controversial than making explicit reference to China's growing capabilities. Similarly, the United

States has emphasized the threat posed by North Korean ballistic missiles to justify its development and deployment of ballistic missile defenses. North Korea's role as a geopolitical buffer that eases security tensions between China and Japan and between China and the United States would obviously disappear after Korean unification. Security concerns may therefore take on a more prominent role in these bilateral relations after unification.

Although China opposes alliances and foreign bases as a matter of principle, Chinese analysts have long acknowledged privately that the U.S. military presence in Asia serves Chinese security interests. In recent years, Chinese officials have made public and private statements to reassure the United States that China does not seek to push the U.S. military out of Asia. Chinese analysts emphasize that Chinese attitudes toward the U.S. military presence in Asia depend on whether U.S. forces are aimed against China or Chinese interests. Chinese officials are especially concerned that U.S. forces and alliances could be used to intervene in a conflict over Taiwan. These attitudes will color Chinese perceptions about a possible U.S. military presence in a unified Korea.

Changes in U.S. military deployments in Asia are likely to exacerbate these Chinese concerns. Although the United States has announced plans to reduce the number of forces deployed in South Korea, Chinese analysts note that the United States is also making efforts to increase its combat power in the Pacific by deploying additional forces to Guam. Some see this as an indication of a shift in U.S. strategic priorities that raises the strategic importance of the Asia-Pacific region. Moreover, the thrust of U.S. global military transformation efforts is to increase the flexibility of U.S. forces and their ability to respond to unexpected regional contingencies. As a result, Chinese fears that U.S. forces in the region might be used to intervene in a Taiwan conflict are likely to intensify. Korean reunification will aggravate these concerns, since a conflict with China over Taiwan would become the most likely regional contingency to require U.S. forces.

Thus, China is highly likely to seek to limit a U.S. military presence in a unified Korea. At a minimum, this would involve efforts to prevent U.S. troops from being based in North Korean territory near China's border. At most, it would involve efforts to pressure Korea to remove all U.S. troops from its territory on the grounds that reunification made their presence unnecessary. The stakes for both countries will be high, since the U.S. military presence in Japan has been justified mainly in terms of the threat posed by North Korea. If U.S. forces leave South Korea after unification, domestic pressures in Japan to reduce the U.S. military presence are likely to increase. It would be awkward politically for Japan to be the sole Asian country hosting large numbers of American troops. Since the regional security stakes will be high for both the United States and China, this issue is likely to be extremely contentious.

CONCLUSION

China's interests on the Korean Peninsula have changed significantly over the last twenty years. China's emphasis on economic development has heightened the importance of South Korea relative to the North and has facilitated strong economic and political ties between Beijing and Seoul. North Korea is now viewed as a problem to be managed rather than as an ally or strategic asset. Nevertheless, China has tried to make the most of its advantageous position as a country with good relations with both North and South Korea. To avoid negative outcomes, China was forced to become more active in efforts to resolve the nuclear crisis, but it has worked hard to establish a process that will discourage extreme actions and contribute to a diplomatic solution. Chinese officials are cautiously optimistic that they will eventually be able to broker a deal that resolves the crisis. However, China places a high priority on maintaining stability and appears willing to live with an agreement that resolves the immediate crisis without fully eliminating North Korea's nuclear potential.

There is less agreement among Chinese analysts about strategies for pursuing longer-term Chinese interests on the Korean Peninsula. This reflects uncertainties about key variables such as the timing and manner of Korean unification, how a unified Korea would behave, China's future role within Asia, and the nature of Sino-U.S. relations. Chinese elites hope that good relations with South Korea mean that a unified Korea will have friendly relations with China. However, Korean unification would end North Korea's role as a geopolitical buffer between the United States and China, turning the future U.S. military presence in Asia (and U.S. military ties with a unified Korea) into contentious issues in which U.S. and Chinese interests are likely to conflict. While cooperation between the United States and China in managing the nuclear crisis has been relatively good, over the long run Korea is likely to become a source of conflict in Sino-U.S. relations. At the same time, the overall state of Sino-U.S. relations will influence the importance each country places on its security interests in Korea and the mix of competition and cooperation in both U.S. and Chinese diplomacy toward the Korean Peninsula.

NOTES

The views expressed in this paper are those of the author and do not reflect the official policy or position of the National Defense University, the Department of Defense, or the U.S. government.

1. The story of China's diplomacy in recognizing South Korea is told in Samuel S. Kim, "The Making of China's Korea Policy in the Age of Reform," in *The Making of Chinese Foreign and Security Policy in the Era of*

Reform, ed. David M. Lampton (Stanford, Calif.: Stanford University Press, 2001), pp. 371–408. Also see Xiaoxiong Yi, "China's Korea Policy: From 'One Korea' to 'Two Koreas,'" *Asian Affairs, An American Review* 22, no. 2 (Summer 1995), pp. 119–40.

2. However, Chinese officials and analysts are still attentive to potential implications that developments in Korea might have for Taiwan. For example, Chinese officials quickly noted that the summit diplomacy that produced Kim Dae Jung's June 2000 visit to Pyongyang was not an appropriate model for rapprochement with Taiwan.

3. If North Korean economic reforms were explicitly patterned on the Chinese model, this might create a new Chinese ideological stake in the success of North Korean reforms. However, North Korea has been reluctant to give China any public credit for inspiring its economic reform efforts.

4. Joby Warrick and Peter Slevin, "Libyan Arms Designs Traced Back to China: Pakistanis Resold Chinese-Provided Plans," *Washington Post,* 15 February 2004, p. A1.

5. You Ji, "China and North Korea: A Fragile Relationship of Strategic Convenience," *Journal of Contemporary China* 10, no. 28 (2001), pp. 387–98.

6. Author's interviews with Chinese officials, July 2004.

7. Victor D. Cha, "Engaging China: Seoul-Beijing *Détente* and Korean Security," *Survival* 41, no. 1 (Spring 1999), pp. 73–98.

8. The chronology in CSIS Pacific Forum's *Comparative Connections* and the quarterly articles on Sino-Korean relations by Scott Snyder are excellent sources for details on these exchanges. See www.csis.org/pacfor/ccejournal.html#csk.

9. Author's interviews with Chinese scholars, July 2004.

10. See David Scofield, "China Puts Korean Spat on the Map," *Asia Times,* 19 August 2004, www.atimes.com/atimes/Korea/FH19Dg01.html.

11. On South Korean views, see Derek J. Mitchell, *Strategy and Sentiment: South Korean Views of the United States and the U.S.-ROK Alliance* (Washington, D.C.: Center for Strategic and International Studies, 2004), www.csis.org/isp/0406mitchell.pdf.

12. South Korean economists are doing detailed studies about how to adopt reforms that will keep North Koreans from heading south in massive numbers after reunification. Some ideas involve fanciful schemes to employ hundreds of thousands of North Korean workers in Russian factories built with South Korean investment.

13. See "South Korea's New Generation: Politics & Social Change," Asian Perspectives Seminar Series, Washington, D.C., 5 May 2003, asiafoundation.org/pdf/southkorea_newgeneration.pdf; and Gordon Fairclough, "Generation Why? The 386ers of Korea Question Old Rules," *Wall Street Journal,* 14 April 2004, p. A1.

14. To be fair, the United States also deserves some blame for the breakdown of the Agreed Framework.

15. See Jia Hao and Zhuang Qubing, "China's Policy toward the Korean Peninsula," *Asian Survey* 32, no. 12 (December 1992), pp. 1137–56; Banning Garrett and Bonnie Glaser, "Looking Across the Yalu: Chinese Assessments of North Korea," *Asian Survey* 35, no. 6 (June 1995), pp. 528–45; and Xiaoming Zhang, "China's Relations with the Korean Peninsula: A Chinese View," *Korea Observer* 32, no. 4 (Winter 2001), pp. 481–500.

16. See Xu Weidi, "Chaoxianbandao heweiji de huajie yu bandao zuochu lengzhan" [Defusing the Nuclear Crisis and Moving the Korean Peninsula away from the Cold War], *Shijie Jingji yu Zhengzhi* [World Economics and Politics], no. 9 (September 2003), pp. 59–64, translation available as FBIS CPP20030925000192, 14 September 2003.

17. For a useful analysis of the U.S. and North Korean paths to the nuclear crisis, see Jonathan D. Pollack, "The United States, North Korea, and the End of the Agreed Framework," *Naval War College Review* 56, no. 3 (Summer 2003), pp. 11–49.

18. Author's interviews, October 2003 and July 2004.

19. Eric A. McVadon, "China's Goals and Strategies for the Korean Peninsula," in *Planning for a Peaceful Korea,* ed. Henry D. Sokolski (Carlisle, Penna.: Strategic Studies Institute, Army War College, February 2001), pp. 160–64.

20. Joseph Kahn and David E. Sanger, "U.S.-Korean Deal on Arms Leaves Key Points Open," *New York Times,* 20 September 2005.

21. See, for example, the remarks of an American intelligence official cited in Seymour M. Hersh, "The Cold Test: What the Administration Knew about Pakistan and the North Korean Nuclear Program," *New Yorker,* 27 January 2003; and leaks about a new U.S. war plan aimed at destabilizing North Korea, cited in Bruce B. Auster, Kevin

Whitelaw, and Thomas Omestad, "Upping the Ante for Kim Jong Il," *U.S. News & World Report* 135, no. 2 (21 July 2003), p. 21.

22. For analyses of U.S. policy toward the Korean nuclear crisis, see Sebastian Harnisch, "U.S.-North Korean Relations under the Bush Administration," *Asian Survey* 42, no. 6 (November/December 2002), pp. 863–74; and Daniel A. Pinkston and Phillip C. Saunders, "Seeing North Korea Clearly: Barriers to a Better U.S. Korea Policy," *Survival* 45, no. 3 (August 2003), pp. 79–102, cns.miis.edu/research/korea/450079.pdf.

23. See Joseph Kahn, "North Korea Signs Nuclear Accord," *New York Times*, 19 September 2005.

24. Author's interviews, July 2004 and July 2005.

25. See David Shambaugh, "China and the Korean Peninsula: Playing for the Long Term," *Washington Quarterly* 26, no. 2 (Spring 2003), pp. 43–56, www.twq.com/03spring/docs/03spring_shambaugh.pdf.

26. China's position on North Korea's right to "peaceful uses" of nuclear energy captures this nuance. Chinese officials at a 2004 U.S.-China arms control conference argued that North Korea had the right to peaceful uses of nuclear energy, while the United States wants to dismantle all North Korean nuclear programs because it sees them all as potential nuclear weapons programs. Peaceful use is an obstacle in the Six-Party Talks, and something that can be discussed in the working group meetings. China feels North Korea should freeze all its nuclear activities first; international inspectors could then decide what should be dismantled and what North Korea could keep under an international inspection regime. China thinks North Korea should have a right to peaceful use only within the NPT framework.

27. For analysis on how to contain the proliferation and regional security consequences of North Korean nuclear weapons if the Six-Party Talks fail, see Phillip C. Saunders, "Responses to a Nuclear North Korea," *KNDU Journal* 8, no. 2 (December 2003), pp. 47–76.

28. For a discussion of Chinese perspectives on unification, see McVadon, "China's Goals and Strategies for the Korean Peninsula," pp. 164–66; and Xiaoxiong Yi, "Ten Years of China-South Korea Relations and Beijing's View on Korean Reunification," *Journal of East Asian Affairs* 16, no. 2 (Fall/Winter 2002), pp. 315–51.

29. For an example, see Zhang Liangui, "China Supports Korean Reunification, Plays Active Neutral Role in Mediating Disputes on Peninsula,"

Dangdai Yatai [Contemporary Asia], in FBIS CPP20040720000203, 15 May 2004.

30. See "DPRK Defector Describes SSD Operations in DPRK-PRC Border Region," FBIS KPP20030423000063, 20 July 2002.

31. One Chinese analyst noted that one reason for the shift was that existing border guards had been based in the area for years and had become involved in smuggling and illegal immigration activities.

32. Available at www.travelchinaguide.com/intro/nationality/korean.

33. South Korea responded to Chinese concerns by drafting the law to exclude Koreans who lived outside Korea in 1948, but a Korean court recently ruled this provision unconstitutional.

34. Author's interviews, July 2004; and McVadon, "China's Goals and Strategies for the Korean Peninsula."

35. For an overview of North Korean WMD capabilities, see "North Korea Profile," www.nti.org/e_research/profiles/NK/index.html.

36. See Tang Shiping, "A Neutral Reunified Korea: A Chinese View," *Journal of East Asian Affairs* 13, no. 2 (Fall/Winter 1999), pp. 464–83; and Xiaoxiong Yi, "A Neutralized Korea? The North-South Rapprochement and China's Korea Policy," *Korea Journal of Defense Analysis* 12, no. 2 (Winter 2000), pp. 71–118.

37. See Jonathan D. Pollack, ed., *Strategic Surprise? U.S.-China Relations in the Early Twenty-first Century* (Newport, R.I.: Naval War College Press, 2003).

38. For an overview of Chinese thinking about the United States, see Phillip C. Saunders, "China's America Watchers: Changing Attitudes toward the United States," *China Quarterly*, no. 161 (March 2000), pp. 41–65; and Denny Roy, "China's Reaction to American Predominance," *Survival* 45, no. 3 (Autumn 2003), pp. 57–78.

39. See Scott Snyder, "The Rise of U.S.-China Rivalry and Its Implications for the Korean Peninsula," in *Korean Security Dynamics in Transition,* ed. Kyung-Ae Park and Dalchoong Kim (New York: Palgrave, 2001), pp. 119–31; and Eric A. McVadon, "China and North Korea: From 'Close as Lips to Teeth' to Taking No Lip," remarks at U.S. State Department Bureau of Intelligence and Research Workshop, China and North Korea, Washington, D.C., 5 March 2004.

12

Dragon in the Eyes of South Korea
Analyzing Korean Perceptions of China

Jae Ho Chung

Among the factors shaping perception, emotion, sentiment, and reputation in international affairs, history has always been a crucial one. However, understanding the historical behavior of different states and their evaluations of relations with counterpart states is seldom straightforward or easy. "Reputation" (whether favorable or hostile) is rarely imprinted in the minds of leaders and citizens. Rather, it represents a deeper process, shaped by historical events and imparted across generations.

Examples abound of historically induced feelings and sentiments between nations and peoples. Anti-Americanism in the Third World and anti-Zionism in the Arab world both constitute relevant examples.[1] Indo-Pakistani and Turkish-Kurdish enmities highlight comparable phenomena in a bilateral context. Antagonistic sentiments and images are often reproduced and reinforced through family and formal education spanning several generations, thus making them highly resistant to change.[2]

East Asian experiences are illustrative of the persistence of these phenomena. For instance, the "Japan problem" has loomed increasingly large since the 1980s, just as the "German question" once did in Europe. Anti-Japanese sentiment has been especially marked in the two Koreas, attributed largely to the thirty-six years of colonial rule during 1910–45, but many of the same sentiments run very deep in China as well.[3] In South Korea, Japan is still the least favored nation, often more hated than North Korea. South Korean citizens insist that Japanese "militarism" should be prevented at all costs. Japan's colonial rule over Korea, which ended six decades ago, is still vividly remembered. Despite the democratic maturation of both societies and their respective alliance ties with the United States, South Korea's old wounds and bitter feelings toward Japan have hardly healed.

By contrast, most South Koreans have almost totally forgotten (if not forgiven) China's military intervention during the Korean War of 1950–53.[4] How do we explain this dichotomy in perceptions? Is it the temporal distance of negative historical events that conditions one nation's sentiment toward another? Since China's intervention against South Korea and the United States occurred more recently, South Koreans should retain more vivid memories of the Korean War than of the colonial era. In turn, this should generate more negative sentiments toward China than toward Japan. But this is not the case. Alternatively, if the duration of a negative event is more crucial, strong anti-Japanese sentiments in South Korea are more understandable, although the time span of Korea's historical (and frequently antagonistic) interactions with China is by no means shorter. Korea's positive, almost unconditionally favorable views of China are thus both intriguing and puzzling.

This essay reviews South Korea's evolving views of China. The assessment will focus principally on three dimensions: (1) key indicators of how the "rise of China" has become manifest in Korea; (2) South Korean perceptions of China in the last fifteen years; and (3) how South Korea's perceptions of China are likely to shape Seoul's strategic thinking in future years.

THE "RISE OF CHINA" OVER KOREA: KEY INDICATORS

"Rise" *(jueqi)* is an appropriate term to depict the process of China's development during the last decade or more. It also coincides closely with the maturation of South Korea's relations with China. Many Chinese scholars and officials, however, object to the concept of "rise" and instead favor either "rejuvenation" *(fuxing)* or the even more neutral characterization of "development" *(fazhan)*.[5] As Wang Gungwu has noted, recent events can be viewed as the fourth rise in Chinese history, following the Han, Tang, and Ming-Qing dynasties.[6] Few analysts dispute that China is again rising, although opinions vary on whether the process will be peaceful and what the consequences might be for East Asia.

The rise of China has been most evident and remarkable in the economic realm. "China market" and "China shock" have become household terms in many parts of the world, including much of Asia and the United States.[7] China's diplomatic accomplishments are also notable. Unlike its initial two decades as a permanent member of the United Nations Security Council, China has recently assumed a much more vigorous and visible role in this body. China has also sponsored its own multilateral organizations, including the Shanghai Cooperation Organization (or the "Shanghai Six") and the Boao Asia Forum. In addition, China has been particularly active in engaging the European Union and the Association of Southeast Asian Nations. China's "great-power diplomacy with responsibilities" *(fu zeren de daguo waijiao)* has also been manifested by Beijing's hosting and facilitating the three- and six-party talks on the North Korean nuclear issue.[8]

Responses to the rise of China have varied significantly. For geopolitical, economic, cultural, and historical reasons, the variations have been particularly marked in Asia. Reactions from Taiwan and Japan have been qualitatively different from those of Singapore and Myanmar. Equally important differences have been evident within various parts of the Southeast Asian region.[9] But the responses have been almost uniformly favorable and receptive in South Korea, with China managing to curry favor with the elites and the general public alike.[10]

Normalization of Sino–South Korean diplomatic relations in August 1992 triggered a continuing process of reconciliation that had long been encouraged by Seoul. South Korea had actively promoted economic détente with China for over a decade, with trade preceding the flag. Bilateral trade quickly expanded from U.S.$19 million in 1979 to U.S.$6.4 billion in 1992. Investment was also permitted beginning in 1988, although its scale remained limited due to the absence of official investment guarantees. Yet the rapid expansion of bilateral economic ties prior to normalization underscored the "special" relationship between the two former adversaries.[11]

In 1993, only a year after normalization, China was already South Korea's third-largest trading partner, following the United States and Japan. In 2001, China became the number-two destination of South Korea's exports, second only to the United States. In 2003, China (excluding Hong Kong and Macao) surpassed the United States as South Korea's top export market. In 2004, four years earlier than Seoul's original forecast, China (excluding Hong Kong and Macao) replaced the United States as South Korea's number-one trading partner. Sino–South Korean trade had grown to U.S.$79 billion by 2004.

Investment is another pillar of Sino–South Korean economic bilateralism. By the time of diplomatic normalization in 1992, South Korea was already the tenth-largest investor in China.[12] By 1995, China had become the leading foreign recipient of South Korean investment. In 1996, 46 percent of South Korea's total outbound investment poured into China.[13] The process slowed during the East Asian financial crisis of 1997–98, but "China fever" soon returned.[14] In 2002, South Korea's investment in China for the first time surpassed its investment in the United States. In 2003, South Korea invested U.S.$1.3 billion in China, becoming the third-largest investor in China, after only

Hong Kong and Japan.[15] As of 2004, South Korea's cumulative investment in China was U.S.$17.9 billion on 13,223 projects, accounting for the largest share (23 percent) of its total outbound investment during 1968–2004.

Table I   **South Korea's Trade Dependency on China**

	China Trade in South Korea's Total Trade (percent)	South Korea's Surplus with China (US$million)
1985	1.9	205
1990	2.8	-715
1995	6.4	1740
2000	9.4	5656
2001	10.8	4887
2002	13.1	6354
2003	15.3	13201
2004	16.6	20193

Source: www.kotis.or.kr/tjgb.

South Korea–China economic relations have been highly profitable for Seoul. Whereas China enjoyed trade surpluses with South Korea prior to normalization, South Korea has reaped huge surpluses ever since. As of 2004, the China trade comprised 16.6 percent of South Korea's total trade, 19.6 percent of its total exports, and 69 percent of Korea's total trade surplus.[16] The trend will very likely continue, as 80.3 percent of the medium-size and small firms surveyed in South Korea in late 2003 preferred to relocate operations to China. Considering that many conglomerates and their parts suppliers have already moved their assembly lines to China, South Korea's economic dependence on China will continue to rise.[17] As Table 1 illustrates, China looms ever larger in South Korean economic calculations. And, as the "garlic battle" in 2000 powerfully demonstrated, even a small fraction of China trade can affect South Korea adversely.[18]

China also weighs heavily in Korean diplomacy. The Chinese shadow had traditionally loomed large over Korea, irrespective of the ebbs and flows of Beijing's influence. The Sino-Japanese War in 1895 over the suzerainty of Korea, Mao's decision in 1950 to intervene in the Korean War despite the continuing civil war and grave domestic problems, and Beijing's agreement in 1997 to participate in the four-party talks testify to China's unequivocal interest in the Korean Peninsula.[19] Now, with much greater power, wealth, prestige, and influence than ever before, China constitutes a formidable diplomatic presence on the peninsula.

Beijing's role in supporting the North Korean economy has also proven highly significant. China's provision of food and energy as grants or at "friendly prices" has been central to the survival of the North Korean regime. It is more difficult to gauge whether and how such aid can be directly translated into explicit Chinese influence over Pyongyang. Kim Jong Il's visits to China in May 2000, January 2001, and May 2004 reflected Pyongyang's efforts to solicit Beijing's support for the North's new policy framework. Beijing's potential influence over Pyongyang, as well as its continued efforts to sustain and facilitate multiparty talks on the nuclear issue, adds to China's pool of resources.[20] But Chinese engagement also highlights the risk to Beijing's efforts should the process fail to produce satisfactory results.

South Korea's security perceptions of China have also undergone major change. To some extent, this may reflect Seoul's preoccupation with sustaining its highly profitable economic interactions with Beijing. Few South Korean security experts openly discuss the military implications of the "rise of China," and even less the potential negative implications. The Defense White Paper, published by South Korea's Ministry of National Defense, generally devotes two to three pages to briefly outlining China's military modernization and another two to three pages to intermilitary exchanges. No trace of security concern is discernible.[21]

Cultural draw has also been a crucial factor in expanding the bilateralism between South Korea and China. Prior to normalization, over 58,000 people had visited between the two countries. The number of two-way visitors rose sharply in subsequent years, to nearly a half-million in 1995 and to over two million in 2003.[22] As of 2003, nearly 180,000 South Koreans were long-term residents in China, including over 35,000 students, accounting for 46 percent of all foreign students in China. Bilateral educational exchanges were officially permitted only in 1993, but the increase in the number of South Korean students in China has been beyond anyone's imagination.[23]

Chinese language study is also becoming very popular in Korea, having already surpassed Japanese in terms of demand among the students, although English continues to be the most favored foreign language. China has also become the third most preferred location for overseas study, after only the United States (39 percent) and Europe. The "China fever" *(hwapung)* in South Korea—along with the "Korean fad" *(hanliu)* in China, particularly with pop culture and language learning—has been mutually reinforcing.[24] China plans to dispatch 600 language instructors, who will teach Chinese at primary and middle schools in South Korea. Furthermore, Seoul was chosen as the first Asian location for a Chinese overseas cultural center.[25]

South Korea's rapprochement with China can therefore be understood within different international relations frameworks. A realist paradigm, for example, draws attention to South Korea's efforts to use Beijing to induce crucial changes in North Korea, as well as to balance vis-à-vis Washington. The liberal perspective that profit maximization is in the best interests of both China and South Korea can also explain Seoul's ever-expanding economic bilateralism with Beijing. China's determination to become a great power has also enhanced the importance of learning and emulation, thereby producing significant changes in its policy vis-à-vis South Korea compared to its earlier (pre-1997) development model.

Something important is still missing, however, in explaining the comprehensive cooperative partnership, including military ties, being forged between South Korea and China.[26] Is there an additional factor or magnet that has pulled the two former enemies together at such a sweeping pace? There are at least two possibilities. At one level, these changes denote certain historically induced sentiments that Koreans in both the South and the North harbor vis-à-vis China. These represent perceptions that are learned and inculcated, rather than being almost hereditary. Alternatively, they may be "wishful expectations," due mainly to the paucity of South Koreans' contact with the "real China." Twenty years from today, if South Koreans still hold the same positive view of China despite more frequent and intensive contact, we may then conclude that the former offers a better explanation.[27]

SOUTH KOREA'S EVOLVING VIEWS OF CHINA: VIEWS OF THE GENERAL PUBLIC

Nationwide opinion surveys conducted during 1988–2004 underscore some pronounced shifts in South Korean attitudes toward China, with South Korean perceptions of China becoming increasingly favorable.[28] Most nationwide surveys indicate that South Korean perceptions of China have been more favorable than perceptions of the United States. Positive South Korean perceptions of China are also inversely correlated with age, while those of the United States were positively correlated with age.[29] As Table 2 suggests, however, the age differentials for the favorable views of China have increasingly narrowed. Public views of what needs to be done in South Korea's relations with the four major powers also demonstrate that China is viewed in ever more favorable terms.[30]

Table 2   **Age Differentials in Positive Views of China (percent)**

	1990	2004a	2004b
20s	46.3	52.7	45.6
30s	36.6	58.8	52.7
40s	33.8	44.3	44.8
50s	26.8	38.4	29.2

Sources: 1990: *Chonhwangi ui hanguk saheo* (The Korean Society in Transition) (Seoul: Institute of Population and Development, 1990), p. 184; 2004a: *Donga Ilbo,* 4 May 2004; 2004b *Hangook gyongje sinmun* (Korea Economic Daily), 12 October 2004.

Table 3, formulated on the basis of nine different (i.e., non-time-series) nationwide opinion surveys conducted during 1996–2004, further highlights that China's rise in the minds of the South Koreans has been real and mostly at the expense of positive perceptions of the United States.[31]

In light of the younger generations' more favorable and optimistic views of China, Beijing's shadow over the Korean Peninsula is likely to continue to expand. Perceptually, the "rise of China" is perhaps far more than an attitude shift for Korea, although the last survey cited—conducted in the aftermath of the South Korea–China row over the Koguryo history controversy—hints at the somewhat fickle nature of public perceptions.

Table 3

	Chose China	Chose U.S.
1996[a]	47	24
1997[b]	56	31
1999[c]	33	22
2000[d]	45	43
2000[e]	53	8
2002[f]	41	30
2003[g]	48	33
2004[h]	61	26
2004[i]	40	54

a. The Ministry of Information Survey (Seoul: MOI, 1996), p. 354. The question: "Which country will become closest to Korea in ten years?"

b. 1997 Sejong Survey (Seoul: Dongseo Research 1997), pp. 11–13. The question: "With which country Korea should strengthen its relations?"

c. *Donga Ilbo*, 1 January 1999. The question: "Which country Korea would be closest to in the twenty-first century?"

d. *Hangook Ilbo*, 9 June 2000. The question: "With which country should Korea cooperate most for the success of the inter-Korean summit?"

e. *Donga Ilbo*, 5 December 2000. The question: "Which country will become most influential in Asia?"

f. *Sisa Journal*, March 2002. The question: "Which of the four major powers do you feel most favorably toward?"

g. *Joongang Ilbo*, 12 February 2003. The question: "Where should South Korea's foreign policy focus be placed?"

h. *Donga Ilbo*, 4 May 2004. The question: "Which country should South Korea regard most important?"

i. *Chosun Ilbo*, 1 January 2005. The question: "Which country do you feel most favorably toward?"

How popular perceptions shape foreign-policy calculations is nonetheless highly complex. It remains entirely possible that popular views will increasingly differ from the Seoul government's policy priorities toward the United States and China. The election of Roh Moo Hyun as South Korea's new president (engineered primarily by voters in their twenties and thirties) in December 2002 created the very real prospect that in the longer term South Korea's foreign policy will give increasing weight to China. By contrast, many in the U.S. government believe that South Korea's "China fever" remains mainly an economic phenomenon.[32] This divergence could become increasingly pronounced over time, affecting the balance in Korea's relations with the United States and China (and the future of the U.S.-Korea alliance) in profound ways.

CHANGING ELITE VIEWS

There appears to be a fine line between the South Korean general public and the policy elite in their respective views of China. South Korean elites have generally been more status quo–oriented, fearing that the "rise of China" will be destabilizing.[33] These more traditional circles exhibit deep-seated concern over China's longer-term intentions toward South Korea. For geopolitical and historical reasons, many South Korean elites cannot help but ponder whether the "rise of China" could ultimately produce a malignant neighbor with parabellum dispositions.

The South Korean elite's ambivalence also has significant bearing upon the "uncivil" faces of China. Maritime piracy and territorial intrusions by Chinese fishing vessels are very often highlighted as an area of concern.[34] China is also portrayed as seriously endangering the environment, particularly in terms of airborne pollutants.[35] Human-rights concerns also loom large in reinforcing the South Korean elite's ambivalence toward China, which, on several occasions since 2000, extradited "refugees" (or "escapees") to North Korea without any assurance of their safety.[36] As South Koreans' human rights awareness has generally been enhanced in recent years, their perceptions of China as "uncivil" have also amplified accordingly. The "refugee" issue is likely to be a continued source of strain in bilateral relations and might even curb the more enthusiastic views of China expressed in some circles.

The "audacity" of Chinese diplomats has also reinforced the negative views that the South Korean elite holds toward China. Prior to the Dalai Lama's first visit to South Korea, scheduled for 2000, Wu Dawei, then China's ambassador to Seoul, warned that "permitting his entry would jeopardize the bilateral relationship, though not to the extent of severed ties." His comments were strongly criticized within South Korea, given that the Dalai Lama paid visits to more than forty countries with which China maintained diplomatic relations. Another example concerned events in the spring of 2004, when the Chinese embassy phoned and faxed members of the National Assembly to prevent them from attending Taiwan President Chen Shui-bian's inauguration in May 2004. The press secretary even threatened to "remember those who insisted on attending it."[37]

Many in Seoul are concerned that a stronger China could increasingly impose its views on South Korea, as the Ming and Qing courts did on Chosun. Particularly given that China is carrying out its "Northeast Project" (*dongbei gongcheng*), which involves incorporating much of Korea's ancient history into China's "local histories" (*difang zhengquanshi*), South Korea's concern with China's "imperial" aspirations is not totally ungrounded. The Koguryo history controversy, in particular, left deep wounds in the minds of South Korean intellectuals.[38]

Despite the sentiments of reservation and ambivalence toward China, the South Korean policy elite is currently going through a crucial set of generational and value changes.[39] According to intensive interviews conducted by an American think tank in 2002 with a new generation of South Korean opinion leaders, 86 percent of the interviewees wished to see South Korea's ties with China further strengthened in the future, while the comparable figure regarding ties with the United States was only 14 percent.[40] This data receives additional support from a poll of South Korean legislators. According to an April 2004 survey of 243 newly elected members of the National Assembly, 55 percent of the 138 "newcomers" to the assembly chose China as the most important target of South Korea's diplomacy in the future. Of the 105 "old timers," 42 percent chose China as the most important target of South Korea's diplomacy.[41] Those from the incumbent party generally showed a higher propensity to choose China than those from opposition forces.[42]

CONCLUDING OBSERVATIONS

As South Korea's dependence on China and the favorable views of China have increased, there are increasing calls to reassess Seoul's overall foreign policy orientation. While such opinions have also been expressed in the past, they were mostly from "progressive" circles and failed to be taken seriously at the time. This time, however, the intensity and magnitude of the challenges to the conventional view have become more formidable.

A *Joongang Ilbo* survey conducted in early 2003, in the aftermath of the presidential election, contained a crucial harbinger of this ongoing debate. Concerning the desirable future direction of South Korea's foreign policy, 59.8 percent of the respondents were in favor of Seoul's detachment from its Washington-centered diplomacy.[43] Throughout 2003, debates and criticisms ensued concerning the Roh Moo Hyun administration's unprecedented strategic soul-searching, a crucial outcome of which was subtly presented in its policy of "cooperative and independent national defense."[44]

The aforementioned survey of the newcomers in the National Assembly also fits in this context. Once the conflicting foreign policy orientations included a partisan dimension, the debates became further politicized and bifurcated.[45] These debates correlated closely with historic declines in U.S.–South Korea relations. The diverging threat perceptions vis-à-vis North Korea, the intricate negotiations over the withdrawal of U.S. forces, the return of bases and defense burden-sharing, and the controversies over the size, location, and timing of Seoul's dispatch of military forces to Iraq have been effective indicators of the state of affairs in U.S.–South Korea relations.[46]

Debates will likely persist, as Seoul's dependence on Beijing is bound to supplant its previous dependence on Washington.[47] At least four key factors will shape future South Korean perceptions of the rise of China. First, the sustained growth of China will certainly affect the range of policy choices available for South Korea. The emergence of "China Inc." with huge market and investment opportunities will draw South Korea increasingly closer, making it more difficult—if not impossible—to coordinate Seoul's economic cooperation (with China) from strategic-security ties (with America).[48] Seoul's attraction to Beijing will also persist, with expanded cooperation in noneconomic areas as well.

Second, the Japan factor may also come into play, further complicating the equation. Many surveys suggest that crucial discrepancies are found between the United States and South Korea in terms of threat perceptions concerning Japan and China. While Japan is always viewed favorably by the United States compared to China (which topped Americans' adversary list for ten successive years), to South Korea the "rise of Japan" is viewed as something worse than the "rise of China."[49] America's continuous assigning of more strategic importance to Japan, without comparable considerations for South Korea's interests, may actually draw South Korea closer to China even without conscious efforts by Beijing at driving a wedge between Seoul and Washington.[50]

Third, much of the perceptual dynamics also rests on China's ability and willingness to regulate its "imperial" air over smaller states in the region. As described earlier, in the eyes of the South Korean elite, the track record of China's modesty has been very mixed.[51] As Seoul's dependence on Beijing further increases, China may become more tempted to use its strengthened leverage vis-à-vis South Korea. The "internalization of border areas" (bianjiang neidihua) encapsulated in the Northeast Project has ample room for unpleasant encounters between both South and North Korea and China.[52]

Fourth, while South Korean elites have traditionally acted upon their psychological dependence on U.S. protection, changes initiated during Kim Dae Jung's presidency have been consolidated under his successor, Roh Moo Hyun. Some of these changes have been hard for the United States to swallow, with its conviction that South Korea should always be grateful for what America did during and after the Korean War. The sheer disparity in the amount of attention the United States and South Korea have paid to each other is a more serious problem: to the United States, as the world superpower, Korea is only a small part of the Asian region in its global strategy, while Washington takes up a huge chunk of Seoul's policy horizon.[53] While in the past a wide array of problems and tension in the alliance was simply taken for granted as a necessary cost of accepting America's defense shield, it is no longer automatically tolerated.[54]

Anti-Americanism is not unique to South Korea, nor is it a new phenomenon there. The fundamental question is whether South Korea's relationship with the United States will worsen to the extent that there is actually room for a third party to interject itself into the political equation. In geopolitical, cultural, and perceptual terms, China is highest on the list of these prospective third parties. Whether Seoul wishes to consider Beijing its strategic alternative—or strategic supplement—is one thing; China's consideration of this as a possibility is quite another. The Security Policy Initiative (SPI) negotiations—that is, how American forces in South Korea are to be restructured in line with the "strategic flexibility" principle—will constitute a major test of how South Korea will position itself between the United States and China.

Viewed from a long-term perspective, the ninety-seven-year (1895–1992) separation between (South) Korea and China appears to be not only very brief in its duration but also highly artificial and, therefore, rather unnatural.[55] The rapprochement and expansion of cooperative relations between South Korea and China are therefore deemed only natural, although the specifics of their processes and implications are no doubt contingent on a wide range of factors. Most notably, unlike the Sino-Japanese War over a hundred years ago, a "war of soft power" has already started in the Korean Peninsula, as South Korea will closely monitor whether the United States or China is more likely to be benign and supportive of its interests in the future.

South Korea is therefore approaching a crossroads in its strategic soul-searching. With so many uncertainties, Seoul may find it increasingly more difficult to determine a strategy that can satisfy all different segments of society while simultaneously addressing different South Korean strategic interests. In the short run, South Korea will continue with the dual strategy of maximizing its benefits from the comprehensive cooperation with China and minimizing its costs from the strained relationship with the United States. The same cannot be said of its long-term strategy, however, which will depend heavily on these four larger factors.

NOTES

1. See, for instance, Jonathan Mercer, *Reputation and International Politics* (Ithaca: Cornell University Press, 1996), chapters 1 and 2.

2. See Rita R. Rogers, "Intergenerational Transmission of Historical Enmity," in *The Psychodynamics of International Relationships*, ed. Vamik D. Volkan et al. (Lexington, Mass.: Lexington Books, 1990), pp. 91–96.

3. By contrast, Taiwan's favorable dispositions toward Japan, compared to those of China and South Korea, warrant further consideration. See, for instance, Shelley Rigger, *Politics in Taiwan: Voting for Democracy* (London: Routledge, 1999), chapters 1–2; and Leo T. S. Ching, *Becoming Japanese: Colonial Taiwan and the Politics of Identity*

Formation (Stanford: Stanford University, 2001), pp. 8–13.

4. While demands for a formal—and more sincere—apology have been a constant issue in South Korean–Japanese relations, no expression of "regret," let alone an apology, was officially offered by China for its military involvement against South Korea during the Korean War. While such demands were made by Seoul during the negotiations for diplomatic normalization in 1992, China never accepted them. See Lee Sang-Ock, *Jonhwangi eui hangook woegyo* (Korea's Diplomacy in an Era of Transition) (Seoul: Life and Dream, 2003), pp. 214–16.

5. See Jiang Xiyuan and Xia Liping, *Zhongguo heping jueqi* (China's Peaceful Rise) (Beijing: Zhongguo shehuikexue chubanshe, 2004), pp. 21–28.

6. See Wang Gungwu, "The Fourth Rise of China: Cultural Implications," *China: An International Journal*, no. 4 (September 2004), pp. 311–22.

7. China's gross domestic product (GDP) has risen fourfold since 1978, making it the world's sixth-largest economy. China also boasts of its status as the world's third-largest trading nation and in 2002 replaced the United States as the world's number-one destination for FDI. See Ted C. Fishman, "The Chinese Century," *New York Times*, 4 July 2004.

8. See, for instance, Li Wen, "Zhongguo de heping jueqi: heyi neng yu heyi wei" (China's Peaceful Rise: How and What For?), *Dangdai yatai* (Contemporary Asia-Pacific), no. 5 (2004), pp. 3–10; and Jae Ho Chung, "China's Korea Policy under the New Leadership: Stealth Changes in the Making?" *Journal of East Asian Affairs* 18, no. 1 (Spring/Summer 2004), pp. 1–18.

9. For variant responses by the East Asian nations, see Alastair I. Johnston and Robert S. Ross, eds., *Engaging China: The Management of an Emerging Power* (London: Routledge, 1999); Herbert Yee and Ian Storey, eds., *China Threat: Perceptions, Myths and Reality* (London: Routledge Curzon, 2002); Zainal A. Yusof, "Malaysia's Response to the China Challenge," Tain-Jy Chen, "Will Taiwan Be Marginalized by China," and Shigeyuki Abe, "Is 'China Fear' Warranted?" in *Asian Economic Papers* 2, no. 2 (Spring/Summer 2003), pp. 46–131; and David Shambaugh, ed., *Power Shift: China and Asia's New Dynamics* (Berkeley: University of California Press, 2005).

10. Jae Ho Chung, "South Korea between Eagle and Dragon: Perceptual Ambivalence and Strategic Dilemma," *Asian Survey* 41, no. 5 (September–October 2001), pp. 783–85; and William Watts, *Next Generation Leaders in the Republic of Korea: Opinion Survey Report and Analysis* (Washington, D.C.: Potomac Associates, 2002), p. 12.

11. See Jae Ho Chung, "South Korea–China Economic Relations: The Current Situation and Its Implications," *Asian Survey* 28, no. 10 (October 1988), pp. 1031–48; and idem, "Sino-South Korean Economic Cooperation:

An Analysis of Domestic and Foreign Entanglements," *Journal of Northeast Asian Studies* 9, no. 2 (Summer 1990), pp. 59–79.

12. *Joongang Ilbo* (Joongang Daily), 10 May 1993.

13. *Munhwa Ilbo* (Munhwa Daily), 20 February 1997.

14. For the adverse impact of the financial crisis, see Song Guanghao, "Jinrong weiji yihoude hanguo duihua zhijie touzi" (Korea's Direct Investment in China after the Financial Crisis), *Dongbeiya luntan* (Northeast Asian Forum), no. 4 (2001), pp. 41–45.

15. The average South Korean investment in China per day is twelve projects worth US$12.6 million. See *Chosun Ilbo* (Chosun Daily), 3 November 2003.

16. In 2003, the surplus with China accounted for 88 percent of South Korea's total surplus. See *Chosun Ilbo*, 1 May 2004.

17. *Maekyung Economy*, 10 December 2003, p. 29; and Dexter Roberts and Moon Ilhwan, "Korea's China Play," *Business Week*, 29 March 2004.

18. See Jae Ho Chung, "From a 'Special Relationship' to a 'Normal Partnership'?: Interpreting the 'Garlic Battle' in Sino-South Korean Relations," *Pacific Affairs* 76, no. 4 (Winter 2003–2004), pp. 549–68.

19. For a rare disclosure of China's intention behind the participation of the four-party talks—to enhance China's influence over the region—see Li Qiang, "Chaoxian bandao wenti sifang huitan de xianzhuang yu qianjing" (The Current Situation of and Prospects for the Four-Party Talks over the Korean Problem), *Dangdai yatai* (Contemporary Asia and the Pacific), no. 3 (1999), pp. 33–37.

20. See Jae Ho Chung, "Korea and China in Northeast Asia, 1948–2002: From Reactive Bifurcation to Complex Interdependence," in *Northeast Asia between Regionalism and Globalization: Korea at the Center*, ed. Charles Armstrong, Samuel S. Kim, Stephen Kotkin, and Gilbert Rozman (Armonk, N.Y.: M. E. Sharpe, 2005).

21. See the Ministry of National Defense of the Republic of Korea, *Defense White Paper 2004* (Seoul: Ministry of National Defense, 2005), pp. 28–30.

22. Sources: *Hanguk gyunghe shinmun*, 21 October 1991; *Munhwa Ilbo*, 20 February 1997; *Chosun Ilbo*, 25 August 1992, 24 August 1997, and 5 January 2003; and www.knto.or.kr.

23. As of 2004, the number of Korean students in the United States was 52,483, the third-largest after India and China. *Donga Ilbo*, 7 Feburary 2005.

24. *Financial Times*, 10 February 2002; and *Donga Ilbo*, 4 May 2004.

25. See *Chosun Ilbo*, 29 January 2005.

26. See Jae Ho Chung, *The Korean-American Alliance and the "Rise of China": A Preliminary Assessment of Perceptual Changes and Strategic Choices* (Stanford, Calif.: Institute for International Studies, February 1999); also available at ldml.stanford.edu/aparcpubsearch.

27. Interpretations along this line entail a danger of "maturation effect" in operation, since both societies may go through crucial changes during these twenty years.

28. Also see Chung, "South Korea between Eagle and Dragon," pp. 783–85.

29. The older generations, with more immediate memories of the Korean War and the Cold War, expressed less affinity for China, while the younger generations were much more positive about it.

30. See Gi-Wook Shin, "South Korean Anti-Americanism: A Comparative Perspective," *Asian Survey* 36, no. 8 (August 1996), p. 795. According to a survey conducted by *Hankyoreh Sinmun* in 1995, those who called for the strengthening of South Korea—U.S. relations reached 33.6 percent, while those for the consolidation of South Korea–China relations reached 71.4 percent. See *Hankyoreh Sinmun*, 15 August 1995. In a 1997 survey, those calling for a strengthened South Korea–U.S. relationship marked 31 percent, while those for a strengthened relationship with China reached 56 percent. See *1997 Sejong Survey* (Seoul: Dongseo Research, 1997), p. 12.

31. This data alone does not suffice to argue that favorable views of China are the result of anti-Americanism, although it certainly is a possibility. South Korea was not alone in witnessing a decline in favorable views of the United States, however. See the Pew Research Center, *What the World Thinks in 2002: How Global Public View Their Lives, Their Countries, The World, America* (4 December 2002), pp. 53–55; people-press.org.

32. For Washington's assessment as such, see Office of Research (Department of State), "For South Koreans, China's Draw Is Mainly Economic," *Opinion Analysis*, M-127-03 30 September 2003). American policy experts appear to be more concerned with political and strategic ramifications of China's rise over South Korea. See Jae Ho Chung, "America's Views of South Korea–China Relations: Public Opinions and Elite Perceptions," *Korean Journal of Defense Analysis* 17, no. 1 (Spring 2005), pp. 213–34.

33. For the generally conservative foreign policy orientations of the South Korean elite, see Sam Sung Lee, "The Korean Society and Foreign Policy," in *Korea in the Age of Globalization and Information*, ed. Yong Soon Yim and Ki-Jung Kim (Seoul: KAIS, 1997), pp. 110–22.

34. See "Special Report," *Weekly Hankook*, 16 December 1999, pp. 48–58.

35. According to a recent study, 49 percent of NOx and 40 percent of SO2 found in South Korea's atmosphere originated from China. See *Donga Ilbo*, 10 August 2004. China's own evaluation is that environmental cooperation between Seoul and Beijing has not been on a par with measures undertaken with Japan, Europe, and the United States. See Xu Songling, "Zhongguo-dongbeiya guojia zhi jian de huanjing hezuo: zhuangkuang fenxi yu pingjia" (Analysis and Evaluation of China's Current Environmental Cooperation with Northeast Asian Countries), *Dongbeiya luntan* (Northeast Asia Forum), no. 1 (2002), p. 51.

36. See *Donga Ilbo*, 13 and 18 October 1999; *Chosun Ilbo*, 27 January 2000; *Wolgan Chosun*, June 2000, pp. 458–72; and *New York Times*, 31 May 2000.

37. See *Chosun Ilbo*, 2 June 2004 and *Donga Ilbo*, 2 June 2004.

38. For such concerns, see Nan Liming, "Hanguo dui zhongguo de wenhua kangyi" (South Korea's Cultural Objection to China), *Yazhou zhoukan* (Asia Weekly), 25 July 2004, pp. 16–17; *Donga Ilbo*, 3 December 2003, 25 August and 25 December 2004; *Joongang Ilbo*, 4 December 2003; and *Washington Post*, 23 September 2004. For the goals of the Northeast Project, see Ma Dazhen, ed., *Zhongguo dongbei bianjiang yanjiu* (Study of China's Northeastern Border Areas) (Beijing: Zhongguo shehuikexue chubanshe, 2003). Also see "Rewriting National History: The 'Zeng Guofan' Phenomenon," in *Cultural Nationalism in Contemporary China*, ed. Yingjie Guo (London: Routledge Curzon, 2004), chapter 3.

39. Over two-thirds (68 percent) of the assembly members in the incumbent Open Party and nearly a half (43 percent) of those in the Grand National Party are newcomers as of April 2004.

40. See Watts, *Next Generation Leaders*, p. 12.

41. See *Donga Ilbo*, 19 April 2004.

42. The figure of those of the Open Party who chose China was 63 percent, while that of the Grand National Party was 33 percent. See *Chosun Ilbo*, 30 April 2004.

43. See the issue of 12 February 2003. Interestingly, concerning the same question, 42.8 percent of the opinion leaders were in favor of South Korea's detachment from U.S.-centered diplomacy.

44. See National Security Council, *Pyonghwa wa bonyongeul wihan dongbuka* (Peace and Prosperity for Northeast Asia) (Seoul: NSC, February 2004).

45. See *Donga Ilbo*, 4 May 2004; *Chosun Ilbo*, 12 May 2004; and *Joongang Ilbo*, 7 May and 23 June 2004. Some academics are even divided between the so-called "Northeast Asian School" and the "American School." See, for instance, Lee Soo-Hoon, "Now, It Is the Era of China," and Chun Chae-Sung, "It Is Still America, not China," in *Chosun Ilbo*, 21 and 25 April 2004.

46. A recent survey of Korea specialists in Washington, D.C., conducted by the Mansfield Foundation and *Kyung Hyang Ilbo* (Kyung Hyang Daily), showed nearly unanimous agreement that the U.S.-Korea alliance is experiencing profound change. See www.mansfieldfdn.org/pubs/pub_pdfs/khsm_summary.pdf.

47. According to a survey conducted by *Chosun Ilbo* in late 2004, 64.6 percent were in favor of independent diplomacy, while 35.4 percent were in favor of strengthened ties with the United States. See the 1 January 2005 issue.

48. For an ominous forecast that China will eventually dominate the Seoul-Beijing relationship, making the former one of its satellites, see "Korea's China Play," *Business Week*, 29 March 2004.

49. See, for instance, *White Paper on the National Consciousness in Korea, China and Japan* (Seoul: KBS, 1996), pp. 431, 436; *1997 Sejong Survey*, p. 11; William Watts, *Americans Look at Asia* (Washington, D.C.: Asia Society Washington Center, 1999), p. 42; Harris Poll No. 8, 31 January 2001, Table 2 at www.harrisinteractive.com; and Jae Ho Chung, *How America Views China–South Korea Bilateralism*, CNAPS Working Paper, Brookings Institution, July 2003, pp. 7, 14–15, 19–20, available at www.brookings.edu/cnaps.

50. During their meeting in 1995, Jiang Zemin and Kim Youngsam jointly spoke at a press conference of their criticism of Japanese historical consciousness. See Gilbert Rozman, *Northeast Asia's Stunted Regionalism: Bilateral Distrust in the Shadow of Globalization* (Cambridge: Cambridge University Press, 2004), p. 170.

51. For China's changing views of South Korea—from a positive example to a negative case to avoid emulating—see Chung, "From a 'Special Relationship' to a 'Normal Partnership'?" pp. 558–60.

52. See Jae Ho Chung, "Dongbuk gongjong eui hyonjaejok euimi wa hanguk woegyo" (The Contemporary Meaning of the "Northeast Project" and Korea's Diplomacy), *Wolgan Joongang* (Monthly Joongang), September 2004; and Shi Jinbao, "Zai duiwai jiaoliu zhong baohu woguo wenhua yichan de chanquan" (On Protecting the Property Rights of Our Cultural Exchanges with Foreign Countries), *Lingdao canyue* (References for Leaders), No. 316 (5 July 2004), pp. 5–6.

53. This is perhaps something that has to be accepted by countries other than the United States, according to Robert Kagan. See *Of Paradise and Power: America and Europe in the New World Order* (New York: Basic, 2002). For the sheer perceptual disparities between Washington and Seoul, see Chung, *How America Views China–South Korea Bilateralism*, pp. 18–20.

54. According to a survey by *Joongang Ilbo* in 2003, 77 percent of the respondents replied that SOFA needed to be amended even if that meant an adverse impact on U.S.-Korea relations. *Joongang Ilbo*, 17 January 2003.

55. For the inherent artificiality of many seemingly obvious watershed periodizations, see Paul A. Cohen, *China Unbound: Evolving Perspectives on the Chinese Past* (London: Routledge Curzon, 2003), pp. 136–41.

13

Power, Money, and Ideas
Japan, China, and the "Korean Shift"

Victor Cha

> *Focus on capabilities instead of numbers. . . . It is no longer relevant to measure America's war-fighting capability by the number of troops and equipment in a particular country or region.*
>
> George W. Bush, 16 August 2004

There are more variables in flux on the Korean peninsula at present than at any time in recent memory. In contrast to the dangerous but enduring stalemate on the peninsula of the past half-century, the peninsula is on the threshold of major change at multiple levels, each carrying high stakes for U.S. and Japanese interests. These include the prospect of a South Korean strategic orientation geared toward a lasting accommodation with China; a fundamental restructuring of the U.S. force presence on the peninsula; and a new strategic balance wrought by a nuclear-armed North Korea, counterbalanced by an increasingly brittle regime in Pyongyang desperate for economic reform.

What are the implications of these changes for Japan's relations with the peninsula, for U.S.-Japan-Korea relations, and for larger power configurations in Northeast Asia? What are Japan's concerns and anxieties with regard to future outcomes on the peninsula? To what extent are Korean outcomes intertwined with, and a potential indicator of, China's rise in the region? This chapter will focus principally on a single major trigger of long-term change: the impending restructuring of U.S. forces in Northeast Asia.[1] I will first present the prevailing interpretation of Japanese concerns—informed by different schools of thought in international relations—about how changes in the

U.S. force structure could affect Tokyo's relations with South Korea. I will then propose an alternative future path that seems just as likely but is somewhat neglected in punditry and commentary. This alternate view takes a longer view of Japan–South Korea relations; it gives more weight to certain factors in Seoul-Tokyo relations than the prevailing view; and it subscribes to a defensive realist view of Japan and South Korea, in contrast to the offensive realist school of thought. I will then extend the defensive realist analysis to Japan's relations with North Korea, arguing that Tokyo has been fairly successful in handling relations with the North, despite a number of impediments.

CHANGES IN U.S. FORCE STRUCTURE

The impending changes in the U.S. peninsular force structure reflect an unusual constellation of forces that compel inevitable, if not imminent, changes to the alliance. The first concerns U.S. strategy. The U.S. troop presence has been tailored to successfully deter North Korean aggression. However, the positioning, training, and equipping of these forces are now less useful to American strategy in East Asia, because they are single-mindedly focused on deterrence, to the exclusion of other military missions. Second, at the same time that U.S. forces are inflexibly tied to one mission, the ROK military has grown more robust and capable of bearing a larger defense burden, a far cry from the feeble force trained by the United States fifty years ago. The third factor concerns demography and democracy. Civil-military tensions over the U.S. military footprint in Korea have grown greatly in recent years. This is not the radical anti-Americanism of the 1980s, but the showcasing of a younger, affluent, and educated generation of Koreans, bred on democracy, who view the United States far less favorably than their elders do.[2] Fourth, the sunshine or engagement policy toward North Korea has had the unintended consequence of worsening perceptions of U.S. troops in the body politic. On the one hand, the exaggerated success of the policy caused the public to be less welcoming of the U.S. presence. On the other, the failure of the policy (measured by the lack of DPRK reciprocation) led to the search for scapegoats, for which the U.S. presence was a ready target.

Finally, larger trends in U.S. security thinking also compelled change. The Pentagon's 100,000-personnel benchmark in Asia has been viewed by experts and the Department of Defense as hindering transformational changes in regional military capabilities. The focus, many reformers argue, should be on military capability, not on a precise number of forces. As the U.S. military continues its transformation into a more expeditionary force increasingly equipped with precision weapons; fully networked command, information, and surveillance systems; and long-range striking ability, U.S. forces stationed in East Asia will of necessity be part of this transformation.

For years, a belief predominated that the United States was too comfortably self-interested with its position on the peninsula to contemplate serious change in its regional deployment patterns, even in the face of mounting anti-American sentiments in Seoul. Events have shown this judgment to be inaccurate. With no imperial aspirations, the United States is prepared to withdraw its military forces in the face of any host nation that does not welcome them. While heightened anti-American sentiment has not helped matters, the constellation of forces described above compels fundamental change.

The elements of the American plan to restructure U.S. forces in Korea are well known.[3] However, the objectives underlying these changes are less well delineated. The August 2004 presidential statements on military transformation, as well as the September 2002 National Security Strategy, provide the larger strategic context for these changes. The post–11 September strategic environment has validated the need for more mobile, agile, yet lethal forces that can be readily deployed globally to combat existential threats wherever they might arise, particularly in relation to terrorism. But the meaning of these changes for the peninsula and Northeast Asia is less apparent.

The objectives of these changes for Korean security can be described in four ways:

- Flexibility: The transformation of forces in Korea is meant to yield an American capability that is flexible: it remains large (and lethal) enough to be militarily significant, but with enough flexibility to handle a broad range of tasks that extend beyond the peninsula.

- Deployability: The transformation of forces in Korea, in combination with other U.S. capabilities in the region (especially those in Japan), are meant to provide an American capability that can react swiftly to regional developments and offer an integrated joint force with the full range of mobility, strike, maneuver, and sustainability that capitalizes on U.S. technological advantages in long-range precision warfare.

- Credibility: The U.S. capability in Korea, in spite of transformation, must still represent and preserve America's traditional alliance commitment to the defense and security of South Korea.

- Unobtrusiveness: A transformed U.S. presence in Korea must also be less obtrusive. The new presence must be equivalent to the old as a symbol of the alliance but possess a footprint that is not perceived as an obstacle to peace in the eyes of the Korean people.

THE "KOREAN SHIFT"

How do these changes in U.S. force posture affect Japan's relations with the ROK? Is the U.S.-Japan-ROK Cold War alliance network (which ironically only became a working trilateral framework in the post–Cold War era) still viable? There are numerous ways of spelling out the implications, but the core causal factor from Japan's perspective is how South Korea responds to the abandonment fears created by U.S. troop reductions. These abandonment fears, despite repeated U.S. efforts at reassuring its Korean ally, are unavoidable.[4] How South Korea responds to these fears, and, in turn, how Japan reacts to South Korean actions will be a pivotal determinant of future pathways for both allies.

One future scenario, prevalent among many experts, might be termed the "Korean shift"—that is, a shift in South Korea's strategic alignments away from a maritime orientation geared to the United States and Japan and toward a continental accommodation with China. This strategic shift reflects three sets of forces. For realism, the Korean shift would follow naturally from the security imperatives created for South Korea by the receding U.S. presence.[5] For Korea, as a small power in a neighborhood of large powers, a decreasing U.S. presence would trigger intense fears of U.S. abandonment. Despite constant U.S. reassurances and despite efforts by South Koreans to accept the "capability, not numbers" argument, abandonment fears would force Seoul to seek security solutions outside the alliance, or supplementary to the alliance. One option is self-help through internal balancing—that is, an enhancement of indigenous military capabilities to the point where the ROK becomes self-sufficient in defense, possibly including a nuclear deterrent. History, however, dictates against this path. Every time Korea has attempted an inward-oriented grand strategy (i.e., the Hermit Kingdom), the results have been far from optimal. Furthermore, South Korean contemplation of a nuclear deterrent potentially entails far-reaching negative diplomatic and strategic consequences. Instead, Korea's geostrategic imperative is to align with one of the major powers. The diminished relevance of the United States as an alternative (either because of U.S. disinterest or because of ambivalence toward the United States among a younger Korean generation) propels South Korea in the direction of China. From a realist perspective, the nature of this security relationship is not determinable—it could range from a formal alliance to a less formal mutual accommodative relationship, or even to a hierarchical arrangement.[6] But the realist model dictates that the perceived U.S. disengagement sets off abandonment dynamics, which in turn cause Korea to seek new balancing alternatives apart from Japan and the United States.

For constructivism, or identity-based arguments about international relations, the Korean shift would be driven by a combination of "new nationalism" (albeit one that still suffers from old pathologies) and historical animosity toward Japan.[7] Arguments about Korea's historical antagonisms with Japan are well known and do not require lengthy explication here.[8] The more important consideration, for our purposes, is the potential link between U.S. disengagement and "new" notions of Korean identity. In addition to the abandonment fears created by the changing U.S. presence, there are parallel South

Korean claims to increased autonomy and independence—that is, a new, younger Korean identity. This notion of a "new" identity, however, exhibits two traits that are not really new: (1) it is still negatively constructed, in the sense of seeking a positive affirmation of self-identity defined exclusively in negative terms (hence, previous Korean identity defined as antiforeign (*tonghak*), anti-Japan, or anticommunism);[9] and (2) the construction of this new identity remains politically contested.[10] For the "new nationalists," Korean identity must be disassociated from approaches linked to the old guard, specifically the Cold War security relationship with America and the economic relationship with Japan. While Japan and the United States suffer in this search for identity, traditional historical affinities toward Beijing position China much more effectively.

Finally, from a liberal perspective, the Korean shift away from the U.S.-Japan framework toward China is enhanced by burgeoning economic ties. From Japan's perspective, the economic picture for Korea has changed dramatically from the Cold War era. In 1995, Korea's total trade with the United States was $54.5 billion, whereas trade with China was $16.5 billion. By 2002, total trade with the United States was $55.8 billion, while that with China stood at $41.1 billion. By 2002, China and the ROK ranked as each other's third-largest trading partner. In 2003, the United States was supplanted by China as the largest export market for South Korean products, a position the United States had held since 1965.[11] Trends indicate that this dynamic should continue. While South Korean exports to the United States grew by 2.7 percent in 2003, those to China grew by 48 percent. In the first quarter of 2004, this trend did not abate, with export growth rates to China increasing by 51 percent.[12] Semiconductor exports to China grew 120 percent compared to 2002. Exports of computer products and mobile telecommunications equipment grew 85 percent. While South Korea faces dumping charges and tariffs on steel from the United States, leading to 27 percent downturns in steel exports, China gobbles South Korean steel, taking in four times more than the United States. (South Korean steel exports to China rose by 60 percent in 2003.)

According to the ROK Ministry of Finance and Economics, China also ranked as South Korea's top investment destination in 2003. While South Korean businesses invested a paltry $50 million in 2003 in Japan, it invested $2.49 billion in China, compared to $730 million in the United States and $700 million in Vietnam.[13] In the first quarter of 2004, ROK investment in China increased by 35 percent, to $725 million, totaling nearly half of all outbound investment (the comparable figure for the investment in the United States was $233 million).[14] Korean economic ties with China will become even more intertwined as Korean companies shift to overseas production. Samsung Electronics, for example, announced that China would become the main production base for its personal computers and flat-panel screens. Hyundai has announced a projected goal of manufacturing a million cars per year in China by 2007.

From Tokyo's perspective, these economic forces have an inexorable gravitational pull. As South Korea's economic livelihood is increasingly linked to Chinese growth and to continued demand for finished products, its political inclinations will be drawn to ever-closer association with China. The Korean government has posited healthy 5 percent economic growth rates, attributable largely to expectations of continued Chinese economic growth and demand for Korean products.[15] (However, economic growth in 2004 and 2005 lagged well behind these projections.) For proponents of economic liberalism, these ties increase economic interdependence between the two countries, make military rivalry or armed conflict virtually unimaginable, and create incentives for cooperation across issue-areas well beyond economics. All these trends increasingly become defined as part of the national interest of Korea. In this sense, grand strategy shifts in Korea are in part driven by the spillover of cooperation in the economic realm.

Thus, across the spectrum of analytic perspectives on international relations, there are compelling arguments for Korea to depart from the long-dominant U.S.-Japan framework. United States military transformation causes Korea to search for alternative security solutions. Power balancing, economic interdependence, and national identity all shape a path toward China and away from Japan and the United States. Arguably, this strategic shift is detrimental to Japanese interests. Critics argue that the Korean shift would not be bad for Japan if it were part of a larger regional dynamic, with China's influence growing vis-à-vis traditionally dominant Japan and America, but with the outcome premised on a more multilateral orientation in Northeast Asia rather than enhanced competition. But this argument is based on heroic and untested assumptions about Sino-Japanese cooperation, and the absence of a geographical, historical, and culturally determined temptation to politically isolate Japan.

OFFENSIVE VERSUS DEFENSIVE REALISM

Japanese concerns about the Korean shift are real, but there is an alternative path that runs counter to the prevailing view and is not often explicated. In part, this is because it operates according to different assumptions about how states interact, particularly with regard to realism. In terms of power relations, the Korean shift scenario is posited on an "offensive realist" view of South Korean fears of U.S. abandonment. Offensive realism argues that states are not status quo–oriented, but instead aggressively seek power for the purposes of survival under anarchy. As John Mearsheimer argues, offensive realists constantly strive for power because "the international system creates powerful incentives for states to look for opportunities to gain power at the expense of rivals, and to take advantage of those situations when the benefits outweigh the costs. A state's ultimate goal is to be the hegemon in the system."[16]

Seoul does not seek to be the hegemon in Northeast Asia. But the Korean shift scenario implicitly assumes that Korea seeks to maximize power in the face of perceived U.S. disengagement. In other words, it seeks to augment national power and maximize security as a response to decreases in power defined by reductions in the U.S. force presence. Moreover, it seeks to maximize its power relative to other powers in the region. Hence, it moves in the direction of the biggest player, China, or toward nuclear self-help.

However, a defensive realist perspective offers a different argument about strategic dilemmas. It also sees the world in competitive, self-help terms. But for defensive realism, survival is best attained by pursuing enough power to maintain a "balance," where no one other power or coalition of powers can threaten the system or one's national security. That is, states seek to maintain a balance of power rather than maximize power as the optimum strategy. Power-seeking states in a defensive realist world seek survival through maintenance of the status quo. They will balance against states that seek too much power and threaten the system. But they are aware that seeking too much power will elicit counterbalancing against them. Power-seeking states in an offensive realist world seek to maximize relative power and are willing to overturn the status quo if necessary. How much power do defensive realists want? Not much more than they already have. How much power do offensive realists want? They want as much as they can get.

If this assumption is applied to Korea, then reactions to U.S. abandonment fears would incline Seoul in the direction of status quo–oriented, rather than revisionist, solutions to its security problems. Notionally, the difference in the two views is whether Korea's reaction is to choose an entirely new security solution in hopes of maximizing power, or to choose a solution that builds on and reconfigures the current model.

THE KOREAN SHIFT REVISITED

Defensive realism does not deny that Japan would be anxious about the Korean shift to China and potential peer competition. This is because realists of all colors are always concerned about relative power. The primary and critical difference is that offensive realism sees South Korea aiming to augment power relative to others by shifting to China's orbit. Defensive realism focuses more on the downside risks. Defensive realists understand that overtly revisionist actions are likely to elicit counterbalancing tendencies, so they would seek to manage power relations and the alliance to minimize peer competition and maintain a stable balance of power. This would imply growing South

Korea's own security capabilities, but still within the framework of the U.S.-Korea-Japan alliance, thereby minimizing insecurity spirals among the three countries.

Power and Balancing

A defensive realist would also be concerned about the risks of drawing too close to China. South Koreans clearly welcomed normalization with Beijing in 1992. By this, along with Soviet normalization in 1990, Seoul succeeded in effectively isolating Pyongyang from its two primary Cold War patrons. In this sense, the existence of the North Korean state has acted as a quasi-buffer for unbridled ROK enthusiasm for relations with Beijing. But realists (particularly defensive realists) appreciate future uncertainty and know that North Korea will not be around forever. In a unification scenario, this buffer disappears, and a united Korea faces the prospect of an eight-hundred-mile contiguous border with a militarily and economically burgeoning China whose intentions are not transparent. Moreover, it faces this situation having shed or greatly curtailed its security relationship with the United States. The possibility therefore arises that the new Korean state might view China with concern and might heavily fortify its northern border.

Comparable threat perceptions are not unthinkable on the Chinese side. Of all the powers in the region, Beijing has the most direct stake in the status quo on the peninsula. Prospective Chinese reactions to a future united Korea were most evident in the early 1990s, when there was much speculation that the DPRK regime could not last. A lengthy 1992 report on future peninsular strategies prepared for the Chinese Communist Party Central Committee asserted that despite Seoul-Beijing normalization, North Korea was still "China's Northeast Asian strategic bulwark." It stated that the North's absorption by the South would have a "devastating psychological impact" on China, and therefore Beijing's priorities center on preventing Korea from becoming "the route for the overthrow of socialism by peaceful means from the West."[17]

As two Chinese analysts have noted, loss of the North would leave China "deprived of an indispensable security buffer proximate to both the nation's capital and to one of its most important industrial regions."[18] A united Korea would present Beijing with the unwanted prospect of another noncompliant power (like Vietnam) on its southern flank with a competing ideological and social system. Moreover, China would not pass lightly on the security implications of such a situation. In the early 1990s, it first expressed concerns about the buildup of South Korean (and Japanese) naval forces, and such concerns are likely to be heightened in the case of a united Korea.[19] As one U.S. specialist has noted, the Chinese perception of a united Korea is far from unadulterated optimism.[20] In the words of a *People's Liberation Army Daily* editorial, "The Korean

Peninsula is at the heart of northeast Asia and its strategic importance is obvious, [so] to control the peninsula is to tightly grasp hold of northeast Asia."[21]

States with contiguous borders, whether intentionally or not, often lapse into competition driven by security fears.[22] In this regard, Japan is fully aware that the most proximate threat to Korea may emanate from China, not Japan. Korea does not have the autonomous capabilities to balance against China; furthermore, while Korea will certainly harbor its share of animosities toward Japan, the relationship (presumably between Tokyo and a united government in Seoul) would still be grounded in decades of normal Japanese–South Korean relations.[23] It would also be grounded in a familiarity bred through common security ties with the United States for the entire post-war and Cold War eras.[24] By contrast, the cumulative experiences underlying the Seoul-Beijing relationship would not extend further back than 1992. Compelled to balance against the more proximate and unfamiliar threat, Korea could look to Japan with greater assurance than is often surmised.

Democracy and Development

From a liberal perspective, the Korean shift scenario focuses on economic interaction with China as the primary causal variable. This cooperation with China stands in the shadow of competition and potential domination. More important, a critical variable for liberalism—political institutions and regime type—operates against the tight arrangement that the Korean shift scenario would predict.

Although the composition of China-ROK trade is complementary today, China's growth is already changing its trade needs and raising competition with Korea. Korea will be faced with a flood of price-competitive Chinese-manufactured goods from industries that increasingly challenge its own firms. Thus, the challenge posed by China is that its sunrise industries increasingly clash with the sunset industries of the more advanced economies in the region. This dynamic will be exacerbated by China's commercial base in Hong Kong and by ties with Taiwan. In addition, liberalization pressures on the ROK market as a result of OECD membership; declining ROK trade surpluses; won appreciation; and rising labor costs could further disadvantage the Korean economy vis-à-vis cheap Chinese imports. The average monthly industrial wage in China is $111, while in Korea it is $1,524.[25] South Korea experienced a period of trade euphoria with China when the Chinese filled most of the demand for South Korea's oil refining, chemical fiber, steel, and container industries. In 2003, for example, container traffic at China's major ports increased 40 percent, which led to a doubling of new ship orders placed with South Korean shipbuilders. But the South Korean economy is vulnerable to losing the leg it increasingly stands on if Chinese demand recedes. The vigor with which ROK finance officials declare that Korea in the long term should reduce exposure and dependence on China is matched by the rush of South Korean companies to fill Chinese orders for the next quarter. The Chinese economy will eventually develop indigenous capacities in many areas they currently fill with external purchases. And when this happens, ROK industries could face acute overcapacity problems.[26]

Finally, tremendous pressure will mount on the Korean economy to avoid getting squeezed out of low- and medium-technology markets taken over by China, while losing pace with higher-technology sectors dominated by Japan. Scott Snyder cites a survey of major South Korean conglomerates in which 43 percent believe that in major industrial fields, South Korea's technological lead over China has been reduced to four to five years; 27 percent believe the lead is one to three years; and 10 percent believe that the lead has entirely diminished.[27] According to Snyder, the South Korean Ministry of Commerce, Industry, and Energy is projecting that Korea's technological leads in key sectors like automobiles, semiconductors, and shipbuilding will significantly diminish by 2010, and that China is already competitive with Korea in household appliances, electronics, and steel.

The vicious circle of Korean economic dependence on China is clear. If China tanks, it takes Korea with it. But if China continues to grow, it will squeeze Korean industry and technology out of international markets, create manufacturing overcapacity on the peninsula, and flood Korean markets with cheap Chinese goods. These considerations give a whole new meaning to the vision of Sino-Korean economic nirvana with Seoul as the economic hub for Northeast Asia. As Snyder observes, "Making South Korea into a regional hub is a way of recognizing that Korea has no choice but to stay ahead of China in the transition from a manufacturing to a service and knowledge-based economy. With China's modernization well under way, Korean economic planners can feel the breath of a stiff competitor at their back; they have no choice but to run harder and faster."[28] Dreams can easily turn into nightmares.

Perhaps the most underestimated and understudied aspect of Korea's future strategic direction concerns political institutions and regime-type variables. The Korean shift scenario assumes that regime type is inconsequential in the political affinity between two nations. But this factor is extremely consequential. When two countries share similar political institutions and political values, there is a familiarity that cannot be replicated in relations between dissimilar regimes. States with comparable electoral institutions, legal structures, concepts of open society, civil liberties, and opportunity tend to externalize their ways of thinking and negotiating with each other. While these attributes are not shared between China and Korea, they are shared to a great extent between Korea and Japan. The two countries represent the success of liberal-democratic values and open market economics in a region of the world that has not yet readily accepted these as universal. In addition, Seoul and Tokyo share a host of broader concerns, including nonproliferation, universal human rights, constitutionalism, antiterrorism, and peacekeeping. Together, they represent the second largest financial contributor (Japan) and third largest military contributor (Korea) to the Iraq reconstruction effort. The two allies also help form the backbone of many global and regional regimes that deal with these problems. Because of democracy and development, Japan and Korea have evolved beyond a relationship that merely stands against a threat, to one that *stands for* something. The relationship's scope is increasingly becoming extra-regional and open-ended rather than parochial and tactical. Political institutions and regime type powerfully affect how countries choose their closest partners. Coupled with the economic dangers inherent in an overreliance on China, there may be less to fret about from the Japanese perspective. This is not to say that Korea will cut off from China. It will continue to seek greater economic interaction with China (as will all of Asia), but will still see its larger strategic interests in a manner similar to the United States and Japan.

The Wildcard of Identity

From a constructivist perspective, the operative question is whether historical animosities toward Japan trump defensive realist and democratic liberalism arguments against the Korean shift. I believe the answer is no. Historical animosity, though extremely important in understanding Japan-Korea relations, does not ultimately explain outcomes. Instead, material factors like power, threats, and political institutions largely determine outcomes.[29]

However, the pathologies inherent in Korea's search for a new nationalism could readily lead in the direction of anti-Japanism. The popularized view of historical affinity toward China does not, by definition, mean that historical animosity toward Japan is a given. The two are not related in zero-sum fashion. As with all history and collective memory, these affinities and animosities are constructions or public narratives that are constantly evolving. Witness the manner in which the construction of China in Korean eyes changed virtually overnight from Cold War adversary to long-estranged friend with normalization in 1992. Moreover, recent disputes over Koguryo are another reminder of the malleability of historical memory.

In sum, a defensive realist perspective offers a more optimistic scenario as Japan ponders future peninsular directions. If Korea seeks status quo–oriented rather than revisionist security solutions as it contends with its abandonment fears, this could move it closer to the U.S.-Japan framework rather than to China. If the democratic consolidation and development that defined South Korea's postwar existence have deeper roots than most people assume, then Japan's position vis-à-vis Korea is brighter than if economic interests alone dictated Korea's direction. Finally, the wild card in the equation relates to Korean national identity, which could evolve in directions contrary to Japanese interests, but without any guarantees that this identity automatically inclines toward China.

JAPAN AND NORTH KOREA: ENGAGEMENT DILEMMAS

Japan's basic dilemma in its relations with North Korea is that actions taken in support of allied engagement with the North may counterintuitively serve to undercut Japan's own interests and policy. There are three dimensions to the problem. The deepest problem for Japanese engagement is the inability to distinguish between DPRK tactics and intentions. Skeptics and optimists agree that Pyongyang's diplomatic offensives reflect a change in tactics largely for the purpose of regime survival. The as-yet-unanswered question is whether a fundamental change in the nature of the regime's intentions has also taken place. All three allies have been willing to accept some opacity on Pyongyang's underlying preferences and to pursue engagement as a means to shape the North's intentions. However, relative to the other allies, Japan has fewer "baskets" of transparency-building issues to elicit a better sense of DPRK intentions. For example, Seoul has a weighty set of issues, including family reunions, infrastructure rejuvenation projects, ministerial meetings, and leadership summits, on which to gauge DPRK intentions. Though to a lesser extent than Seoul, Washington also has a larger basket, including MIA remains, where DPRK concessions offer a window on whether intentions rather than tactics are changing. However, for Japan, the comparable basket is substantially lighter. The abductee issue was a potential vehicle by which to communicate political goodwill, but even with DPRK concessions, two problems arise: (1) the public's outspoken anger drowns out any concessions by Pyongyang; and (2) the issue provides little value in terms of understanding North Korea's nuclear weapons intentions. Similarly, the abduction issue has been a major impediment to normalization talks, but actions by Pyongyang to resolve this issue do not convey a sense of costs to Pyongyang, or build confidence of change in the North's aggressive intentions vis-à-vis Japan.

One possible response by Japan would be for Tokyo to expand the range of issues on which it could engage the DPRK. However, historical animosities place inherent limits on the available issues. In all likelihood, the DPRK is undergoing significant internal adjustment, as the domestic images of Seoul experienced rapid reevaluation after the June 2000 summit. To effect a similar transformation with Japan is difficult, particularly if DPRK identity and national purpose needs to be constructed negatively (i.e., against an adversary). If one of the primary causes for historical reconciliation between Japan and South Korea was the ROK's development and democratization, then this offers a positive example of what is missing from the prospective reconciliation formula between Japan and the North. This assessment does not deny that normalization may still occur between Tokyo and Pyongyang, but it does mean that historical reconciliation will not. Hence a normalization settlement would result in a situation similar to Japan-ROK relations in 1965, when security and economic incentives dictated normalization but perceptions and attitudes remained highly antagonistic. From the Japanese perspective, this begs two questions: why press for normalization if Japan still remains demonized in DPRK rhetoric; and why press for normalization if residual historical enmity ensures that a settlement will provide little insight into DPRK intentions?

Japan's engagement dilemmas are equally apparent with regard to the North's chemical and biological weapons (CBW) threat. Next to the ballistic missile and nuclear weapons threats posed by the North, the CBW threat (estimated to be the third-largest stockpile, behind that of the United States and Russia) is an intense, but less publicly expressed, concern in Japan. However, neither U.S.-DPRK bilateral discussions nor the ROK-DPRK dialogue includes this issue. The reasoning is twofold: (1) addressing the missile threat can by default address the CBW threat (i.e., by negating the primary means of delivery); and (2) because U.S. war-planning on the peninsula includes potential CBW use by the North, such threats are viewed in the context of conventional force negotiations, should these ever occur. While both rationales make sense, neither is comforting from a Japanese perspective. The former in particular does not address the likelihood of unconventional means of delivering CBW, a fact not lost on the Japanese, in view of the Aum Shinrikyo sarin gas attack.

Some might ask: who cares if Japan is left behind? If, by some means, a deal with the DPRK encompassing the nuclear programs and long-range missiles is achieved without progress on shorter-range missiles and chemical and biological weapons, then this is not bad. The problem is that it is impossible to get the latter without the former. The biggest carrot for successful U.S.-ROK engagement with the North is Japanese financial support, in the form of either a normalization settlement or Tokyo's consent to billions of dollars in IMF–World Bank loans for Pyongyang.

Given this structural dilemma, Japanese Prime Minister Koizumi's second summit meeting with North Korean leader Kim Jong Il in May 2004 was reasonably useful. These results could be measured along three dimensions: (1) inching closer to restarting a Japan-DPRK normalization dialogue; (2) validation of Japan's firmer stance toward Pyongyang; and (3) enhancing the strength of Washington-Tokyo consultations on the nuclear issue. The summit produced the return of two children of Kaoru and Yukiko Hasuike and the three children of Yasushi and Fukie Chimura, ending the nineteen-month separation after the repatriation to Japan of the abductees. Kim Jong Il also reportedly agreed to reopen investigations into ten other disputed cases (eight were initially reported dead, and two of these were denied by Pyongyang earlier). The North Korean leader also agreed to maintain a moratorium on missile test launches.

In return, Japan committed to providing two hundred fifty thousand tons of food aid to the UN World Food Program appeal for North Korea (the first such disbursement since 2001), as well as ten million dollars' worth of medical supplies. Koizumi urged Kim to accept international inspections of all its nuclear weapons programs and Pyongyang's return to the NPT regime. He renewed Japan's (perennial) request for the extradition of leftist radicals who defected after hijacking a Japan Airlines (JAL) plane in 1970 and may have been involved in other abduction cases involving Japanese nationals. Japan also provided assurances of Tokyo's continued adherence to the 2002 Pyongyang declaration, which in operational diplomatic terms means that Japan has no intention to impose sanctions on the DPRK.

Koizumi's return from Pyongyang was received by many in Washington, Seoul, and Tokyo in highly critical terms. Critics blasted Koizumi's inability to secure the release of all of the relatives of the Japanese abductees while giving millions in medicine, humanitarian aid, and food. Moreover, the lack of any more definitive commitment by Kim to dismantling the North's nuclear weapons programs disappointed many observers. The token restatement of mutual adherence to the principles of the 2002 Pyongyang declaration, critics argued, only highlighted the absence of any substantive progress on the issue. A *Yomiuri Shimbun* editorial, for example, decried the summit as making "no headway in resolving the abduction, nuclear, missile or any other issues related to Northeast Asia's peace and security." *Mainichi Shimbun* blasted Koizumi for playing Japan's "trump card" (i.e., a second visit) and getting nothing in return.[30] Katsuya Okada, head of the Democratic Party of Japan (DPJ), criticized as "a major diplomatic blunder" Koizumi's pledge to Kim that Japan would not implement economic sanctions.[31]

But the results of Koizumi's trip were not half-bad. It earned Koizumi a moderate (but not major) boost in domestic popularity. His inability to secure the release of all the abductees' relatives was not for lack of trying. Preparatory meetings in April took place involving unofficial talks in Beijing with Taku Yamasaki, former vice president of the Liberal Democratic Party, and Lower House member Katsuei Hirasawa. In May these were followed by bilateral talks involving Mitoji Yabunaka (director-general of Asian and Oceanian affairs) and Deputy Foreign Minister Hitoshi Tanaka in Beijing. Both sets of talks did much of the heavy lifting for the summit's results. Shortly after Tanaka and Yabunaka's return from Beijing, success in convincing LDP Secretary-General Shinzo Abe (a hawk on North Korea) to accept the provision of food aid was another critical step in fostering the summit's outcome. Although criticisms came from certain circles for not getting more on the abductee issue, there is no denying that the summit made progress on this huge impediment in Japan-DPRK relations.

Second, moderate pressure on the Pyongyang regime works. Since Kim Jong Il's ill-fated confession in September 2002 to his country's abductions of Japanese nationals, Tokyo has been pressing for the release of these individuals and their relatives. Japan's suspension of rice aid to North Korea (effective since 2001, when Japan provided $104 million through the World Food Program) remained firm largely because of this unresolved issue. Critics should not be asking why Koizumi reinstated food aid (which has been held in abeyance as a result of the abductee issue); instead, they should be asking why North Korea agreed this time to return the relatives when they had previously spurned Tokyo's entreaties.

The answer lies not in weakness, but in the firmer stance adopted by both the United States and Japan in curtailing North Korean illicit activities. In January 2004, the Diet passed foreign exchange legislation that would allow Japan—without a UN resolution—to cut off financial remittances to the North or to impose an import ban on North Korean goods. Shortly thereafter, a second piece of legislation banning North Korean port calls was debated, accompanied by a three-month export ban on domestic trading companies potentially selling dual-use uranium enrichment materials to the North. Furthermore, Tokyo continues to play a central role in the U.S.-led Proliferation Security Initiative (PSI), which aims to curtail illicit transfer of WMD–related materials. In short, the food provided by Koizumi was always there for the taking if Kim Jong Il wanted it. What elicited the North's flexibility was not just U.S. and Japanese carrots, but their sticks.

From Washington's perspective, it was not entirely bad that the summit's results were not wildly applauded by the Japanese public. The ambivalence over Koizumi's second trip pales in comparison to his first trip, which boosted his approval ratings by some 30 points to nearly 70 percent, according to some media polls in Japan. The lukewarm public reaction thus solves the "moral hazard" problem of DPRK diplomacy and the abductee issue—that is, it ensures that Koizumi will not be tempted by short-term domestic-popularity gains to move too far afield from the American position. It would have been much more worrying for Americans if Koizumi's summit had produced the same results to resounding applause in Japan, because this would have created greater incentive for Japan to be more flexible without receiving much in return.

ENGAGEMENT FROM STRENGTH, NOT WEAKNESS

The net effect of Koizumi's second trip to Pyongyang, therefore, was far less problematic than many observers reported. Pyongyang's efforts to drive a wedge in U.S.-Japan relations had proven unsuccessful. The summit proved that the American and Japanese engagement strategy based on both carrots and sticks was effective in eliciting DPRK flexibility. The summit therefore validated engagement based on strength, not on weakness. The fact that the Diet passed key legislation allowing Japan to ban port calls by the DPRK ferry *Mangyongbong* to Niigata the week after the Pyongyang trip underscores this conclusion. Muscular engagement made the messages brought by Koizumi to President Bush at the G-8 Summit at Sea Island more credible. According to press reports, Koizumi told the President that he had posed stark choices for Kim Jong Il. The Prime Minister reportedly told Kim that DPRK gains from nuclear weapons pale in comparison to the prospective gains from dismantling all such programs. A Japanese premier who poses these choices as his parliament prepares legislation for potential sanctions is infinitely more credible than one who rationalizes engagement with North Korea because his country cannot afford another crisis with the regime.

Prime Minister Koizumi relayed to President Bush that he believed North Korea was truly ready for talks, rather than bluster only. The fact that this advice registered with the President not only attests to Bush's trust in Koizumi's judgment, but also was the key factor that prompted the U.S. proposal to Pyongyang at the June 2004 Six-Party Talks in Beijing. Indeed, the similarity in Japan's talking points to the U.S. position was self-evident: (1) North Korea must freeze all nuclear programs, including uranium enrichment programs; (2) North Korea must disclose information on all its nuclear programs; (3) this freeze must entail effective verification; and (4) Japan is ready to contribute to international energy assistance for North Korea only if these conditions are satisfied and if this freeze is a part of an agreement to dismantle North Korea's nuclear programs.

North Korea's protracted boycott of the six-party process following the June round may have been vexing to some, but it highlighted Pyongyang's inability to detach Tokyo from its closely coordinated diplomatic stance with Washington. By hewing to a policy that would not reward the North as an inducement to return to the nuclear negotiations, Japan contributed directly to Pyongyang's decision to return to the talks thirteen months later, and to assent to the denuclearization statement of September 2005, as well as the renewed commitment by both countries to pursue normalization. However, as the bilateral meeting between the representatives of Japan and the DPRK in Beijing made clear, Tokyo would not compensate Pyongyang without credible evidence that the North had undertaken the strategic decision that would make normalization possible.

Given the stakes for all parties, negotiations with Pyongyang are likely to prove contentious and protracted, even assuming that all involved in the six-party process are prepared to move toward agreement. But progress can be achieved only if Japan and its diplomatic and security partners maintain common cause, and only when the DPRK fully and finally grasps what it must do if it expects to become a credible participant in Northeast Asian politics and economics. Short of this latter step, Japan has no alternative but to persist in its present prudent course, even if it necessarily defers the normal relations that it seeks with North Korea.

NOTES

I prepared the original version of this paper prior to joining the National Security Council at the White House as a Director for Asian Affairs, on public service leave from Georgetown University. All opinions and judgments in the paper are my own and should not be attributed to the U.S. government or to any governmental agencies.

1. This exercise requires that many other variables or forces for change be held constant. Although suboptimal, it is the best way to understand the future relations in systematic rather than haphazard fashion.

2. Derek Mitchell, ed., *Strategy and Sentiment: Korean Views of the United States and the U.S.-ROK Alliance* (Washington, D.C.: CSIS, June 2004); Eric Larson and Norman Levin, *Ambivalent Allies? A Study of South Korean Attitudes Toward the U.S.*, RAND TR-141-SRF (Santa Monica: RAND, March 2004); Victor Cha, "America and South Korea: The Ambivalent Alliance," *Current History*, no. 279 (September 2003).

3. "American Forces in South Korea—The End of an Era?" IISS *Strategic Comments* 9, no. 5 (July 2003); "U.S. Troop Withdrawals from South Korea—Beginnings of the End of the Alliance?" IISS *Strategic Comments* 10, no. 4 (June 2004).

4. Even if the United States provides reassurances and conveys the "capabilities, not numbers" argument credibly, certain attribution error dynamics ensure that some form of abandonment fears remain likely. See Jonathan Mercer, *Reputation in International Politics* (Ithaca, N.Y.: Cornell University Press, 1996), pp. 59–69; and Victor Cha, "Mistaken Attribution: The United States and Inter-Korean Relations," *Asia-Pacific Review* 9, no. 2 (2002), pp. 45–60.

5. Realism generally posits that international relations operate under a condition of anarchy, where nation-states are the primary actors and such states are egoistic and self-help-oriented. Security is the primary consideration in an anarchic world, and strategic choice is dominated by concerns about attaining and retaining relative power over others. Realism therefore generally posits a very competitive view of international relations where states constantly jockey for power and position. The world is zero-sum, in the sense that gains by one can only be made at the expense of another.

6. On the last of these, see David C. Kang, "Getting Asia Wrong: The Need for New Analytic Frameworks," *International Security* 27, no. 4 (Summer 2003), pp. 57–85.

7. Constructivism holds that self-help is not automatic under anarchy but the product of social construction and interaction. State behavior reflects societal norms, the ideational context, and identity, not solely power. Constructivists believe that states can go beyond cooperation based on shared interest to establish a cohesive community based on shared identities.

8. This view argues that deep-seated enmity and psychological barriers stemming from the turbulent histories shared by the two peoples is the primary cause of friction. Although disputes date back to the late-sixteenth-century Hideyoshi invasions, the defining event in a modern context was Korea's colonial subjugation to Japan from 1910 to 1945. Occupation policies sought to assimilate the Koreans through the banning of their language,

adoption of Japanese surnames, and coerced worshiping of the Shinto state religion. The colonial police (many of whom were Korean) intruded extensively into every aspect of society and suppressed attempts at resistance, often brutally. Many colonial subjects were drafted into the military for the Japanese war effort. Even more were forced into labor conscription programs that abruptly mass-migrated nearly 20 percent of the rural population to low-skill mining and factory occupations in northern Korea, Manchuria, Sakhalin, and Japan under subhuman working conditions. All were the object of social discrimination and relegation to the lowest strata of society. In spite of these heavy-handed policies, the occupation period also brought some benefits to Korea. Colonial policies aided the development of educational systems, an efficient government bureaucracy, and modernized agriculture and infrastructure. Distilled from this history is a peculiar "admiration-enmity" complex. On the side of admiration is the view in Korea of Japanese organization, efficiency, and economic prowess as models to be emulated and aspired to. Similarly, Japanese liken Korea's modern development to that of a younger sibling—one to be nurtured and through which Japan vicariously relives its own earlier successes. In spite of this mutual admiration, it is the enmity stemming from the colonial period that dominates. See Victor Cha, *Alignment Despite Antagonism* (Stanford, Calif.: Stanford University Press, 1999), chap. 2.

9. Hahm Chaibong, "The Two South Koreas: A House Divided," *Washington Quarterly* 28, no. 3 (Summer 2005), pp. 57–72.

10. This latter dynamic has been evident in South Korea today over the ch'in il p'a (friends of Japan) controversy. The attempts to claim a new Korean nationalist identity by delegitimizing past and current politicians associated with Japan is an example of a construction of national identity that still lacks positive definitions, as well as the entanglement of this construction with domestic politics.

11. Korea International Trade Association, *Bridging the Pacific*, no. 34 (January 2004).

12. Andrew Ward, "Seoul's Links with U.S. Under Threat," *Financial Times*, 30 April 2004.

13. *Korea Insight* (Korea Economic Institute) 6, no. 2 (February 2004).

14. Ward, "Seoul's Links with U.S. Under Threat."

15. For example, when Chinese oil imports increased by 30 percent and container traffic at Chinese ports increased by 40 percent in 2003, this contributed to a doubling of orders for ships for South Korean shipbuilders. James Brooke, "Koreans Look to China, Seeing a Market and a Monster," *New York Times*, 10 February 2004.

16. John Mearsheimer, *The Tragedy of Great Power Politics* (New York: Norton, 2001), p. 21.

17. See Korean coverage of the report in *Mal* ([Free] Speech), October 1994, in *FBIS-EAS*, 94-245, 21 December 1994, pp. 38–46.

18. Jia Hao and Zhuang Qubing, "China's Policy Toward the Korean Peninsula," *Asian Survey* 32, no. 2 (December 1992), p. 1137.

19. "Chinese Military Wary of Naval Buildup of Japan, Korea," *Korea Herald*, 10 November 1992.

20. "From a longer-term perspective, China is apprehensive about potential threats to its interests from a reunified Korea. In the economic sphere, Beijing is wary of competition from a united Korean economic powerhouse. Politically, the Chinese are uncertain about the role that a united Korea might play in the region and worried that Japan could eventually dominate the peninsula and undermine China's growing influence in Korea. Militarily, the prospect of a reunified Korea with at least a potential if not an actual nuclear capability is also cause for Chinese concern. In addition, some Chinese foresee the possibility that a reunified Korea would seek to reclaim Chinese territory bordering Korea that both North and South view as the birthplace of the Korean nation." Bonnie Glaser, "China's Security Perceptions: Interests and Ambitions," *Asian Survey* 33, no. 3 (March 1993), pp. 261–62.

21. *People's Liberation Army Daily*, Editorial, 10 July 2000.

22. John Mearsheimer, "The Case for a Ukrainian Nuclear Deterrent," *Foreign Affairs* 72, no. 3 (Summer 1993), p. 54.

23. For arguments regarding Japan–South Korea cooperation implicitly as a hedge against China, see Hideshi Takesada, "Korea-Japan Defense Cooperation: Prospects and Issues"; Hiroyasu Akutsu, "Strengthening the U.S.-Centered Hub-and-Spokes System in Northeast Asia"; and Hisahiko Okazaki, "Japan-South Korea Security Cooperation: A View towards the Future"; all in *Korea-Japan Security Relations: Prescriptive Studies*, ed. Sang-Woo Rhee and Tae-Hyo Kim (Seoul: New Asia Research Institute, 2000), resp. pp. 131–33, 146–51, 123–40. Also Narushige Michishita,

"Alliances after Peace in Korea," *Survival* 41, no. 3 (Autumn 1999), pp. 68–83.

24. While these relations do not constitute "institutions" in the formal sense of a European NATO or the EU, they do breed a familiarity between Japanese and Korean leaders. For a related point on how such institutions engendered a familiarity among European leaders that mollified anxieties about German reunification, see Aaron Friedberg, "Ripe for Rivalry: Prospects for Peace in a Multipolar Asia," *International Security* 18, no. 3 (Winter 1993/1994), p. 13. On the need for building on this baseline of familiarity, see Kang Choi, "Korea-Japan Security Cooperation in the Post-Unification Era," in *Korea-Japan Security Relations*, ed. Rhee and Kim, p. 293.

25. Brooke, "Koreans Look to China, Seeing a Market and a Monster."

26. For example, the China State Shipbuilding Corporation broke ground in 2003 on a shipyard project that will surpass Korean Hyundai Heavy Industries' position as the top global shipbuilder.

27. Scott Snyder, "Beijing in the Driver's Seat? China's Rising Influence on the Two Koreas," *Pacific Forum CSIS Comparative Connections* (4th Quarter 2002), www.csis.org/pacfor/cc/0204Qchina_skorea.htm.

28. Scott Snyder, "Clash, Crash, and Cash," *Pacific Forum CSIS Comparative Connections* (2nd quarter 2002) www.csis.org/pacfor/cc/0202Qchina_skorea.htm.

29. Cha, *Alignment Despite Antagonism*.

30. Quoted in James Brooke, "Koizumi's Trip Gets Lukewarm Reviews," *New York Times,* 24 May 2004.

31. "LDP'S Abe Cool on Summit, DPJ's Okada Slams Results," *Japan Times,* 23 May 2004.

14

Sino-Japanese Competition over the Korean Peninsula
The Nuclear Crisis as a Turning Point

Gilbert Rozman

Chinese and Japanese writings on Korea are both becoming more forward-looking, but they do not reflect a frank assessment of internal debates. Prime Minister Junichiro Koizumi's 22 May 2004 visit to Pyongyang (his second visit to the North in less than two years) rekindled an essential discussion in Japan on that nation's strategy in bilateral relations and in the Six-Party Talks in Beijing,[1] despite the reluctance of many to question Bush administration policy openly when the alliance is deemed essential. After nearly two years of obsession with abducted citizens and family members left behind, the wider context had finally drawn some attention. Signs of belated and still highly constrained flexibility from North Korea and the United States in advance of the Six-Party Talks in late June 2004 and on the heels of Kim Jong Il's visit to Beijing in mid-April intensified Chinese analysis of how the nuclear crisis could be brought to a conclusion.[2] Although this optimism proved premature, it had opened a window of debate on the strategic implications of the crisis, even if continued censorship limited direct criticism of North Korea. In place of sterile explanations of who wants a nuclear North Korea or who favors reunification, the focus in both China and Japan began to shift to how a gradual process of confederation in which the North remains an active force could benefit each country's interests.

As Sino-Japanese relations have become increasingly competitive and even rancorous, both sides agree that the stakes in triangular relations with the Korean Peninsula are rising. Even if the one-year hiatus after the third round of the Six-Party Talks slowed the debate in each country, there was already a start to forward-looking discussion well before the fourth round's Joint Statement of 19 September 2005.

East Asians are conscious of their region's past as the history of three kingdoms: China, fountainhead of tradition and dominant influence; Korea, transmitter of tradition and testing grounds for ambitions at critical times; and Japan, leader in modernization but marred by a record of militarization. Under the spell of a long-popular Chinese novel, *History of the Three Kingdoms*, readers throughout the region regard triangular relations as a strategic challenge demanding diplomatic cunning, alliance building, military preparedness, and long-range tactics. Since the end of the Cold War, China and Japan have resumed their regional competition, with the added twist that the United States and Russia, which had carved Korea in two, also remain intent on playing a role in shaping its destiny. The region is returning to triangularity at its core, but one entity is still split and two additional states loom in the background. China and Japan must deal with a defiant North Korea, shape relations with an emboldened South Korea, and draw on the distant but overwhelming power of the United States as well as a Russia insistent on a continued role. This is a formidable environment for strategic thinking, complicated by the fact that the two countries are being drawn closer in economic integration amid widespread talk of the positive prospects for regionalism, putting Korea at the "hub" of Northeast Asia.[3]

The Chinese and the Japanese draw different lessons from the history of Korea. When Korea is divided or under Japanese control, Chinese calculate that their country cannot avoid trouble or even being drawn into wars. In the seventh century, sixteenth century, and nineteenth century, and again in the 1950s, China fought over Korea in such situations. In contrast, Japanese believe that a Korea under Chinese influence means an Asian continent dominated by China, leaving their country isolated. For each aspiring power, no other neighbor has so much historical meaning or so much near-term potential to undercut its prospects. As Korea moves toward unification, its centrality between the two will keep growing. If Tokyo defensively prefers to slow unification, Beijing increasingly supports a gradual process that props up the North while using unification as a lever for regional security.

For a quarter-century, through the 1980s, Japan tried to find leverage on the Korean Peninsula; but it was constrained by the dominant role of the United States in South Korea and the difficulty of achieving a breakthrough with North Korea in the Cold War atmosphere.[4] The situation for China on the peninsula was similar: it could not outflank the Soviet Union as the North's main security guarantor, and it was unwilling to accept the regional consequences of pursuing normalization with South Korea.[5] Thus, when Tokyo and Beijing started to improve bilateral ties in 1972, neither had reason to be concerned about the other's influence on Korea or the potential for using the peninsula to transform the Northeast Asian region. This situation changed after China's normalization with South Korea in 1992; and it changed again, more abruptly, in 2000 with the Sunshine Policy of Kim Dae Jung and in 2002 with the renewed nuclear weapons gambit of Kim Jong Il. As the leaders of Korea grew more assertive, administrations in China and Japan, still watchful of the policies of the United States, searched for a new strategic approach to the entire Korean Peninsula.[6]

At the beginning of the 1990s, China had gained the edge in reintegrating the Korean Peninsula, and that advantage widened as it joined the United States as one of four parties resolving the nuclear crisis of 1993–94, endorsed the Sunshine Policy in 1999–2000, and became the mediator in the three-party and six-party talks of 2003–2005. Japan scrambled to keep pace, relying on its virtual three-way alliance with the United States and South Korea as well as pursuing prenormalization talks with North Korea. In September 2002, Koizumi boldly visited Pyongyang, but within weeks the nuclear crisis had burst into the spotlight and the abduction issue had spiraled out of control. In spring 2004, as the nuclear showdown momentarily seemed to approach more meaningful negotiations, Koizumi's second visit began to position Japan to contend against China. Competition over the Korean Peninsula took place against the backdrop of a broader rivalry for leadership in the emerging Northeast Asian region. In 2004 and 2005, open contention between China and Japan intensified, and uncertainty over North Korea loomed as the battleground. While observers were mostly preoccupied with immediate flare-ups irritating bilateral relations, the biggest stakes for security had reverted to the critically situated Korean Peninsula.

The first objective of Beijing and Tokyo was not to lose the rough equilibrium in Korea as a result of changes that followed the Cold War. In the early 1990s, North Korea was shaken by a loss of support from Moscow, China was isolated by sanctions in response to the June 4 oppression at Tiananmen, and Japan was confidently preparing to "reenter Asia." It seemed that Japan would gain an advantage on the peninsula, as it was trying to reach a deal with the regime in Pyongyang while aiming to use its immense economic clout in support of regionalism. The Kakuei Tanaka line toward China and North Korea, subsequently revived by Masayoshi Ohira, gained new life with Shin Kanemaru, although he was not prime minister and did not wield enough power to manage the resultant backlash. Yet, in each case, Liberal Democratic Party (LDP) leaders—to the satisfaction of Japan's political left—alienated Seoul as they looked for balance on the peninsula.

Doubting that Tokyo could be trusted as regional leader, Seoul, in turn, was eagerly courting the Beijing leadership. Alert to an opportunity and fearful that it would lose clout to Tokyo, Beijing switched course, recognizing the South and shifting part of its trade with the North to market principles. Economic ties with South Korea progressed with remarkable speed, and soon bilateral relations warmed to the point that the Japanese, unable to make headway in talks with the North, were growing nervous that they were losing their advantage. Yet, considering itself betrayed, North Korea provided little leverage for China against the other powers. Thus, through 1998, competition mainly took the form of striving to win the goodwill of the South Koreans, and China proved more adept than Japan. In October 1998, however, the Japanese gained reassurance when Kim Dae Jung promised to set history aside—unlike his predecessor Kim Young Sam, who had joined Jiang Zemin in warning Japan over its failure to reflect on historical lessons. Apart from the nuclear crisis in 1993–94, which gave rise to the four-party talks that included China but not Japan, the Koreas did not become the focus of much diplomatic maneuvering. Each side had avoided any serious loss of influence. The decade of the 1990s was but a prelude; Korea took center stage in 2000.[7]

Kim Dae Jung's Sunshine Policy set in motion a more intense quest for clout, with ambitious objectives linked to a new security framework and regionalism. Although most observers focused on the effort to entice the North from its shell, the stakes were much larger. While Kim Dae Jung took the initiative, China's leaders exerted a large role in the background. In contrast, Japan was having little success in talks with the North and had become the most marginalized of the four outside powers.[8] China had obviously gained a greater edge over Japan. However, all recognized that no effort to address security concerns or engage the North could exclude a large financial role for Japan. The U.S. role will, of course, help to determine the outcome. If, in his swan song, Bill Clinton had brokered a deal with Kim Jong Il, Japan might have ridden on his coattails to make its own arrangements with the North. Now many nervously feared that, as in the 1994 agreement, Japan would be left with a large bill without having a voice in the outcome.[9] If some Japanese held out major hopes for a free-trade agreement with South Korea, others realized that Tokyo was the more eager party, while Seoul anticipated that China would be included before long. But Sino–South Korean economic ties are rising so fast that Japan continues to lose its earlier advantage.

The contrasting strategy of George Bush to strengthen the U.S.-Japan alliance appeared to shift the balance in Northeast Asia back to Tokyo. In theory, this could leave China more contained, North Korea more isolated, and Japan with a green light to build on U.S. support to improve ties with South Korea while also limiting China's chance of reunification with Taiwan and strategic partnership with Russia. The Japanese therefore redoubled efforts to achieve a breakthrough summit with North Korea, whose options had narrowed. Yet, ties with the South floundered before revived tensions over history,[10] and they gained only modest impetus from the more positive mood that came from shared success and from jointly hosting the World Cup. While many Japanese were confident that they had turned the corner with the South Koreans, especially through the South's cultural opening to Japan and a rush of tourism, Korean media and politicians acknowledged no such breakthrough. After September 11, the United States accommodated China more as a partner in the war against terror. When Bush labeled North Korea part of the "axis of evil" in January 2002, some in Japan may have seen an opportunity for taking advantage of the North's isolation, but the confrontational atmosphere drove the North closer to China and Russia instead. Meanwhile, growing alienation from the United States in South Korea left the Koizumi regime with dependence and diminished leverage as Bush's junior partner. In addition to sticking close to the United States, Japanese sought more options for "reentering Asia."

The nuclear crisis of 2002–2005 has upped the stakes for Sino-Japanese competition over the Korean peninsula. Instead of being wooed by Seoul and persuaded by Washington to join a process of integration, Pyongyang was flaunting its destructive potential and challenging other countries to stop it or to yield under pressure. Moreover, Seoul and Moscow were insisting that a compromise was within reach without pressure, as Beijing gained the preferential role of mediator, culminating in the six-party declaration of September 2005. Without a war, the outcome would likely be a more secure North Korea with international assistance and security guarantees, enabling it to gain a voice in regional geopolitics.

Tokyo feared the consequences of this process, but it could not resist becoming engaged, especially as Beijing shuttled between the adversaries and then began to relish its new diplomatic weight and the benefits of a potential breakthrough. Increasingly in 2003 and glaringly throughout 2004, the United States lost leverage because it did not find a way to keep pressure on the North and refused to offer enough incentives to convince the other four parties, as well as the North, that it had a plan. By June 2004, there was mounting speculation that the possibilities for some kind of freeze had surpassed those for unambiguous elimination of all nuclear programs in the North, leaving a security dilemma that would endure.[11] With North Korea boycotting the talks for thirteen months following the June round of talks, the stalemate persisted. Despite the resumption of contentious but more productive negotiations during the summer of 2005, it remains highly doubtful that the nuclear threat will be fully resolved in one or two years, even with a statement of principles diminishing the crisis atmosphere.

The North Korean nuclear crisis convinced Japan, which in September 2002 had plans to develop an independent diplomacy to the North,[12] as well as Russia, which in January 2003 made an unsuccessful attempt to become the mediator between the North and the United States, that they must coordinate closely with a more influential power.

Soon Japan chose the United States and Russia chose China. Preoccupied with Iraq over the nearly three years that a standoff with the North has persisted, the United States tried to buy time by accepting China as the main mediator. In February–April 2003 China proved that it could bring the North to three-party talks. In June–August it derailed U.S. efforts to build a coalition of pressure or naval inspections by persuading the North to accept six-party talks. Then in October–December China induced the North to consider a package deal as part of another planned six-party meeting, but the United States backed away. To a degree, China salvaged the effort in replacement talks convened in February 2004 that were followed by the establishment of a working group and by back-to-back visits to Beijing by Dick Cheney and Kim Jong Il. In the background, China and Japan each were looking beyond the immediate nuclear crisis to position themselves in the long-term struggle to shape regionalism and the security environment in Northeast Asia to their national objectives. The overall global initiative remained with the United States, but in Northeast Asia the United States had accepted the need for multilateralism and found its means of control limited.

Expectations of momentum in the talks proved overoptimistic. Though the U.S. stance in the June talks seemingly acknowledged that it was isolated in trying to pressure the North and lacked a strategy that could entice the North, it would take another year and Condoleezza Rice's move from the White House to the State Department before a more forward-looking approach fully materialized and bore some initial fruit. Japan remained preoccupied by hostages left behind in the North, with many doubting Koizumi's motives and denigrating his strategic thinking.[13] After Koizumi visited Pyongyang in May, he met with Roh Moo Hyun on Cheju Island in July, and the two pledged to meet twice a year, as both sides sought increased coordination. Both were seeking to adjust their strategies, even as they had to await larger shifts in U.S. strategy.

CHINESE REASONING ABOUT THE NUCLEAR CRISIS

China and Japan had different security objectives in the nuclear crisis. China sought to transform the regional security order, reducing U.S. hegemony and, to the extent possible, undercutting America's bilateral alliances. It feared that pressure on the North, jointly advocated by the United States and Japan in May–July 2003, would threaten to extend U.S. hegemony.[14] Having persuaded Pyongyang to take part in three-party talks in April, the leaders of China pressed even harder in July to broaden the process to six-party talks and derail the pressure building from the United States and its allies. Now Japan as well as Russia and South Korea had a place at the table, and by joining these talks Japan was accepting the need for a multilateral framework that gave China a pivotal role and left the triangular consultations with the United States and South Korea struggling to prove their relevance.

Chinese analysts explained that the crisis had arisen because the United States broke the Agreed Framework, while insisting that the United States and Japan were less interested in ending the nuclear danger than in realizing narrow national interests not favorable to China or to North Korea.[15] Chinese assessments were quick to focus on the broad context, not only the need to keep Japan and others from pursuit of nuclear weapons but also the reestablishment of a power balance that would draw Russia closer, keep North Korea and the United States apart, and widen the divide between South Korea and both the United States and Japan. As strategic planners debate how to proceed, China occupies the pivotal position and has no intention of relinquishing it.

China's view of North Korean diplomacy grew more favorable in the first half of 2004. In contrast to cultivating an image through most of 2003 as an even-handed mediator that was prepared to pressure a recalcitrant North, China had shifted to the stance that pressure on the North is not needed.[16] The North was seen as ready for a deal that would serve both its national interests and regional stability. As the United States stalled, with little sign of compromising on its fundamental goals, China eyed a long-term security framework in which all of the powers would guarantee the survival of the North (meeting varied security concerns) without imposing regime change. In the face of U.S. unilateralism, China became more multilateral. It valued the annual ASEAN Regional Forum (ARF) talks, championed the Shanghai Cooperation Organization (SCO) framework that it had initiated, and apparently favored turning the Six-Party Talks into a regular Northeast Asian security cooperation exchange. The United States, in turn, had little choice but to couch its unilateralism in multilateral language and respect diplomacy based on close consultations that might edge toward a compromise solution, while China, by taking pressure off the table, narrowed the multilateralism that it accepted. With Japan tailing the United States and Russia tailing China as South Korea searched for its voice, multilateralism was circumscribed. Yet, behind the scenes, prospects for genuine multilateral negotiations were rising, and China was positioned to play a more prominent role than Japan—a judgment amply confirmed when more serious negotiations began in July 2005.

Chinese describe a North Korea that serves China's interests well. It is not afraid of pressure, while being united, proud, and strong-willed. It demands equality in foreign relations, as well as respect. This suggests that China has no way to persuade the North to abandon its nuclear program without a deal that is in its national interests, but also that China cannot even make progress by overtly parading its own reform successes. Instead, it and others must patiently and indirectly expose the North to the gains within its reach and then wait for it to draw its own conclusions. Chinese also depict Kim Jong Il as anxious to develop his country and reasonable about what must be done once conditions are created that provide for national security. He is not rigid; but he feels totally vulnerable and must have a security guarantee to proceed with reforms he recognizes as inevitable. Rather than behaving as a wild man who might recklessly endanger the region, Kim is seen as a realist who is playing a weak hand for specific goals that China can accept. By showing respect to Kim, especially on a personal basis, the United States could find that a deal is within reach and obtain the best possible payoff.[17] Of course, this message coincides with China's interest in a security outcome that exposes the weakness of the U.S. position and lays the foundation for multi-lateralism in which South Korea is preoccupied with appealing to the goodwill of the North and Japan has little choice but to subscribe to the process.

The parties to the nuclear crisis talks also vary in their time frames. Beijing has the most deliberate approach, calling for patience to achieve gradual progress, word for word and action for action in reconciling differences and building trust. The United States, however, does not expect to develop a trustworthy relationship with North Korea, fearing that any outcome other than a quick, decisive resolution of the crisis would allow deception by the North and no "complete, verifiable, irreversible dismantlement." Given the great gap be-tween the two sides, few expected that periodic signs of tactical flexibility would yield a definitive outcome. Continuing to view the United States more than North Korea as the problem, the Chinese braced for a long wait. The six-party agreement on principles was thus a necessary but very preliminary first step in a highly protracted process.

In adopting a "good-neighbor" ethic toward Asian countries, the Chinese hammer home the price of arrogance. This serves both to underscore the contrast with the Bush administration and to draw attention to Japan's failure to respect the lessons of history. Beijing is staking its claim to regional leadership on cultivating traditional ties of friendship, showing respect in personal relations with leaders, generously providing assistance, and making clear the importance of peace and development as shared goals. Chinese spokesmen note that as long as the North has nuclear weapons it cannot ex-pect to have the favorable external environment needed for development, but they place most of the responsibility on the United States to persuade the North by meeting its fundamental needs: by promising no preemptive strike, stopping pressure for re-gime change, removing obstacles to normal economic growth, and developing a cli-mate of cooperation and trust. Not only does Beijing seek to use U.S. reliance on its help as a lever for a more accommodating U.S. position on Taiwan, it also wants to en-sure that the Korean outcome will contribute to positive momentum for the political reintegration of China and for the regional balance of power.

The Chinese posture in the Korean crisis is shaped by internal analysis that the U.S.-Japanese alliance since Bush took office is directed at a long-term military alliance to contain China.[18] Even if there will be some differences between a Japan seeking more independence and a United States wanting to exert more control, a shared view of regional security is likely to check frictions, as seen in the North Korean crisis. The way the crisis ends could be critical. If the United States is no longer tied down in Iraq and Japan has revised its constitution as it upgrades its military, China may face a more formidable combination. Although Hu Jintao had first responded to this growing challenge with a cautious strategy to reassure others of China's peaceful and cooperative intentions, by 2004 the leadership was more critical of both Japan and the United States. Indeed, the Koguryo controversy over the summer of 2004 also revealed insensitivity to the Koreas.

Behind the surface remarks claiming Sino-U.S. relations are the best ever are debates in each country about the fragility of relations, too often described in terms of the mood at a few meetings between top leaders. But Chinese fears that a second Bush administration would press China to force the North to act without reasonable compromises have not been realized; instead, the U.S. negotiating stance is increasingly depending on Chinese leadership of the six-party process.

Chinese officials thus remain optimistic about the endgame to the nuclear crisis, even if they retain some doubts about U.S. acceptance of what seems inevitable to Beijing. The resolution will be in stages and emphasize enticements to the North, including security guarantees and ample economic assistance. North Korea will agree to end its nuclear programs, even if doubts will remain about its compliance and the value of verification. South Korea will become absorbed in managing gradual economic integration with the North. Japan will finally offer substantial economic assistance, but it will not gain much influence. The United States will lose its special security role on the peninsula, but it may maintain its military presence for a time. Sino-Russian cooperation over Korea will persist. All of these outcomes will suit China well, stabilizing the region and laying the foundation for a security framework and a balance of powers that facilitate rising Chinese influence. Without an obvious security threat, the United States will turn its attention elsewhere and Japan will have no choice but to agree to regional arrangements that leave it without "perpetual separation" and political clout.[19]

Indeed, many analysts see the North Korean—U.S. standoff less as a struggle over WMD and more as a contest over control of Northeast Asia. In this view, the United States is using the North to reassert control over a region that may be slipping from its grasp due to the rise of China and a realignment of South Korea toward it, movement toward rapprochement of North and South Korea with the United States on the sidelines, Russian reassertion in Northeast Asia of a great-power role and new willing-ness to reach an accommodation with China, and perhaps, eventually, Japanese explo-ration of an independent diplomacy toward North Korea. Even if the nuclear issue is settled, these issues will remain. Indeed, they will come to the fore. Continued crisis, however, lets the United States maintain the appearance of keeping the initiative in the region as it embraces Japan closer and leaves South Korea in an exposed position.

China's growing role has come with encouragement from others. Early in the decade South Korea was eager for China to help get the North to talk. In 1994, the United States pressed China to assist in the first nuclear crisis, although it grew concerned that Seoul was giving Beijing a greater strategic role, as reflected in comments by the South Korean ambassador to China in March that later were downgraded into his personal views.[20] In the Perry Process of 1999 and the Sunshine Policy that followed, China again found itself the target of others trying to gain the ear of the North. In 2003–2005 China retook center stage, agreeing with the United States to work for a nonnuclear North Korea, with South Korea to oppose sanctions or a military response, and with Russia to coordinate closely. Roh Moo Hyun's ever-larger accommodation with China persisted as the South's relations with Japan deteriorated sharply in 2005, seemingly in parallel with the deterioration of Sino-Japanese relations. Not only were Sino–South Korean economic relations becoming ascendant, security cooperation was also advanc-ing. Yet, in the midst of the announced redeployment of U.S. troops in the South, Roh took care not to let left-leaning Uri allies undercut the U.S. alliance.

To China, Japan's motives on the Korean Peninsula are suspect. Although welcoming Koizumi's 22 May visit to Pyongyang, while blaming the United States for merely stall-ing, the Chinese warned that Japan seeks perpetual separation as a means to avoid tak-ing historical responsibility and as justification for becoming a military power. Yet they argued in 2004 that Japan cannot accept the U.S. intention of relying on pressure that could lead to a limited military strike and that Japan more than the United States seeks normalized ties with the North.[21] While these views may hold some promise, many in China fear that Japan's leaders seek to break through the fetters of their postwar status, for which North Korea has been giving them an excuse and could continue to do so.[22]

JAPANESE REASONING ABOUT THE NUCLEAR CRISIS

Japanese are generally aware that the two extreme ways of viewing Northeast Asia are equally far-fetched. The idea that U.S. unipolarity and unconstrained power operates in this region has no basis in fact. If the United States were to act by itself against North Korea, it would alienate the entire region and diminish its influence in shaping the future of the Korean Peninsula. Also, the idea that China is on the verge of gaining regional dominance flies in the face of a reality where no country wants China's influence to increase appreciably and all are prepared to strike deals with at least some of the others to prevent it. U.S. power is significant, and Russian power, backed by its geographical presence and WMD prowess, is not meager, but China and Japan have a wide array of assets to shape the evolution of this region, which all four powers consider to be in the forefront of their legitimate spheres of influence. Since Japan is closer to the United States and can engage Russia effectively, it is positioned to match the influence China wields for at least some time to come. Yet Japanese foreign policy has been slow to make use of its assets and to combine its U.S. backing with a regional strategy, even allowing emotionalism over kidnapped citizens and their family members to eclipse strategy.

Both China and Japan are nervous about Korean unification, but Japan is much more so. Some Chinese feared an extension of U.S. power or found parallels in Vietnam, which after unification in the 1970s turned from ally to enemy. Yet the mainstream has recalculated that a unified Korea will be too dependent economically and too weak in its political and security options to distance itself from China. In contrast, many in Japan expect a unifying Korea to become more nationalistic against their country and to favor ties with China. They had taken South Korea for granted as a state limited by the threat from the North and unable to leave the U.S. embrace, but now they are scrambling to find a way to retain influence and to develop a direct connection to North Korea. As Japan sees it, China would use its greater clout in Korea to dominate the region. As China sees it, Japan's strategy is to contain China and use China's rise and fears about Korea to reassert itself as a political and military great power.[23] Doubts about each other's motives have not dissipated, and in reliance on the United States the Japanese have found relative comfort that has delayed recognition of the urgency of thinking strategically.

Japanese conservatives were initially optimistic in the summer of 2003 that pressure, even including China's participation, would work against North Korea. Calling for intensified pressure through sanctions and a United Nations Security Council resolution and under the forceful lead of Shinzo Abe, they argued that the North could be isolated from international society and the crisis resolved.[24] Yet, while many called for an end to the "benign neglect" that had allowed the North to sustain itself by means of more than 1,400 vessels a year to Japanese ports, most had little sense of a real threat that required a strategic role for Japan instead of just letting the United States take care of it. Increasingly, Koizumi's political fate depended on his diplomacy, and he chose to cast his lot with the emotional reaction toward the abductions and the family members left behind, as well as the need for more information on victims who had not returned. Japan became part of the Six-Party Talks, and it pressed for new legislation that could cut the economic gains to the North. Yet the futility of this strategy was soon clear. No progress was made on the abductees. Pressure on the North was not working, as its trade with both China and South Korea increased. Most important, the United States became discredited in its handling of Iraq and lacked credibility in its inflexible posture toward North Korea, with little indication that it could bring pressure to bear. Koizumi needed a new approach.

For a time in the early 1990s, even after the Kanemaru trip failed, some in the LDP pursued a breakthrough with North Korea. Koichi Kato became associated with this secret initiative, which worried Kim Young Sam.[25] The nuclear crisis of 1993–94 halted this effort, and fear of a missile threat in 1998 slowed any efforts at resuming it. Hiromu Nonaka continued to serve as a powerful LDP pipeline to Pyongyang, but the decline of the left and the strengthening of pro-U.S. influence in the LDP dampened new initiatives. If some may see the Koizumi visits to Pyongyang as carrying on this tradition, most regard them as having more modest goals less challenging to South Korea or the United States.

In Japan, many doubt U.S. management of the nuclear crisis as well as the Iraqi War and its aftermath. Not only does the declining left wing insist that Japan needs an Asian balance to the United States, centered in South Korea and linked to better ties with China, but many on the right also are uncomfortable with sole reliance on U.S. power that is offering no clear direction on Korea and is being discredited in Iraq. Koizumi's trip to Pyongyang in late May 2004 renewed Japan's independent diplomacy after one and a half years of obsessing over the abductees, but it offered little near-term prospect of leverage in the Six-Party Talks. In November 2005, after being interrupted for a year due to a dispute over whether the remains of an abducted Japanese citizen were genuine, bilateral talks resumed with North Korea and speculation resumed about the prospects for a breakthrough. Having led the LDP to a resounding election success in September and building on the progress in the Six-Party Talks, Koizumi had a new opportunity. A new agreement with the United States on relocating forces and strengthening the military alliance bolstered his position. Yet North Korea might seek to divide Japan and the United States, and Koizumi might be eager for notable progress with at least one country in Northeast Asia. The situation would depend, first of all, on whether some agreement were reached on implementation of the agreed principles in the Six-Party Talks.

When Kim Young Sam was president, Japan made little headway in relations with either South or North Korea. He was seen as quick to use the history issue, making it easy for emotionalism on both sides to intensify, while China persisted with less fanfare in upgrading ties with the South and making itself indispensable to the North. After Kim Dae Jung took office, Japanese–South Korean ties advanced sharply, but the main thrust of Kim's Sunshine Policy was to widen the divide between Seoul's warmth to Pyongyang coupled with reliance on Beijing and Tokyo's alienation from both. Events in the South keep tilting the balance in relations from Japan to China. Not only has China overtaken Japan as a trading partner and has South Korea's position on Korean reunification come to resemble China's, but to the politicians who had been working closely with the Japanese in an influential interparliamentary group, the parliamentary elections of 15 April 2004 caused an "earthquake" unlike anything in the past thirty years. The leadership, including former Prime Minister Kim Jong Pil, fell, as did two-thirds of the membership on the Korean side. Informal diplomacy involving Koreans who studied Japanese under the Occupation and had shared an aversion to communism was reaching a dead end. The newly elected parliamentarians feel closer to China than to Japan or the United States; they blame Japanese for cooperating with American neoconservatism in isolating North Korea, insisting on discussing the abductions issue at the Six-Party Talks, and, more than before, acting in ways that bring history to the forefront.[26] This shift in South Korea was the backdrop to a sharp deterioration in relations in 2005 when Roh Moo Hyun reacted with strident criticisms to a perceived Japanese reassertion of claims to Tokdo/Takeshima island and new middle-school textbooks seen as whitewashing history.

Until this new tension, South Korean ties were becoming the launching pad for improved North Korean ties. In Japan a third boom in relations with South Korea is under way, though more at a mass than elite level. The new trend follows the late 1980s boom from democratization and the Seoul Olympics and the turn-of-the-century boom from Kim Dae Jung's October 1998 agreement to drop the "history card," followed by the buildup and celebration of the cohosted World Cup. The third boom may have started with the pop culture of young people and shopping trips, but it has widened into housewives mad about the Korean drama *Winter Sonata,* leading them to make tours of Korean shooting locations and even to what one newspaper calls an epoch-making rise in the study of the Korean language.[27] Yet the Japanese right warned as early as 2004 that South Korea's National Assembly, driven by pro–North Korean tendencies, is playing on anti-Japanese sentiments in a new law that is aimed at tracking down collaborators of sixty years ago and whose scope is being enlarged after the April election purge of pro-Japanese assemblymen.[28] Japanese are also conscious of polls in the South that show not only that China is the friendliest country toward unification, but also that Japan is seen as the least friendly, far below the figures for the United States and Russia.[29]

At the time of each summit with leaders of North or South Korea, a fresh debate has opened over the future of Japan's relations with the peninsula. Following the May 2004 summit with Kim Jong Il in Pyongyang, Japanese commentators charged that the return of five hostages without progress on the fate of ten suspected hostages and on nuclear weapons and missiles was too small a return for the excessive cost to Japan in humanitarian grain and medicines. Yet public opinion valued the restarting of normalization talks and the move to put Japan back in the picture in further negotiations. For the North this meeting was needed to overcome hardened Japanese public opinion. In short, both sides deemed it necessary preparation for the endgame that still awaits.[30]

Some Japanese recognized that only by realizing the return of the family members by means of assistance to the North could Japan move ahead to normalization talks as well as gain leverage in pressing the North to soften its position on the nuclear issue.[31] Japanese also fretted about worsening political relations with China and South Korea.[32] As the U.S. position in Iraq deteriorated, some suggested that Japan was being restricted by its alliance and needed to reactivate its diplomacy in Asia, which includes recognizing that mutual interdependence is deepening and that South Korea is taking the initiative in forging a community.[33] Yet, others saw little bounce for Koizumi from his visit to Pyongyang and little sign that he was preparing bolder action. Indeed, many said that he had gone with the narrow goal of winning votes for the LDP in the July Upper House elections and prolonging his own term as prime minister.

Many in Japan saw it as their country's responsibility to convince North Korea to abandon nuclear weapons. Considering the U.S. position to be inflexible regime change, they applauded Koizumi's visit to Pyongyang as opening the way to broad negotiations.[34] Some suggested that Koizumi's visit moved Japan away from pressure on the North toward talks on normalization.[35] One view held that North Korea doubted that China could influence the United States to negotiate and was turning to Bush's friend Koizumi, who had real influence in Washington.[36] In other circles there was concern that Koizumi's visit put Japan on a track of compromise with the North that would raise concerns in the United States and leave the United States completely isolated in the Six-Party Talks.[37] A debate was at last joined.

Some saw North Korea, with encouragement from China, outmaneuvering the United States through diplomacy, and Japan responding to recognize this reality. Instead of the United States succeeding in its strategy of rallying five states united against the North, coupled with economic pressure that would force Pyongyang to give up its nuclear programs, the North divided the group of five and garnered ever more economic support.[38] China's approach in favor of a compromise solution favorable to the continuation of the Kim Jong Il regime offered incentives to all parties and played upon the danger of instability or a stalemate, while the United States had neither carrots nor sticks to gain support.

Japanese sources on the left accentuated Tokyo's leverage on Pyongyang. In the *Asahi Shimbun*, for instance, articles kept appearing insisting that only Japan and the United States could meet the North's needs, the former for economic assistance and the latter for security. In this view, soft power with a forward strategic outlook must overcome emotionalism or nationalism.[39] In contrast, even media at the center blamed Japan's past laxity for sustaining the North and granting criminal groups a large role in bilateral economic ties.[40] Some on the right insisted Japan could do a lot on its own to pressure the North by cutting these long-standing ties,[41] and some further to the right grew upset that early in 2004 Koizumi sent the wrong message when he reverted to secret diplomacy with the North without applying new laws allowing more pressure against economic relations.[42]

In the July 2004 Cheju island summit of Koizumi and Roh Moo Hyun, Japanese speculated about how, now that rival proposals of the United States and North Korea offered the prospect of real negotiations, Japan might work together with the South to shape the outcome. It had two advantages: being in the middle between the hard posture of the United States and the soft leanings of the South, Japan could become the pivot in the triangle; and being essential for an economically shaky South to address the economic instability in the North, it could become vital to the South's strategy. Yet it had to face leadership in Seoul that mainly wanted Japan's support for its own plans for the nuclear crisis, as well as distrust linked to the Yasukuni shrine visits and other divisive issues. Although the two leaders announced a new stage of "shuttle diplomacy" with two bilateral summits a year from 2005, this did not ensure that a common approach would be developed.[43] Indeed, the June 2005 summit was a chilly affair, mostly devoted to Roh lecturing Koizumi on Japan's historical transgressions and why they must not be ignored.

One uncertainty is the choice of an axis of North Korean development. Would it be through the first designated free-trade zone of Rajin-Sonbong along the eastern coast to Vladivostok, an option touted in talk of an iron silk road from Pusan to Moscow and beyond and of a parallel natural gas pipeline? Yet this is a costly approach, requiring long-term confidence in the North as well as Japanese-Russian understanding on how regionalism should evolve. Or would the axis be through Pyongyang to the second and third designated free-trade zones of Kaesong and Sinuiju, and on to northeast China, which would favor China and reduce the distance to both populated areas and Europe?[44] Japanese strategizing had little likelihood of countering China's advantage. In April 2004, Kim Jong Il spoke of linking the Sinuiju free trade area to China's new development program for the northeast provinces, and Premier Wen Jiabao responded approvingly.[45] In contrast, in August the United States registered concern over technology transfer to the North through Kaesong, troubling South Koreans but likely garnering Japanese support.

CONCLUSION

After the Asian financial crisis South Korea's economy opened significantly, and it drew closer to the economies of both China and Japan. Through the ASEAN +3 process, it also gained a pivotal role in the increasingly formalized meetings of the three Northeast Asian states. From 1999 Japan pressed for an FTA with South Korea, leaving it unclear if and when China might qualify to join. Given that the South also was dropping barriers to Japanese culture, hopes in Japan were rising. On the left, the emphasis was on a full Japanese–South Korean partnership: promoting together the concept of an "East Asian community," recognizing the rising political presence of China in the host role for the Six-Party Talks, and coping with the withdrawal of one-third of the U.S. troops in the South.[46] On the right the reaction was mixed, fearing the South for its lingering critique of Japan, its naiveté toward the North, and its enthusiasm for China. Neither side of the political spectrum pointed Japan toward a strategic approach that could work, and the two visits by Koizumi to Pyongyang only hinted at a new approach to the North.

The most dynamic economic force for South Korea was Chinese magnetism as a market and venue for investments. These ties facilitated China's growing strategic role in promoting a gradual reform process in North Korea as the nuclear crisis is resolved. While China was cultivating the image of a neutral and indispensable broker supportive of reunification, Japan had become tagged with the image of a nation that was obsessed with the emotional issue of divided families owing to abductions and insistent that it could tighten the flow of money to the North but that had little leverage and deep fear about reintegration. Only with Koizumi's visit to Pyongyang in May 2004 did Japanese sense that their voice counted not just in the North but also in the United States, which followed with a more flexible policy. From the Koizumi visit to the United States in May 2003 to the Koizumi visit to Pyongyang in May 2004, Tokyo had followed Washington's lead in regarding pressure as no less important than dialogue, but it seemed to be realizing that there was no coherent and effective strategy for pressure. Having gained a seat at the Six-Party Talks, it had no success raising the issue of abductions as it watched Beijing play the pivotal role. If dialogue were to prevail, the Japanese feared that they would have little say. The abduction issue had to be put aside, and bilateral talks with the North had to parallel the Six-Party Talks in order for Japan's economic clout to matter.

Assuming the crisis could be resolved, the Japanese were accepting the prospect of a secure dictatorship retaining power in the North, relaxing its military threat in stages, and setting its own pace for economic and political reform. It would be buttressed by Chinese commitment to its survival, Russian eagerness to use it as an *entrée* into the region, South Korean enthusiasm for helping their brethren, and even U.S. agreement to offer a security guarantee in order to defuse a nuclear threat. With trilateral cooperation frayed by South Korean distrust of Japan and the U.S. inability to manage a multilateral approach through a unilateralist mentality, some in Japan started to look anew at balancing ties with the two Koreas and transforming the Six-Party Talks into a long-term security framework in the region. Yet, in contrast to far-reaching Chinese strategic thinking, the Japanese struggled to overcome right-wing nationalism opposed to compromise with the North and left-wing nationalism uncritical of the growing nexus of China, Russia, and North Korea. It could not play a role as mediator between the United States and North Korea,[47] and it had yet to design any alternative to following closely in the shadow of the United States.

China's assistance to North Korea changed in the spring of 2004 from emergency aid for survival to long-term support for economic construction and linkage with reform of state-owned enterprises in northeast China. Likewise, its view of the Six-Party Talks shifted to establishing a security framework for the region. If Japan's posture seemed to change from staying in synch with the United States to pressing for its own direct connection to the North, with an option for a more independent role,[48] the reality was little consensus and more delay until the United States acted. Each waited for the United States to make its next move. After the United States accepted a compromise statement at the fourth round of Six-Party Talks, Hu Jintao visited Pyongyang on 28–30 October 2005 and upgraded economic relations even as his aides spoke of a positive North Korean attitude to the coming round of talks, while all Koizumi could do was to launch new bilateral talks with the North and wait for a signal from the Six-Party Talks that an opening really existed.

China had gained a central role in orchestrating the outcome of the North Korean nuclear crisis, with at least four goals in mind. First, it aimed to increase its indispensable standing, convincing the South Koreans by the end of 2002 that the road to Pyongyang goes through Beijing, making the United States from early 2003 rely on it first in three-party talks and then in six-party talks, forging a close partnership on this issue with Russia in the fall of 2003, and becoming the venue for preliminary meetings as well as the intermediary when in March 2004 it informed Tokyo of Pyongyang's interest in a second summit.[49] Second, an objective for Beijing was to sponsor the political and economic survival of the Kim Jong Il regime, deeming that desirable for China's approach to the reintegration of Korea and for the survival of the communist regime in China. Already in June 2004 China sent its first economic inspection mission to the North, including enterprise managers.[50] Third, it was looking ahead to a new security framework, blocking containment and cooperating in a gradual reduction of North Korea's potential threat through joint efforts, rather than through pressure tactics that would strengthen the U.S.-Japan alliance. Fourth, the Chinese were eyeing a joint economic program for the North, linked to the South as well as to China, that would boost Northeast Asian regionalism.

China cultivates the image of a neutral broker, strenuously navigating between the United States and North Korea and deserving gratitude for each step along the way. Japan counters with the image of a firm backer of the United States on matters of security and human rights. Yet both states are driving forces for outcomes that may not be the best for the United States. China and the United States agree on a nonnuclear North Korea and a peaceful resolution of the crisis, but they disagree on the process and pace of demilitarization, the use of pressure to transform the regime, the security framework that should emerge, and ultimately the balance of regionalism and globalization. Japan and the United States agree on most of these matters, but Japan may be more opposed to a deal that enhances China's position, or may be more willing to accept a degree of regionalism that may challenge United States–led globalization. The critical questions are not who wants a nuclear North or who wants reunification soon, but who is interested in using an active North Korea to shape the region. China is, the United States is not, and Japan may be, depending on its North Korean and South Korean ties.

American strategists need to put North Korean crisis resolution in the context of a gradual process of Korean reintegration, and that, in turn, into a framework of steps that will allow for some type of regionalism that balances China and Japan and can be consistent with U.S. security interests. The September 2005 declaration may represent the first tentative steps in this process. Thus, the Six-Party Talks should not be seen as a sideshow in lieu of bilateral negotiations between Washington and Pyongyang, but as the start of an enduring venue for reconciling conflicting notions of security in a region poised to exert greater influence in the global system. The United States has ample reason to continue to regard Japan as the indispensable ally in shaping this region. However, this is not the same as being blind to whatever strategy Japan's right-wing may choose in the assumption that Japan will follow whatever the United States dictates. More consideration is needed on how Japanese-Russian ties can serve regional security and how the Sino–South Korean–Japanese triangle at the core of regionalism can be guided in ways supportive of globalization and long-term security. Japanese realism is becoming more pronounced, focusing on the U.S. alliance, but it is not secure. U.S. realism must overcome neoconservatism if it is to have the flexibility to work with China and keep Japan close in maneuvering over North Korea. A coordinated U.S.-Japan strategy toward North Korea will require new thinking by both.

NOTES

I am grateful to the National Council on Eurasian and East European Research for supporting my research on the reintegration of the Korean Peninsula, centering not only on Russia but also on China, Japan, and South Korea. I want to thank Shigeyuki Iwaki for assistance in finding Japanese materials, and to thank experts at many institutes in Beijing, Changchun, and elsewhere for help with access to materials and interviews.

1. Nakayama Tsunehiko, "Hanzentosenu shusho hocho no seika," *Jiji Top Confidential,* 6 July 2004, pp. 15–19.

2. Jiang Xiyuan, "Chaoxian wenti yu Dongbeiya anquan hezuo kuangjia qianjing," *Dongbeiya luntan,* no. 3 (2004), pp. 44–48.

3. Gilbert Rozman, *Northeast Asia's Stunted Regionalism: Bilateral Distrust in the Shadow of Globalization* (Cambridge: Cambridge University Press, 2004); Charles Armstrong, Gilbert Rozman, Samuel Kim, and Stephen Kotkin, eds., *Korea at the Center: Dynamics of Regionalism in Northeast Asia* (Armonk, N.Y.: M.E. Sharpe, 2005).

4. Victor D. Cha, *Alignment Despite Antagonism: The US-Korea-Japan Security Triangle* (Stanford, Calif.: Stanford University Press, 1999).

5. Chae-Jin Lee, *China and Korea: Dynamic Relations* (Stanford, Calif.: Hoover Press, 1996).

6. Gilbert Rozman, "The Geopolitics of the North Korean Nuclear Crisis," in *Strategic Asia 2003–04: Fragility and Crisis,* ed. Richard J. Ellings and Aaron L. Friedberg (Seattle: The National Bureau of Asian Research, 2003), pp. 245–61.

7. Samuel S. Kim, ed., *The International Relations of Northeast Asia* (Lanham: Rowman & Littlefield, 2004); Nicholas Eberstadt and Richard J. Ellings, eds., *Korea's Future and the Great Powers* (Seattle: National Bureau of Asian Research, 2001); Young-Sun Lee and Masao Okonogi, eds., *Japan and Korean Unification* (Seoul: Yonsei University Press, 1999).

8. Tae-Hwan Kwak and Seung-Ho Joo, eds., *The Korean Peace Process and the Four Powers* (Aldershot, U.K.: Ashgate, 2003).

9. Shigemura Toshimitsu, *Kitachosen no gaiko senryaku* (Tokyo: Kodansha gendai shinsho, 2000); Nishioka Tsutomu, *Kim Jong-il & Kim Dae Jung* (Tokyo: PHP, 2000).

10. Gilbert Rozman, "Japan and South Korea: Should the U.S. Be Worried about Their New Spat in 2001?" *Pacific Review* 15, no. 1 (2002), pp. 1–28.

11. Kim Yongsu, "Nanboku shuno kaidan de juka shoikonda Kankoku," *Sekai shuho,* 22 June 2004, p. 25.

12. Gilbert Rozman, "Japan's North Korean Initiative and U.S.-Japanese Relations," *Orbis* 47, no. 3 (Summer 2003), pp. 527–39.

13. There was much criticism of the 22 May trip as serving only to distract Japanese from Koizumi's political troubles and to provide a boost for the LDP before the Upper House elections in July. See Osami Kunihira, "Yokoda Megumi san shosoku joho," *Gendai* (July 2004), pp. 130–35.

14. *Mainichi shimbun,* 15 July 2003, p. 6.

15. Lu Guoxue, "Yibo sanzhe de Chaomei zhengduan," in *Quanqiu zhengzhi yu anquan baogao,* ed. Li Shenming and Wang Yizhou (Beijing: Shehuikexue wenxian chubanshe, 2004), pp. 161–84.

16. In visits to China seven months apart, in October 2003 and May 2004, I found the contrast striking.

17. This is a composite message from dozens of interviews of Chinese experts and officials.

18. Contrasts in the coverage of international relations in public Chinese sources and internal or secret ones have varied over times, and my impression is that the gap has widened again on issues of security raised here.

19. Zhang Liangui, "Chaoxian bandao de tongyi yu Zhongguo," *Dangdai Yatai* (May 2004), p. 34.

20. *Chosun Ilbo*, 31 March 1994, as reported in Chong Jae-Ho, "Between Dragon and Eagle," unpublished manuscript.

21. Jiang Xiyuan, "Chaohe wenti yu Dongbeiya anquan hezuo kuangjia qianjing," *Dongbeiya luntan*, no. 3 (2004), pp. 44–46.

22. Wan Hongfang, "Koizumi zhizhenghou xiang 'zhengzhi daguo' chuan mian tuijin de guiji," *Guoji ciliao xinxi*, no. 4 (2004), pp. 24–27.

23. *Shijie jingji yu zhengzhi*, May 2004, p. 44.

24. *Sankei shimbun*, 15 July 2003, p. 1.

25. *Asahi shimbun*, 18 July 2004, p. 6.

26. *Asahi shimbun*, 26 May 2004, p. 15.

27. *Tokyo shimbun*, 3 July 2004, p. 24.

28. *Sankei shimbun*, 15 July 2004, p. 6.

29. *Sankei shimbun*, 9 June 2004, p. 7.

30. Hideshi Takesada, "Bokatsu kaiketsu ni muke senryakuteki kosho o," *Jiji Top Confidential*, 8 June 2004, pp. 2–5.

31. *Nihon keizai shimbun*, 7 May 2004, p. 2.

32. Makoto Sasaki, "Nitchu, Nikkan kankei no 'seirei bunatsu,'" *Jiji Top Confidential*, 9 April 2004, pp. 12–15.

33. Li Jongwon, "Hokuto Ajia o 'sozo no kyodotai' ni," *Ronza* (May 2003), pp. 173–79.

34. *Yomiuri shimbun*, 2 June 2004, p. 12.

35. *Mainichi shimbun*, 2 June 2004, p. 5.

36. *Mainichi shimbun*, 21 May 2004, p. 5.

37. *Sankei shimbun*, 15 May 2004, p. 2.

38. Kenneth Quinones, "6kakoku kyogi ni nozomu Kitachosen no takaku senryaku," *Sekai shuho*, 29 June 2004, pp. 6–9.

39. *Asahi shimbun*, 6 March 2003, p. 15; *Asahi shimbun*, 12 June 2004, p. 30.

40. *Nihon keizai shimbun*, 10 June 2003.

41. *Yomiuri shimbun*, 10 June 2004.

42. *Sankei shimbun*, 3 April 2004, p. 3.

43. *Hokkaido shimbun*, 18 July 2004, p. 2.

44. Pierre Chartier, "The Northern Corridor of the Trans-Asian Railway," *Erina Report* 58 (July 2004), pp. 10–29.

45. Haruki Wada, "Nitcho kokkyo kosho saikai igai ni michi wa nai," *Sekai*, July 2004, p. 140.

46. *Asahi shimbun*, 22 July 2004, p. 2.

47. Li Jongwon, "Kako o tokashi, mirai o kizuku," *Ronza* (July 2004), p. 14.

48. Hisashi Hirai, "Okiku ugokihajimeta Tohoku Ajia no kozu," *Foresight* (July 2004), pp. 22–23.

49. "Nitcho shuno kaidan o jitsugensaseta Hu Jintao no atsuryoku," *Gendai* (July 2004), p. 29.

50. Ibid., p. 31.

15

The Past Is the Future
Russia and the Korean Peninsula

Alexandre Y. Mansourov

The year 2004 marked the 140th anniversary of the beginning of voluntary migration of Koreans to the Russian Far East, the 120th anniversary of the establishment of Russian-Korean diplomatic relations, the 100th anniversary of the Russo-Japanese naval battle and the heroic tragedy of the Russian navy cruiser *Varyag* in February 1904 near the coast of Korea at Inchon, as well as the 55th anniversary of the first Soviet-DPRK agreement on economic and cultural cooperation, signed in Moscow on 17 March 1949. These symbolic events of great historical significance were widely marked in Russia, the ROK, and the DPRK throughout the year.

BALANCING ACT OF THE RUSSIAN BEAR

A balanced and even-handed policy toward the Korean Peninsula remains a major priority of Russian foreign policy in the Asia-Pacific region. During his first term, President Vladimir Putin was able to overcome the ideological barriers of the Cold War separating Moscow and Seoul and the political animosity of the post–Cold War era dividing Moscow and Pyongyang. He reached a good deal of mutual understanding with the political leadership of both Korean states, which allowed Russia to discuss any problems, including the most controversial ones, in a constructive and partner-like manner. Although Moscow seems to favor Seoul, it sees no evil in any part of the peninsula and pursues a well-calibrated two-Korea policy. President Putin officially visited Seoul in February 2001 and Pyongyang in July 2001. These visits led to the development of relations of "constructive and mutually complementary partnership" between

Russia and the Republic of Korea, as well as "traditional friendly and cooperative relations" between Russia and the DPRK, in all fields, especially in political dialogue, trade and investment, and the development of military ties and military-technical cooperation, as highlighted in the joint statements signed during these visits.

President Putin met with ROK President Roh Moo Hyun at the APEC summit in Bangkok in October 2003 and at the APEC summit in Chile in November 2004, as well as during Mr. Roh's official visit to Russia in September 2004. Russian Foreign Minister Lavrov visited both Pyongyang and Seoul in July 2004. The main topics in the ongoing political dialogue center on the situation on the Korean Peninsula, joint efforts to settle the North Korean nuclear weapons issue, and a wide range of international cooperation activities. In their discussions with South and North Korean representatives, Russian government officials play the intermediary role. Moscow promotes the multilateral six-party approach and package solution to the nuclear problem, stressing the vital national interests of both Korean states and other parties, including security guarantees and inducements for the socioeconomic development of the DPRK, that must be seriously taken into account.

RUSSIAN INTERESTS AND POLICY TOWARD THE TWO KOREAS

Russian policymaking concerning the DPRK tends to be passive, reactive, and cautious, demonstrating a great deal of continuity and little innovation. Radical policy departures occur only as a result of ad hoc personal interventions by the top political leadership of the country. As a rule, policy formulation and implementation is left to midranking government officials at various ministries and agencies and is rarely elevated to the level of national leadership or even significant public debate. Official Russian policy toward North Korea has traditionally been subordinated to domestic political demands and the broader goals of Russian diplomacy in Northeast Asia, and thus is secondary to and dependent on the policy goals and dynamics of Russian-American, Russian-Chinese, and Russian-Japanese relations, as well as some transnational security concerns.

Russia's principal strategic objectives in dealing with the DPRK are as follows:

- Preserving international peace ("unjust peace is better than just war," or "keep it quiet down there")
- Maintaining domestic political stability ("known evil is better than unknown evil")
- Promoting regional socioeconomic development ("a well-fed people is less dangerous than a hungry people")
- Securing Russian participation in Korean affairs ("participate in everything, but do not enter anything")[1]

- Safeguarding Russian interests on the Korean Peninsula ("if not for now, then for future generations")
- Global power balancing (use North Korea as strategic leverage in relations with the United States, China, and Japan).

However, Russia has a deeper set of principal stakes on the peninsula, especially related to the North Korean nuclear issue.

Partial Denuclearization of the Korean Peninsula

"Nuclear weapons and proliferation," no—"Nuclear power for peaceful use," yes

The Russian government does not share with the United States a comparable sense of urgency over the North Korean nuclear weapons development programs. Nor is Moscow willing to accept at face value the U.S. allegations about the existence of the DPRK's highly enriched uranium (HEU) program in violation of the Agreed Framework. Russian officials argue that Pyongyang largely abided by its obligations under the Agreed Framework and is receiving the short end of the stick, which, ironically, confirms their long-held belief that Washington was never serious about providing Pyongyang with alternative sources of nuclear power for peaceful use. Washington's arbitrary decision not to certify Pyongyang's compliance with the Agreed Framework is interpreted as a manifestation of a growing U.S. tendency toward unilateralism and increasing reliance on the use of force, instead of the rule of law, in international affairs. They also believe that the ROK's 2004 revelations about its clandestine experiments with plutonium reprocessing and uranium enrichment in 1982 and January–February 2000, respectively, have created additional difficulties in the nuclear negotiations.

Russian government officials were frustrated with and worried about the dramatic shifts in U.S. policy toward the DPRK evident during President Bush's first term in office. The general belief is that the U.S. designation of the DPRK as part of the "axis of evil," despite clear signs of positive domestic evolution in the North in recent years, seriously undermined President Roh Moo Hyun's peace and prosperity policy, thereby damaging the prospects for peace, stability, and inter-Korean reconciliation. Without naming names, Moscow tends to hold the United States responsible for the protracted absence of dialogue and escalation of tension between Washington and Pyongyang. U.S. unilateral actions in Iraq are said to have had a "very negative" impact on the North Korean problem. At the same time, Moscow questions the applicability of the Libyan model to the DPRK's case. Russian officials are heartened by the signs of U.S. flexibility evident during 2005, including direct dealings between Washington and

Pyongyang and the issuance of the denuclearization statement at the September 2005 round of the Six-Party Talks, though they do not yet see a comprehensive break-through, only a different attitude about negotiation.

The Russian government continues to believe that with all its flaws, the 1994 Geneva Agreed Framework and the Korean Peninsula Energy Development Organization (KEDO)-run light water reactor (LWR) project did contribute to managing produc-tively, if not resolving, the North Korean nuclear problem. A nuclear freeze in the DPRK, monitored by the International Atomic Energy Agency (IAEA) and the interna-tional community, and implementation of cooperative security alternatives to military confrontation and nuclear armament on the peninsula were deemed far preferable to an unconstrained weapons program in the North. Moscow believes that the "Agreed Framework Light" or "Agreed Framework Plus" is still better than "everything mi-nus," because without the Agreed Framework and a nuclear freeze, all nations sur-rounding the peninsula are worse off and are back to "square one," facing a renewed North Korean nuclear challenge, as they did a decade before.[2]

Officially, Moscow regards the DPRK's nuclear problem as part of a larger strategic problem of global nuclear proliferation. As one of the three depository states of the 1963 Nuclear Nonproliferation Treaty (NPT) and a United Nations Security Council (UNSC) permanent member-state, Russia strives to strengthen the global NPT regime by con-vincing the threshold states, including the DPRK, not to go nuclear, through the multi-lateral strategic arms control process and a mixture of bilateral incentives and sanctions. Should North Korea choose to forgo the nuclear weapons option, Moscow appears to be willing to resume its scientific-technical cooperation in the field of nuclear technology used for peaceful purposes with Pyongyang, as it had been doing until 1993.

From the nuclear nonproliferation standpoint, Moscow regards the current situation as much worse than the status quo ante that existed before October 2002. At that time, the DPRK was still an NPT member; the nuclear freeze was in place at the Yongbyon nuclear complex; and IAEA inspectors and surveillance and measuring equipment were monitoring North Korean compliance with the DPRK's international obligations under the IAEA, NPT, and Agreed Framework provisions. In contrast (and despite the September 2005 declaration), the DPRK is no longer a member of the NPT and IAEA; the IAEA inspectors and monitoring equipment are no longer present in the country; and the international community is much less certain about the status of North Korea's nuclear programs. In addition, there is a concern about the possibility of a civilian nu-clear accident occurring at one of the unsafeguarded North Korean nuclear facilities, and possible uncontrolled repercussions for Russia and the rest of the world. Clearly, the integrity and credibility of the global nuclear nonproliferation regime suffers greatly from the DPRK's decision to withdraw and resume its unsupervised, prohibited nuclear activities. Russia therefore believes that the course of unilateral DPRK actions must be reversed at the earliest possible time, but this will be contingent on U.S. actions and initiatives as well as decisions by the North.

Some prominent Russian military strategists believe that if North Korea carries out a nuclear test, the Kim Jong Il regime will have only several months to arm its missiles with nuclear warheads. By that time, the international community will have had to make a decision whether to let another nuclear state emerge at one end of the "axis of evil" or take preemptive measures to disarm it by force. They do not believe that Russia will ever agree to a joint decision in favor of the use of force on its border. Therefore, as one prominent Russian strategist predicts, "the United States may decide, at its sole discretion, to attack North Korea's missile launchers and nuclear warhead manufacturing facilities."[3] But, as another strategist notes, "any military conflict may have extremely disastrous consequences," concluding that the "existence of a nuclear DPRK that behaves responsibly may be a preferable choice to war."[4]

At the same time, Moscow regards the North Korean nuclear crisis as a part of the historical legacy of the Cold War–era hostility and confrontation between the United States and North Korea. Russia feels very strongly that full normalization of bilateral relations and creation of political trust between the DPRK and the United States, and the DPRK and Japan, are essential to lasting peace and stability on the peninsula. These would then be followed by the establishment of a new international security regime ensuring peace, stability, and socioeconomic development on the peninsula, "unlocking" the North Korean nuclear problem and reducing the risk of a "nuclear chain reaction" and uncontrolled escalation of tensions in Northeast Asia.

The Russian government supports the main principles of the "package solution" on the basis of the "simultaneous or coordinated" action and "words for words and actions for actions" principle, as outlined by the DPRK.[5] The congruence of the Russian-DPRK views was revealed in public in the aftermath of Russian Deputy Foreign Minister Losyukov's mission to Pyongyang on 17–21 January 2003. The two governments proposed that the essence of the "new package deal" should consist of three main elements, including, first, maintenance of the nuclear-free status on the Korean Peninsula and strict compliance of Korean states with their NPT obligations; second, credible security assurances for the DPRK in one form or another (bilateral, multilateral, written, oral, etc.); and, third, resumption of economic and humanitarian programs aimed at promoting domestic socioeconomic changes in the North and strong support for the policy of constructive engagement with the DPRK.[6] All components are reflected in the September 2005 declaration at the Six-Party Talks, but the declaration remains a statement of broad principles, not a road map or action plan.

In deference to Pyongyang's position, the Russian government took a very cautious stance on the question of referring the North Korean nuclear issue to the UNSC, stressing that "quiet diplomacy" and multilateral negotiations, not "political pressure" or "military option," must be the main venue for the diplomatic resolution of the crisis. Moreover, Russian President Putin and Chinese President Hu Jintao agreed on a Joint Declaration on the Korean Question in May 2003, stating that "any forceful pressure or use of force scenarios to solve the existing problems on the Korean Peninsula will be unacceptable to Russia and China." Both sides confirmed their principled desire to see the Korean Peninsula nuclear-free and in peace, and reiterated the need to provide security assurances to the DPRK and create a favorable international environment for its social and economic development.

On 10 December 2004, Russian Defense Minister Sergey Ivanov stated, "Russia is seriously concerned about the situation on the Korean Peninsula. We believe that the DPRK's decision to withdraw from the NPT can weaken considerably the efforts of the international community aimed at strengthening the WMD nonproliferation regimes. [The] Russian military-political leadership still believes that the Korean Peninsula must remain nuclear-free. One must do everything possible to ensure that the DPRK's nuclear program be limited by peaceful framework and [the] nonproliferation regime. I cannot comment on the question whether or not the DPRK possesses nuclear weapons." Having reportedly learned two days in advance from its trusted sources in Pyongyang about the DPRK's 10 February 2005 announcement of its claim to nuclear weapons, the Russian government expressed only "regret and concern." It faulted the statement of the DPRK Ministry of Foreign Affairs (MOFA) announcing Pyongyang's decision to build up a nuclear weapons arsenal and to suspend its participation in the Six-Party Talks, because it did not "correspond to the goal of denuclearization of the Korean Peninsula declared by the DPRK."

The resumption of the Six-Party Talks in the summer of 2005 was clearly viewed by Russian officials as a positive and essential step in averting a larger crisis, with Washington and Pyongyang both obligated to further negotiations. However, in contrast to the United States, Russia, together with China, places a higher priority on the peaceful resolution of the North Korean nuclear crisis than on the process of the denuclearization of the peninsula per se. In other words, "for the sake of peace," Moscow and Beijing are ready to prolong the process of North Korea's dismantlement and abandonment of the nuclear weapons program for as long as necessary—perhaps even into the indefinite future.[7]

Missile Proliferation Control

"For self-defense," yes—"For sale," no

For decades, the former Soviet Union was one of the primary sponsors and facilitators of the "indigenous development" of the DPRK missile program, as a proxy strategic deterrent force against the United States, Japan, and, possibly, China. At present, the Russian government is content with the DPRK government's 6 August 2001 statement that the North Korean "missile program is of peaceful character and is not designed to pose a military threat to any country, which demonstrates respect for the DPRK's sovereignty," which is interpreted as meaning "no military threat to Russia." This provision is clearly reflected in the Russian-DPRK Pyongyang Declaration of July 2000 and Moscow Declaration of August 2001.

However, because of its fundamental interest in enhancing the global missile nonproliferation regime, Moscow continues to encourage Pyongyang to show restraint in new missile development, to refrain from missile sales overseas, and to abide by its unilateral moratorium on missile launches, as well as to talk to the United States regarding the resolution of the "missile issue." The Kremlin is on the record as willing to contribute its assistance to any reasonable "buy-out" deal on the missile issue between the DPRK and the international community. At the same time, upholding the DPRK's sovereign right to self-defense, Moscow is unlikely to denounce Pyongyang or impose any sanctions against it should the DPRK walk away from its long-standing missile moratorium, conduct new missile tests, or resist any negotiations aimed at eliminating its missile development program. This policy is heralded as one of the demonstrations of Moscow's so-called balanced approach toward the Korean Peninsula.[8]

Notwithstanding official policy, some Russian nonproliferation experts take a more sinister view, arguing that one of the distinctive features of the DPRK's missile program is its close linkage with the nuclear weapons development program. They are worried not only about the increasing range of North Korean missiles now under development, but also about their growing payloads and accuracy. They speculate it may take North Korea a relatively short period of time to move from the first nuclear test to arming a certain number of intermediate-range ballistic missiles with nuclear warheads. In their judgment, the North Korean missile threat is twofold. First, there is a danger of DPRK preventive nuclear missile strikes against regional powers aligned with the United States in the event of escalation of hostilities between Washington and Pyongyang. Second, the DPRK is a known exporter of missiles to other countries with so-called problem regimes, and, therefore, one cannot exclude the possibility of the transfer of nuclear-tipped missiles from Pyongyang to its overseas customers in the future. Consequently, these ardent proponents of nuclear and missile nonproliferation urge the Russian government to consider the possibility of Russian participation in the counterproliferation efforts of the international community aimed at halting and dismantling the DPRK's nuclear and missile development programs.[9]

CONVENTIONAL ARMS CONTROL AND REDUCTION

"Defensive self-sufficiency," yes—"Offensive self-defense," no

Moscow has always supported the idea of conventional arms control and reductions on the Korean Peninsula, stating that these confidence-building measures will help reduce tensions across the DMZ, allowing the DPRK to "earn the peace dividend" by saving money on defense spending, facilitating "defense conversion" in the North Korean military-industrial complex, and possibly creating propitious conditions for the transformation of the armistice agreement into a peace treaty. Moscow advocates the principles of reciprocity, transparency, and verifiability in the process of conventional arms control and reduction on the Korean Peninsula.

Russia does not regard the DPRK as a source of direct military threat or any kind of terrorist threat.[10] Moscow is keen to preserve a certain degree of military balance and "reasonable defensive self-sufficiency" on the Korean Peninsula. Military-technical cooperation between Russia and North Korea has been anemic in the past decade. In April 2001, the DPRK defense minister visited Moscow and signed an intergovernmental agreement on military-technical cooperation between the two defense ministries. The content of the agreement is unknown. Russia is no longer eager or able to rearm the Korean People's Army almost for free, which is what the DPRK wants and what the Soviet Union used to do. Despite persistent rumors about unofficial Russian technical assistance to the DPRK missile development program, given the financial constraints facing both governments, Moscow is only willing to help Pyongyang repair and properly maintain some of the obsolete Soviet armaments and military equipment already present in the North, without demanding any serious payment in return.[11] This gloomy reality, however, contradicts one of Russia's undeclared goals on the peninsula—namely, to maintain a certain balance of military power between the two Koreas.

Occasionally, senior Russian officials express their willingness to supply enough military hardware to the North to allow it to enjoy a degree of "reasonable defensive self-sufficiency." On 28 June 2001, the then–Deputy Foreign Minister Alexander Losyukov stated that "Russian-DPRK military-technical cooperation has a well thought-out character and will be based on the principle of reasonable defensive self-sufficiency.

The DPRK is a sovereign state that, naturally, has the right to self-defense, has the right to have a certain military potential, which would suit its national interests and could protect the country from any eventualities in the international environment. In South Korea, as you know, there is a certain military potential, including the presence of foreign troops. It is only natural that the DPRK must have confidence that it will be able to protect itself, should any extraordinary circumstances arise. The DPRK must have a certain defense potential." On 10 December 2004, Russian Defense Minister Sergey Ivanov stated the "the Russian Federation is a lawful successor of the Soviet Union. Therefore, we fulfill all the obligations earlier assumed before our foreign partners. This concerns also our cooperation with other states in military and military-technical fields. We will continue it until there exist mutual interests of all parties concerned. We will, of course, take into account existing international norms regulating this process. Our cooperation with the DPRK is not an exception. Since 1991 it has been limited mostly to the delivery of spare parts to the Soviet-made military equipment and armaments." It is estimated to range from fifty to one hundred million U.S. dollars annually. But it warrants mention that Russian–South Korean military-technical cooperation has reached US$700 million, which causes great concern to the military leadership of the Korean People's Army (KPA) and contributes to latent anti-Russian sentiment in Pyongyang's political circles.

FOREIGN TROOP PRESENCE

"Yankees go home, no Chinese welcome"

The official Russian position on the current role and future status of the U.S. forces on the Korean Peninsula has been consistently negative and has changed little since the end of the Cold War, although it is more diplomatic, less pronounced, and based on a new post–Cold War justification.

The removal of the foreign (read U.S.) military presence from the Korean Peninsula remains one of the basic principles of Russian policy in Korea, because it is supposed to serve the goal of enhancing stability and security on the Korean Peninsula. Although Russian officials recognize that the question of the U.S. military presence in the ROK belongs to the realm of bilateral relations between Seoul and Washington and even concede that the ROK-U.S. Mutual Defense Treaty appears to contribute to the maintenance of peace and stability on the Korean Peninsula, they still consider the deployment of U.S. troops in the ROK as against fundamental Russian national interests. They describe it in a novel way as an anachronism of the Cold War that must be eliminated. They are echoed by many Russian Korea experts who "consider it necessary to put an end to foreign military presence in Korea after its possible reunification since it can be directed only against Russia (and also China)."[12]

In his interviews to the *Yomiuri Shimbun* and Kyodo News Agency on 18 July 2000, President Putin stated, "The issues concerning the presence and status of the U.S. troops on the Korean Peninsula carry significant weight for maintaining the security in Northeast Asia, a region vital for Russia's national interests. While we acknowledge the legitimacy of the inalienable rights of the Northeast Asian nations to national and collective self-defense in accordance with the U.N. Charter, we also believe that the realization of these rights should fully correspond to the common interests of relaxing military-political confrontation, strengthening the climate of trust and dialogue in the region, without creating any threats to anyone's security." This nuanced and ambiguous position reflects a very lukewarm, albeit not outright negative, attitude toward the continuation of the American military presence in Korea.

In the Moscow declaration signed by the Russian leader and Kim Jong Il on 6 August 2001, the Russian government expressed its understanding of the DPRK's fears and concerns regarding the threat that the U.S. forces in South Korea pose to the North Korean state, as well as the North Korean position that "the withdrawal of the U.S. forces from South Korea is an urgent problem, the resolution of which can no longer be delayed in the interests of safeguarding peace and security on the Korean Peninsula and in Northeast Asia."[13] (There are no foreign forces stationed in the North.) Russian leaders completely discount the statements from Washington (if now far less from Seoul) about Pyongyang's aggressive military intentions. They believe that the North Korean leadership is preoccupied with regime survival amidst a profound economic crisis. They share the DPRK's position that a reduction in, or better, a pullout of U.S. forces in the ROK will create a completely different situation on the peninsula, which will undoubtedly lead to a real reduction in tension and greater security and stability on the Korean Peninsula. Therefore, they welcomed the U.S. decision to withdraw 12,500 U.S. troops from the peninsula by 2008 and to relocate some of the remaining units from their current forward positions to consolidated bases south of Seoul in Osan and Pyongtaek. They do not see any reason for U.S. forces to remain on the peninsula after Korean reunification.[14]

Access to Ports, Airspace, and the Exclusive Economic Zone

The Russian Pacific Fleet has always sought access to the DPRK's warm-water ports of Rajin and Wonsan along the eastern littoral. The Russian Pacific Air Force is interested in acquiring overflight rights across DPRK airspace, which Pyongyang granted to Moscow briefly in the late 1980s. The Russian Ministry of Agriculture and various Far

Eastern fishing concerns are interested in extending Russia's fishing rights and catch quotas in the DPRK's exclusive economic zone (EEZ) adjacent to the Russian EEZ.

Access to Strategic Natural Deposits and the Atomic Energy Industry Market

From the liberation of Korea in August 1945 until the collapse of the USSR, the relevant Soviet organizations maintained access to strategic natural deposits, especially natural uranium ore, in the DPRK. It is safe to assume that after the resolution of the nuclear crisis, the Russian atomic energy industry will seek to reassert Russian interests in further exploration of the DPRK's uranium ore reserves.

The Russian government showed lukewarm interest in official participation in the activities of KEDO because its proposed place and role in KEDO was not regarded as adequate to the level of development of the Russian atomic energy industry. It did not satisfy the interests of the Russian nuclear energy establishment and failed to reflect the rich experience accumulated by the former Soviet Union in cooperation with the DPRK in the nuclear energy field. This notwithstanding, the Russian government believes it is useful to promote bilateral cooperation between various Russian organizations under the Ministry of Atomic Energy (Minatom) and its Korean counterparts in searching for various ways of involving the Russian atomic energy industry. On the assumption that North Korea rejoins the NPT and IAEA, this could include the future construction of a nuclear power plant at Kumpo, in the form of Russian shipments of nuclear fuel, components, and equipment. In general, the Russian atomic energy industry establishment is ready to discuss an alternative approach to the resolution of the DPRK's persistent energy deficit problem: should Pyongyang and KEDO agree, Moscow will be willing to construct a nuclear power plant with two 1,000-MW(e) LWRs on its side of the Russian-DPRK border with KEDO financing. The problem is that neither North Korea nor KEDO has any interest in the Russian proposal, and KEDO's future looks especially problematic.[15]

Three Myths: Promoting Regional Economic Growth and Infrastructure Development

Although Russian trade with North Korea is still insignificant by historical standards, South Korea is one of Russia's important trading partners. In 2003, the trade turnover rose to US$4.18 billion, from US$2.11 billion in 1998. In 2004, it reached almost six billion U.S. dollars. In 2003, exports from Russia to South Korea were estimated at US$2.52 billion (an increase of 13.7 percent compared to 2002), and imports at US$1.66 billion (an increase of 55.7 percent). Russia exports mostly aluminum, special equipment, marine products, cast iron, rolling steel, and cellulose, and a little bit of machinery and equipment (2.35 percent), while importing machinery and transport equipment (31.9 percent), chemicals (25.6 percent), electronics (15.7 percent), food and agriculture raw materials (9.6 percent), and textiles (9.5 percent). The ROK invested only US$205.7 million in 135 projects in Russia, including US$44.6 million in direct investments, 56 percent of which is concentrated in the construction industry.

Within the framework of the Russian-Korean Commission on Economic and Scientific-Technical Cooperation,[16] the Russian government expressed considerable interest in attracting ROK investment for such large investment projects as the construction of a Lotte business center in Moscow (expected investment could reach three hundred million U.S dollars), the participation of LG Corporation in the construction of a large oil-refining plant in Tatarstan (expected investment could reach one billion U.S. dollars), and the ROK scientific-industrial park in the Nakhodka Special Economic Zone. To facilitate bilateral trade and ROK investments in Russia, Moscow agreed to sign an intergovernmental agreement on restructuring and repayment of the US$1.47 billion Russian debt to the Republic of Korea, which was followed by the resumption of cooperation in the banking sector.[17] In November 2004, Russia and the ROK successfully completed bilateral talks on Russian admission into the World Trade Organization (WTO). There are good prospects for bilateral cooperation in joint space exploration,[18] in the energy sector, including the future shipment of Russian gas to the Korean market,[19] and in the fishing industry.

Moscow is demonstrating some interest in promoting trilateral cooperation between Russia, South Korea, and North Korea, especially in the rehabilitation and modernization of more than fifty industrial facilities built in the DPRK with Soviet technical assistance (in power engineering, ferrous and nonferrous metallurgy, mechanical engineering, and other spheres), as well as in connecting the future Trans-Korean Railroad to the Trans-Siberian Railroad. Russian–North Korean economic cooperation has been minuscule since 1991, averaging one hundred to one hundred fifty million U.S. dollars in annual bilateral trade, and it has poor prospects in the foreseeable future. There are three widely held myths about the possible roles for Russia in the economic rehabilitation of the DPRK—the "railroad myth," the "pipeline myth," and the "enterprise recovery myth." None of these three megaprojects is likely to be implemented any time soon, because obstacles are too high, stakes are too low, and the interests concerned are just too marginal for their overall success.

The idea of connecting the Russian Trans-Siberian Railway and the Trans-Korean Railway is appealing on the surface, but it has to overcome plenty of invisible shoals to reach port. The geopolitical risks involving North Korean cooperation are severe. Opposition from various interest groups in Russia and the ROK, including environmentalists, port authorities in Nakhodka and Pusan, maritime trade unions, and local governments in the Maritime Province and in the ROK coastal areas, is strong and vociferous. Financial incentives for the quasi-privatized Russian Railway General Stock Company (created in lieu of the former Russian Ministry of Railway Transportation) to invest almost eight hundred million U.S. dollars in the reconstruction of the North Korean railway system without Russian government subsidies, which are unlikely to be forthcoming, are minuscule compared to its other investment priorities and plans regarding the railway maintenance work and expansion plans in other parts of Russia. At the same time, potential benefits, in terms of the projected transit revenues and accompanied local development, seem to be still uncertain.

Various gas pipeline construction projects, designed to link the Kovykta gas condensate field in the Irkutsk region (three possible routes) or the Srednevilyuiskoye and Chayandinskoye gas condensate fields in the Yakutsk region (two possible routes) of Eastern Siberia to the ROK via the People's Republic of China (PRC) or the DPRK, appear to face intractable long-term hurdles. Projected investment costs are exorbitant (eighteen billion U.S. dollars for the Kovykta gas pipeline alone); neither private syndicates nor any regional government is willing to pay it forward now. Political opposition from local governments and the general public, policy stonewalling from environmentalist groups, corporate feuds and legal battles among key Russian players, geopolitical risk involving North Korean cheating and uncooperative behavior, alternative offers from Japan, and the liquid natural gas (LNG) alternative—all these factors dim the prospects for the construction of any gas pipeline via North Korea any time soon.

Despite repeated promises, Russia cannot help North Korea rehabilitate most of its Soviet-built industrial enterprises. Some of them are beyond recovery or have nothing left to recover due to a decade-long industrial decline and mass larceny. Others are obsolete and face technological extinction. Some flagship enterprises may face steep competition from South Korea (like the Chongjin Iron and Metal Works competing against global metallurgy leader Pohang Iron and Metals Combine) and consequent Russian sensitivity to Seoul's views arising from Russia's "two-Korea policy." Pyongyang's reluctance to swap certain valuable industrial assets for its long-overdue debt obligations also undermines Russian willingness to finance industrial enterprise recovery in the DPRK. Besides, many of the old state-owned enterprises should not be rehabilitated at all, because the industrial structure of a new economy of the future may be very different from the old one.

Thus, in all three areas of Russia's potential large-scale economic assistance and cooperation with the DPRK—the TSR-TKR railroad cooperation, natural gas pipeline construction, and state-owned enterprise recovery—the barriers and risks appear to be too high, the potential payoffs too low, and the political interests too insignificant to push the process forward. Ongoing structural economic reforms in North Korea complicate the decision-making environment and raise the cost of entry and exit for any Russian player interested in the exploration of the North Korean markets. ROK decision making and its own inter-Korean reconciliation and integration priorities and plans have a negative impact on the Russian–North Korean economic cooperation, as well.

The Russian government and private sector have therefore adopted a wait-and-see attitude toward various challenges and opportunities emanating from the Korean Peninsula. They prefer to wait until Korean unification as a way to manage geopolitical and business risks arising in the two Koreas. It is increasingly obvious that there will be neither Russian-sponsored construction of a railway or gas pipeline via the territory of the DPRK, nor any substantial Russian investments in the North Korean industry, until Korean reconciliation and reunification. Russia has no more money to throw into the "hermit money pit."

Debt Settlement (Can Wait)

The defaulted North Korean debt to Russia (about US$5 billion) is one of the obstacles to any major improvement in bilateral economic relations. Moscow has been reluctant to offer any kind of debt relief to Pyongyang, citing its obligations before the London and Paris Clubs and taking into account its own debt to the ROK (about US$1.47 billion), which could be offset by the North Korean debt obligations in the event of Korean reunification. However, Russia's restructuring of Syrian debt (Moscow forgave US$9.7 billion of a US$13 billion debt owed by Damascus, despite Washington's objections) may indicate a new willingness in the Kremlin, despite the objections of the Ministry of Finance, to forgo immediate economic benefit for the sake of substantial political influence and long-term geopolitical advantage. If such a new policy is applied to North Korea in the future, the chances of Kim Jong Il's regime muddling through successfully and surviving may increase significantly in the long run.

A Good Idea, to Be Promoted: Economic Reform

Many Russian Korea watchers praise the acceleration of the North Korean reforms and encourage more economic and humanitarian assistance and support from South Korea. Most Russians understand that the Dear Leader's regime is totalitarian in nature, and they do not particularly like it because they had their own terrible historical experience with Stalinist totalitarianism. But the Russian government is against any regime change through foreign intervention or "export of democratic revolution" to North

Korea. The ongoing economic liberalization and political decompression in Pyong-yang is likely to gradually soften up the regime beyond recognition, and with time the Kim clan is sure to pass away from the historical scene, thereby opening the floodgates of Korean unification. Russians stress that the process must unfold naturally, without foreign military intervention.

In the meantime, these domestic socioeconomic changes may contribute to increasing mutual trade and investment between the DPRK and Russia, which should be welcomed and encouraged by all means. Moscow is likely to continue its efforts to convince the North Korean leaders that domestic change is good, that it should not necessarily be threatening to their survival, and that the more open and market-oriented they become, the more benefits they are likely to receive in terms of the advancement of their economy, social welfare, and national security.

An Internal Matter: Improvement of Human Rights

Many Russian Korea specialists tend to dismiss American moralizing regarding Kim Jong Il's regime. They believe that the U.S. hard-line policy—embodied in adamant insistence on North Korea's unconditional unilateral nuclear disarmament and talk about "regime change," exemplified by the North Korea Human Rights Act of 2004—fortifies the siege mentality in Pyongyang, does no good for the human rights of ordinary North Koreans, and only strengthens Kim Jong Il's regime. Intensified international hostility around the DPRK simply allows the government to impose harsher security measures on the society, puts the KPA at the center stage of domestic politics at the expense of other social and political forces, drains productive resources away from economic reform and development, and increases popular support for and domestic legitimacy of Kim Jong Il. The specialists consider human rights to be an internal matter of the sovereign North Korean state and, by and large, none of Russia's business.

In general, Russia has rarely been concerned about the humanitarian situation in North Korea, especially famine, mass population migration, and human rights, and has never been a large humanitarian donor there. Part of this policy derives from history, including its own; part of it can be explained by ideological tradition; and part of it is rooted in biased policy analysis. Whatever the reasons for such humanitarian neglect, humanitarian aid and humanitarian involvement seem to be the least often used tools of Russian diplomacy on the Korean Peninsula, to the regret of Seoul and the measured delight of Pyongyang. The Kremlin does not give a penny about North Korea's economy or its people; it cares only about good working relations and mutual understanding with its leaders and its national security apparatus.

Local News: Curtailing Illegitimate North Korean Activities inside Russia

Russian local law-enforcement authorities occasionally have to deal with various criminal activities (for instance, counterfeit foreign currency, drug trafficking, human smuggling, inhumane treatment of labor, murder, espionage) linked to North Korean officials stationed in or transiting Russia, and North Korean migrant laborers employed in the timber sector, construction industry, transportation facilities, agriculture, and service businesses, especially in the Russian Far East. Although these incidents may get some coverage in the local press, they almost never get the attention or due consideration of the central government in Moscow.

We Hardly Care: The Recovery of Japanese Abductees

Russian officials believe that Kim Jong Il showed considerable goodwill during his September 2002 summit meeting with Japanese Prime Minister Koizumi by admitting the fact of and taking responsibility for the abduction of Japanese citizens by the DPRK's special security forces in the late 1970s and early 1980s. It was a difficult political decision for Kim domestically, because he had to cross his father, criticize his legacy, and put the blame on some parts of the security establishment; but he did it anyway in hopes of expediting the normalization of DPRK-Japanese relations. Regrettably, his courageous decision backfired in Japan, and Kim Jong Il had to pay a double price. Russian officials assume that now that Kim Jong Il has turned the page at a political level, the recovery of Japanese abductees is a purely technical matter that should be handled by experts.

However, Moscow also believes that the Japanese should be reasonable and refrain from repoliticizing and pushing their position on the abductions issue to the extreme, because North Koreans also have legitimate issues of historical justice to be settled with Japan. Russians share the North Korean negative view of Japanese colonial rule of Korea, which created deep scars and bitter memories in the Korean mind, as well as leaving the still-unresolved issues of symbolic significance (apology, return of cultural treasures), issues of practical value (compensation for property loss, damages, reparations, etc.), and issues of moral gravity (forced abduction of Korean labor, comfort women, and so on). But Russians care very little about the return of the remaining Japanese abductees and prefer to keep this whole issue away from the multilateral negotiation agenda with the DPRK.

MULTILATERAL PEACEFUL COOPERATION ON
NORTH KOREA–RELATED PROBLEMS

Despite the September 2005 statement of principles on Korean denuclearization, many Russian experts are relatively pessimistic about the prospects for the Six-Party Talks. They tend to predict a continuation of the status quo, which may be occasionally adjusted at the margins during the on-again, off-again rounds of slow negotiations, accompanied by the clandestine development of North Korean nuclear weapons.[20] They expect such multilateral talks to head slowly toward an unannounced death, like the unsuccessful four-party peace talks of 1997–99.

At worst, the experts predict a collapse scenario for the Beijing Six-Party Talks. In particular, these talks are believed to be a venue for both Washington and Pyongyang to buy time for further advancement of their respective "sinister aggressive plans" (vis-à-vis each other) and an opportunity to delegitimize their respective opponent in the eyes of the international community of nations: "See, we told you so. . . . We made concessions time and again, but they just refused to listen and compromise." At the end of the day, they expect that the United States may succeed in delegitimizing the North Korean regime in front of other participants, especially its Chinese partner.

Consequently, Russian experts believe that Washington may try to use the talks to form an ad hoc multilateral anti-DPRK coercive coalition of the "intimidated" (ROK and PRC), "the weak" (Russia), and "the greedy" (Japan) and may attempt to bring down the North Korean regime by intensifying blockades, increasing international pressure, and using force if necessary, thereby resolving the North Korean security crisis once and for all. They urge the Russian government to resist this trend. The Russian MOFA half-heartedly endorsed the Geneva talks, the four-party peace talks, and the KEDO mission in the DPRK throughout the 1990s, and expressed conditional diplomatic support for the three-party peace talks in Beijing in April 2003. Now Russia is actively participating in the six-party North Korean crisis resolution process. Its goal in the Beijing process is to be an "honest broker" that strives to achieve denuclearization of the Korean Peninsula, to facilitate the provision of credible assurances of mutual nonaggression and confidence-building measures across the DMZ, and to advance better governance based on democratic values and free markets in North Korea. But the reality is that Moscow is acting as a cheerleader for the Dear Leader in Beijing.

The Russian government seems to allow for the possibility of three scenarios developing on the Korean Peninsula in the wake of the Beijing process, namely, the "bad," "the ugly," and a "difficult one, but with a happy ending." The "bad" scenario would be the continuation of the current stalemate—"neither war nor peace"—with no one willing to make any compromises while the DPRK continues to slowly but steadily build up its nuclear arsenal to the displeasure of its neighbors. The "ugly" scenario would involve the complete breakdown of talks, followed by the escalation of tensions and a nuclear arms race with possible military hostilities on the horizon, which is hardly acceptable to Russia. Lastly, the "difficult scenario with a happy ending" would mean productive Six-Party Talks resulting in a "new package deal" opening the way for a nuclear-free zone on the Korean Peninsula with reliable security assurances for all states involved. Clearly, among the three possible approaches to the North Korean nuclear crisis mentioned above—inaction, confrontation, or engagement—Russia strongly favors constructive engagement, though it remains skeptical that either the United States or North Korea is fully committed to this process.

A MILITARY OPTION?

Some Russian military experts believe that, in contrast to Iraq or Yugoslavia, the United States lacks a fundamental economic or political interest in initiating a major war in Korea. There is no oil in the DPRK—it is poor, hungry, and underdeveloped (in the words of one expert, "there is nothing to plunder in the North"), and despite its official label of a "terror-sponsoring nation," Pyongyang is not known for extremist Muslim connections. Washington also does not want to have any serious trouble with Beijing at present. In addition, they consider Pyongyang's suspected "nuclear arsenal" and artillery forces located near the DMZ sufficient military deterrents, able to prevent a U.S. military attack against North Korea. Precision strikes from offshore bases alone are unlikely to resolve the Korean crisis, whereas Washington is clearly not interested in any protracted large-scale military conflict on the peninsula. Moreover, seeming American failure in rebuilding post-war Iraq has put a damper on any highly coercive U.S. options in Korea.

However, other military analysts argue that the United States could not care less about Korea, and if the Bush administration were to decide to attack the North preemptively, it would be mostly for domestic reasons and causes unrelated to the Korean Peninsula. In that case, Washington is not going to ask anyone's permission, including the United Nations, ROK, Russia, or even China, and is likely to strike first when the U.S. Forces Korea, U.S. Forces Japan, and augmentation forces are militarily and logistically ready for a major sustainable offensive operation. In their opinion, American war-planners are not afraid of Kim Jong Il's imaginary "nuclear deterrent," or of his rusting long-range artillery tubes. They are likely to carpet-bomb everything from nuclear facilities to Kim Jong Il's palaces, as they did in Iraq, and then parachute ROK special forces into all major North Korean cities and key installations in order to "reunite" the country from within. Given all these expert opinions that by and large allow for the possibility of war in Korea and in light of the escalating DPRK-U.S. confrontation, it is no wonder that in mid-August 2003, the Russian General Staff and Pacific Command conducted large-scale joint civilian and military exercises designed, among many other things, to test Russian operational response to the possibility of the outbreak of hostilities on the Korean Peninsula.

Whatever happens on the Korean Peninsula in the immediate future and in the years to come, it is clear that Russia's national security interests and its economic and political interests will be directly affected. Therefore, the Russian government seeks to pursue an active, balanced engagement policy vis-à-vis both Korean states through separate bilateral channels, within various multilateral frameworks, including the Six-Party Talks, and in cooperation with third parties, especially China.

To be sure, Russia is the only party to the Six-Party Talks that is not directly blackmailed by Pyongyang. It will not support any attempt by the North Korean leaders to blackmail Seoul in militarily aggressive terms, because of the counterproductive nature of such activities and because of Russian expanding national interests in the South. Nor will Moscow encourage any kind of head-on challenge by Pyongyang against Washington, because of the devastating consequences for the North and the highly destabilizing impact on all of Northeast Asia.

But Russia will remain receptive to Kim Jong Il's personal overtures and pleas for political, diplomatic, and military-technical support, and, possibly, expanded economic assistance. Although Russia will not deploy its forces, as it did during the Korean War, to defend Kim Jong Il, Moscow appears to be committed to providing enough spare parts for defensive weapons to Pyongyang to ensure the North Korean regime's "defensive self-sufficiency" and the restoration of the North's credible military deterrent capability. Russia is certain to withhold its support for any kind of coercive international coalition aimed at crushing militarily its North Korean friend and neighbor.

THE UNIFICATION OPTION

The Russian government seems to assume that a slow-moving process of Korean reintegration and eventual reunification was initiated at the historic inter-Korean summit on 15 June 2000. The process is rather unstable and erratic because of frequent fluctuations in North Korea's security position, financial difficulties and political squabbling inside the ROK, and the U.S. policy that seems designed to slow down Korean reunification. But, in this official view, the two Koreas are on their way to formal political unification, and the process, which reached the stage of "practical irreversibility," is likely only to accelerate in the years to come.

To position itself to benefit from its friendly and close relationship with whoever comes to power in a unified Korea, Russia strives to keep up the reunification momentum by creating an appropriate balance in its separate relations with Seoul and Pyongyang, mediating inter-Korean differences, and by hampering the further development of the inter-Korean processes in accordance with the perceived scenarios of mounting American domination, Japanese stonewalling, and further Chinese expansion.

Russia's basic principles toward the formation of a unified government in Korea are based on its own experience with democratic transition and lessons learned from Korean decolonization past. They are designed to prevent civil war, maintain internal stability and civil peace, protect law and order, and promote new policies and values desired by a new regime. They are as follows:

- Forgive and forget, rather than prosecute and punish the old party and military elites and security apparatus in the North.

- Share power with and, whenever possible, work through former local administrative elites on a regional and administrative basis, rather than install a colonial-style, hostile and alien southern administration or U.S.-led military rule in the North.

- Retire current North Korean political elites from public life and allow for new ones to form, to be proportionately represented with full political rights in a unified political system, as well as slowly but steadily reeducate and retrain the North Korean administrative and managerial classes.

- Facilitate early evacuation of Kim Jong Il and his family to one of the friendly neighboring countries to avoid unnecessary violence and secure a strategic advantage.

In general, many Russian academic experts believe that "the DPRK's unification formula, which calls for the creation of a neutral non-aligned unified state on the peninsula, looks more attractive from the standpoint of Russia's long-term security interests than South Korea's commitment to the U.S. military presence even after the reunification of Korea."[21] But they concede that, in the future, the more Seoul moves away from Washington and displays greater autonomy and independence in its foreign and security policies, the more incentives there will be for Moscow to shift from its "balanced policy approach" toward two Korean states in favor of a preferential relationship with the ascending Republic of Korea.[22]

A STRATEGIC PLAYER WITH LOW ECONOMIC STAKES

The Korean Peninsula still occupies a relatively minor place in Russian strategic thinking about Russia's national interests around the world, and in the Far East in particular. In that sense, the past is the future for Russia in Korea. The beginning of the 21st century is likely to resemble the turn of the 19th century. Russian interests on the Korean Peninsula seem to be predominantly strategic rather than economic. Russian-Korean relations are certain to be secondary and subordinated to Russian-American, Russian-Chinese, and Russian-Japanese relations in Northeast Asia. Further, the eccentricities of North Korea are part of the problem. If one looks at the Russia–South Korea economic exchange, one can see that it is still wanting (at about US$2.7–3.5 billion annual trade turnover only), despite the fact that both countries have open market economies. The problem is that Korea is a relatively small country with limited markets and resources that is located just too far away from main Russian economic and population centers. Besides, Russia simply has too little money to spend and invest on the peninsula, especially given its preoccupation with its own post-communist economic transition and glaring socioeconomic underdevelopment and underinvestment in Siberia and the Far East.

In the meantime, Russia seems to be content to play three roles in North Korea. First, Moscow offers a degree of international legitimacy to the North Korean leaders through periodic Putin–Kim Jong Il summits and other high-level exchanges. Second, Russia may serve yet again as a developmental model to emulate, demonstrating to Kim Jong Il how he can take his country from the Gorbachev-style political decompression and economic liberalization to Putin-style militocratic state monopoly capitalism, bypassing the Yeltsin-era plunder of national assets, political chaos and social destruction. Third, given Kim Jong Il's birthright to Russian citizenship, Russia can still provide physical protection to the DPRK's leaders in the event of emergency (like King Kojong's flight to the Russian legation in 1896–1897 to escape from Japanese prosecution), in order to ensure a bloodless transition and a friendly new government in a united Korea.

Russia is thus a strategic player with limited economic stakes in Korea. Both the maintenance of the existing status quo and unification are acceptable policy alternatives to Moscow, as long as Russian influence is preserved in Pyongyang and Seoul, and no other great power (either China or the United States) is able to establish its dominance over the entire peninsula, while the North-South reconciliation is rapidly intensifying and the U.S. influence is increasingly marginalized and neutralized.

NOTES

The views expressed in this article are personal views of the author, and they do not represent the official positions of the U.S. government, the Department of Defense, and the Asia-Pacific Center for Security Studies.

1. The Russian Foreign Policy Concept adopted by President Putin on 10 July 2000 states, "Russian government shall concentrate its efforts on ensuring Russian participation on the basis of the equality of rights in the resolution of the Korean problem and on maintaining balanced relations with both Korean states."

2. See Alexander Matsegora, presentation at the Joint Seminar on "Russian-American Partnership for Security on the Korean Peninsula," sponsored by the Carnegie Endowment for International Peace and the Moscow State Institute of International Relations (MGIMO) and held on 17 November 2004 at the Carnegie Moscow Center.

3. See Vladimir Dvorkin, "Russian Debate on the Nonproliferation of Weapons of Mass Destruction and Delivery Vehicles," discussion paper for the Belfer Center for Science and International Affairs, April 2004, p. 17. Major General (Ret.) Dvorkin is the head of research at the Center for Strategic Nuclear Forces, Russian Academy of Military Sciences.

4. See Georgi Bulychev, "Is There Any Prospects for the Negotiating Settlement of the 'Korean Crisis' in the Six-Party Format?" *Korus Forum*, nos. 11–12 (2003), p. 13.

5. See Gennady Evstafiev, "WMD Nonproliferation: Some Problems and Risks," *Nuclear Control* 10, no. 1 (71) (Spring 2004), p. 69.

6. See Yevgeni Primakov, "How Real Is a Nuclear North Korea?" minutes of a workshop held by Yevgeni Primakov at MGIMO, Moscow, in November 2003; *Russia in Global Affairs*, 18 February 2004, p. 2, at www.eng .globalaffairs.ru/printver/518.html.

7. See Andrei Grebenschikov, "Problem of the North Korean 'Challenge': View from Russia," *Nuclear Control* 10, no. 2 (Spring 2004), p. 115.

8. See Yuri Fedotov, "New Developments on the Korean Peninsula and Russia's Interests," *Issues of Security* 5, no. 17 (September 2001), pp. 7–8.

9. See Vladimir Dvorkin and Alexander Scherbakov, "North Korea's Missile Dreams," *Issues of Security*, no. 2 (March 2003), pp. 3–4.

10. See Grebenschikov, "Problem of the North Korean 'Challenge,'" p. 110.

11. See interview by I. I. Klebanov, Deputy Prime Minister of Russia, *ITAR-TASS*, Moscow, 28 February 2001.

12. See Alexander Zhebin, "Russia's Efforts for Reconciliation and Peace in Korea," a paper delivered at the Second World Congress of Korean Studies, Pyongyang, 3–7 August 2004, p. 4. Dr. Zhebin is director of the Center for Korean Research at the Institute of Far Eastern Studies, Russian Academy of Sciences.

13. See the Moscow Joint Declaration signed by President Putin and Chairman Kim Jong Il during the latter's historical train trip to Russia in August 2001.

14. See Valery I. Denisov, "Inter-Korean Settlement and Russian Interests," *International Affairs*, no. 1 (2002), pp. 59–60. Also see Valery E. Sukhinin, "Inter-Korean Reconciliation and Rapprochement: A View from Russia," paper presented at the APCSS conference on Korean Reconciliation held in Honolulu, Hawaii, on 1–3 March 2005.

15. See Anatoli Luchin, "About KEDO Activities," *Nuclear Control* 8, no. 5 (September-October 2002), p. 56.

16. The commission has held six annual sessions since its formation in 1998.

17. It is worth mentioning that in 2004, the Export-Import Bank of Korea began to finance South Korean exporters through Russian commercial banks. The ExIm Bank concluded an agreement with Rosbank for the US$30 million credit facility. It is also in the process of negotiations with Alfa Bank for a US$50 million loan.

18. During President Roh Moo Hyun's four-day trip to Russia, the two governments reportedly signed an agreement on space technology transfer. The agreement would allow the ROK to develop its own rocket to launch satellites into orbit and put one of the country's astronauts in space on a Russian spacecraft in the years to come. Russia also agreed to build a rocket-launch facility for civilian satellites in Goheung, South Jeolla province, in the ROK by 2007. See "Russia to Send South Korea Joint Satellite Project Proposal," *Asia Pulse*, 22 September 2004, and "Korea and Russia Agree on Space Launch Facility," *Joongang Ilbo*, 28 October 2004.

19. In 2000, Russia and ROK signed the intergovernmental agreement on energy cooperation. Following this agreement, Rusiya Petroleum (a TNK-BP-led consortium), South Korea's state-owned Korea Gas Corporation (Kogas), and the Chinese National Petroleum Company (CNPC) announced plans to construct a pipeline connecting Russia's Kovykta field to China's northeastern provinces and across the Yellow Sea to South Korea. The plan calls for a 1.2-Bcf-per-year pipeline that would deliver roughly two-thirds of its gas annually to China while delivering the rest to South Korea and, in smaller quantities, to the domestic market en route. The partners expect that the pipeline could come online in 2008.

20. See Primakov, "How Real Is a Nuclear North Korea?" p. 5.

21. See Zhebin, "Russia's Efforts for Reconciliation," p. 4.

22. See Grebenschikov, "Problem of the North Korean 'Challenge,'" p. 111.

PART SIX

Policy Implications for
the United States

16

The Korea-U.S. Alliance
A Problematic Future

William T. Pendley

Since the end of the Cold War, international politics has undergone a radical transition marked by globalization, the expansion of democracy, and increased dangers from nuclear proliferation and radical Islamic terrorism. Most of the former communist states have rushed to reform their failed political and economic systems and integrate with the world community and the global economic system. The most significant national security threats for the United States in this new era are the potential for the proliferation of weapons of mass destruction (WMD) to failing states or terrorist organizations, and radical Islam's support for terrorism across the wide crescent from North Africa to Southeast Asia.[1]

The survival of North Korea and a divided Korean Peninsula are legacies of the Cold War, as are the unresolved Chinese civil war and the backward regimes that cling to power in Cuba, Vietnam, and Laos. The Iron Curtain is but a pile of rusted scrap metal; most of the Warsaw Pact nations that once were isolated behind it are either in NATO or seeking to join it or the European Union. The national security threat posed by the superpower confrontation, with its proxy wars and nuclear weapon arms race, is now history. Despite being leftovers from another era, the unresolved Chinese civil war and the divided Korean Peninsula still have the potential to erupt with such force as to end a half-century of peace in Northeast Asia and to involve the United States in a major conflict that is not in its national interest.

The Korea-U.S. alliance was critical for ensuring the independence of South Korea and the maintenance of peace on the Korean Peninsula throughout the Cold War. The purpose and objectives of the alliance were clearly defined. To remain relevant over time, however, an alliance's purpose and objectives must support the current political, security, and economic interests of both parties at acceptable cost. With the end of the Cold War and the collapse of both the Soviet Union and the international support structure of the Pyongyang regime, many have come to question the future structure and role of the Korea-U.S. alliance.[2] Some even question its continued relevance or intrinsic value.

No matter what the preferences of the two parties, the future of the Korea-U.S. alliance will not be determined solely by the governments in Seoul and Washington. Quite probably, events beyond their control will shape the future of the alliance. This chapter will discuss five factors that will influence or determine the future of the alliance: (1) events in North Korea; (2) perceptions in South Korea; (3) South Korea–U.S. relations: (4) relationships with China; and (5) U.S. national priorities. The focus will be on potential scenarios and trends and their impact on the alliance's future. Finally, the steps that Seoul and Washington could take to strengthen and modernize the alliance, thereby helping preserve its relevance and value, will be examined.

FACTORS SHAPING THE ALLIANCE'S FUTURE

Events in North Korea

The North Korean leadership has faced some exceedingly difficult choices since the end of the Cold War and the collapse of its international support system. Despite its commitment to *juche,* or self-reliance, North Korea throughout its history has depended on external support for its survival. With the collapse of the Soviet Union and the normalization of China's relations with Seoul, external support for Pyongyang was greatly reduced. Additionally, there developed a widespread tendency in capitals around the world to write off the regime in Pyongyang as largely irrelevant and to predict its rapid exit from the world stage. To regain the external support it required, the North Korean regime had to restore its international relevance.

Initially the regime launched a diplomatic offensive designed to reduce tensions on the Korean Peninsula through agreements with Seoul that could open up renewed contacts with Tokyo and a dialogue with Washington. In 1990, the Korean People's Army (KPA) agreed to repatriate sixteen sets of war remains to a U.S. Congressional delegation visiting Panmunjom, as part of a renewed effort begun in 1985 to encourage bilateral contacts with the United States using the POW/MIA issue.[3] An Agreement on Reconciliation, Nonaggression and Exchange between the North and South negotiated in 1991 entered into force on 19 February 1992.[4] Pyongyang's objective through this warming period was to secure greater access to international assistance. It even acknowledged its severe food shortages and economic problems to gain increased humanitarian relief. North Korean diplomatic efforts met with some initial success from late 1989 through early 1992.

During the 1980s, Pyongyang had also continued the development of nuclear weapons, despite having ratified the Nonproliferation Treaty (NPT) in 1985.[5] As part of its diplomatic offensive, Pyongyang signed a joint denuclearization agreement with Seoul in 1991. It later concluded a Safeguards Agreement with the International Atomic Energy Agency (IAEA) and allowed international inspections of its declared nuclear facilities, including its reprocessing facility. While signing agreements reduced tensions and decreased international pressure, the effective implementation of those agreements was thwarted wherever possible. Known nuclear waste sites were concealed and not declared. North-South joint inspections of suspected nuclear facilities to implement the Joint Declaration for Denuclearization of the Korean Peninsula were never carried out by the Joint Nuclear Control Commission. The excuse was that IAEA inspections made such joint inspections unnecessary.[6]

Pyongyang erred, however, in believing that IAEA inspectors could be deceived as they had been in Iraq prior to the Gulf War. Soon it became obvious that this was a new IAEA, determined not to be embarrassed again.[7] Despite extensive North Korean efforts prior to inspections to clean up the nuclear facilities and doctor records, evidence was uncovered that records on reprocessing had been falsified and that the North was not fully accounting for reprocessed material. Access to known nuclear waste sites would have further verified both the falsifications and the extent of the reprocessing effort, so the North denied such access. Cooperation was drying up by late 1992 as the North attempted to conceal the extent of its nuclear weapons program.

By the end of 1992, Pyongyang's diplomatic offensive was failing to increase the level of international support. By early 1993, IAEA disclosures of North Korean deception were both embarrassing the regime and converting any prospects for increased aid into the potential for tougher international sanctions.[8] There were still some in the West and in South Korea who continued to doubt that the North had a nuclear weapons program, but their numbers were shrinking and their influence waning as evidence of the nuclear program mounted. North Korea's economic situation was also continuing to deteriorate, and its diplomatic offensive was turning into a disaster for the regime.[9]

In early 1993, Pyongyang's leadership sensed a possible opportunity to reverse its fortunes. It believed that new administrations in Seoul and Washington might possibly prove weaker than their predecessors. North Korea chose to test both, with a strategy of brinkmanship and crisis creation. It was not a totally new strategy, but one that had been tested before and would be used again. On 12 March 1993, Pyongyang suddenly declared that it was leaving the NPT and would be expelling the IAEA inspectors. As it so often does, it used the justification of being threatened by the United States, citing the Team Spirit military exercises of the Korea-U.S. alliance that had been routinely conducted for years.[10]

Brinkmanship proved more effective than even the North Korean leadership probably anticipated.[11] By generating a crisis atmosphere, Pyongyang produced pressure in Washington, Seoul, and Tokyo to rush to negotiations. Preconditions for negotiating sessions were routinely announced but promptly discarded each time as North Korea turned up the heat.[12] Sanctions were a hollow threat and not supported in the region.[13] With the visit of former President Carter to Pyongyang in June 1994, the Clinton administration had effectively lost control of the negotiating process.[14] In less than sixteen months Pyongyang had an agreement providing annual aid and two new light water nuclear reactors (LWRs), to be constructed and paid for primarily by South Korea and Japan. The agreement also allowed Pyongyang to retain its current nuclear facilities and stored reactor rods that could be reprocessed in the future. Most important, the lack of an immediate requirement for a full accounting of its reprocessed material or access to nuclear waste sites enabled North Korea to retain ambiguity about its longer-term nuclear intentions.

By refusing to include South Korea and Japan in the negotiations and placing the United States in the position of negotiating its allies' equities at the table, Pyongyang created strains in the Korea-U.S. alliance[15] and in the U.S. relationship with Japan.[16] The United States even provided a letter of guarantee that the North Koreans had demanded from President Clinton placing ultimate responsibility for fulfilling the agreement on the United States alone. Because the structure of the agreement was an Agreed Framework, it required coordinated mutual actions and thus tied the two parties together in continuing negotiations if implementation was to succeed. The North Korean leadership was astute in using this arrangement to extract additional aid throughout the life of the Agreed Framework.

The only real immediate requirements for North Korea were to freeze its nuclear program, retain the reactor rods in storage, discontinue all reprocessing activities, and allow international monitoring. At the time the agreement was reached, it was considered a buyout of the North Korean nuclear weapons program, though later it was more accurately described as a rental program requiring periodic payments. The Clinton administration tried to put the best face on the agreement by declaring that it had prevented a renewed Korean conflict, and some key officials rationalized that the North Korean regime would not survive the decade. The reality, however, was that brinkmanship and crisis creation had been a highly successful policy in increasing aid for North Korea, all the while allowing it to maintain its nuclear ambiguity and (in the absence of intrusive international verification arrangements) the opportunity to continue a clandestine nuclear weapons program.

Emboldened by its success, North Korea tore up most of what remained of the Armistice Agreement by unilaterally withdrawing in 1994 from the Military Armistice Commission (MAC). North Korea had refused since 1991 to deal with the South Korean Senior Member of the United Nations MAC delegation appointed by the commander of the United Nations Command (UNC), insisting instead on dealing only with U.S. general officers.[17] Once again its unilateral action resulted in success, as the United States and South Korea agreed to a new venue of four-party talks to address the issue of a peace treaty for Korea to replace the Armistice Agreement. These talks went nowhere, but they did allow Pyongyang to extract additional aid as the price for North Korean attendance.

During the 1990s North Korea not only reestablished its relevance but also largely called the shots in relations with Seoul, Washington, and Tokyo. With its economy still a basket case, it received significant infusions of international aid, including from Washington. Despite the difficulties faced by some U.S. friends and allies after the Asian financial crisis of 1997, North Korea was the United States' major aid recipient in Asia during the decade.[18] By 2001, however, Pyongyang's policies and strategy faced new challenges. Deadlines in the Agreed Framework for increased accountability and removal of the reactor rods were rapidly approaching if the LWRs under construction were to be completed. Additionally, intelligence gained from the breaking up of a global nuclear technology ring originating in Pakistan verified that Pyongyang continued to seek nuclear weapons through development of a uranium enrichment capability.

The election of a new administration in the United States resulted in an early review of Korea policy.[19] It was clear that the Bush administration would not provide aid to North Korea for merely showing up at meetings, but would insist on substantive progress in exchange for any future aid. No attempt was made to hide the contempt the new U.S. leadership held for the regime in Pyongyang, which it identified as part of the "Axis of Evil." The U.S. administration acted promptly to confront Pyongyang on the uranium enrichment program and, when that intelligence was confirmed, to cut off oil shipments under the Agreed Framework.[20]

Pyongyang's reactions to its new challenges were initially inconsistent. Given its judgment that the United States was deeply engaged in the Middle East and that the new hard-line policies of the United States toward Pyongyang were not supported in Seoul and possibly even in Tokyo, Pyongyang returned to the strategy of brinkmanship and crisis creation that had worked so well in 1993. It reactivated the mothballed nuclear reactor, removed the reactor rods from their storage ponds, and demanded increased aid and a formal nonaggression treaty for a mere return to a nuclear freeze. It claimed that between January and June of 2003 it had reprocessed the reactor rods "for peaceful uses."[21] Many in the United States and in Seoul and Tokyo reacted as they had before, pushing for the United States to immediately open bilateral negotiations with Pyongyang.

For a time it appeared that the North's policy would once again succeed. However, the new U.S. administration remained firm, insisting that any new negotiations be multilateral and any new agreement should require not merely a freeze but the complete, verifiable, and irreversible dismantlement (CVID) of North Korea's nuclear weapons programs. The lessons from 1993–94 and subsequent developments would not be ignored. North Korea rejected the U.S. position but, faced with increasing Chinese pressure, was forced to accept multilateral negotiations. The talks have since evolved from an initial trilateral meeting in Beijing to six-party talks, with working group meetings and direct meetings on the side between the U.S and North Korean representatives, culminating in a September 2005 declaration, signed by all six parties, to realize the goal of a denuclearized Korean Peninsula. The process would entail full disclosure of all of Pyongyang's nuclear weapons activities and the North's rejoining the NPT and IAEA, in exchange for various security and economic guarantees and the opportunity to participate fully in Northeast Asian politics, including normalized relations with both Washington and Tokyo. These are very grandiose goals, and it remains to be seen whether and how they will be achieved. But the United States and its partners at the talks have succeeded in making these multilateral commitments, thereby avoiding the trap of enabling North Korea to define the issue as a purely bilateral matter between Washington and Pyongyang.

The nuclear weapons issue and the related issue of ballistic missile development clearly remain central to future U.S.–North Korea relations. The U.S. concerns are not narrowly focused on security on the Korean Peninsula or even Northeast Asia but are global. The dangers of a successful North Korean nuclear weapons program are amplified by the nature of the regime and the economic condition of the country. The nightmare scenario is not a few nuclear weapons in North Korea but an active reprocessing or enrichment program that would allow Pyongyang to provide weapons-grade nuclear material to the highest bidder. The nature of the regime and its past record do not allow much faith to be put in any assurances that it would not provide such material to rogue states or terrorist organizations. Its desperate economic conditions are a strong incentive to sell whatever it can to whoever will buy for hard currency and energy resources.

The Korea-U.S. alliance has a high stake in the success of the current negotiations. If an agreement that ends the above nightmare scenario cannot be achieved through negotiation with positive incentives, and if North Korea continues its current nuclear weapons development, the United States will be forced at some point to act forcefully to prevent the worst case. There is a broad range of potential actions that the United States might employ, from increased sanctions through military strikes on known facilities. Any coercive option or combination of options that the United States might pursue must be strong enough to convince Pyongyang to give up its nuclear weapons program, with adequate verification, and abandon its brinkmanship strategy. For a coercive option to be adequate to achieve those objectives, it will also carry the risk of a renewed conflict on the Korean Peninsula.

No nation wants to see renewed warfare, and the North Korean regime would probably not survive such a conflict. Because of its inherent vulnerabilities in any war and past suffering, Seoul in particular seeks to maintain the peace at almost any price. Tokyo and Beijing fear being drawn into any renewed conflict. The United States recognizes that the use of force generated by unilateral American actions would be potentially disastrous for its relationships and alliances in Northeast Asia. However, if negotiations ultimately fail, Pyongyang may cross a "red line" that so directly threatens U.S. security that forceful action is required despite the clear potential for major adverse consequences. North Korean actions and U.S. reactions on the nuclear weapons issue thus could pose a significant threat to the Korea-U.S. alliance and to continued peace in Northeast Asia. Even the process of negotiations and the development of negotiating positions allow North Korea the opportunity to attempt to drive a wedge between Washington and Seoul and to damage the alliance.

The Korea-U.S. alliance is strongest when faced with a common threat that is acknowledged by both Seoul and Washington. Whenever there is no shared perception or acceptance of the threat, the alliance is weakened. A prolonged divergence of views between Seoul and Washington that reflects a conflict of their interests rather than a common interest on policy toward North Korea could end the alliance. North Korea's nuclear weapons issue is one that could create that result. Thus, North Korea's actions on this critical issue could determine the future of the Korea-U.S. alliance.

While North Korea's nuclear weapons program is the most pressing issue that could affect the future of the alliance, it is not the only area where future developments in North Korea may prove critical. There is always the possibility of internal change in North Korea, whether the change is positive or negative, peaceful or violent. Some argue that positive change is already under way in North Korea, while others maintain that change is not possible without removal of the regime. The internal and external pressures on the North make change inevitable, and attempts to resist change create their own dynamic.

The most optimistic scenario for future events in North Korea centers on a movement toward real reform that follows the example of China. There have been some tentative steps in that direction. To date, the depth and range of reform are far too shallow and much too narrow to confirm a real commitment by the leadership in Pyongyang. It will take far more than a few highly controlled showcase projects, such as the Tongil Market or the Kaesong free trade area, to establish a credible trend. It will require a more serious effort to welcome and protect foreign investment and to remove the restrictions on management-labor relations that have been imposed in the past. It will require major agricultural reforms. It will require an expansion of economic and personal freedom for the people of North Korea that the regime has never before tolerated. These are not impossible steps for a regime in Pyongyang to take, but they are difficult steps. If the regime can continue to extort direct cash payments, food aid, and energy assistance for attending negotiating sessions or summits and from projects like the Hyundai initiative and the POW/MIA recovery operations that involve no real reform efforts, they can delay the difficult decisions.

If events in North Korea move progressively toward attaining the optimistic scenario, the opening of the society to outside influences and the inevitable development of a broader middle class could reflect the experience of China. North Korea could move toward greater integration into the international community and a growing interdependence, which often leads to less aggressive foreign and national security policies. Such a scenario would also likely entail an expanded and mutually beneficial relationship with South Korea. With such a change in North Korea there is also the probability that the threat would actually diminish, or at least that tensions would be reduced to the point that threat perceptions would largely disappear.

The purpose of the Korea-U.S. alliance, from its inception, has been to contain and deter North Korea and allow the rebuilding and development of South Korea. U.S. policy toward North Korea after 1953 was largely a miniature version of the containment policy for the Soviet Union and China. By isolating and containing those regimes it was hoped that they would change their policies and integrate as positive players in the international community—or, failing that, that the regimes themselves would collapse. In both China and the Soviet Union the policies changed over time. In the Soviet Union, regime collapse also followed. If positive change takes place in North Korea and the optimistic scenario is achieved, U.S. policy and the Korea-U.S. alliance will have been a success. Such an outcome could make the alliance unnecessary or result in highly significant changes in the structure even if it continues.

There are also far less favorable scenarios for how events will evolve in North Korea. Even the optimistic reform scenario could end in violence or turmoil. A more probable scenario is that at some point there will be a regime change in the North. It could come about by natural causes, it could be the result of a coup d'état, or it could be an internal conflict between factions in the party and army seeking control during a leadership transition. Without a significant change in economic conditions, a revolutionary movement may emerge within the party, the army, or the society at large, producing a leader to challenge the regime. A North Korea plunged into chaos and factional violence could cause severe strains in the Korea-U.S. alliance. The United States would be reluctant to be drawn into a very dangerous and uncertain situation and fearful of possible Chinese reaction to such intervention as well. Moreover, the government in Seoul would be under much greater domestic pressure to intervene if its aid was sought by one faction or if there were widespread bloodshed and executions.

Short of a repeat of 1950, with a North Korean invasion or attack on the South (which is a highly improbable scenario), events in North Korea over the next decade are unlikely to strengthen the Korea-U.S. alliance. More probably, those events will cause significant strains and, coupled with other factors, could lead to a severing or severe weakening of the alliance. Even if the future in the North is largely a continuation of the status quo with a negotiated agreement reached on the nuclear weapons issue, North Korea can be expected to attempt at every opportunity to weaken or break the alliance. Because of its success in the past, Pyongyang should be expected to continue attempting to establish a bilateral relationship with Washington that marginalizes Seoul, or, conversely, playing on concerns held by many in South Korea about the dangers of a war caused by unilateral U.S. actions.

Perceptions in South Korea

Regardless of how events may actually transpire in North Korea, the future of the Korea-U.S. alliance will also be shaped by the perceptions and attitudes of the South Korean people. How they interpret events in the North, as well as actions by the U.S. government in response to those events, will directly affect their level of support for the alliance. The conclusions they reach on the principal threats to their own peace and prosperity will play out in the domestic politics of the nation. The people of South Korea live today in peace and at a level of prosperity and personal freedom unequaled in their history. Such conditions tend to reinforce support for low-risk strategies. Over half a century after the Korean War, many South Koreans tend to discount the North Korean threat.[22] Some even believe that the North would not use nuclear weapons against the South.[23] This assumption appears naive to those who remember the horrors committed against people in the South during the 1950 North Korean invasion, or to those aware of the repression Pyongyang imposes on its own people. Perceptions often develop, however, with the ability to block out contrary facts and historical experience. The perception of a North Korean threat is a necessary foundation for the Korea-U.S. alliance. Without such a threat, it is difficult to justify either the presence of U.S. forces in South Korea or the continuation of the alliance.

The older generation that lived during the Japanese occupation and the Korean War remains grateful for an America that liberated the nation twice and assisted in its rebuilding. That generation continues largely to support the alliance, but it is passing from the scene. Politics is increasingly dominated by those born in the 1950s or even later, with no memory of the earlier period. As a result, many share a far different perception of America's role in Korea. They blame the United States for the division of Korea and believe that the United States continues to support a divided Korean Peninsula.[24] They hold America responsible for the military rule that they lived under from the 1960s to the late 1980s.

Like all perceptions, there is a grain of truth to these views. The United States did initially support the division of Korea for purposes of accepting the Japanese surrender, and it did prevent the North Koreans from unifying the peninsula by force in 1950–53. Of all the major powers in the region, however, the United States has been the strongest advocate of a unified democratic Korea. By contrast, China provides a safety net for North Korea to assure its survival as a buffer state. While other neighbors give lip service to unification, they are concerned that a unified Korea will once again become the object of regional competition for influence. While the United States did support the military leadership of South Korea during the Cold War when an effective democratic alternative did not appear possible, it was the United States that pushed for respect for human rights and the political transition that resulted in the democratic political system that is in place today.[25] The United States has unfortunately not made its case convincing enough to eliminate the negative perceptions held by large numbers of the younger generations.

The Korean people are a proud people with a long history. No population wants to see foreign troops based in its country unless absolutely necessary. Given the location of U.S.

military bases in some former Japanese facilities and the growth of bases during and after the Korean War, the U.S. military presence has remained widespread and highly visible, even in the heart of Seoul. The U.S. domination of the military command structure of the Korea-U.S. alliance and attempts to maintain effective operational control of South Korean troops over half a century after the Armistice Agreement has reinforced the negative perception held by many.[26] All these factors strengthen for some the perception that the alliance is a one-way street designed more to benefit U.S. interests than Korean interests.

There is anti-Americanism in South Korea, though it waxes and wanes with events.[27] There are the infrequent but highly damaging cases of misconduct by American servicemen that take place off base and are highlighted in the Korean press. There are automobile and training accidents. Even routine training exercises often affect the daily lives of Korean citizens. There are a percentage of "ugly Americans" who visit or are stationed in Korea. There are even senior visitors who make derogatory remarks about the country, its people, or its culture in the back seats of sedans driven by KATUSA (Korean Augumentation to the U.S. Army) drivers. Because their drivers are Korean, visitors may forget that most have some college education and clearly understand English. The driver will probably not forget the comments, and his perception of Americans suffers. Many American servicemen and servicewomen and others offset some of the anti-Americanism by working hard in communities and in their relationships with individual Koreans to make a difference during their time in Korea.

South Korean perceptions are not framed just by experience but are influenced by family and associates, one's education, and what is read and seen in the press and other media. Some of these influences are positive for Americans, the alliance, and U.S. policy, but many are not. While North Korean propaganda has never been highly effective in the South, it has been able to exploit and reinforce negative perceptions generated from events or other sources. The American media, which seldom portrays a positive image of the United States, its policies, or its leadership, is widely watched and read in South Korea. The impact of the "CNN factor" on U.S. foreign policy decisions is often discussed in the United States. By contrast, seldom discussed or recognized is the damage done to U.S. interests abroad by the influence of the adversary culture on U.S. media and its negative reporting on the United States, its policies, and its leadership.[28]

South Koreans generally admire America for its democratic traditions, personal freedoms, and economic success, even while at times disagreeing with the policies the United States pursues. Polls underline that admiration even when they oppose a specific policy, as in the case of the war in Iraq. Many have been educated in the United States, have traveled there, or have relatives there, which gives them a far better understanding of the United States and its people than Americans have of Korea. All these factors help to shape South Korean perceptions of the Korean-U.S. alliance and its value to them. The two most important factors in shaping that perception will be South Koreans' analysis of the threat and their assessment of whether U.S. strategy and policy result in the alliance's protecting their peace and prosperity or putting it at unnecessary risk. South Korean perceptions thus may support or oppose the Korea-U.S. alliance in the future, and U.S. actions will be a major factor in determining the outcome. This requires a high degree of sensitivity in the formation of strategy and implementation of policy in East Asia and close coordination with the South Korean government, both of which have often been lacking in the past.

U.S.–South Korea Relations

U.S.–South Korea relations cover a wide range of economic, security, and political areas, but the military alliance has been the critical cornerstone of the relationship, with security issues dominating the relationship over more than half a century. But the economic development of South Korea has assumed an increasing importance in bilateral relations. South Korea is now a major trading partner of the United States, and, in many cases, a significant economic competitor. Economic disputes, therefore, have the potential to damage the overall relationship. In the aftermath of the Asian economic crisis of 1997 and the collapse of large *chaebols*, militant Korean unions have protested the breakup and acquisition of companies. U.S. firms have been involved in some of those acquisition disputes, as recently demonstrated in the Citibank takeover of AmKor Bank. Some in Korea also believe that the United States has attempted to take advantage of the Korean economic problems and failed to step forward with more help for Korea in the 1997 economic crisis.

The political relationship has at times also been difficult. There has been a lack of chemistry between the new democratic political leaders in Seoul and American administrations. There were open rifts with the Kim Young Sam administration during the negotiations of the Agreed Framework. The emphasis of Kim Dae Jung on the Sunshine Policy and the steps taken in implementation of that policy were often not wholeheartedly supported by the United States.[29] The continued disagreements between the Roh administration and the Bush administration over policy toward North Korea are widely known.

With the evolution of democratic government in Seoul, public opinion is now a major factor in determining Seoul's policies. While there were human rights issues during the period of military rule, economic and political differences could often be muted by the security relationship. Public opinion was highly controlled and manipulated. Ironically, the very success of U.S. policy and of the Korea-U.S. alliance in fostering and protecting the emergence of a democratic, peaceful, and prosperous South Korea has complicated the bilateral relationship. However, the South Korean government has been a reliable ally for the United States during difficult times. It stood with the United States during the Vietnam War, and it has been a reliable ally in the war on terrorism and the Iraq conflict. Unlike Spain and the Philippines, it has stood firm in maintaining its troops in Iraq even in the face of the kidnapping and killing of a young South Korean citizen by terrorists.

The U.S.–South Korea relationship has, over time, been a very positive one. When there are strains in the relationship, they generally reflect a lack of coordination prior to one side or the other's taking unilateral actions. The security relationship has a far more robust, institutionalized system of routine consultation and coordination than the political and economic relationships. This system has enhanced the Korea-U.S. alliance and strengthens it even during periods of political or economic strain. There will continue to be differences over economic relations, strategy in dealing with North Korea, modernization of the military relationship, and specific elements of both U.S. and South Korean foreign policy. These do not appear to be insurmountable problems, nor will they threaten the future of the Korea-U.S. alliance as long as there is established a strong system of consultation and coordination.

Relations with China

Chinese diplomacy has been extremely active around the nation's periphery for more than two decades. These efforts have been geared to resolving outstanding territorial issues, reinforcing peace and stability, and increasing Chinese influence. Chinese diplomacy has supported the priority Chinese objective of economic development by working to reinforce a stable and peaceful regional environment in which the economy could grow. That diplomacy has been very effective throughout the region and has enhanced the Chinese influence on the Korean Peninsula.[30] China is the only nation that has significant influence in both Seoul and Pyongyang.[31]

With North Korea, China has maintained a basic safety net of economic and international support that has ensured the survival of the regime as a buffer state during a difficult period for Pyongyang. While China's aid may be indispensable and provides leverage, China's influence is not unlimited, since the withdrawal of that aid could produce the very conditions of turmoil and chaos it is designed to prevent. China encourages reform and accommodation in North Korea that serve Chinese national interests, but it cannot dictate policy in Pyongyang.

China is also very careful not to position itself between the two Koreas and thus reduce its influence in either Seoul or Pyongyang. This has proved difficult at times, with the problem of refugees and defectors who flee North Korea through China. When placed in a situation that potentially positions it between North and South, China has usually been astute in handing off the issue to the Korean parties and accepting their resolution. In the 1993 nuclear weapons crisis, China was quick to reject U.S. requests to take the initiative and instead moved to the sidelines, forcing the United States to take the leading position in negotiations with North Korea. In the renewed nuclear crisis, however, China's involvement at all levels has been much more direct and hands-on, underscoring the risks to China's larger interests.

In its ties with Seoul, Beijing has created a positive atmosphere that has facilitated a mutually beneficial economic relationship. South Korea has provided capital investment and technology transfer to China, and trade has flourished for both countries. Both nations favor low-risk strategies in dealing with issues that have the potential to generate renewed conflict on the Korean Peninsula. Both favor a nonnuclear Korea. Both tend to discount any North Korean threat more than either Japan or the United States. Both share concerns about the potential for the future expansion of military roles by Japan. China by its nonthreatening posture enjoys a very positive image in South Korea that is reinforced by a wide spectrum of common interests.[32] Thus, China has positioned itself well on the Korean Peninsula. It has maintained a buffer state in North Korea at limited cost and with international assistance. At the same time, it has developed a strong positive relationship with Seoul. That relationship is economically beneficial but also ensures continuing Chinese influence if North Korea should collapse or unification be achieved.

China's relationship with the United States is more complex and thus a greater challenge for Chinese diplomacy. Despite periodic tensions and mutual wariness, relations have recovered from the low point of the EP-3 incident of 2001[33] and the sobering Taiwan Strait confrontation of 1996. The history of U.S.-China relations since 1949 could be characterized as America's "Long March," with long periods of struggle, including even a conflict in Korea, interspersed with brief interludes of relaxation and cooperation.[34] China is currently cooperating in the war on terrorism and while not supporting the war in Iraq has generally not obstructed U.S. efforts there or at the United Nations. China has its own concerns with radical Islamic support for terrorism, given the vulnerability of its Islamic minority living under Han domination in various areas of the country.[35] Despite U.S. objections, it has also tried to disguise its crackdown on legitimate dissent as part of the war on terrorism.

Unlike in the nuclear weapons crisis of 1993, China has taken a leading role in negotiations with North Korea during the current crisis. China and the United States share a common interest in a nuclear weapon–free Korea without a ballistic missile capability. While the interests are common, the motivations are very different. U.S. motivations relate primarily to proliferation. China does not want to see nuclear weapons in Korea for quite different reasons. First, such a development could lead Japan to seek nuclear weapons and its own deterrent force. Second, there is the clear danger that if North Korea were to continue its nuclear weapons program the United States could take forceful action, leading to a renewed conflict in Korea. China would not be able to avoid the costly consequences of such a war even if it avoided being directly drawn into the conflict. At a minimum, it could expect a massive humanitarian crisis created by refugees fleeing to northeast China. Missile development by North Korea reinforces the rationale for missile defense systems in the United States and Japan that could undermine the effectiveness of China's limited nuclear deterrent. Expanded deployment of missile defense systems in Japan and the United States could force a greatly increased investment in expanding its deterrent force, which China does not want to undertake.

China and the United States, as major exporting nations, also share a common interest in the health of the international economic system. Despite that common interest, there are growing tensions in the U.S.-China economic relationship. China is now the largest factor in the U.S. trade deficit, with the imbalance likely to approach or even surpass $200 billion in 2005. China's economic growth and growing demand for oil is a major factor in current high energy costs. China's demand is driving up the cost of all major commodities at the same time it is driving down the costs to consumers of most manufactured goods. This squeeze threatens U.S. manufacturers. China is now the leading producer of steel in the world and is beginning to move into many high-technology areas. On the positive side, China's domestic market is now becoming a major engine of growth and China is a major investor in U.S. treasuries that support the current U.S. deficit at very low interest rates. These factors encourage continued U.S. pressures on China to revalue its currency, and this is likely to remain a highly contentious issue between both countries.[36]

While economic issues may strain the U.S.-China relationship, the pivotal issue in the relationship is always Taiwan. Economic issues can generally be resolved through the World Trade Organization (WTO) or bilateral negotiations, but the United States has been in the middle of the unfinished Chinese civil war for over half a century with no satisfactory solution in sight. The United States, as the guarantor of Taiwan's de facto independence, virtually stands alone in preventing the return of Taiwan to Chinese sovereignty. Over the last decade, the United States sold over twenty billion dollars in military equipment, including the sale of 150 F-16 fighters, to Taiwan. Washington's argument that such sales give Taipei the confidence necessary to negotiate with Beijing rings hollow in Beijing, where American support for Taiwan is considered to strengthen the independence movement on the island.

Most nations in Asia, including the U.S. allies in South Korea and Japan, do not want to see a conflict triggered over the issue of Taiwan's independence. At the same time, these same nations rely on the United States to restrain the parties on both sides of the Taiwan Strait. This task has become increasingly difficult since the return of Hong Kong and Macao to China and with the growth of Taiwanese nationalism on the island. The Taiwan issue could destroy the U.S.-China relationship, despite the best efforts of both China and the United States. Korea (despite its impressive economic development and political progress) remains a smaller fish in a Northeast Asia pond filled with large sharks. It has no interest in seeing a breakdown of U.S.-China relations, or even worse, a conflict over the future of Taiwan. U.S.-China relations therefore have the potential to negatively affect the future of the Korea-U.S. alliance if those relations should collapse or become severely strained while South Korea continues to enjoy good relations with Beijing.

China is indeed the Middle Kingdom in the security equation in Northeast Asia. China's role will be a major factor in the future of the Korean Peninsula. That role will be guided primarily by Chinese national interests but will also be influenced by its evolving relationships with North Korea, South Korea, and the United States. If South Korea and the United States effectively manage their relationships with China and keep each other fully informed on the status of the relationship, their alliance should be largely unaffected. If, however, the parties fail in the management of their relationships with China or act unilaterally without consultation, the alliance could be endangered.

U.S. National Priorities

Another major factor that could affect the future of the Korea-U.S. alliance is a shift in U.S. national priorities. There is no doubt that U.S. national security interests are focused on preventing further proliferation of weapons of mass destruction and defeating—or, at a minimum, protecting the United States and its interests from—the threat of radical Islamic terrorism. Korea remains important at this time to U.S. national security interests primarily because of the potential threat of proliferation posed by the North Korean nuclear weapons program. Deterrence and containment of North Korea, which have been the main purpose of the Korea-U.S. alliance, remain important in the current context but have not been successful in preventing the North Korean nuclear weapons program. Some could even argue that the more isolated and surrounded Pyongyang feels, the more paranoid and desperate it becomes. In dealing with the North Korean nuclear weapons issue, the United States may begin to distance itself from the Korea-U.S. alliance. This could be the case in the event of successful negotiations or if the United States determines that it must take unilateral actions that the alliance will not support.

The alliance could be viewed as imposing more restraint on the United States than on North Korea. Critics could argue that while the North Korean threat is becoming more serious and the North Koreans are moving forward with proliferation activities, U.S. hands are tied by the alliance. Some have been convinced for some time that South Korea, with twice the population and many times the economy of the North, should be capable of providing for its own national defense.[37] If South Korean support or efforts seem inadequate and the Korea-U.S. alliance seems no longer to benefit changing U.S. security interests, pressures could mount for a radical restructuring of the alliance, including the removal of the U.S. military presence in South Korea or a termination of the alliance.

The alliance structures and deterrence and containment policies that worked so well in the cases of the Soviet Union and China were implemented with a degree of imagination and flexibility that probably accounts for their success. Except for a brief period from 1989 to early 1992, no such imagination and flexibility mark recent U.S. policy with respect to Korea. Whatever changes in policy have taken place have been in response to North Korean unilateral actions or forced by initiatives in Seoul. An alliance that fails to adjust to the new realities on the Korean Peninsula may not survive.

More threatening to the future of the alliance would be an American public that grows weary of its international responsibilities and engagement. The world is far more messy and dangerous in this new era than during the Cold War. Americans tend to want quick fixes for problems and rapid disengagement with limited costs. Its long-term commitments in Korea, Japan, and Germany at the end of conflicts there might appear to be exceptions, but those commitments were not costly in human terms, and even the financial costs were shared by others. The Persian Gulf War is the type of brief military conflict and commitment that Americans support. Both the economic and human costs were limited and again shared by others. By contrast, Korea and Vietnam became unpopular wars as the costs rose and victory in the traditional sense proved elusive. America steered clear of Rwanda and Bosnia, where the risks seemed high, and quickly withdrew from Somalia as the costs mounted.

Despite the rapid initial U.S. military success, the liberation of the Iraqi people, the removal of Saddam Hussein, and the establishment of a provisional Iraqi government that is actively trying to establish a democracy while fighting terrorists and remnants of the Baathist regime, American media routinely characterize intervention in Iraq as a failure. Some even try to compare Iraq to U.S. involvement in Vietnam, though the comparison is highly forced. The United States and Iraq are bearing the major costs of both military operations and the rebuilding of Iraq. With the exception of Great Britain, there has been no substantial sharing of human and economic costs by major U.S. allies, even in the rebuilding and stabilization phase. With no WMD discovered in Iraq, the lack of substantial support from some major European allies, and continuing U.S. casualties, public support for the intervention in Iraq has declined significantly. This result, while not surprising, is disappointing in view of the fact that the liberation of Iraq and the establishment of a representative government in Iraq could change the strategic geography in the Middle East. The liberation of twenty-five million Iraqis is, by itself, the most significant human rights achievement since the collapse of the Iron Curtain.

Regardless of the final outcome in Iraq or the results of the offensive strategy under way against terrorist sanctuaries, attacks by radical Islamic terrorists will continue. There will also undoubtedly be additional terrorist attacks within the United States or against U.S. interests abroad. A nation that is a major trading state and also a diverse and open society that values its civil rights and individual rights of privacy cannot eliminate all vulnerability to such attacks. At some point it is quite possible that the American people, disgusted by the lack of support and efforts of others internationally, will turn inward, devoting both their resources and their technology to implementing a fortress-America type of strategy. Such a response would trigger a major disengagement abroad that could end the Korea-U.S. alliance.

The domestic situation in the United States could be another major influence.[38] After the Cold War, the American people yearned for and expected a period of relaxation to address domestic issues. As the Cold War ended they had faced a recession and there were mounting concerns about health care, social security, public education, Medicare, an aging physical infrastructure, high deficits, and the ability to remain economically competitive in a global economy. Economic growth returned in the 1990s and temporarily erased the deficits, but the other issues were not seriously addressed, and when the economic bubble burst at the end of the 1990s, recession returned in 2000. Even as the economy has again partially recovered, the same issues persist, especially with the renewed ballooning of the federal deficit and mounting pressures to address problems at home. Thus, in future years, domestic priorities may top the agenda of most

Americans.[39] Disengagement and a defensive strategy may be increasingly appealing, and support for continued U.S. commitments abroad may significantly decline. Such a shift in U.S. national priorities would threaten the Korea-U.S. alliance.

The United States today is a deeply divided nation politically, with no agreed national strategy in place.[40] The new era is not a comfortable one for America. Because of the fundamental change in the security threats that the United States faces and the continuing domestic issues that need to be addressed, a major review of American strategy and priorities cannot be avoided much longer. The new strategy that emerges and the national priorities that it sets will affect not only the Korea-U.S. alliance but America's relations around the globe.

BUILDING A FIRMER FOUNDATION FOR THE ALLIANCE

The underlying assumption of this chapter is that the Korea-U.S. alliance remains valuable to Seoul and Washington and that both countries want to sustain the security relationship in the future. The challenge is whether policies can be implemented and the alliance can be modernized to offset those factors that work against its survival. The alliance value is not only found in its crucial underpinning of deterrence against any rerun of North Korean aggression. Its larger strategic value is as a foundation for a positive U.S.-Korea relationship in the decades ahead.

Events in North Korea are not controllable by Seoul and Washington, but their reactions to those events are. Given the current nuclear weapons issue and the countless scenarios that may unfold in North Korea, it is absolutely essential to improve the coordination of policies. Merely improving routine consultation, while necessary, is inadequate. The two nations cannot be involved in multilateral negotiations that are using the lure of economic assistance as a major incentive to end North Korea's nuclear weapons program while at the same time one party concludes a bilateral agreement on more secondary issues that provides much needed assistance to Pyongyang. While aid may have been appropriate during the period when Pyongyang was within the NPT and abiding by the provisions of the Agreed Framework, it is not appropriate given North Korea's current policies and withdrawal from both agreements. These are matters for both countries to address fully and frankly with one another.

If the Korea-U.S. alliance is to be strengthened, it is imperative that consultations and coordination not just be a preparation for negotiating sessions. There must be consultations to determine what should be the coordinated political, economic, and military responses to the wide range of policies and scenarios that may develop in North Korea.[41] Without such a level of consultation and coordination there will continue to be ad hoc responses taken in Washington or Seoul that undercut both support for the alliance and potential progress in broader negotiations with Pyongyang.

South Koreans' perceptions of the alliance will be more positive if they see the evidence of increased consultation and coordination between Seoul and Washington. Support of the Korea-U.S. alliance will also require the political leadership in Seoul to stand firm when required. Seoul cannot continue to force the United States to play "bad cop" to its "good cop" in all dealings with North Korea. The United States will also need to accept that as a price for the long-term health of the alliance, there will be restraints on U.S. options in dealing with North Korea.

Another major influence on South Korean perceptions will be the readiness of the United States to alter the command structure of the military alliance and reduce the footprint of American forces in Korea. There are initiatives in the Future of the Alliance discussions under way between the ROK Ministry of National Defense and the U.S. Department of Defense to move along that path, and these initiatives will need to become realities. As Secretary of Defense Rumsfeld has repeatedly emphasized, deterrence is based not on numbers but on capabilities. It is also based on the shared sense of common cause in the alliance, which must be demonstrated by the close consultation and coordination of the parties.

Because of the dangers on the Korean Peninsula, U.S.-South Korean relations take on an importance that would not normally be justified with a state the size of South Korea. The stakes make it important that high-level U.S. government officials traveling to Northeast Asia visit Seoul when traveling to Tokyo or Beijing. While security interests may be at the heart of the relationship, smooth economic and political relations are also extremely important in reinforcing the value of the alliance. Extensive consultation and coordination at all levels can help avoid contentious political and economic issues, or at least mitigate their fallout on support for the alliance.

In the management of the trilateral U.S.–China–South Korea relationship, it is important for Washington not to view a close Beijing-Seoul relationship as threatening to the Korea-U.S. alliance. In many ways just the opposite is true. The closer the Beijing-Seoul relationship, the more probable it is that China will use its influence to restrain North Korea, which is consistent with the purposes of the alliance. Any effort to approach the trilateral relationship as a competition for influence in Seoul or a zero-sum game will likely backfire. Such an effort places Seoul in an impossible situation that will not strengthen the alliance.

Seoul needs to review its own national history to break through some of the euphoria that often characterizes its view of China. Just as it historically has sought to maintain predominant influence in Korea to hold off Japanese, Russian, or other outside influences, China seeks to attain the same position today. There are consistencies in Chinese national interests in Korea that will not always reflect Korea's best interests. At the same time, South Korea needs to maintain its positive relationship with China to ensure its own political, economic, and security interests.

U.S. relations with China will continue to have a major effect on developments in Korea. A positive relationship facilitates cooperation on dealing with issues related to North Korea. Likewise, a positive U.S.-China relationship tends to be a restraining factor on unilateral actions by all three parties to the Taiwan Strait confrontation. Successful management of its relationship with China and specifically the Taiwan issue is the greatest challenge that the United States faces in the region. The potential for a conflict over the future of Taiwan poses a great danger to U.S.-China relations and to U.S. relations throughout East Asia, including the Korea-U.S. alliance.

Since the early 1970s the policy of containment for China has been replaced by a strategy of engagement, with the objective of peacefully integrating China into the international system as a positive player. Because of the uncertainty of China's future role, the U.S. strategy has been a hedging strategy that emphasizes engagement while also strengthening existing alliances in East Asia.[42] If the future relationship is characterized by cooperation and competition rather than confrontation, the U.S. strategy for China will have been a success.[43] South Korea, like most nations in East Asia, remains hopeful that that will be the case, and the future of the alliance with the United States would benefit from such an outcome.

MODERNIZING THE ALLIANCE

Two major considerations must be included in any plans to modernize the Korea-U.S. alliance for the 21st century. The first is the absolute requirement to maintain deterrence and the capability to fight and win any renewed conflict on the Korean Peninsula. The second is to fashion an alliance that will promote a long-term positive relationship between the United States and Korea. For effective deterrence, it is critical that Pyongyang recognizes that it will be defeated and the regime will not survive if a new conflict erupts in Korea. Deterrence is not based on the number of U.S. troops in South Korea. Maintaining a U.S. force structure on the ground in South Korea is an important message of commitment that reinforces deterrence, but the numbers are not the measure of deterrence. The overall capability of the South Korean armed forces and U.S. forces to prevail in any new conflict is what deters. Deterrence is enhanced by U.S. air and naval power and its long-range strike capability. Deterrence is demonstrated in joint and combined exercises and further enhanced by the capability for rapid reinforcement and logistics support. Most important, deterrence is made credible by the strength of the bonds within the alliance. This is one of the reasons that Pyongyang's policies so often attempt to sever those bonds.

Announced plans to move a forward element of the I Corps staff to Japan, the repositioning of some selected U.S. forces to Guam, and the activation of missile defense batteries in Alaska all reinforce deterrence in Korea. Key facilities in Japan, including air and naval forces and the U.S. Marine presence, support deterrence. The integration of air and missile defense systems in Japan is also a part of the deterrence equation. The qualitative improvements of South Korean, U.S., and Japanese forces demonstrate a clear intention to prevail in any new conflict on the Korean Peninsula. Deterrence is robust, and it is critical that it remain unquestioned and undiminished.

Some question why it is necessary or prudent to reduce U.S. troop levels, return bases to the South Korean government, and revise the command structures in the alliance. The answer is simple, yet extremely important. If the U.S. seeks a long-term positive relationship with Korea, it is essential to update the alliance, which has had no major revision in the military structure since 1978. It is important to implement the U.S. transition from a leading role to a supporting role in the military alliance similar to the role it has in its alliance with Japan. By that transition the United States recognizes the changes on the Korean Peninsula and that South Korea is quite capable of providing for its own defense with the support of the United States.

The vast majority of military forces within the Combined Forces Command (CFC), which is the war-fighting command, are Korean. CFC should be commanded by a South Korean general officer, who should also be the designated Ground Force Commander. There is arrogance in the often present but unstated assumption that the South Koreans are incapable of assuming the leading role in maintaining their own security. Rejecting that arrogance and transitioning from a leading to a supporting role in the security alliance is a critical step for Washington in building the foundation for a long-term positive relationship with Korea.

Given that North Korea has unilaterally torn up the Armistice Agreement and left the Military Armistice Commission (MAC), it is time to deactivate the United Nations Command (UNC) and give the South Korean government responsibility for maintaining the cease-fire along the fortified frontier that masquerades as a Demilitarized Zone (DMZ). The cease-fire and DMZ are all that really remain of the Armistice Agreement reached at the end of the Korean War.

The deactivation (rather than disestablishment) of the UNC would allow its reactivation at any time by the U.S. government as the Executive Agent for the UN Security

Council, without any formal action by the UN Security Council. The Commander, U.S. Army Pacific (USARPAC), as a four-star billet, could be the designated UNC Commander, who would take overall command of the Korean theater in the event of a renewal of hostilities. The UNC could be routinely reactivated for major exercises to ensure that any transition in command would be smooth and the capability for rapid reinforcement maintained. The South Korean commander of the CFC would be designated the Deputy UNC Commander responsible for the maintenance of the cease-fire. If North Korea agrees at some point to return to the MAC, the UNC element of the MAC could also be reinstated.

The designation of Commander USARPAC as the UNC Commander when activated would allow concentration on planning the strategy and execution of a theater campaign for any renewed conflict on the Korean Peninsula and on the planning for critical reinforcement and logistics support. At the same time, this commander's rank and position would increase his prestige in the Asia-Pacific region, allowing him to exercise a more important role in the interface with armed forces' leaders in the region. While U.S. military power in the U.S. Pacific Command is largely air and naval, most of the military leadership in the region is army. Giving an enhanced position to the Commander U.S. Army, Pacific should enhance U.S. military-to-military relationships and U.S. influence on security matters.

More than formal changes in the command structure of the CFC and UNC are required to achieve a genuine U.S. transition from a leading to a supporting role. Roles and missions within the alliance need to be clearly defined and assigned. South Korea's role should be to provide forces capable, with the support of U.S. air and naval forces, of initially halting any invasion north of Seoul. The initial U.S. role would therefore be concentrated in the Fifth and Seventh Air Forces, long-range strategic air power, and the Seventh Fleet. The United States and South Korea would provide shared logistics support for the CFC, which requires an emphasis on strengthening the rapid reinforcement capability and the facilities necessary to support such reinforcement. Interoperability would remain essential for effective logistics support. The United States would continue to assist South Korea in fielding effective air and missile defense systems and would continue to support combined intelligence centers. U.S. ground force reinforcement would be designed to augment and complement South Korean capabilities. A clear definition of roles and missions facilitates more effective and efficient allocation of the resources available for defense in both the U.S. and South Korean defense budgets.

By implementing a transition plan, the United States dramatically reduces the requirement for U.S. bases and facilities in South Korea. Steps taken in the transition send a clear message to the South Korean people that, while U.S. forces in Korea and the Korea-U.S. alliance are designed to prevent North Korea from intimidating the South or unifying the country by force, they are not there to stand in the way of peaceful re-unification or of South Korea taking charge of its own security. Likewise, those same steps send a clear message to Pyongyang that it must deal with Seoul on security issues within the framework set by the 1991–92 North-South agreements.

A modernized Korea-U.S. alliance is an essential step in maintaining deterrence, en-suring the ability to fight and win any renewed conflict in Korea, and ensuring a posi-tive U.S.–South Korean relationship for the future. Modernization of the alliance requires an implementation plan, agreed to by both parties, for phased actions to shift the United States from a leading to a supporting role in the military relationship and to reduce the footprint of U.S. forces in Korea. It can only be achieved by a commit-ment in Seoul and Washington to move forward in the relationship with carefully co-ordinated planning. Such planning was in place in the late 1980s[44] but only covered the period up to 1995 in detail and was shelved with the growing nuclear weapons crisis in 1992.[45] Events since 1993 and the importance of the U.S.-Korean relationship require moving forward now with the modernization of the Korea-U.S. alliance for the new century.

CONCLUSIONS

Despite the best efforts of both countries, the future of the Korea-U.S. alliance could prove problematic. Many of the key factors that will determine that future are not di-rectly controlled by Seoul or Washington. However, through the policies that they put in place and the actions that they take, the two parties to the alliance can influence the future of the alliance in important and potentially decisive ways. They can work to-gether within the multilateral negotiations to resolve the nuclear weapons issue. They can coordinate their efforts and those of the international community to promote change in North Korea. They can refuse to allow North Korea to dictate the terms of engagement or the pace of change on the Korean Peninsula. They can cooperate in ef-forts to reinforce a positive perception of the alliance among the South Korean people. They can expand the formal consultation and coordination within the U.S.–South Korean relationship while at the same time deepening the level of informal contacts. They can work together on their respective relations with Beijing to encourage its inte-gration into the regional and global systems as a positive player and support its initia-tives on multilateralism. Both Seoul and Washington can continue to support Beijing's efforts to promote moderation and reform in North Korea.

Modernization of the security alliance will be essential to its longer-term viability. Future security ties must reflect the changes in South Korea and on the Korean Peninsula of the past several decades. Seoul and Washington control the steps that need to be taken in that modernization. It is important to fully implement the transition of the United States from the leading to a supporting role in the military relationship. This will allow a significant reduction in the broad footprint of U.S. forces and facilities in South Korea. It will strengthen military capabilities through a clear definition of roles and missions and a more effective allocation of resources. It will also force North Korea to recognize that it must deal directly with Seoul on security and confidence-building measures on the Korean Peninsula and it can no longer use the U.S. military position in South Korea as a means to drive a wedge between the allies or to marginalize the South. In addition, it will send a message to the South Korean people that the alliance recognizes their ability to provide for their own security with U.S. support and is not the tool of U.S. interests or a barrier to future unification. Most important, modernization of the security alliance builds a more solid foundation for the future of a positive U.S.-Korean relationship.

While efforts are under way within the Six-Party Talks to ensure a nuclear weapon–free Korean Peninsula, it is equally important for Seoul and Washington to develop a coordinated plan for the future of the Korea-U.S. alliance. During America's future national strategy debates, a coordinated plan will support those in the United States who believe that while the United States must remain globally engaged, it must also require increased efforts from U.S. allies that reflect agreement on common purposes and directions. File cabinets and academic libraries are full of studies, but it is now time to move beyond studies to the development of an agreed plan and the timely initiation of actions to implement such a plan. A failure to move forward endangers both the future of the Korea-U.S. alliance and the prospects for a long-term positive relationship between the United States and Korea.

NOTES

1. James Schlesinger, "A Test by Terrorism," *National Interest,* no. 65-S (Thanksgiving 2001), pp. 5–10.

2. Doug Bandow, "Old Wine in New Bottles: The Pentagon's East Asia Security Strategy Report," *International Journal of Korean Studies* 3, no. 1 (Spring/Summer 1999), pp. 74–76; and Selig S. Harrison, "Time to Leave Korea?" *Foreign Affairs* 80, no. 2 (March/April 2001), pp. 52–78.

However, Harrison is heavily courted by Pyongyang and often supports DPRK policy positions.

3. *History of the Headquarters, United Nations Command—Korea, 1 January 1990–31 December 1990* (Seoul: United Nations Command, c. 1991), p. 29.

4. For details see ROK National Unification Board, *Intra-Korea Agreements* (Seoul: National Unification Board, 1992), p. 15.

5. North Korea had brought its experimental reactor on line by 1986, and in 1987 it began construction of its reprocessing plant, capable of reprocessing 200 tons of spent fuel a year.

6. For a discussion of the incentives and disincentives for a North Korean nuclear weapons program, see William C. Martel and William T. Pendley, *Nuclear Coexistence: Rethinking U.S. Policy to Promote Stability in an Era of Proliferation* (Montgomery, Ala.: Air War College, 1994), pp. 86–93.

7. Paul Lewis, "U.N. Maps Plan to Nab Atomic Cheats," *New York Times,* 11 October 1991, p. A10; and Michael R. Gordon, "U.N. Agency Rejects Offer by North Korea," *New York Times,* 7 December 1993, p. A6.

8. R. Jeffrey Smith, "N. Korea and the Bomb: High Tech Hide and Seek," *Washington Post,* 27 April 1993, p. A1.

9. See Nicholas Eberstadt, "Economic Recovery in the DPRK: Status and Prospects," *International Journal of Korean Studies* 4, no. 1 (Fall/Winter 2000), pp. 15–35.

10. Sam Jameson, "North Korea Quits Treaty to Halt Spread of Nuclear Arms," *Los Angeles Times,* 12 March 1993, p. A4; and David Sanger, "North Korea Fighting Inspections, Renounces Nuclear Arms Treaty," *New York Times,* 12 March 1993, p. A1.

11. Don Oberdorfer, *The Two Koreas: A Contemporary History* (Reading, Mass.: Addison-Wesley, 1997), pp. 286–87.

12. R. Jeffrey Smith, "U.S. Weighs N. Korean Incentives," *Washington Post,* 17 November 1993, p. A31; and Michael R. Gordon, "Korea Speeds Nuclear Fuel Removal Impeding Inspection," *New York Times,* 28 May 1993, p. A3.

13. Patrick E. Tyler, "China Tells Why It Opposes Korea Sanctions," *New York Times,* 13 June 1994, p. A5; and Thomas W. Lippman, "North Korea Could Prove Sanction-Proof," *Washington Post,* 25 December 1993, p. A30.

14. Douglas Brinkley, *The Unfinished Presidency: Jimmy Carter's Journey Beyond the White House* (New York: Viking, 1998), pp. 403–405.

15. Song-Hee Lee, "The North Korean Nuclear Issue Between Washington and Seoul: Differences in Perceptions and Policy Priorities," *Journal of East Asian Affairs* 11, no. 2 (1997), pp. 334–36.

16. Susumu Awanohara, "Uphill Battle: Japan Finds Few Friends in Clinton White House," *Far Eastern Economic Review,* 2 June 1994, pp. 30–31; and David E. Sanger, "Tokyo Reluctant to Levy Sanctions on North Koreans," *New York Times,* 9 June 1994, p. A1.

17. The U.S. government effectively accepted the North Korean conditions by negotiating bilaterally in both the shootdown of the OH-58 helicopter in December 1994 and the North Korean submarine intrusion in 1996.

18. Tang Whan Park reports U.S. aid at $270 million per year with a cumulative aid commitment of about $1 billion. Park, "Bringing Peace in from Without: How to End the Cold War in Korea," *International Journal of Korean Studies* 4, no. 1 (Fall/Winter 2000), p. 8.

19. Victor D. Cha, "Korea's Place in the Axis," *Foreign Affairs* 81, no. 3 (May–June 2002), pp. 79–92.

20. Jonathan D. Pollack, "The United States, North Korea and the End of the Agreed Framework," *Naval War College Review* 56, no. 3 (Summer 2003), pp. 35–36.

21. See Siegfried S. Hecker's report on his visit of 8 January 2004 to the Yongbyon Nuclear Scientific Research Center in North Korea, delivered to the Senate Committee on Foreign Relations, 21 January 2004.

22. Anthony Faiola, "As Tensions Subside Between Two Koreas, U.S. Strives to Adjust," *Washington Post,* 25 July 2004.

23. This is disputed by a North Korean senior colonel who defected in 1995. See Ju-whal Choi, "An Inside Perspective: North Korea's Unalterable Stance," *East Asian Review* 11, no. 4 (Winter 1999), pp. 95–96.

24. Chong-So Ku, "Two-Korea Strategy of the United States Should be Halted," *Seoul Wolgon Chosun,* September 1996, in FBIS, East Asia Daily Report, 1 September 1996, Serial SK0109044996, pp. 188–97.

25. William Stueck, "Democratization in Korea: The United States Role, 1980 and 1987," *International Journal of Korean Studies* 2, no. 1 (Fall/Winter 1998), pp. 1–26.

26. Young Koo Cha, "U.S. Forces in Korea: Their Roles and Future," in *The Future of South Korean–U.S. Security Relations,* ed. William Taylor et al. (Boulder, Colo.: Westview, 1989), pp. 145–53.

27. Nicholas Eberstadt, "Our Other Korea Problem," *National Interest* 69 (Fall 2002), pp. 110–18.

28. For a discussion of the adversary culture so often reflected in the U.S. media and movies, see Paul Hollander, "The Resilience of the Adversary Culture," *National Interest*, no. 68 (Summer 2002), pp. 101–12; and Michael Medved, "That's Entertainment: Hollywood's Contribution to Anti-Americanism Abroad," ibid., pp. 5–14.

29. For a positive review of the Kim Dae Jung engagement policy for North Korea, see Jong-seok Lee, "Dismantling the Sole Remaining Cold War Structure and the Engagement Policy," *East Asia Review* 12, no. 1 (Spring 2000), pp. 81–99.

30. For an excellent discussion of the trilateral relationship of China, Korea, and the United States see Sung-joo Han, "The Emerging Triangle: Korea Between China and the United States," *East Asia Review* 12, no. 1 (Spring 2000), pp. 3–29.

31. For a historic treatment of China's relations with Korea see Il-keun Park, "Chinese Foreign Policy and the Korean Peninsula," *International Journal of Korean Studies* 3, no. 1 (Spring/Summer 1999), pp. 116–35.

32. For the argument that South Korea may be slipping into the Chinese orbit as a result of economic activity and U.S. accommodations with the North, see Warren I. Cohen, "Compromised in Korea: Redeemed by the Clinton Administration," *Foreign Affairs* 76, no. 3 (May/June 1997), p. 112.

33. For an overview of the EP-3 incident see John Keefe, *Anatomy of the EP-3 Incident, April 2001* (Alexandria, Va.: CNA Project Asia, 26 October 2001).

34. For a review of the current U.S.-China relationship, see David M. Lampton, "The Stealth Normalization of U.S.-China Relations," *National Interest* 73 (Fall 2003), pp. 37–48.

35. Charles Horner, "The Other Orientalism: China's Islamist Problem," *National Interest*, no. 67 (Spring 2002), pp. 37–45.

36. For an overview of the factors influencing both cooperation and competition in the U.S.-China relationship, see David Shambaugh, "Facing Reality in China Policy," *Foreign Affairs* 80, no. 1 (January–February 2001), pp. 50–64.

37. Doug Bandow, "America's Korean Protectorate in a Changed World: Time to Disengage," in *The U.S.-South Korean Alliance: Time for a Change*, ed. Doug Bandow and Ted Galen Carpenter (New Brunswick, N.J.: Transaction Publishers, 1992).

38. Niall Ferguson and Lawrence J. Kotlikoff, "Going Critical: American Power and the Consequences of Fiscal Overreach," *National Interest* 73 (Fall 2003), pp. 22–32.

39. Peter G. Peterson, "Riding for a Fall," *Foreign Affairs* 83, no. 5 (September/October 2004), pp. 111–25.

40. For an overview of recent U.S. strategy, see Colin L. Powell, "A Strategy of Partnerships," *Foreign Affairs* 83, no. 1 (January/February 2004), pp. 22–34.

41. Adopting the recommendations in the Perry Report contained in William Perry, *Review of United States Policy Toward North Korea: Findings and Recommendations* (Washington, D.C.: U.S. Department of State, October 1999), would support this effort.

42. For a cautionary assessment of the future Chinese regional role, see John J. Mearsheimer, "The Future of the American Pacifier," *Foreign Affairs* 80, no. 5 (September/October 2001), pp. 53–58.

43. Zbigniew Brzezinski, "Living With China," *National Interest* 59 (Spring 2000), pp. 5–21.

44. Department of Defense, *A Strategic Framework for the Asian Pacific Rim: Looking Toward the 21st Century, a Report to the Congress* (Washington, D.C.: Assistant Secretary of Defense, International Security Affairs, 1990), pp. 9–10.

45. Department of Defense, *A Strategic Framework for the Asian Pacific Rim: A Report to Congress* (Washington, D.C.: Assistant Secretary of Defense, International Security Affairs, 1992), p. 20.

About the Authors

Seung Joo Baek is Chief, North Korea Studies Division, Center for Security and Strategy, Korea Institute for Defense Analysis, Seoul.

Victor Cha is Associate Professor of Government and Politics and D.S. Song Korea Foundation Chair in Asian Studies, Georgetown University. He is presently on leave, serving as a Director for Asian Affairs at the National Security Council, The White House.

Jae Ho Chung is Professor and Chair, Department of International Relations, Seoul National University.

Nicholas Eberstadt is Henry Wendt Chair in Political Economy at the American Enterprise Institute, Washington, D.C.

Yong Sup Han is Director, Research Institute on National Security Affairs, Korea National Defense University, Seoul.

Byung-Kook Kim is Professor of Political Science and Director, East Asian Institute, Korea University, Seoul.

Andrei Lankov is Lecturer at the China and Korea Center, Australian National University, Canberra. He is presently on leave at Kookmin University, Seoul.

Phillip Wonhyuk Lim is Fellow, Korea Development Institute, Seoul. He is presently a Visiting Fellow at the Center for Northeast Asian Policy Studies at the Brookings Institution, Washington, D.C.

Alexandre Y. Mansourov is Associate Professor in the College of Security Studies, Asia-Pacific Center for Security Studies, Honolulu.

Narushige Michishita is Senior Research Fellow at the National Institute of Defense Studies, Tokyo.

Marcus Noland is Senior Fellow at the Institute for International Economics, Washington, D.C.

William T. Pendley, RADM U.S. Navy (Ret.), is an independent consultant on Asia-Pacific affairs and former Acting Assistant Secretary of Defense for International Security Affairs.

Jonathan D. Pollack is Professor of Asian-Pacific Studies and Chairman of the Asia-Pacific Studies Group, Naval War College, Newport, R.I.

Gilbert Rozman is Musgrave Professor of Sociology, Princeton University.

Phillip C. Saunders is Senior Research Fellow, Institute for National Strategic Studies, National Defense University, Washington, D.C.

Robert A. Scalapino is Robson Professor of Government Emeritus and Director Emeritus, Institute of East Asian Studies, University of California at Berkeley.

The Strategic Research Department

One of the departments in the Center for Naval Warfare Studies of the Naval War College, the Strategic Research Department (SRD) focuses on the major strategic and policy issues affecting U.S. national security interests and the role of the U.S. Navy in advancing these interests. The department's primary research agenda encompasses: (1) the long-term political, economic, military, and technological forces that are reshaping international security as a whole; (2) prospective alternatives in U.S. grand strategy, with particular attention to the role of seapower; (3) security trends and the development of national military capabilities in the regions of primary concern to U.S. national security; (4) major technological and industrial changes that are transforming the defense capabilities and military doctrines of the United States and other major powers; and (5) the future utility and limitations of military power as an instrument of national policy, and its implications for the developments of the U.S. Navy. SRD employs a multidisciplinary approach in its research, integrating various analytic and methodological tools.

The Asia-Pacific Studies Group

The Asia-Pacific Studies Group (APSG) acts as a catalyst, coordinator, and implementer of research supporting the Navy, the U.S. Pacific Command, and other elements of the U.S. government responsible for formulating policy and strategy and for planning related to Asia and the Pacific. It draws together personnel of the Naval War College and the Navy Warfare Development Command engaged in work on Asia and the Pacific. Many of its members have either lived, studied, or served in the region. In addition to assisting U.S. national security policy makers, the APSG serves as the Naval War College's principal forum for addressing a full range of Asia-Pacific strategy and policy issues. The APSG has also initiated a long-term collaborative research relationship with the Maritime Staff College of the Japan Maritime Self Defense Force.